IN THE
BLINK OF
AN EYE

IN THE BLINK OF AN EYE

THE FBI

INVESTIGATION OF

TWA FLIGHT 800

PAT MILTON

RANDOM HOUSE NEW YORK

RANDOM HOUSE and colophon are registered trademarks of Random House, Inc.

Library of Congress Cataloging-in-Publication Data
Milton, Pat.
In the blink of an eye : the FBI investigation
of TWA flight 800 / Pat Milton.
p. cm.
ISBN 0-375-50086-3
1. Aircraft accidents—New York (State)—Long Island Region.
2. Aircraft Accidents—North Atlantic Ocean.   3. Aircraft accidents—
Investigation—United States.   4. Terrorism.   I. Title.
TL553.5.M55   1999
363.12'465'0974721—dc21   99-25359

Random House website address: www.atrandom.com
Printed in the United States of America on acid-free paper

Book design by Barbara M. Bachman
BVG 01

FOR THE 230 PEOPLE

WHO LOST THEIR LIVES AND

THE MEN AND WOMEN WHO

TRIED TO FIND OUT WHY

————————

HE WHO LEARNS MUST SUFFER.

AND EVEN IN OUR SLEEP,

PAIN THAT CANNOT FORGET

FALLS DROP BY DROP UPON THE HEART,

AND IN OUR OWN DESPAIR,

AGAINST OUR WILL, COMES WISDOM

TO US BY THE AWFUL GRACE OF GOD.

—AESCHYLUS
(often quoted by Robert Kennedy
following the death of his brother
President John Kennedy)

FOREWORD

The reader of this book should understand at the outset what it is—and what it most assuredly is not. It is not an encyclopedic account of the crash of TWA Flight 800 and its aftermath, laden with technical details. Nor does it propose a theory of why Flight 800 exploded in the sky off Long Island, New York, in the early evening of July 17, 1996, a crash that remains, three years after it occurred, the greatest mystery in aviation history.

Instead, this book was written to take readers into the heart of the largest, most complex criminal investigation in the history of the FBI, an agency as secretive as it is proud. During the sixteen months in which more than seven hundred agents worked day and night to make sense of the Flight 800 disaster, the FBI was severely limited by law as to what it could share with the public about its findings—and its frustrations. Because of those curbs, and for lack of evidence, the bureau could not share its overarching fear: that the crash of Flight 800 might be the second or third strike in a terrorist war against the United States perpetrated by an undeclared enemy. This book shows how a team of dedicated law enforcement professionals responded to what they truly believed may have been an act of war.

More broadly, *In the Blink of an Eye* shows how a nation and its people—including hundreds of volunteers—responded to a catastrophic event. For all those citizens, investigators, and workers from numerous agencies, as well as for journalists covering the story, this investigation was unique.

This book took nearly three years to research and write, in part because information was gathered from scores of sources, many of them at the top levels of government. Sometimes cooperation was immediate; at other times, it took weeks or months of pursuit. Inevitably, the central character is James Kallstrom, head of the FBI investigation into the crash. While his cooperation was invaluable, much of the story was developed through other sources.

Many of the anecdotes and conversations have been re-created; to ensure accuracy, the memory, notes, and calendars of the participants have been compared and rechecked. I have attempted to preserve the language of the main characters, reflecting their speech and attitudes.

In all, more than three hundred people were interviewed, many numerous times, and many on a not-for-attribution basis. Those people interviewed included FBI agents; FBI lab scientists and explosives experts; investigators from Suffolk County, Nassau County, New York City, and other New York State police departments; ATF and Secret Service agents; missile experts; members of the Joint Chiefs of Staff; White House officials; State Department and Pentagon officials; members of Congress; metallurgists; NTSB investigators and officials; federal prosecutors; FAA officials; U.S. Navy officers; U.S. Navy and law enforcement divers; Coast Guardsmen; Red Cross and other volunteers; workers at Boeing and TWA; 747 pilots; conspiracy theorists; and victims' family members.

In the end, the book was produced from hundreds of hours of taped conversations and thousands of pages of notes, maps, documents, affidavits, and reports.

In retrospect, I can safely say that no one who worked closely on this investigation was unchanged by it. At the start, investigators were driven almost solely by the desire to learn the cause of the disaster and, if it proved to have been a crime, find the criminals. Over time, lessons about life—its preciousness, its transience, its capacity to change in the blink of an eye—consumed every agent and expert involved as much as the myriad tantalizing pieces of evidence and the wreckage of the plane itself. In the lingering aftermath of a disaster, old rules and habits are put aside; priorities change; lives open up; compassion and courage emerge.

This is a story of heroism in a cynical world, of ordinary men and women, thrust into an extraordinary event, who rose to the challenge. And it is, in the end, an American story, of Americans working to help and protect one another, and their country. And it is the story of how a touch of grace was brought to a terrible tragedy.

CONTENTS

IN THE
BLINK OF
AN EYE

CHAPTER 1

THE BEEPERS

At 8:45 P.M. on July 17, 1996, the last toasts of a very private dinner were raised within a mahogany-paneled private dining room of the Friars Club on East Fifty-fifth Street in Manhattan. The guest of honor was a short, compactly built former Marine named Ray Kelly: ex–police commissioner of New York City, newly named undersecretary of the U.S. Treasury in charge of U.S. Customs, the Secret Service, ATF, and other law enforcement branches. The dinner was an intimate one, as befitted a vestpocket-size club that occupied a single brownstone. About thirty guests sat on either side of Kelly at a horseshoe-shaped banquet table. Most were men: top brass in the New York police department, the FBI, the CIA, and the Secret Service. But among them were a few women judges and prosecutors. The men kept their jackets on and their ties pulled tight, the women remained in their business suits, but a sense of fun, even mischief, pervaded the room. The Friars Club was one place where a public official could have a glass of port with dessert, light up a cigar, and tell an off-color story without having to read about it the next morning in the *Daily News*.

As the guests were leaving—law enforcement dinners tended to start and end early, even at the Friars—the gently insistent sound of beepers began chirping from every direction. The guests exited, perhaps a bit more quickly than usual, to their waiting cars to return the calls, not yet aware that they were all about to get the same message.

One of the biggest men in the group—six feet tall, solidly built—managed to look rumpled in his newly pressed suit as he trotted toward his car. With the easy warmth by which his colleagues had come to know him, James Keith Kallstrom mumbled a few quick good-byes, slid behind the wheel of his navy blue Crown Victoria, and called the familiar number that had lit up his beeper: the FBI duty agent in downtown Manhattan. As he dialed, he unbuttoned his collar and yanked his tie loose. Turning north on Madison Avenue, he glanced at his watch. The time was 8:55 P.M.

Seconds later, Kallstrom, the FBI's assistant director in charge—the highest-ranking agent in the field—was racing toward the southbound FDR Drive, his siren blaring, his red dashboard light whirling, his headlights flashing. "The FAA's telling us there was no unusual communication from the crew, nothing. No distress calls." Traffic was thin at this hour, and Kallstrom was able to weave in and around the scattered taxis and Charge-and-Ride limousines. In the FBI's New York office, his fast driving habits were notorious. Everyone conceded he was good at the wheel; everyone knew he'd scored high in the FBI's tactical driving courses, and that he was a race-car and motorcycle enthusiast. But the New York agents also did anything they could to avoid riding with him. The work was dangerous enough as it was.

No distress calls? Kallstrom turned the air-conditioning up. With the back of his hand, he brushed the sweat from his brow and ran his fingers through his thick black hair. Commercial jets don't just fall out of the sky by accident. Kallstrom thought there was a good chance it was a bomb. Ever since the World Trade Center bombing three years before, he'd dreaded the next attack. You could beef up security, wiretap even more suspected terrorists, but Kallstrom knew the real lesson of the World Trade Center: You couldn't cover every possibility. You never knew what was going to happen next. One thing was sure: If a 747 and its passengers had just been downed by sabotage, the world had changed. No plane had ever been downed by terrorists in the United States before.

Hurtling down the FDR Drive, Kallstrom punched an unlisted Virginia home number into the secure phone set on the floor beside his seat. "Louie, we have a 747 down in the water just off the south shore of Long Island," he said tersely in his lingering Boston accent.

"Any survivors, Jimmy?" Louis Freeh, the FBI's director, was more than a colleague on a first-name basis with his New York bureau chief. Years ago, Freeh had worked for Kallstrom as a field agent. When he'd left the FBI to become a federal prosecutor, he and Kallstrom continued to work together to convict Mafia bosses.

"I've got agents headed over to the Coast Guard station in East Moriches. They're sending boats out from there. So far we just don't know."

"Anything you need, you got it, you know that, right?"

"Right."

Within minutes, the news had been passed up the line: from Freeh to Attorney General Janet Reno, from Reno to White House chief of staff Leon Panetta, from Panetta to President Clinton. Kallstrom's next call was to his number-two man, Tom Pickard, whom he instructed to call John O'Neill, head of the FBI's counterterrorism unit in Washington. O'Neill then called the president's special assistant on terrorism, Richard Clarke. And that was how it worked: From Kallstrom's car phone, the White House was now alerted and on the case.

Kallstrom's beeper went off again. He pulled it up from his belt and squinted at the number. It was his own. When his wife answered, he started to explain, but she cut him off. "I know," she said. "Call Charlie."

"Charlie Christopher?"

"He thinks Janet was working that flight."

Charlie Christopher was a fellow FBI agent and Kallstrom's close friend. He had been an usher at Charlie's wedding when he married Janet Wolf thirteen years ago. Janet had been a TWA flight attendant for twenty-five years. She adored her work—so much that she had put off marriage to Charlie for ten years, until he agreed she could keep flying after they had children. As an attendant, she was meticulous but also exuberant and fun, and not above coming back to the stewards' station to whisper, "Wait'll you see that hairdo in 32-F!" The Kallstroms, like all her friends, had been awed by her knowledge of restaurants and shops in cities around the world. She would walk into a tucked-away jewelry store in Vienna, and the proprietor would beam. "Ah, Janet! I've got a new pair of earrings I know you'll love." Kallstrom clutched the steering wheel tighter as he heard Charlie pick up.

"Hey, Charlie, it's Jim."

Charlie was frantic. "She's on that plane, Jim. She wasn't supposed to be, but she was." Usually, Janet worked Friday's Flight 800, returning from Paris on Sunday night. This week, she'd changed shifts with a coworker so she could be back in time to help twelve-year-old Charles pack and see him off to Boy Scout camp. "What can you tell me?" Charlie pleaded.

Kallstrom swallowed hard. "The Coast Guard is out there in full force, county police, it's a full-scale rescue effort, Charlie," he said. "That's all I know so far."

"Please, Jim, you'll do all you can, right?"

"Everything. Everything. You have my word, Charlie. Just stay there. I'll call you."

As Kallstrom sped toward the FBI's New York office at 26 Federal Plaza, Richard Clarke was driving nearly as fast through the streets of Washington, D.C., to the White House. Clarke, special assistant to the president on terrorism, was wearing the same polo shirt and shorts he'd had on when the FBI's John O'Neill called him at his Virginia home. If his worst fear proved true, there was no time to waste changing clothes.

Hurrying past the West Wing security guards to the White House Situation Room, Clarke began making the necessary calls to stage an emergency video teleconference of the coordinating security group on terrorism, known as CSG. The teleconference would be held in the Situation Room, on the first floor. From monitors in their respective offices, terrorism experts from all relevant federal agencies would participate: the Pentagon, the CIA, the FBI, the State Department, the Secret Service, the Justice Department, the Joint Chiefs of Staff, and, for this crisis, the FAA. Clarke was CSG's chairman.

Convening an emergency video conference underscored the atmosphere of deep concern—considerably greater than the press and public knew. The fact was that recent classified intelligence reports indicated the Iranian government was planning a wave of major terrorist attacks against the United States. There was a lot of evidence. A conclave of international terrorists in Tehran had made the threat seem not only more dire but more imminent. Clarke's hunch was that attacks might be timed to coincide with, or even to disrupt, the upcoming summer Olympics in Atlanta. Quietly, President Clinton had placed the country on the highest state of security since the early days of the Cuban Missile Crisis. He had also instructed the Joint Chiefs of Staff to work up a retaliation strike plan. The "contingency plan," he called it. In an Oval Office meeting just days before, Clinton had made clear that if a link between an attack and specific state-sponsored terrorists could be proven, he wanted the plan to be severe. He was still frustrated by the ineffectualness of America's response to an assassination attempt on former president George Bush while Bush was traveling in the Middle East. Clinton had ordered Saddam Hussein's Iraqi intelligence headquarters bombed, but in retrospect, the president and his advisors decided that blowing up a few buildings did little to deter terrorism. "I don't want a lukewarm plan," Clinton said. It was agreed that the response to state-sponsored terrorism resulting in large numbers of American fatalities must be a massive, full-scale series of attacks that inflicted on the enemy ten times the damage it had caused.

Now, literally out of the blue, a commercial jet with 230 passengers and crew had exploded in midair and crashed into the Atlantic, less than ten miles south of Long Island. Was this an Iranian attack?

The video conference began at 10:00 P.M. About forty people were packed into the Situation Room itself. On one wall were eight closed-circuit television sets hooked up to eight different agencies, whose terrorism experts were similarly convened. Clarke began by conveying the first sketchy details he'd received from the FBI and FAA. He emphasized that the pilots of Flight 800 had not reported any mechanical problem with the plane and appeared oblivious to any danger before the explosion. Almost instantaneously, the plane had burst into a fireball, Clarke related, which was extremely unusual.

Over the next hours, the FBI would tell Clarke, a few eyewitnesses had reported seeing streaks of light in the sky before the explosion. The words "missile" and "bomb" began to be used in wide-ranging discussions during more video conferences throughout the night. The experts considered various countries that might have sponsored an attack, and ticked off a number of freelance radical groups that had been active in the last few years. Just three weeks before, the Khobar Towers apartment complex, a U.S. military residence near Dhahran, Saudi Arabia, had been bombed, resulting in nineteen deaths. The experts wondered if Khobar Towers was Iran's first strike or if it was the first attack in a campaign by certain independent militant Islamic fundamentalists; could TWA Flight 800 have been their next move? A flight from New York to Paris seemed an odd choice for a Middle Eastern terrorist, though perhaps a terrorist with a missile may have been trying to hit a flight headed at about the same time from Kennedy Airport to Israel.

Over at the Pentagon, experts began looking at charts and maps to gauge what kinds of missiles, if any, had the range to hit a plane at Flight 800's altitude and distance from shore. To many, the missile theory seemed far-fetched. Why would a terrorist go to the trouble to smuggle a missile into the United States and fire it at a plane three miles in the air? As a plan, it seemed messy, unreliable, and complicated—far more so than a bomb. Yet until shown otherwise, the FBI had to assume the worst. What if a missile had downed Flight 800, and the terrorists involved were even now planning to take out more commercial jets in the next days, or even hours? What steps could be taken to prevent another attack?

In ongoing teleconferences, the FAA pointed out that deterrence would be almost impossible, because planes fly low over large areas of land on their takeoffs and approaches for landing. If a threat was confirmed, those large swaths of land would have to be secured by the National Guard or local police. Should all commercial flights be grounded until those areas were deemed safe? If so, how long should such security be kept in place? The scale of such a plan, as Clarke observed ruefully, would very likely bring air transportation in the United States to a complete halt, throwing the country into turmoil and crippling the economy. In the long run, some experts suggested, a missile-jamming device like the one on the president's plane, Air Force One, might have to be installed on every commercial aircraft. The jammer on Air Force One, a 747, disabled the electronics within an oncoming missile and forced it off its path. The device could be made available for commercial planes, but at staggering cost.

At about three in the morning, a call came from Tony Lake, the national security advisor and Clarke's boss. Lake, in his office just above the White House Situation Room, had just received a call from the president, who was in his living quarters. "Yes, Tony?" Clarke said.

Lake said he had just spoken with the president, who in his slightly hoarse voice with the famous Arkansas accent but with none of the easygoing manner he showed in public, had relayed the following message:

"Dust off the contingency plan."

A perfect summer day was just tapering toward dusk on July 17, 1996, as Petty Officer Ken Seebeck eased his twenty-eight-foot patrol boat up to the dock of the U.S. Coast Guard station at Shinnecock Inlet. Somewhere nearby was the highway, thick with summer traffic, that bisected Long Island's 130 miles of flat landscape from Manhattan to Montauk Point; around the inlet were summer towns crowded with sun-warmed strollers in search of drinks and dinner. The Coast Guard station at Shinnecock stood apart from all that. A white brick building with standard-issue red roof and dormers, it occupied the end of its own grassy peninsula. On the sand bar to the south that protects the inlet from the pounding Atlantic, a row of summer houses could be discerned, along with a seafood joint or two. Nothing else here appeared to have changed since the station was built in 1942, when wartime fears of German invasion helped give rise to a string of stations, much like this one, along Long Island's shore. Indeed, the only reminder that a modern world pulsed beyond was the regular drone of jets overhead, coming into or taking off from John F. Kennedy International Airport, sixty miles—or ten minutes—to the west.

Ordinarily, Petty Officer Seebeck ended his shift at the next Coast Guard station, fourteen miles west in East Moriches. That was where he was based, and it was from there, earlier in the day, that he and his three-man crew had taken their boat into the Atlantic to rescue the crew of a sailboat so becalmed that it was, as sailors put it, "locked in irons." The guardsmen had towed the sailboat and its grateful crew three hours to the nearest marina, which happened to be in Hampton Bays, on the inlet, then stopped at Shinnecock to refuel before heading back to end a shift that had begun at 7:30 A.M.

The time, Seebeck noted, was exactly 8:31 P.M.

Lean and fit, with short-cropped blond hair and a steady gaze, Seebeck had an air of command that made him seem older than his twenty-seven years. Nothing dramatic had happened in his four years of service, but he loved the Coast Guard life, and planned to reenlist. He liked having his own boat and overseeing a crew of three young guardsmen, none older than nineteen. After several months of working together, the crew was performing as a real unit, and that pleased him. Teaching the recruits made him feel responsible—grown-up. So did being a husband and the father of a two-year-old son.

Seebeck's thoughts were just turning to dinner when an officer flung open the station door. "You guys better get over to East Moriches," he called out. "Something big is going on."

Seebeck jumped into his boat and turned the marine radio to channel 16, the principal public-access frequency. He heard a boater shouting about a ball of falling light. Other voices followed, confirming the report, both from other boats and from ashore. Through the crackle of static and the crispness of two-way radio talk, Seebeck sensed an unusual undertone of excitement in the voices. When he looked toward the ocean, he saw what looked like an Air National Guard helicopter several miles offshore, dropping phosphorous flares over the water. Still, he thought little of it. The chopper was probably engaged in a routine rescue drill. In fact, it was hovering within the very coordinates where such exercises were most commonly conducted. If someone had really seen a "ball of light," Seebeck imagined it might be the wing of an incoming plane reflecting the sun's last rays as it banked west for Kennedy Airport.

Seebeck called the East Moriches Coast Guard station and got fellow petty officer Danny Phee. "Danny, it's Ken. What's up?"

"Go secure, Ken."

Seebeck switched from channel 16 to the secure line used only by the Coast Guard. "What the hell's going on?"

"We have a commercial airliner in the water. Right in the middle of Jaws." Jaws was the name the guardsmen had given to the coordinates where the exercises were held.

"Roger. Anything further?" Seebeck spoke as calmly as if his wife had just asked him to pick up a loaf of bread on the way home. He was cool by nature, cooler for his Coast Guard training, and this was no time to get worked up, not with his young crew. He called the three into the cabin to tell them where they were headed and why. "Guys," he said, "this is going to get pretty nasty." Seebeck sounded as if he knew what to expect, but that, too, was Coast Guard training. The truth was he had no idea.

With his tank full, Seebeck switched on the boat's twin 225-horsepower outboards and pushed his throttle steadily forward. The boat roared away from the dock and across the inlet at nearly fifty miles an hour. Aside from the engines you might find in a professional racer, these were about as powerful as outboards get. Seebeck had never pushed them all out in these waters before; he could do it now only because there was no chop at all.

As the boat sliced past the Tiana Beach sand bar into the open Atlantic, Seebeck's crew dug out first-aid supplies—bandages, thermal blankets, oxygen tanks—and assembled them on the well deck by the stern. "Confirming the site at 40-39.39 north by 072-38.47 west," the radio crackled. On an ocean nearly as calm as the inlet, Seebeck headed southwest about eight miles offshore and roughly in a line with the town of East Moriches, where the lone Air National Guard helicopter Seebeck had seen before was still hovering, shooting more phosphorous into the deepening dusk.

All at once, the acrid bite of jet fuel enveloped the guardsmen. It burned their eyes and stung their throats. This was nothing like the reassuring smell of gasoline at a corner filling station. It was more like kerosene flaming up from a barbecue grill—a suffocating smell that even the headwind from the speeding boat did little to mitigate. Dead ahead, Seebeck and his crew could see black smoke, but for nearly ten minutes, nothing else appeared on the water.

"Oh my God."

Seebeck's eighteen-year-old crew member, Jarrl Pellinen, was the one who spoke. The others stared in silence, transfixed, as they saw the huge tail section of a commercial jet, atilt in the water at 45 degrees, gleaming in the glare of a mile-long wall of fire. On the tail, the guardsmen could plainly see the letters TWA. Seebeck counted maybe forty windows along the wrecked section of fuselage that adjoined the tail, though even as he looked, another window, then another, slid under the fiery surface. Half a mile away was the Coast Guard cutter *Adak*, which happened to be in the area on a routine fishing patrol off Long Island. Seebeck could see its officers on the bridge, scanning the site with binoculars. Though the sky was still light, the *Adak*'s crew had turned on large searchlights and was combing the water for survivors even as they lowered the cutter's nineteen-foot rescue boat. Other than that, Seebeck's vessel was the first to reach the scene.

As Seebeck's crew approached the site, the smell grew sharper, not just of kerosene but with the rotten-egg stench of burning sulfur. Smoke was billowing black and thick; Seebeck thought it looked impenetrable. He felt his throat tighten. He thought he might gag. From half a mile away, he could feel the searing heat of the fire. Smaller fires, no less furious, rose like molten lava from black pools of jet fuel and chunks of the plane. As they edged closer, the guardsmen could also see a carpet of debris stretching in every direction: smoldering hunks of the fuselage, seat cushions, life preservers still in their plastic casings, stacks of Styrofoam cups, clothing, suitcases, airline pillows, and video camcorders. A half-full baby bottle bobbed on a light swell as if the swell were a cradle. There were passports and drivers' licenses with photos of faces. Amid these objects, here and there, floated larger lumps. Seebeck realized these were human bodies.

By now it was 9:20 P.M. The sun had set, but the sky was eerily lit by searchlights from the chopper and the *Adak*, by the brilliant white phosphorous flares, and by the flames. As it happened, the searchlight on Seebeck's own boat wasn't working. He wasn't accustomed to being out on the water at night. Instead, while he steered slowly toward the flaming debris, his three crewmen beamed large flashlights toward the sinking fuselage. Their beams caught the floating bodies, paused for a moment, then passed on. Most of the bodies were nude. "What happened to their clothes?" one of the young guardsmen asked Seebeck.

"Maybe blown off by the pressure as they fell," Seebeck said. "Maybe burned off. I don't know."

The dead ones could wait, Seebeck told his men. "Search for survivors." Slowly, the men played their beams over the chaos of debris and along the receding windows of the plane's rear section as it continued to slide slowly beneath the surface. Could they see faces at the windows, imploring the guardsmen to save them? Still the length of a football field away, kept back by the wall of fire, the men saw only blackened circles of glass: thirty, then twenty, then ten. In the garish orange light, the plane's tail appeared as a ghastly cross in a floating cemetery. Then, as the men watched, the tail with its red-and-white TWA logo broke off from the rest of the fuselage and fell back onto the sea, jutting up like a shark's fin. The last windows slid out of view, headed down to the ocean floor, 120 feet below.

Suddenly, the boat's engines sputtered. Seebeck shot a glance at Sam Miller, the crewman nearest him. Both knew what that meant. Before Seebeck could turn the ignition key to "off," the engines went dead.

Gently but inexorably, the boat drifted toward the wall of fire. Seebeck's crewmen raised the heavy 225s, trying to focus on the task at hand. The propellers, as Seebeck had suspected, had become tangled in cables and electrical wiring from the shattered plane. Grimly, Seebeck radioed the *Adak* for help. "We need a tow or we'll fry." Even as he spoke, the boat lifted on a low swell that then thrust it dangerously toward a patch of flame. He couldn't believe this. An hour ago, he had been a small-town guardsman on routine patrol, wondering what his wife was making for dinner. Now he felt like a wartime commander in a brutal, close-pitched firefight, facing a life-and-death decision. Were his men safer in the boat, or should he order them overboard before the boat was engulfed in flames?

Two minutes ticked by, then three. As the boat nudged closer to the wall of fire, he saw that the flames were actually higher and fiercer than they had seemed from a distance. With professional detachment, Seebeck estimated they rose nearly thirty feet from the water's surface. But even as he guessed, he was having a harder time maintaining his professional cool.

"I think I've got it," shouted Miller. With his pocketknife, he'd managed to hack through the wiry mess and was carefully extricating the propeller blades. "Thank God," Seebeck muttered under his breath as Pellinen lowered the engines into the water. He lit the ignition; the engines coughed, gasped, and rumbled back to life.

His heart still pounding, Seebeck threw the throttle in reverse and slowly backed away from the flames. He knew now that the boat, though covered with oily soot, wouldn't burn as long as he kept it ten feet or more from the fires, but what if the propellers became enmeshed in another clump of wiring?

In the flare-lit night, Seebeck steered slowly around the flames, edging closer to where the vanished rear cabin section had been. Could anyone have survived? Could anyone be so lucky as to fall from an exploding plane into a fiery sea and live? Seebeck thought of the poor souls who jumped from the New York bridges: They were dead on impact every time. Even as he kept his men scanning the water for signs of life, he knew the effort was probably hopeless. "Let's start pulling them in," he said, heartsick at the sight of the nearest float-ing bodies. He couldn't think of anything else to do.

As the boat approached the first body, the men pulled on plastic surgical gloves. With the engines idling, Seebeck and the third guardsman, Craig Achilli, reached over the boat's low gunwales. Seebeck took an arm, the nine-teen-year-old guardsman a leg. Because of the surgical gloves, they couldn't feel the texture of the corpse's skin, but the coldness of death came through. The body was a woman's, nude, perhaps in her thirties. It was hard to tell. Her hair was a mess, and her features contorted, perhaps by the sudden change in cabin pressure as the plane went down. She looked almost unscathed, yet as they pulled her onto the deck, they could tell that most of her bones were bro-ken. She was as limp as a rag doll.

Since the woman had been floating facedown, mouth-to-mouth resuscita-tion was probably useless. Still, Seebeck held her wrist for a moment, hoping for a pulse. Then he rolled the woman over on her stomach. That way, she almost seemed to be sleeping. Gently, he covered her with a blanket.

Seebeck eased the boat toward the next floating body, a fat man still par-tially clothed. "Grab him by the belt buckle," Seebeck shouted. Pellinen seized the fancy buckle of an expensive leather belt and helped haul the body over the gunwale. Slid onto the deck, he looked up wide-eyed at the crew, his mouth open, as if crying out.

Other Coast Guard boats were nearby now, pulling up more bodies. Most, like the woman, were nude. Some seemed calm—dead, perhaps, before they could react. Other faces, like the fat man's, were frozen in shock. Many of the bodies showed no signs of injury. Others were terribly disfigured, their faces deeply gashed, limbs torn off. The back of one man's head was sheared off, the brains gone, the skull an empty bowl. A couple of bodies were decapitated. One man's stomach was ripped, the intestines spilling out. Several were burned, apparently from the flaming oil on the water's surface.

As the damaged bodies were brought aboard, many Coast Guardsmen vom-ited over their boats' gunwales. When they had finished retching, they turned back to their work, their stomachs heaving but empty. The work was awful, but they felt worse not helping, even for a minute or two.

The men on Seebeck's boat spoke to one another hardly at all. There was lit-tle to say but "over there" or "here now." In the cabin, the marine radio crack-led with dozens of voices. "There're so many bodies," Seebeck heard over and over again. "So many bodies." Some voices came from other Coast Guard boats that had converged on the scene, or from the Suffolk County police boats that Seebeck could see silhouetted against the flames, their crews, like his, pulling bodies aboard. What seemed like dozens of private fishing boats had also appeared, lit not only by the flames but by the Coast Guard cutter *Adak*, as well as by the half-dozen helicopters that now hovered overhead, beaming their searchlights and adding to the marine radio babble.

An exchange over the marine radio made the Coast Guardsmen pause in their work. The crew of one boat had found a man faceup in the water and pulled him aboard, thinking he might be alive. Other boaters drew alongside to watch as a guardsman leaned over the man, pinching his nose and blowing air into his mouth while another guardsman pushed on his chest to force air out. The guardsman, vigorously working on the prostrate figure, transfixed the other crews as they watched the frantic silhouette lighted by the flares on the water behind them. To find even one survivor, they now knew, would give this dreadful exercise meaning. But then the hopeful voices on the radio fell still, and the guardsman stopped bobbing. The crews in the neighboring boats went back to work. On another boat, a shout went up when an arm was seen reaching up from the water, as if beckoning the rescuers over, but the arm turned out to be a sliced-off limb, wedged at an odd angle in the debris.

By 11:30 P.M., half a dozen bodies lay on Seebeck's deck. He arranged by marine radio to pass them over to another Coast Guard or Suffolk County police boat, which would shuttle them back to a temporary morgue set up at the station in East Moriches. Moments later, a TV news crew, with camera lights blazing, pulled alongside Seebeck's boat. Seebeck and his men had to shield their eyes. A woman reporter leaned down from the boat's high deck, her makeup intact, a pleased-to-meet-you smile glued to her face. She glanced quickly at the bodies and turned to Seebeck, still smiling. "Excuse me," the reporter asked as the cameras panned the Coast Guard boat's deck. "Could you just tell us how you are feeling right now?"

Furious, Seebeck shouted, "Turn off the lights." Then louder, "Turn off the damn lights!"

"Officer, this is news," the reporter said. "Please just give us two minutes and we'll be out of here. Have you found any survivors?"

"If you want to help, get aboard and help," Seebeck said. "If not, get the hell out of here." Still, the cameras whirred, zooming in on the bodies. "How would you feel if someone you loved turned up like this on TV?" Seebeck shouted at her. "Turn them off!"

The lights clicked off, and the whirring stopped. Trying to hide her frustration, the reporter signaled her crew to move on. "We're just trying to do a job," she said. "If you were home watching TV, you'd want to know what was happening, too."

"This is different," Seebeck said, but his words were lost in the roar of the engines. Suddenly exhausted, he leaned for a moment against the side of his boat and closed his eyes.

Less than a mile away, Tom Cashman, a retired electrician, was struggling with the same feelings on the deck of his fifty-foot charter boat, the *Rogue*. Soon after 9:00 P.M., he had seen the first bulletins on a tavern television near his home in Center Moriches. "TWA Flight 800, New York–JFK to Charles de Gaulle Airport, Paris, is down in the water off Long Island. No word yet on passengers and crew." A tough, tall man with a fisherman's leathery skin, Cashman was a U.S. Navy veteran who had served on a ship off Korea. One of his missions was to help recover American pilots downed by enemy fire. One December night in the 1980s, he'd also rescued three fishermen from the frigid waters off Long Island when he'd heard on the marine radio that their boat was sinking. At sixty-four, Cashman still radiated the can-do attitude he'd learned in the military, but it was more than that. If you had a boat, and people were in trouble, you helped.

Cashman slid off his bar stool to call his son, Matt, and six or eight friends who might join him. When he reached Liz Corrigan, she told him her husband wasn't home. When Cashman told her why he'd called, she volunteered to go herself. "Sure, I guess," Cashman replied, taken aback. He hadn't thought of having a woman aboard, but then a woman might be better at comforting survivors, especially if any were children. Liz ran around the corner to the house of her twenty-five-year-old sister, Patty Soper, and knocked hard on the door. Patty knew about boats. Liz told her the news in gasps. "Plane crash . . . Tom Cashman said . . . in the water. . . . We have to go. . . ."

The two women drove quickly to the marina where the *Rogue* was tied up and joined the seven men who had responded to Tom's call. From her own family's boat in a slip nearby, Patty grabbed some blankets to warm the survivors. The early report Cashman had seen mentioned inflated life rafts and life preservers, even an inflatable slide. Perhaps most of the passengers had survived. For Patty, who earlier that day had quit her job as assistant manager at a rental-car company and felt pretty glum, the crash suddenly put everything into perspective. How could she care about the job now? People's lives were at stake.

For the half hour that it took for the big charter boat to churn out of the inlet and into the sea, she felt oddly exhilarated. Then she saw the flames and smelled suffocating jet fuel. "I hope nobody lights a cigarette," she muttered. At Cashman's suggestion, she and Liz joined him on the bridge to film the bizarre scene with a video camera. She zoomed in on floating debris: CDs, attaché cases, backpacks, shoes, suitcases, passports, two upside-down seats bouncing gently in the water, and several three-foot-long green oxygen containers floating by like huge Coke bottles. Then, as they drew closer to the site, they came upon their first body, floating facedown in the water. Stunned, Patty clicked off the camera and put it away.

"Don't look at their faces—you'll be reminded of someone you know," Matt Cashman called out as other bodies came into view. Matt was right, Patty thought later. How did he know that? But by then it was too late: The faces were already burned into her mind.

Cashman had rescued pilots off Korea, one or two at a time, but that was nothing like the carnage he was witnessing this night. He was badly shaken, but tried not to show it. "We've got to keep focused," he said to his ashen crew members. "We've got to keep our emotions screwed down tight. If we don't, we won't be able to save anybody. Okay? The point is to save lives here."

The *Rogue* was among the first pleasure boats to reach the crash site, arriving around 10:00 P.M. It didn't take long for Cashman and his crew to come to the same sickening realization that Seebeck had reached. It would be a miracle if anybody survived this crash. The only thing to do was start hauling in bodies.

"I don't know if I can do this," Liz said, biting her lip.

"Liz, don't think about it," Cashman said. "Don't think at all if you can help it. Just put yourself on automatic and do it, because right now these people need our help."

The *Rogue* was not alone for long. Soon, dozens of other private vessels—fishing boats and motor yachts—converged on the scene. If a morbid curiosity had impelled any of the boaters to the scene, it was not in evidence. Local residents, who an hour before had been watching television in carpeted dens or grilling burgers in their backyards, were hauling bodies with grim dedication. The gathering news crews caught random images of the boaters from a distance but could not begin to convey the dull horror that moved them as they worked amid the wall of fire in the desperate hope of saving lives. By 11:30 P.M., as the flames began to ebb, what kept them going was the shared resolve to do right by the dead.

Repeatedly, Cashman urged his crew to preserve the dignity of the bodies they dragged aboard. "Be gentle with them. Be careful with them. They're human," he said. He knew Long Island fishermen are accustomed to dragging tuna and shark and marlin across their decks with gaff hooks as big as scythes. From his bridge on fishing trips, Cashman would often look down to see streams of blood rolling across his deck from the day's catch. Now, for all the care he and his crew took, he saw blood trickling from four victims, their bodies mere sacks of bones. Patty lay one blanket beneath them, and with another she covered them. A woman's hands protruded from the blankets; Cashman noticed that her fingernails were gaily painted in an elaborate design.

Nearby, a black-and-red commercial fishing boat, about one hundred feet long with a rotating crane, pulled up to a pleasure cruiser a few yards away. Over the marine radio, boaters heard the larger boat's captain instructing the smaller boat to hand over bodies. The crane swung over with a fifty-gallon green garbage can attached to its hook. The boaters were asked to place bodies in the garbage can. Some were disgusted. No way would they do that. "We'll take them back to East Moriches ourselves," Cashman told his crew.

His aim was to haul up as many bodies as he could find, but then Patty shone a spotlight on a large, twisted piece of fuselage and noticed a pair of small, black sneakers hanging from it. At first Cashman thought he was looking at a doll. Then he edged closer and saw that the doll was a young girl, swaddled by a piece of fuselage. Patty, still shining a light down from the bridge, saw the little body before her older sister did and tried to shield Liz, who had a daughter about the same age, from the sight. "Liz, it's a little girl, don't look," Patty said. The men reached over the side and with their bare hands pried the child free, bending back the jagged aluminum skin that had somehow enveloped her as Patty kept her light trained on the body to help the men work. Unlike most of the victims, the girl was still clothed, protected by the fuselage wrapped around her like the arms of a tin man. Along with her black sneakers, she wore overalls and a denim jacket. Patty found herself praying for the girl, for her body to have suffered no pain, and for her soul to have gone to heaven the instant she died.

From the bridge, Patty watched one of the men gently place a blanket over the child's body. The man looked to her like a proud father, tucking her in for the night. For a moment or two, he knelt beside her, his head bowed, his shoulders heaving. Until then, Patty had been barely able to hold her feelings in, but neither she nor Liz could stop the tears that came now as the man below stretched the blanket up over the girl's head and made a sign of the cross over her covered body.

That was when Cashman turned the *Rogue* back toward East Moriches. He could have stayed several hours longer; he knew his crew would have worked through the night, but what he wanted to do more than anything was get that little girl home as soon as he could.

———

At 8:30 P.M., thirty miles west of the crash site in a small inboard boat in the Great South Bay, sheltered by the long sand bar of Fire Island, George Gabriel, chief of the Long Island office of the FBI, lay waiting for a fish to bite. He had chosen to drop anchor directly under the Robert Moses Bridge connecting Fire Island to Long Island. After nearly nearly three hours, he and his nine-year-old son, Matthew, had felt a tug at last. As his wristwatch ticked forward to the fateful moment of 8:31 P.M., Gabriel whispered, "Hold it steady now." The line drew taut. "Don't let it go slack."

"I've got it, Dad," Matthew said. As Matthew tugged at the striper he'd hooked, he noticed a flash on the eastern horizon. "Look, Dad, fireworks."

This was Matthew's first nighttime fishing trip, and the striped bass was a big one, so he gave the fireworks no further thought. His father, a big man who had once played college football, noticed that the burst looked more like the gas-fueled fire of an exploding tanker than any fireworks he'd ever seen: an orange glow that formed a plume as it fell toward the sea. But from thirty miles away, he could hear no explosion; the plume might even be an advertising gimmick, he thought, like those airborne banners conveyed by little prop planes over the Long Island beaches on sunny weekends. Besides, Gabriel was distracted by the fish, too. He and Matthew had worked hard for this moment, readying the lines, scattering chopped clams into the water to draw the fish. Hooting, they pulled the striper aboard, flipped it into the cooler, and rebaited the line.

In the boat with them was their friend John Gleeson, a federal court judge who had been the prosecutor at the trial of mob boss John Gotti two years before. Gabriel had been the FBI agent at Gleeson's side during that trial. As it happened, the agent who had engineered the wiretaps that convicted Gotti was now the head of the whole New York office, James Kallstrom.

The next tug on the line came about twenty minutes later. Gabriel bent over his son, his big hands steadying the boy's grip as the fish struggled to free itself. Suddenly, his beeper sounded. "Oh, man, of all times for that . . ." He handed Matthew over to Gleeson, pulled out his cell phone, and called the number of Inspector Bill Kiley at the Suffolk County police headquarters. As he did, he looked at his watch. It was just 9:00 P.M.

All Kiley knew was that a plane had crashed in the ocean off East Moriches and that Suffolk County police boats had headed out to investigate. He was calling Gabriel because that was the protocol for emergencies: Notify the FBI. Of course, thought Gabriel: The fiery light we thought was fireworks. . . . Gabriel's own protocol was to call his boss, Lewis Schiliro, head of the New York office's criminal investigation division. Punching the numbers on his cell phone as his son tugged at the line, he found Schiliro's wife at home. She explained that she had just come from the hospital. Her son had been hit hard in the face by a baseball earlier that evening, and her husband was still at the emergency room. Rather than beep Schiliro, Gabriel called the New York duty agent. "Mr. Kallstrom's on his way down here," the duty agent told him. "He's told us to open the Command Post, and he said to tell any agents reporting in to stand by."

Again the beeper sounded. Gabriel looked at the number. Christ, he thought. Kallstrom. With a 911 next to it—beeper shorthand for call right away.

"Where are you?" Kallstrom wasn't one to bother with niceties in a crisis.

"What do you need?" Gabriel answered, hedging.

"There's a plane crash off Long Island. A goddamn 747. I need someone out to East Moriches right away. Where are you?"

Gabriel was off duty and knew he had every right to be out fishing, but that didn't keep him from feeling sheepish. "Fishing," he said with a sigh, "out on Great South Bay."

"What?"

"It'll just take me thirty minutes to get back," Gabriel said.

"Get moving!" Kallstrom shouted. "East Moriches; the plane's ten miles out. And it sure doesn't look like an accident."

"Right."

Gabriel gunned the inboard before Matthew could reel in his line. As his boat cut across the bay, he beeped four of his agents. When they called in, he told them to meet him at his home in Bay Shore. In fifteen minutes—half the usual time—he was tying up his boat at the Bay Shore marina. By the time he pulled up in front of his driveway, the agents were waiting for him; so was his wife, with the look of exasperated concern he'd come to expect when emergency calls came. "Plane down, don't know any more," he said as Matthew and Judge Gleeson got out of the car and the agents piled in. Gabriel pulled on a SWAT-team shirt that he had taken from the trunk, and told his family, "Don't know when I'll be back. Probably not tomorrow. I'll let you know."

His wife nodded, her arms folded across her chest.

The car started out of the driveway, then stopped. Gabriel stuck his head out the window and looked back. "Oh—so, honey?" he said to his wife. "Tomorrow? Will you clean the boat? It's disgusting."

With a nod to the guards at the underground garage security desk of 26 Federal Plaza, Jim Kallstrom hurried into the elevator. His office was on the twenty-eighth floor, but tonight he pressed for twenty-six. When he stepped out of the elevator, he punched his ID number into the security-code box, and before the wooden double doors had swung fully open, hurried into the emergency crisis center known as the Command Post.

Behind a long reception counter, three duty agents manned the phones in rotating shifts, twenty-four hours a day, to handle everyday traffic and serve as a first-response team in emergencies. To their right was the Command Post itself: a room about as wide and nearly as long as a basketball court, though not as high-ceilinged. The track-lit room was defined by three, long, semicircular workstations built on ascending levels. Kallstrom and his three top deputies—each was known as a special agent in charge, or SAC—sat along the highest row, while other agents manned the tiers below. The Command Post resembled NASA's Mission Control Center in Houston and as in Houston, the descending tiers faced a number of large screens on the opposite wall: for teleconferencing, for data display, and for watching twenty-four-hour newscasts.

The room, far removed from anything known in the conservative J. Edgar

Hoover era, was filled with some of the most sophisticated investigative equipment operated by the FBI. Rows of mainframe computers were tapped into impressive databanks of cross-referenced "intel"—intelligence information—and the phones on the top-tier desks were equipped with secure lines, as were the high-speed fax machines against the wall. The New York office was the FBI's largest, as capable of tracking complex financial scams on Wall Street and spies at the United Nations as it was in dogging New York's Mafia figures engaged in thuggery and worldwide racketeering. It was from the Command Post in New York that Kallstrom, then head of Special Operations, Pickard, and the now-renowned FBI–NYPD Joint Terrorism Task Force had conducted investigations that led to the arrest of Ramzi Yousef, the World Trade Center bomber, and the blind terrorist Sheik Omar Abdel-Rahman. The agents assigned to the New York office were an elite force. As a result, they were said to have a New York attitude—scoffing at Washington bureaucracy, doing things their way. Agents in small FBI field offices put one black-shod foot in front of the other. Agents in the New York office swaggered.

By the time Kallstrom strode in, the Command Post was up and running. Some twenty-five agents were already at their stations. The boss's presence charged the room; you could see the difference in the way the agents seemed to come to attention as he entered. Kallstrom was a bear of a man brimming with fierce energy, whose sparkling green eyes invariably flashed the message: We'll win, I promise. His voice boomed over the ringing telephones and urgent chatter. "Call Kennedy Airport," he told one agent. "I want to know everything the FAA knows." He pointed at two other agents. "Get ahold of TWA. Get the manifest of the plane. Let's start an information flow." A third agent was assigned to be in touch with agents at SIOC, the Strategic Information Operation Center, a vaultlike chamber sealed off by heavy steel doors at the FBI's headquarters in Washington, a few blocks from the White House. From SIOC, O'Neill had already opened up lines of communication with CIA, the Pentagon, the Justice and State departments, and other government agencies in order to feed Kallstrom and the task force information they needed. It was an important link for Kallstrom, and he had confidence in O'Neill, a smart agent who knew how to get it done.

Kallstrom hardly needed to state the obvious: that the crash appeared to be the result of terrorism. The midair explosion of Pan Am Flight 103 over Lockerbie, Scotland, on December 21, 1988, served as an obvious precedent: A bomb placed on that flight by terrorists had killed 259 people. Terrorism had been the chief topic of a four-day, high-level FBI National Academy Training Session just concluded that morning in New York City, one that Kallstrom and many of the agents in the room had attended. "The same day we learn how to prevent it, it happens," one agent muttered in disbelief.

"Where's Tom?" Kallstrom bellowed.

A tall man with salt-and-pepper hair and a brown mustache slid into the station beside Kallstrom's, unfazed after a high-speed drive from his home in Montclair, New Jersey. At forty-five, Tom Pickard looked like a college professor. Cerebral, subdued, and rather colorless at first meeting, he was an accountant by training and brought an accountant's obsession with detail to his work. Yet he had the driest wit of any senior agent, and a boyish enthusiasm about his work that often made him seem more like an academy graduate than Kallstrom's chief deputy. Pickard radiated the quiet satisfaction of a man who was doing what he always wanted to do. In a sense, he was following in his mother's footsteps; she had aspired to be an FBI agent at a time when only men were allowed. Self-deprecating, low-key, and smart, he was one of the fastest-rising agents in the FBI. He had distinguished himself as an undercover agent during the Abscam investigation, in which congressmen were nabbed for taking bribes. Currently he was one of Kallstrom's chief deputies and the head of the New York National Security Division, in which capacity he oversaw all terrorism and espionage cases. Pickard had the quiet gift of being able to connect easily with anyone. He was also the one agent willing to ride in a car with his boss at the wheel. Though he and Kallstrom never socialized after work—never even shared a beer at a downtown bar—Pickard was the colleague on whom Kallstrom relied most and to whom, in his own bearish, often profane way, he was most deferential.

Kallstrom nodded at Pickard without saying hello. "Get Rapid Start fired up," he said. Pickard set down the overnight bag he always kept packed and ready for Command Post duty. The Rapid Start software, designed especially by the FBI, provided the Command Post with instant access to information being compiled by every agent in the field. "We're reviewing intercepts," Pickard said.

"Good. Let me know if you come up with anything," Kallstrom responded. On the floor below, several agents were already poring over the transcripts of recently wiretapped conversations conducted by suspected terrorists of various groups around the United States, particularly in New York and New Jersey. On the drive in, Pickard had thought of a half-dozen possible suspects who might have downed Flight 800. Their conversations were tapped routinely by agents with judicial orders to detect terrorist operations in the offing.

"Are you sure there was no Mayday from the pilots?" Pickard asked Kallstrom.

"Absolutely: no Mayday."

To Pickard, that was significant. A mechanical failure, he thought, could not possibly occur so quickly that the pilots wouldn't become aware of it and report it, but a well-placed bomb could knock out a plane's communication instantly. The subject had been discussed among terrorism experts for years.

In any investigation of a catastrophe, the key is to move very, very fast. Kallstrom had to assume that suspects, leads, evidence, and even routine information were scattering. What the FBI did in the next few hours would be critical to the investigation. One of his first moves from his car was to ask Pickard to call the FBI–NYPD Joint Terrorism Task Force. Pickard reached agent Neil Herman, head of the task force and an expert on terrorists, at his home in Westchester. "What are you thinking?" Pickard asked.

"I'm thinking Yousef," said Herman of the mastermind behind the World Trade Center bombing. He'd been on the phone, already putting his agents in place; he would come down to the Command Post when he'd done all he could from home.

With the FBI and the Joint Terrorism Task Force both up and running, Kallstrom now began recruiting other agencies to help, starting with the U.S. Bureau of Alcohol, Tobacco, and Firearms, to help search the wreckage for traces of explosive material, and the Immigration and Naturalization Service, to help cross-reference the arrivals or departures of suspected terrorists. He put out an all-bureau directive for FBI agents with expertise in high-tech electronics and explosives; as they arrived, Kallstrom and Pickard assigned them to various teams. Other agents were dispatched to the big East Coast airports in New York, Boston, and Washington. A terrorist might even now be fleeing the country—as Ramzi Yousef had done the night of the World Trade Center bombing. Kallstrom wanted agents to secure lists of all passengers on flights to and from every U.S. international airport, starting from twenty-four hours ago: As he knew from bitter experience with Yousef, airlines delete each day's records the next day for lack of storage space. If Flight 800 was the first or second strike in a campaign of terrorism by Iran or some freelance group, a plane from one of those airports might also be the next target.

"Any credit calls?" he shouted over to one agent. The agent shook his head. Nearly ninety minutes had passed since the crash, and no terrorist group had called the FBI or any other U.S. enforcement agency to take credit for the crash as a political act. There weren't even any crank calls. That was frustrating, but no longer unusual. A decade or more ago, virtually every terrorist act was followed by a claim; usually, the problem was sorting out which of a dozen or more calls and faxes was the genuine article. The point of terrorism, after all, was to make the link between a terrorist group and its violent acts clear to all concerned—to provoke terror for political gain. But recently, terrorist groups, especially some Middle Eastern ones, had seemed almost to prefer not making claims. Inflicting damage on the United States, rather than advancing an agenda of their own, had become the point.

"We need to put out a press release," Kallstrom told Joe Valiquette, the New York office's seasoned press spokesman. "It should say that the FBI along with the Joint Terrorism Task Force have begun investigating the circumstances surrounding the destruction of Flight 800 based on its jurisdiction to investigate crime aboard an aircraft. Make sure you say that we are not prepared to declare this a terrorist incident. We need to let the public know we are eager for anything they might have seen."

Within seconds of its release, the statement was echoing back from the television screens in the Command Post wall and being put high up in newspaper accounts of the crash as a first official recognition that terrorism was suspected.

"The manifest is coming through from O'Neill," Pickard reported. He scanned it, then grimaced. "How can there be seven hundred names here?"

"It's the overall list of everyone who made a reservation for the flight," O'Neill explained on the phone. "It includes people who never bought a ticket or showed up for departure. The FAA says a verified list will take a few hours."

"Tell them to be faster than that—a lot faster," Pickard said.

Though a complete radar picture of Flight 800's final moments would also take the FAA some time to compile, a preliminary tape from Kennedy Airport revealed an odd series of blips near the plane in the seconds before the crash. An FBI agent at Kennedy Airport had driven back to the Command Post, his siren wailing, with the printout of the tape. The FAA was also rushing a copy of the tape with the mysterious blips over to the White House. Kallstrom and Pickard pored over the white grid-lined paper. Red diamonds identified TWA Flight 800, showing the plane's altitude and flight path a moment before the crash. Beside the diamonds was a swirling line of blue slash marks. Could the swirl be a missile? It very well could be, the FAA advised the FBI, but it could also be a computer glitch, or a "ghost blip"—a visual error on that particular tape. A blip or a glitch was not common, nor was it rare. The FAA would have to study it more carefully and compare it to other tapes of Flight 800 from different locations as they came in.

From the lowest echelon of the Command Post, a young agent named Pam Culos looked up from the Flight 800 cargo list she'd been studying. "Hey, guys," she shouted out a moment later. "There was AIDS blood on that plane." Culos then alerted agents at the East Moriches Coast Guard station who, over the marine radio, warned boaters at the crash site not to handle any floating cargo that looked as if it might contain vials of blood.

By now, Lewis Schiliro, the criminal-division head whose son had received stitches from a baseball injury, was at the East Moriches Coast Guard station coordinating a force of agents that would grow, by midnight, to nearly two hundred. Technically, Long Island was the purview of George Gabriel, the agent who had been out fishing with his son. Schiliro was one of Kallstrom's three top deputies, or SACs, who usually worked several floors beneath his boss at 26 Federal Plaza, and he had a place along the highest tier of the Command

Post. The criminal division covered every kind of crime except terrorism: anything from Latin American drug trafficking to Mafia racketeering to Wall Street white-collar crime. But Schiliro happened to live on Long Island. For Kallstrom, having Schiliro near the crash site was his first, and so far only, break of the night. A gentle, unassuming man who managed to be paternal even with much older men, Schiliro was one of the smartest agents in the field, who brought an unusual degree of creativity to the analysis of a crime. His son's injury notwithstanding, he was a serious baseball fan.

"Have you found any eyewitnesses yet?" Kallstrom asked Schiliro. "We need to talk to these people."

On one of the three wall-size screens in the Command Post, CNN reporters were already doing just that. Eyewitnesses were saying they'd seen streaks of light in the sky near the plane before it exploded. The New York FBI office had received five or six calls from Long Island residents reporting flarelike objects in the sky before the blast—too big, they said, to be flares. Commercial and private pilots flying in the area had also filed reports with the FAA of streaks of light prior to the blast.

A missile hadn't been Kallstrom's first thought, but it certainly could explain the streaks of light. "Shit," he muttered. "Could something have hit this plane?" To the public it would sound outlandish, but planes, including commercial airliners, had been shot down by missiles elsewhere in the world over the last two decades, among them an Iranian plane mistakenly shot down in the Persian Gulf by an American cruiser. For years, intelligence experts had discussed the possibility that an enemy missile might shoot down a commercial jetliner in the United States. Kallstrom told Pickard to have the U.S. Department of Defense line up missile experts to brief FBI agents in the morning. "I want to know everything there is to know about a missile," he said. "I also want to know what was out there—all military planes and choppers and what they were doing, all commercial and private planes, too."

A missile might be a random act of terrorism; it might be a tragic misfire from a U.S. military plane or vessel; it might also be an act of war. Kallstrom felt his gut tighten as it had nearly thirty years ago under fire in Vietnam. His body was hardening, a natural reflex that kicked in when he had to take control, but he had far more troops to manage now than he'd had when he served as a Marine captain. In fact, the way he was juggling tasks now reminded him of a summer job he'd had as a short-order cook when he was sixteen years old, at a restaurant on Cape Cod. The restaurant was next to a Catholic church, and on Sunday mornings when Mass let out, the waitresses would step up toward the kitchen and yell out forty orders at once. Kallstrom, his fingers blistered from spattering hot grease, would slap two dozen eggs on the grill, dip out pancake batter, get the orders going all at once, and serve them up on plates still hot from the dishwasher, one after another onto the counter of the narrow pickup window, with the waitresses glaring as they scooped them up. It was Hazel barking orders then. It was Kallstrom barking orders now.

"Let's get all senior people into the side office," Kallstrom said to Pickard. Before he joined the meeting, he made one more call.

Charlie Christopher picked up the phone on the first ring. When he heard Kallstrom's voice, he felt a surge of hope. "Any word yet, Jim?"

"It doesn't look good, Charlie. No survivors have been found yet, and it's pitch-black on the ocean now. But we've had helicopter reports of life rafts sighted."

"I know Janet; she's a survivor, Jim. I know she's alive."

"I know how scrappy she is, Charlie. If there's any chance, you know she's got it."

Cradling the receiver gently, Kallstrom put his head in his hands and detected the faint odor of cigar smoke on his sleeve. The Friars Club dinner seemed days, not hours, ago, and the day seemed more like a week. He'd started it at 4:30 A.M., as he always did, and had driven from his home in Connecticut to 26 Federal Plaza. It was now just after midnight. He knew he wouldn't get home that night—he'd already told his wife—and that if he grabbed an hour or two of sleep on the sofa in his twenty-eighth-floor office before dawn, he'd be lucky. The Marines had taught him that he could get by on a few hours of sleep a night for as long as a week. Perhaps he still could. But at this point, sleep was the least of his concerns.

———

Set within the Command Post was a scuffed-up conference room with tattered maps, worn leather chairs, and an old brown wooden desk. Kallstrom took the leather seat at the desk. Pickard sat on one side of him. George Andrew, an assistant special agent in charge (ASAC) under Pickard, sat on the other; Andrew was the antithesis of Pickard, excitable and outspoken enough to challenge Kallstrom when he saw fit, even as fellow agents slid down a notch in their chairs and Kallstrom grimaced, but Andrew was also respected as a workaholic and much liked. Half a dozen other men filled out the room.

"Let's get started," Kallstrom said. "We have a plane crash like nothing we've ever seen before, and we're hearing talk about missiles. What do you think?"

"Well, it's obvious we have to start with Yousef," Andrew declared.

The image in everyone's mind was of the clever, intense Kuwaiti who had not only masterminded the World Trade Center bombing but plotted to blow twelve U.S. commercial jetliners out of the sky within a single forty-eight-hour period. Ramzi Yousef had learned to take advantage of America's false sense of security on September 1, 1992, when he walked off a jet from Pakistan and strolled through Kennedy International Airport like a confident tourist. He had no right to be in the country, but he knew the magic words: "I want asylum." From a war-torn country like Pakistan, where human rights were routinely abused in the name of Islam, claiming to be a political prisoner was always a plausible story, and usually paid off. This case was no exception.

Immigration agents saw no need to track Yousef—he had made no threats and committed no crimes—and so he settled without notice in Jersey City, amid an enclave of Middle Eastern expatriates, some of whom were, in fact, known radicals being tracked by the FBI. With the help of at least one confederate, he began to fulfill his mission by building a bomb—one that the FBI's rueful technicians would declare highly ingenious—using mundane substances easily bought over the counter at local stores. Eventually, he recruited more helpers, perhaps as many as eight, to transport the one-thousand-pound bomb by rented panel truck into the underground garage of the World Trade Center on February 26, 1993. The bomb went off as planned, killing six people, injuring more than a thousand, and creating a half-billion-dollar hole half the size of a football field. Experts believed that virtually no bomb, no matter where it was placed, even closer to a crucial support beam, could have brought the entire building down.

Within hours of the blast, Yousef was on a jet back to Pakistan. His quick escape from the United States after the World Trade Center bombing had haunted Kallstrom, Pickard, and the others; it haunted them even now, after his arrest. While Yousef had proved to be something of a lone wolf, acting out his personal hatred of the United States apparently without help from any particular state or group, he was idolized by a wide scattering of other militant radicals, from Afghani rebels to followers of Sheik Abdel-Rahman.

Of those, the sheik's followers seemed the most logical suspects. Galvanized by the World Trade Center bombing, the sheik had incited his followers to bomb the United Nations, FBI headquarters in New York, and the major tunnels linking New York and New Jersey, as well as the George Washington Bridge. Recently convicted of conspiracy for plotting to blow up these city landmarks, the sheik had threatened the judge at his sentencing, hinting at retaliation and giving his blessing to aggression against the United States.

"Let's check if anyone's visited our friends in prison," Kallstrom said of Yousef and the sheik. Under law, the prisoners could not be denied visits from their lawyers and legal assistants. A few followers of the sheik had become paralegals to gain access to him in a high-security federal medical center in Missouri. Kallstrom knew this. He also directed his agents to check the phone calls and recent mail received or sent by the two terrorists.

"Any threats from other groups?" Pickard asked the others. Most agents were unaware, as yet, of just how high a state of alert Washington had initiated, and of the recent movements among Middle Eastern terrorists that had helped provoke it. They did wonder if the ongoing Yousef trial, in a courthouse two blocks away from FBI headquarters, had prompted sympathizers to target a commercial plane. But as the agents confirmed, no actual threats had been called in to the FBI. To be sure, Pickard ordered teletype inquiries sent to the other fifty-five FBI offices throughout the United States and to embassies around the world.

"What about the Olympics?" Kallstrom asked of the other reason for Washington's high state of alert. That very evening, a pre-Olympics ceremony had been conducted in Atlanta; Charlie Christopher had been watching it on television when the first report of the crash came as a bulletin across the bottom of the screen. What if one of Yousef's cohorts had bombed Flight 800 as a prelude to more terrorism when the games began? There seemed little more to be done: The FBI had agents all over Atlanta, and New York's special operations bureau had dispatched a team of divers to search for bombs in a lake outside the city where water sports were scheduled. The specter of Olympics terrorism was no less haunting for that.

That morning, as it happened, Kallstrom's third SAC, Joe Cantamessa, had set off for Atlanta in an FBI car filled with tanks and other equipment for the divers, whom he would oversee for the duration of the games. But now Kallstrom needed Cantamessa back in New York. He'd beeped him as he was checking in for the night at a Motel 6 in Greensboro, North Carolina, and felt better just for hearing Cantamessa's cocky voice on the line.

"How fast can you get your ass up here?" Kallstrom bellowed.

"I'll start driving right now," Cantamessa said coolly.

"Why not fly?"

"Because nothing but birds will be flying out of Greensboro's airport at this hour, that's why."

The two had worked closely together for twenty years, reeling in one Mafia kingpin after another. Both were surveillance experts; Kallstrom had served as the first head of a special operations bureau set up to take on the Mafia with aggressive electronic surveillance, and Cantamessa had succeeded him. Kallstrom felt better just knowing his old partner would be on the team by morning.

"How about intel on any characters coming into the States or leaving?" Kallstrom asked the senior team. Such movement, the agents knew, sometimes indicated a terrorist mission in the works.

"Not that I know of yet," said Pickard. He had wondered that himself, and had already asked the team reviewing intelligence to check if anyone had fallen out of sight recently. Perhaps by comparing intel reports, a pattern of movement would become clear.

Among other things, Kallstrom wanted to know everything there was to know about the plane and anyone associated with it. Apparently it was twenty-five years old. What was its history? Its full service record? How did that record compare to those of other 747-100 planes? Most important, what was that particular plane's recent flight record, beginning with the last half-dozen trips it had made? So far, the agents knew only that its last departure had been from Athens, Greece. Kallstrom wanted a manifest of all passengers who had flown to Athens on the previous flight, and all those who had flown from Athens to New York.

Kallstrom also wanted a rundown on everyone else who had access to the plane after it landed in New York: cleaning personnel, baggage handlers, fuelers, inspectors, caterers. In addition, he wanted the identities of everyone who had worked at Kennedy Airport the night of the explosion. There were fifty-five thousand employees at Kennedy Airport alone. Kallstrom wanted to know who was on duty, who was not, and who should have been on duty but didn't show up.

"And where's that amended manifest of Flight 800 passengers?"

Pickard had it now. His agents had begun checking the names against the FBI database to see if any known terrorists were on board. They were also checking to see if anyone on board might have seemed a target of assassination: a highly protected trial witness, perhaps, or a foreign diplomat or other dignitary. The list of names would also be sent on to the Secret Service, the CIA, and other intelligence agencies overseas for similar checks. Later, the families of each victim would be interviewed. Had any of the passengers been threatened somehow? Was any passenger involved in a lovers' triangle? Were any of the passengers clinically depressed, perhaps suicidal? Could the loss of a loved one or job have triggered an irrational act? All these possibilities would be pursued 230 times—for every passenger and crew member.

"And the cargo?"

George Andrew said he'd get agents to check out what cargo, in addition to passenger luggage, had been put aboard the flight. There was that early report that a shipment of HIV-positive blood had been en route to Paris for medical research analysis; could something else have been slipped in with it?

As Kallstrom continued to field ideas from the Terrorism Task Force investigators, Tom Pickard took a break from the group and walked down the hallway alone. He was worried. What if a known terrorist had been aboard Flight 800— one whom Pickard's counterterrorism group should have been tracking but missed? What if the intercepts revealed a clue to the bombing, one that his agents had overlooked? Or what if a code word for "bomb" or "airliner" was used by some terrorist in a wiretapped conversation that had been misunderstood by agents? Even if not, the crash certainly looked like terrorism, and terrorism was Pickard's responsibility. Could his agents have done more? Could he have ridden them harder? Was Flight 800 his fault?

Pickard took a deep breath and reentered the room. Then it hit him: Kallstrom, who had ultimate responsibility for everything in the New York FBI, must be tormented by the same thoughts—and worse. Yet there he was, channeling his energy not into fear, but into finding answers. Pickard felt better for that, and as he looked around the room at his colleagues, he could see that they, too, were pumped up by their leader. They all knew his record—it was little short of legendary—but they also knew how hard he had worked to break those cases and how personally he took the work. He was a boss who'd risen in the ranks not by bureaucratic maneuvering or luck but by doing better, with more heart, than anyone else. In fact, his hatred of bureaucracy was so intense and so well known that other agents often wondered what lay behind it.

As a boss, Kallstrom could be tough, but only if he thought you weren't doing your best. If you worked flat out, you knew Kallstrom would back you up as fiercely as a fellow Marine in a foxhole. He might yell at you if you made a mistake, but you knew the storm would pass, and the mistake would be forgiven. The truth was that his men didn't merely respect him; they adored him, and none more so than Tom Pickard.

"One other thing you should know," Kallstrom said. "Washington is treating this as a potential act of war. And, gentlemen, you've all become generals. I want this to be the most thorough investigation ever conducted on U.S. soil. If a terrorist downed this plane, we're going to catch him. Make it absolutely clear to everybody: Not one piece of evidence will be overlooked."

Sometime later, Kallstrom ducked into the men's room to splash water on his face. In the mirror, his eyes were red, his face heavy. He had been nearly thirty years younger as a Marine, back when he stayed up nights at a stretch. The Marines, he liked to say, had given him "three of his four sides." They had toughened him, taught him the Corps values—courage, character, leadership, and loyalty—and sent him to the front lines of the Vietnam War during the worst of the Tet offensive. Somehow this week—and maybe for a long, long while—he would have to feel that young and strong again.

Back in his Command Post seat, he dialed Louis Freeh's number for a second time that night. "They're telling us the plane fell from about thirteen thousand feet," he said, "and it's been hours now without a survivor reported. I don't think anyone made it alive."

"Just do what you have to do, Jimmy. Whatever you need . . ."

"We put out the press release and have received more calls about streaks in the sky," Kallstrom said. "We are talking with DOD about missiles. I'll touch base in a couple of hours." Kallstrom hung up the phone and looked absently at his watch. It was 3:00 A.M. He realized he had shaken his boss out of a sound sleep.

———

Two hours after the explosion, a dozen bodies were already lined up in a temporary morgue in a boathouse at the water's edge. The bodies were laid out on Red Cross blankets for identification, and then the grim work of tagging the bodies began.

As the Suffolk County homicide detectives assigned to the job were starting to work, two young women burst into the boathouse to join them. Karen LoPresto was a twenty-eight-year-old sonogram technician; with her was her thirty-one-year-old roommate, Lucy Lagravinese. Both were members of an emergency forensic team trained for disasters; when they saw the TV reports of the crash, they rushed from their East Moriches apartment to help. Before entering the boathouse, they peered in at the bodies, some in body bags, some exposed, and wondered if they had the stamina to go in. To Lagravinese, it looked like a horror movie, but worse. "Every one of them is somebody's daughter or mother or son," she whispered to LoPresto. Lagravinese wept quietly for a moment, then took a deep breath and entered.

The women were given clipboards and told to record the data about the dead that the detectives dictated to them. The body bags were opened one by one, the bodies photographed and numbered. Close-up pictures were taken of any jewelry or belongings that might help identify the victim, as were scars, tattoos, or other distinguishing details. One of the bodies that stayed in LoPresto's memory was that of a woman with long, wet, stringy hair and a broken front tooth; days later, she would be startled to see a photograph on the morgue wall of a beautiful bride smiling broadly with her husband in front of a white limousine, and realize that was the woman she had seen in the boathouse. She saw another body so crushed that only a telltale braid indicated it was a woman. Farther down the same row she saw a young girl with a few dollars tucked into her sock, probably money her parents had given her at the last moment to spend in Paris. Across the room, she spotted another young girl covered with sparkling glitter. Why the glitter, she wondered?

As she followed the detectives down the silent rows, LoPresto recalled a movie about a plane crash she had seen in which an angel comes on board while the plane is still flying and gathers up the souls, leaving behind the bodies. It was just a movie, she knew, but the image comforted her a bit. "It's just the shells of their souls," she told herself. Most upsetting, for her, were the bodies of the plane's crew. How many times had she been scared by turbulence on a plane and been reassured by a warmly professional flight attendant? Yet all the confidence and experience that this flight crew must have radiated, too, had been shattered by a force so much greater than any of them could comprehend.

Soon after sunrise, the bodies in the boathouse were readied for transport to the county morgue. LoPresto and Lagravinese found seats on some concrete steps near the water and took a break. They were overwhelmed. So many lives snuffed out in an instant. So many other lives changed in the blink of an eye. That was when they noticed the luggage and backpacks lined up on the dock and the letters and diaries scattered on the ground nearby, drying in the early light. Among the debris was a blue teddy bear and a large, stuffed Tweety Bird with a broken leg. Someone had patched the broken leg back to the bird's body with surgical tape.

From where they sat, the women might have seen the running lights of the *Rogue* moving slowly back into East Moriches Inlet. Tom Cashman, the *Rogue*'s captain, saw no need to hurry now. Besides, gliding through the darkness with the ebbing fires of the crash site nearly out of view felt oddly comforting to the crew. They rode in silence on the flat sea, numb with grief, shock, fatigue. Cashman, who had headed out hoping to save lives, just wanted this night to end, and yet he dreaded reaching the Coast Guard station in East Moriches. The blankets on top of the bodies would have to come off; the bodies would have to be moved. When they were moved, he wondered, where would they go?

As the *Rogue* approached the Coast Guard dock, Cashman saw what looked like hundreds of uniformed police, ambulance workers, and investigators. The ones who stepped forward to meet the boat were covered from head to toe in white biohazard jumpsuits. One of the white-suited men motioned for him to back his boat into the dock, then tossed him several packs of disinfectant and some brushes. Gently, he asked the crew members to scrub their hands, arms, and legs before disembarking.

As they stepped off the boat, an FBI agent asked the crew their names and took down the name and registration number of the boat.

"What about the bodies?" Cashman asked.

"We'll take care of them," the FBI agent said.

The agent led Cashman's crew to the far side of the dock, where stress management counselors were waiting to treat them if they needed to talk about what they had gone through. Wearily, Cashman and his crew declined the offer.

Then the FBI agent passed them over to a young Suffolk County police officer, who led the men to a row of portable shower stalls set up outside the station, the women to others, and directed them to take off their clothes and scrub themselves down with bleach and disinfectant. The officer told them there was danger of contamination from the burning fuel and debris, or possible exposure to disease from the victims. Cashman did not strip entirely but scrubbed the blood off his knees. When he looked back at his boat, he saw four Suffolk County police officers carrying the bodies he had brought to shore, one by one, into a temporary morgue set up in the station's boathouse. "Be careful with that little girl," he called out. Beside the boathouse were two metal refrigerator trucks waiting to carry tagged bodies to the county morgue. The men in white jumpsuits then hosed down the *Rogue*, though like most of the other pleasure boaters who'd brought in bodies, Cashman would find bits of congealed blood and flesh here and there on the deck the next day. Entangled in the propeller he would find a dress. He remembered the wartime credo: Never leave your dead on the battlefield. Maybe the crash was the start of a war, maybe it wasn't, but the dead had needed bringing back all the same. He wasn't sorry he'd gone.

Among the hundreds of workers lining the dock was a chief in the Suffolk County police department, Joe Monteith, a highly respected official whom Cashman recognized. It seemed inappropriate to wave to the man, but for whatever reason—fatigue perhaps—Cashman found himself looking back at Monteith several times, his hands clasped behind him as he stood to the side of the workers. Suddenly, without changing his grim expression, Monteith unlocked his hands and gave Cashman the thumbs-up. To Cashman, the gesture meant everything: that he and his crew had done all they could, and that the police appreciated it. It was the only good feeling Cashman had all night, and it made him cry.

Patty Soper was exhausted and afraid of collapsing. When she had scrubbed down and got back in her clothes, someone handed her a slip of paper advising her that she might suffer nightmares in the coming weeks. The warning proved prescient. A few days later, on a television program about the crash, she would see a family video of the little girl in black sneakers. The girl was laughing. Patty recognized her as one of the bodies she'd pulled up that night. Over the next few months, the image of the girl laughing was what she saw just before she woke up, sweat-drenched, in the dark. Or else she imagined what the passengers of Flight 800 experienced before the plane hit the water, alive on the way down. For months afterward, she would find comfort on the docks in the company of boaters who had also been out there that night. You could just stand there with them, looking out at the inlet and the ocean beyond; you didn't need to talk at all.

By dawn, the pleasure boats were gone from the crash site, herded back to shore by the Coast Guard. All the bodies floating on the surface had been brought into the boathouse morgue, tagged, and put in body bags: 104 bodies, 70 of them women.

Of the Coast Guard and Suffolk County police boats that remained at the site, one was Petty Officer Ken Seebeck's twenty-eight-foot patrol boat. Seebeck and his crew had been out on the water all night, harvesting the dead. Every so often, a Suffolk County police boat would sidle up to them, and more bodies would be passed over the gunwales for transport back to the dock. By 8:00 A.M., when they finally headed in, Seebeck was pretty sure he and his men had retrieved twenty-four bodies in all, though there might have been one or two more. There were no more to be seen; that was the main thing.

As the patrol boat approached the Coast Guard dock in East Moriches, Seebeck was astounded by the size of the crowd. There had to be two thousand people milling about, amid police cars, ambulances, television news trucks, and more. Like the pleasure boaters, he was greeted by officers in white suits and given disinfectant, bleach, and brushes. He and his men hosed down the boat first, scrubbed the soot and scorch marks off the sides, then set to cleaning themselves. That was when his young crew members, their longest shift done, began at last to sob.

Seebeck held his own emotions in that morning. He even held them in as he recounted the horrors of the night to his wife when he returned home. He was a guardsman, after all, a member of the U.S. military. He had a crew to lead and a boat to tend. He had responsibilities.

A few days later, Seebeck entered a local bike shop to pick up some parts. The owner was old enough to be his father. "You did a good job out there, young man," the owner said softly. "Everybody's grateful to you."

On the ten-minute ride back home, Seebeck finally wept.

———

In the hours since Lewis Schiliro had arrived at the station, he had spent much of his time trying to coordinate the FBI's efforts with those of the various agencies on the scene. The county police launches were shuttling back and forth to collect bodies from the other boats and bring them back to the dockside morgue. Guardsmen were either out on the water, hauling in bodies, or helping in the morgue. FBI agents were responding to calls from eyewitnesses and fanning out through the area to find others and to begin initial checks at marinas. Gabriel, having arrived so quickly from his fishing trip, had commandeered one of the station's few telephone lines for FBI use; for that, Schiliro was especially grateful, since the dozens of cell phones on the site now made it almost impossible to get a cellular call through.

A little before midnight, Schiliro and Gabriel borrowed an Air National Guard helicopter and went up together to inspect the crash site. By now, there was little to see in the glare of powerful floodlights from a dozen choppers one hundred feet above the water: just innumerable bits of debris and a few fragments of the fuselage. The wall of fire had subsided to a low-burning fuel slick—long, narrow, and black—and several small fires still dotted the surface, enough to cast a faint orange glow in the dark. Looking down on the ghastly scene, with the smell of jet fuel harshly pervasive even now, Schiliro felt sure that an explosion had downed the plane, and that the explosion was no accident.

At Kallstrom's direction, Schiliro spent his next hours trying to "rope off" a potential crime scene in the Atlantic Ocean—not an easy task. It meant starting to herd the pleasure boaters back to the Coast Guard station, carefully recording and storing any debris they brought in, and keeping other private boats from joining the search. Then, as the Coast Guard and Suffolk County police went about the arduous task of harvesting any debris still afloat, the FBI agents began tagging all the debris as potential criminal evidence. As Kallstrom had emphasized, all debris would have to be painstakingly tracked, and every hand that touched each piece noted. Otherwise, if the debris yielded clues that resulted in the arrest and trial of terrorists, defense lawyers could shoot holes through the prosecution's case.

By dawn, Schiliro and Gabriel were tired, but neither of them paused long enough to feel the depth of his fatigue. They were so preoccupied that they paid no attention to the roar of the Air National Guard Black Hawk helicopter carrying their boss. When the chopper set down in the station's parking lot, no one came out to greet its two passengers.

Schiliro looked up from his precious phone to see Kallstrom and Pickard at the door of the second-floor Coast Guard office appropriated for FBI use. "Good job, Lew," Kallstrom said, and put a hand on Schiliro's shoulder. Schiliro gave him a weary smile and sighed. Suddenly, he was grateful not to be the one in charge anymore.

CHAPTER 2

ORDINARY FLIGHT, EXTRAORDINARY PEOPLE

The banner headline across the front page of *The New York Times* on July 18, 1996, stunned every reader who had failed to turn on a television or radio the night before. For all, it set the crash into perspective as a catastrophe of historic proportions. TWA Flight 800 was one of the worst plane disasters ever to occur in United States airspace, worse even than the crash of a ValuJet DC-9 jet over the Everglades just two months before, in which 109 people had died. Over time, the sinking of the *Titanic* would come to seem a closer historical comparison.

Most of a century separated TWA Flight 800 from the *Titanic*, and so did the manner of this destruction. Flight 800 had exploded in a fiery ball and sunk in flaming waters, while the *Titanic* had hit an iceberg and gone down in the freezing waters off Greenland. For the victims, these were fates as different, literally, as fire and ice. But the 747 that took off as Flight 800 that July night was the *Titanic*'s jet-age counterpart: an airship, the grandest of its class, as the *Titanic* was of its own. Both vessels had been designed for Atlantic crossings, and both were declared indestructible, in part because of their vast size. On both, there was a general air of festivity about traveling from one side of the Western world to the other, and on both there were distinct classes of passengers, kept strictly apart. The coach section of a 747 carried more affluent passengers, as a rule, than did the steerage of an oceanliner, but that only underscored a reason that TWA Flight 800 might have affected readers of the *Times* even more than the *Titanic*'s sinking did in 1912: They could have been on it.

Until Flight 800, air disasters had seemed remote to most Americans. Seventeen 747s had been destroyed by accident, half a dozen more by bombs by July 1996. Yet the accidents tended to occur in distant venues like the Canary Islands, where 582 people had died in 1977 when two 747s, one belonging to Pan Am and the other to KLM, collided on a runway—still the highest death toll from an airplane disaster. In 1983, Soviet fighters shot down a Korean Airlines 747, killing 269 people. Sabotage had occurred, occasionally, closer to U.S. shores: A bomb in the cargo hold of an Air-India Boeing 747 had exploded off the coast of Ireland in June 1985, killing all 329 aboard, while Pan Am Flight 103 had been taken down by a pound of plastic explosives concealed inside a Toshiba cassette recorder that exploded soon after takeoff over Lockerbie, Scotland, in December 1988; the death toll that time had been 259. But even these tragedies had happened on the other side of the ocean. As for the ValuJet crash on May 11, 1996, it had seemed distant in another way. Relatively few people had heard of ValuJet; fewer had ever flown in one of its planes. Fairly or not, the image that the name "ValuJet" conjured was of a tin box with wings, filled with economy flyers en route from the shopping malls and subdivisions of paved-over Florida.

From the first reports that the *Times* and other daily newspapers around the world were able to deliver on July 18, 1996, it was clear that the passengers of TWA Flight 800 were a different sort. A TWA flight from New York to Paris on any given night would have included its share of successful people: the sort of passengers who had business on two continents, as well as those affluent enough to take ocean-spanning trips for fun. Those on this particular flight seemed an unusual group even by that standard. Several names on the passenger manifest were prominent enough in their fields that a wide array of readers recognized them. Others, from the first sketchy biographical details, would have stood out in any crowd. The stories of how each had come to be on Flight 800 contained the same chillingly mundane mix of fate and circumstance that might have put any other *Times* readers in their place.

Jack O'Hara, an Emmy-winning executive for ABC's *Wide World of Sports,* had just lost his job in a corporate restructuring, but was on his way to Paris for his last assignment: to oversee coverage of the Tour de France bicycle race. To ease his well-known fear of flying, as well as the sting of his dismissal, ABC had paid to have his wife and thirteen-year-old daughter fly with him; the plan was for them to enjoy a short vacation in Paris when the work was done. Marcel Dadi, France's best-known country music guitarist, was returning from a weekend in Nashville, Tennessee, where he had been honored at the Country Music Hall of Fame. Constance Coiner, an English professor at the State University of New York, Binghamton, was allowing herself the luxury of a vacation in France after receiving tenure; with her was her twelve-year-old daughter, Ana Duarte-Coiner, an accomplished pianist who had been honored in the spring as one of Binghamton's most impressive students. Jed Johnson, an interior designer who had begun his career by working for Andy Warhol and had gone on to do homes for Yves Saint-Laurent, Mick Jagger, and Richard Gere, among others, was about to push his career to new heights with the opening of shops in Paris, London, and New York. Kirk Rhein, chief executive of the Danielson Holding Company, was on his way to close an $80 million deal. Rico Puhlman, a veteran fashion photographer for *Harper's Bazaar*, was going to Paris to shoot a magazine story. Kristina Skjold, a twenty-four-year-old from Sweden, spoke seven languages and had just finished business school in Paris, to which she was returning to pick up her degree; she had already started a distributorship in New York for a Swedish brand of bottled water called Malmberg.

More than a few passengers also appeared to have boarded Flight 800 at major turning points in their lives. With their sudden deaths, their stories assumed a terrible drama.

Sixteen teenagers from Montoursville, Pennsylvania, were bound for Paris as members of their high school French club. Montoursville is a modest mid-state town with a population not much over five thousand, yet the parents of its students had managed for decades to send one or another of the school's clubs on trips every year, raising the money through bake sales, car washes, and the like. For most students, a town-sponsored trip provided their first glimpse of a world beyond the business loop of Route 180. For months before, it fired their imaginations and brought to life the subjects they were studying in their clubs. Students didn't have to belong to a club to go on a club trip, however. If they were eager enough to go, a way could usually be found to send them. So it was with Rance Hettler and the girl he'd come to like in a hurry, Amanda Karschner.

Six-foot-three, blond, and well built, Rance McKenzie Hettler was the school's football and track star. He was also a leader in antidrug and antialcohol youth programs in his community. His ambition, often stated, was to become an FBI agent. A few days before the trip to France, Rance's mother, Jackie, had seen Amanda Karschner, a stunningly attractive high school track star, sitting in her car with her mother. Jackie knew the young woman was making the trip. Like Rance, Amanda was no longer in the French Club but was going to Paris anyway. Mrs. Hettler approached the car and greeted Amanda's mother, Pam, whom she hardly knew. She said hello to Amanda, who was seated next to her mother on the passenger side.

"Are you all packed and ready to go?" Jackie Hettler asked.

Amanda broke into a beaming smile and nodded energetically, her long blond hair whipping her shoulders.

Jackie didn't know her son had taken a keen liking to Amanda, but Amanda's mother did. Her daughter had been telling her how much she liked Rance, who was a year older. They had met at track meets.

Rance had a sense of humor, yet he was as earnestly responsible as any parent could wish a young man to be. On July 16, he cooked dinner for his family because his mother was feeling ill. The next morning, he got up early and drove to his grandmother to say good-bye, then visited his two great aunts. Later, along with his mother and sister, he stopped at his father's office.

"Rance, I don't know about you going on this trip," Gary Hettler told his son.

"Oh, Gary, he'll be fine," Jackie admonished him.

The prospect of having his son an ocean away made Gary nervous. He didn't want to spoil Rance's trip, though, so he smiled, hugged him, and told him to be careful.

At the Montoursville high school, a bus was waiting to take Rance, Amanda, fourteen other students, and five chaperons to New York's Kennedy International Airport, a three-hour drive. Before climbing aboard the bus, the excited students posed for group pictures. Then Rance hugged his mother, picked her up, swung her around, and gave her a peck on the lips. "Mom, I love you," he said. He gave his little sister, Katie, a good-bye squeeze, winked proudly at her, and boarded the bus. On the steps, he turned back to yell out, "Don't worry, Mom. I'll be fine. I'll call you from Pareeeeee."

Then Pam Karschner, who was standing a few yards away from the Hettlers, called out, "Rancey, watch out for Mandee."

Rance cupped his hand around his mouth and called out, "I'll take care of her, Mrs. Karschner. I'll just throw her in the ocean." Rance and Amanda laughed as they climbed into the bus. They sat next to each other and waved through the window to their mothers. Clearly, the two were at least as interested in spending time with each other as they were in exploring Paris.

As the students rode off, a more seasoned romance was taking a decisive turn on the front steps of a stylish brownstone in the East Eighties in Manhattan. Heidi Snow, a willowy twenty-four-year-old with white-blond hair and big brown eyes, was listening to her boyfriend of two years ask her to marry him as a livery car waited at the curb to take him to Kennedy Airport to board TWA Flight 800.

Heidi had noticed Michel Breistroff two years earlier in a restaurant on Martha's Vineyard, the quintessential summer island just off Cape Cod. He was a tall, handsome man coming downstairs with an athlete's limber step, in a dark windbreaker that didn't conceal his muscular build. Heidi was so smitten that she made a point to cross his path, a bold move for a shy woman who rarely spoke above a whisper. "Hi," he said. "What's your name?"

Born and raised in France, Michel was a senior at Harvard working toward a degree in biological anthropology. His prowess as an ice-hockey player had delayed his matriculation—after high school, he had played professionally on a Canadian minor-league team—and now he was putting his career ambitions in science on hold. Not long before, he had nearly won a spot on the French Olympic team, and was determined to make the cut next time. That summer, he was teaching hockey on Martha's Vineyard in association with Harvard. Heidi, who had returned home to Boston after college at the University of Wisconsin in Madison and was on the Vineyard for a summer of fun, planned to move to Manhattan to work toward a stockbroker's license. By the time she did, she and Michel were spending every possible moment together. "You are my mirror, Heidi," Michel would tell her, "so everything I do has a reflection and therefore a purpose."

Over the last several months, the two had grown closer. At Christmas, Michel had surprised Heidi by flying over from France, where he was skating for the national hockey team, to Boston, where Heidi was spending the holiday with her family, though he had only twenty-four hours between games. On this mid-July day, they were just back from a short vacation in the Florida Keys, where Michel had mentioned, not for the first time, his fear of flying. Another fear was of dark ocean water. At the Vineyard, he'd stayed out of the surf altogether; he and Heidi preferred the Keys, where the water was turquoise-blue and clear to the bottom. On the plane back, he'd talked tensely of the ValuJet crash. Not only had the passengers suffered the worst fate he could imagine; they'd disappeared into the dark, marshy water of the Everglades. "If I had to die in a crash," he told Heidi, "I'd rather crash on the ground." And he hoped, he said, that if he did die that way, he wouldn't be alone. Going down alone with no one to hold on to: That was, to Michel, an unimaginable horror.

Heidi thought his spirits may have been affected by the flu they'd both caught. Now, as Michel was preparing to return to Europe to start playing on a professional German team, he and Heidi felt better. With his head clear but his heart heavy at the prospect of leaving, he paused on Heidi's doorstep to ask the most important question of his young life.

Heidi beamed. "I would love to be your wife," she whispered in reply.

But Heidi's answer failed to ease Michel's anxiety. "When?" he asked. He wanted to know right away. Heidi could sense his urgency, and she thought it odd. There was no reason, she thought, why a wedding date had to be decided right now. "One year or two years?" he pressed.

"One year," Heidi answered.

Michel reached around and held her tight.

As he climbed into the livery car that Heidi had ordered for his trip to the airport, he turned toward her one last time, blew a kiss, and waved. Heidi kept waving back even after the car was out of sight.

———

Earlier in the day, Pam Lychner had flown up from Houston with her two daughters, ten-year-old Shannon and eight-year-old Katie. Pam was a former TWA flight attendant with thick blond hair who had more grit than her delicate looks might have suggested. In 1990, she testified against a twice-convicted sex molester who had attacked her, and two years later, when he was up for parole, she persuaded the parole board to keep him locked up. Lychner then worked with two other women to create Justice For All, a Houston-based advocacy group that lobbied successfully against early release for prisoners and convinced judges to let crime victims address their assailants in court after a guilty verdict.

Her career at TWA ended with a buyout during a corporate downsizing. The buyout included lifetime free travel passes for her and her family. Recently, she and her husband, Joe, who had taken a new job in Houston, had planned an ambitious series of educational trips—now that their daughters were old enough—starting with Israel and Egypt. The four-day trip to Paris was sort of a preseries lark, inspired by a poolside chat during a visit from Pam's good friend Paula Carven, with whom she had worked as a TWA flight attendant. Paula and her nine-year-old son, Jay, decided to accompany Pam and her daughters.

At the last minute, Joe Lychner's job kept him from joining his family. As Pam and the girls were waiting to board the plane, they called Joe at his office in Houston. "Pam from New York," his secretary said.

Joe was in a meeting and said, "I can't talk now. Tell her to call when she gets to Paris." Instead, the secretary told Pam to try back in fifteen minutes. "I think the meeting is wrapping up," she said. A quarter of an hour later, the meeting had ended—and Joe was bolting out the door to a business dinner. "Why not stick around five minutes?" the secretary suggested. "I bet she'll call by then."

Joe did—and Pam did. In the background, Joe could hear the children's excited voices.

"I'm going to miss you guys," Joe said quietly.

"Don't worry," Pam said with a laugh. "We'll be back to see you on Sunday."

Meanwhile, Paula Carven saw that her son, Jay, was chatting with a girl from Arizona. She was eleven-year-old Larkyn Dwyer, an accomplished rider who owned two horses, Red and Scotty, which she kept in a stable at her family's large home just north of Phoenix. She loved animals, and told her parents she wanted to be a veterinarian when she grew up.

As confident as Larkyn was on the back of a horse, she felt much less so about the prospect of her first plane trip alone. She was going to visit a friend whose family had moved from Phoenix to Paris, and she had vowed to stand under the Eiffel Tower on her birthday—August 14. But now that her family had brought her to the airport after a stay at their vacation home in the Adirondacks, she realized she was scared, especially after her father hugged her good-bye and rushed off to make a flight back to Phoenix. Her mother and her fourteen-year-old brother were getting ready to leave by car for Connecticut to visit relatives. From the stricken look on Larkyn's face, her mother could see that her daughter needed someone to reassure her.

"Oh, don't you worry. I'll keep an eye on her."

Her mother looked up to see a TWA flight attendant, a handsome woman in her late forties, put her hand on Larkyn's denim-jacketed shoulder, which made her brighten immediately. "I'm Janet Christopher," the flight attendant introduced herself. "I've got a son named Charles about this one's age. Eleven?"

Larkyn nodded vigorously.

Janet looked at Larkyn's ticket. "Hey, this is great!" she said. "I'm in first class, too. In fact, you can sit right near me when we take off, if you like, and I'll keep an eye on you the whole way."

Larkyn tugged her red L.L. Bean knapsack tight and took Janet's extended hand. Just then, a desk clerk at the TWA booth for Flight 800 picked up the microphone and announced that Flight 800 was boarding first class: the first call for Flight 800.

Larkyn's mother last glimpsed her daughter with her hand in Janet's, turning to wave good-bye as the two of them boarded the plane together.

The Boeing 747 that would be designated TWA Flight 800 had arrived as Flight 881 from Athens shortly after 5:00 p.m.—an hour later than scheduled due to air-traffic-control problems at Hellenikon International Airport. The plane was carrying 349 passengers and 17 crew. Of the passengers, 109 were Bosnian refugees, including two infants; 64 were Greek; and 178 were Americans or from other nations. Despite the late arrival, the ground crews at Kennedy Airport had more than enough time to prepare the jumbo jetliner for its scheduled 7:00 p.m. flight to Paris.

As the passengers from Athens disembarked, their luggage was unloaded from the cargo holds below. Inside the cabin, meals for first-class passengers— a choice of lobster or rack of lamb—were being loaded into the galleys as cleaning crews went from row to row, vacuuming and tidying up. Out on the tarmac, a fueler revved up his pumper truck to begin drawing jet fuel from an underground tank to fill the 747's two huge wing tanks. Instructions on his chart called for him not to put fuel in the plane's center fuel tank, a tank about the size of a one-car garage.

In its first twenty minutes in the air, the plane would burn 10,000 pounds of fuel. By the time it reached Paris, it would use most of the 176,600 pounds of fuel it carried on board. Nearly all its fuel would come from the two wing tanks. Only 50 gallons remained in the 13,000-gallon center fuel tank, a residual amount that barely covered its bottom. On an overseas flight from west to east, a plane is pushed along by the prevailing tailwinds, so much so that it needs only about two thirds of its fuel capacity. Filling the third tank would only add dead weight, causing the aircraft to burn even more fuel in the process. Besides, the trip to Paris was six hours, a relatively short overseas hop. For the flight home, when a 747 had to fight those same winds, all three fuel tanks would be filled. By the time it landed, much of that fuel would be gone. Within the last twenty-four hours, the plane that would end as Flight 800 had started from Kennedy Airport with its center tank nearly empty, and left Athens with all tanks full. Jets were refueled this way hundreds of times a day at major airports all over the world.

At the TWA terminal's Gate 27, rows of plastic seats were filling with Paris-bound passengers and well-wishers, including a number of standby hopefuls—among them the Lychners and the Carvens, who, as TWA pass-holders, had to let the airline fill all the seats it could with paying passengers before being allowed on themselves. Paula Carven and Pam Lychner had originally planned to leave Thursday, but switched to Wednesday a few days before, thinking they would stand a better chance of getting on a midweek flight. At one point, the flight had been sold out, but inevitably some passengers had canceled, and now they were optimistic.

A trio of Italian men were fuming as they checked in at the last minute for Flight 800 at the ticket counter near the gate. Their flight to Kennedy had arrived late, and they had missed their connecting flight to Rome. There was one more nonstop flight to Rome that night, but it was full. Reluctantly, they agreed to board Flight 800 and fly on to Rome from Paris.

As they lined up at Gate 27 to board the flight, a TWA attendant hurried over to tell them three seats had opened up on the nonstop Rome flight. It was leaving in a few minutes. Did they want to be switched, or were they now content to stay on Flight 800?

The only hitch, the representative observed, was that their luggage was already checked in for Flight 800, packed into one of the plane's eleven cargo bins and loaded onto the plane. Their luggage could not be removed. Despite airline policy, she said, and given the circumstances, officials would allow the luggage to continue on the flight without them. Would the men mind if their luggage reached Rome the next day? They hesitated: It would mean a trip back to the Rome airport. Still, to avoid a stop in Paris. . . . After a moment's debate, the men decided to switch to Flight 840, and hurried off to the new gate, their voices, in exuberant Italian, trailing behind them.

Meanwhile, another passenger was complaining at the check-in desk about the delay. "I'm traveling on United from now on!" the man exclaimed. "I have an appointment in Paris I can't miss." He headed for a men's room with his carry-on luggage—and emerged, about half an hour later, dressed as a woman. Neatly coiffed, with understated makeup and jewelry, he walked briskly on high heels back into the waiting area and took a seat. The students from Montoursville were stunned.

As the passengers waited in their seats, Captain Ralph Kevorkian of Garden Grove, California, and the copilot, Captain Steve Snyder of Stratford, Connecticut, passed through the waiting area, into the jetway, and onto the plane. In recent years, Kevorkian had taken a lot of kidding about his name, but he was a genial, confident man and laughed at the jokes. He was also a very experienced pilot who had flown in the U.S. Air Force and worked for TWA since 1965. In retrospect, it would seem odd that the flight tonight was his first as captain of a 747, but Kevorkian had logged 5,000 hours in 747s, either as a copilot or as another member of the flight crew, and 18,791 hours in the air all told as a commercial pilot. He had a perfect safety record. So did instructor-pilot Snyder, who had flown with TWA since 1964 and logged, in that time, 17,263 hours, including 2,821 hours as captain of a 747. Snyder would be seated to the right of the pilot as Kevorkian's instructor, a routine monitoring procedure required by the FAA and the airline since it was Kevorkian's first 747 flight in the captain's seat.

The cockpit on a 747 sits on a level above the main cabin, in what looks from a distance like the head of a huge mechanical bird. In a jump seat behind Kevorkian and Snyder was the flight's senior engineer, Richard Campbell, from Ridgefield, Connecticut. Campbell had more than 18,500 hours flying time with TWA, including 3,873 on 747s and 2,390 as flight engineer. Close to retirement at sixty-three, he was acting as instructor–flight engineer for Oliver Krick, twenty-five, from St. Louis, Missouri, who was to make his first flight as engineer in a 747, having obtained his engineering certificate less than a month before.

This was a representative crew in every way. Most of its members had decades of experience, the most seasoned backing up the only slightly less seasoned, with a young recruit also under guidance in the most junior position to gain experience exactly as flight protocol required. Together, the flight-crew members had more than one hundred years' flying time, as much as or more than any other crew one might find on a commercial airline.

As the pilots went through the first of their safety checks, thirteen flight attendants and a flight service manager gathered for the flight. Among them was twenty-three-year-old Jill Ziemkiewicz from Rutherford, New Jersey, who had joined TWA two months earlier and was participating in her first international flight. Jacques Charbonnier, a silver-haired Frenchman with piercing blue eyes, who was also fluent in English, Italian, and Spanish, was the flight service manager. Charbonnier had worked the New York–to–Paris route side by side with his wife, Connie, for almost a quarter of a century. Although he was now sixty-five, he was waiting until Connie turned fifty next year so they could retire together. The couple, who lived in a renovated carriage house in Northport, Long Island, usually worked the first-class cabin, serving passengers as if they were guests in their own home. And then there was Janet

Christopher, who would have been on Friday's Flight 800 but had switched with attendant Donna George so she could be back to see her twelve-year-old son, Charles, receive the Boy Scout Order of the Arrow. Donna was just as pleased to make the switch. Her own son, Eddie, who had won the Heisman trophy earlier in the year for his outstanding football season at Ohio State University, was to sign with the Houston Oilers. She wanted to be in Houston for the big event.

As was her custom, Janet called home while the other attendants boarded. She had tried to reach Charlie a few minutes before, but he hadn't yet arrived home from the FBI's New York office. If she missed him, it would be the first time they'd ever failed to talk before a flight. Once again her son, Charles, picked up. "Hey, Mom, great timing, Dad's just pulling in the driveway."

Janet heard the screen door banging in the background and her husband's steps as he approached the phone. "Hi, darlin'."

Janet and Charlie talked about where Janet would stay in Paris, and when exactly she'd be home. She said she was sorry that one of the fathers had picked up Charles for Boy Scouts at 10:30 that morning rather than at noon, as usual; she would have liked to have spent the late morning with him, talking about his plans for Boy Scout camp in the upcoming days.

As Janet was talking, the Charbonniers, who knew the Christophers well, came up behind her and took the phone from her hand. "Oh come on, Charlie; come with us to Paris. You can't work *all* the time," Charbonnier said as his wife, Connie, echoed the plea. Janet had tried for three days to get her husband and son on the flight, not only to give her family a minivacation but so they could all spend time with the Charbonniers, who had flown with Janet for years. But the computer showed that the flight was full.

"I've got to go, honey," Janet said, laughing, when she reclaimed the phone.

"Come on, Janet, I love you, let's talk some more," Charlie teased.

"No, really, I've got to go, they're about to call first-class passengers."

Sighing, Charlie gave Janet his standard send-off. "Well, you tell that damn pilot that if he gets you hurt, I'm going to kick his ass."

"Okay, I'll talk to you tomorrow from Paris," Janet said softly.

"Hey, wait—what kind of a plane do you have?"

"A good one, a 747," she said. "Love ya," she added, then hung up and hurried over to the gate. That was when she noticed Larkyn Dwyer looking a little apprehensive, and strode over to take her in hand.

The time was 6:05 P.M. From the plane, Captain Kevorkian called the counter attendants at the gate to make their first boarding announcement. As far as he knew, the plane was still due to depart at 7:00 P.M. A few first-class passengers were climbing the spiral stair to the small, second-floor cabin of just eight comfortable seats that lay directly behind the cockpit. Janet Christopher and the Charbonniers were awaiting passengers in the main first-class section below.

Captains Kevorkian and Snyder were still going through a first series of safety checks; later, when the plane rolled out to the runway, they would conduct another. As they did their initial checks, Snyder looked down at the 971 lights, gauges, and switches in the cockpit, and noticed a warning light alerting the crew that the temperature had risen in one of the cargo compartments.

"I'll check it out," said Campbell, the instructor–flight engineer. He took the stairs down to the main first-class cabin, then stepped onto the jetway to a door leading outside. He punched in his code to disarm the door and descended the metal steps that led to the tarmac below, where the cargo handlers were loading luggage.

"Does it feel hotter than usual in there?" he shouted over the rumble of the 747's warming engines.

"It's hot, all right," the worker shouted back. "My shirt's completely soaked from being in the 'B' hold."

Still, Campbell knew it was not unusual for cargo holds to heat up on a plane that sat on the tarmac in warm weather, especially with the jumbo jet's air-conditioning units, which resembled large, black beer kegs under the center fuel tank, running steadily. For a moment, he watched as the handlers loaded cargo into the rear storage hold. Every international flight had its share of odd items. On Flight 800, there were seventeen cash registers that had been shipped by sea from Yokohama, Japan, to Los Angeles, then flown to Kennedy Airport to be taken to Paris. A shipment of live turtles was being sent to a turtle farm outside of Paris. A French theatrical troupe had ordered eight hundred pounds of glitter, in various bright colors, each color in its own large box. More typical were the bags of air mail, U.S. State Department pouches, airplane parts and supplies, newspapers, and magazines. After surveying all this and satisfying himself that the heat in the cargo hold was not a problem, Campbell climbed back up the stairs and into the plane.

As Campbell returned to the cockpit, the pilots got word from the ground crew that two unusual bits of cargo were being placed aboard. A small, sealed container of vials of HIV-positive blood samples, packed in dry ice, was to be put in a cargo section at the rear of the plane. The blood was being sent to a research laboratory in Paris. At the same time, a Styrofoam cooler carrying human corneas was placed in the cockpit. The Medical Eye Bank of Maryland in Baltimore was sending the corneas to a doctor in Marseilles, who was going to perform a transplant on an Italian patient. The pilots disliked surprises as a rule, but the last-minute additions meant that Flight 800 was now a "lifeguard" flight, considered an air ambulance with potentially life-saving cargo for medicine and research, and would be given takeoff and landing priorities.

The hope of a quick takeoff was short-lived, however. A routine cross-check of baggage had turned up a mismatch: One of the numbers on a bag failed to match the baggage numbers for the passenger who had checked it, which meant that the ground crew would have to make sure the passenger was on board and check the bag to be sure it didn't contain a bomb. The process took an hour.

As they waited, Snyder asked flight engineer Krick to recheck ATIS, the automatic terminal information system, which provided the latest flight conditions, including current weather, wind speed and direction, and density altitude readings at Kennedy Airport. The temperature at the airport was 71 degrees but higher on the blacktop apron. The dew point was 68 degrees. Winds were from the south-southwest at four knots, and the barometric pressure read 30.09. Visibility was twenty-five miles—about as far as the eye can see.

Below the cockpit in the cabin, the passengers fidgeted and opened their air valves, putting more stress on the air-conditioning units below. At least the cabin was not filled to capacity, as had been expected. A TWA flight from Chicago to New York had been delayed by mechanical problems, and 150 passengers scheduled to fly on to Paris on Flight 800 had missed their connection. Grounded at O'Hare International Airport, they must, at the moment, have been very frustrated.

Just after 8:00 P.M., nearly an hour after its scheduled departure, Flight 800 was given permission to push back from the gate. The pilots completed their final preflight checks. At 8:02 P.M., the plane with tail number N93119 pushed back from Gate 27. With its passengers, flight crew, and cargo, it weighed 590,441 pounds, well under the maximum for a 747 of 734,000 pounds. The plane taxied toward runway 22-R with only three of its four engines fired up, a standard practice to conserve fuel. "Have a good flight, 800," a TWA ground crewman radioed the pilots. "See ya," Ollie Krick, the flight engineer, replied.

The pilots went through their last checks. "Five hundred and ninety thousand seven-seventy-one takeoff EPRs set at point-three-three bugs set and cross-checked at one-fifty-three."

"Set and cross-checked."

"Stabilizer trim?"

"Is set at six-point-one."

"Flight recorder?"

"On."

"Beacon lights?"

"Are on."

"Probe heat?"

"On."

"Flight controls?"

"Checked."

"Autobrakes?"

"Armed."

"Now you can start it."

"Yaw dampers?"

"On."

"Transponder?"

"That's checked."

So it went until 8:17:21 P.M., when the control tower told Flight 800 to taxi into position for takeoff and hold. "Flight attendants please be seated for takeoff," Krick announced.

At 8:18:21 P.M., the control tower cleared Flight 800 for takeoff. A moment later, with all four engines at full throttle, it rolled down runway 22-R and lifted off the ground, heading east in a wide arc. A few seconds after that, Captain Kevorkian gave the command to "gear up." Copilot Snyder lifted the metal lever that retracted the big wheels into the belly of the jumbo jetliner.

The plane climbed into the sky over the Rockaway beaches of Brooklyn at about 287 MPH, or 250 knots, typical for a jumbo jet shortly after takeoff. Gradually, it increased its speed to 344 MPH, or 300 knots. Passengers gazing out their windows could see the houses across Long Island and the serpentine highways that defined this narrow stretch of land, still pulsing with the flow of summer traffic.

At less than 10,000 feet, the plane soared through light scattered clouds. The pilot pulled the nose up, and the plane climbed rapidly, so rapidly that it seemed to have a mind of its own as the 747's four massive engines achieved full power. Then the plane slowed a bit. "Seems like a homesick angel here . . . awesome," Kevorkian said softly at 8:24:30 P.M.

"It's bleeding off airspeed, that's why," said Snyder. The "homesick angel," in other words, was pushing heavenward at full climb thrust but also slowing slightly as it climbed. The temporary slowing was what Snyder meant by "bleeding off airspeed."

At 8:24:41 P.M., copilot Snyder radioed the New York air-traffic-control center for permission to climb. "New York Center, TWA's lifeguard 800 heavy, eight thousand two hundred climbing one one thousand." The "lifeguard" reference was to the cargo of human corneas that gave Flight 800 priority in the air; "heavy" denoted its size as a 747 jumbo jet and warned smaller planes to stay clear of the turbulence created by its turbo fan-jet engines. The plane was at 8,200 feet, and Snyder was asking for permission to climb to 11,000 feet, expressed as "one one thousand" to denote ten thousand plus one thousand.

The reply came not from New York's air-traffic controllers but from Boston's, because Flight 800 had already moved into Boston Center's outlying jurisdiction. "TWA 800 Boston Center roger climb and maintain one three thousand."

Eleven seconds later, Snyder repeated the command to confirm the instructions. "TWA 800 heavy. Climb and maintain one three thousand." A half minute later, he added the rate of climb: "TWA 800 heavy, ah, about ah, two thousand feet a minute here until accelerating out of ten thousand."

Boston gave the go-ahead to keep rising. "Roger, sir, climb and maintain flight level one-niner-zero and expedite through fifteen." But a minute later the controllers changed the instruction. "TWA 800, amend the altitude. Maintain one three thousand. Thirteen thousand only for now," the controller said. The amendment was to keep Flight 800 clear of a USAir flight passing overhead.

At 8:25:59 P.M., Krick said, "Thrust, go on cross-feed?" "Yeah," said Kevorkian. This was an instruction to open a connecting tube between the fuel tanks in either wing to allow all four engines to draw evenly from both wing tanks so as to balance the plane. Between the wing tanks, directly under the belly of the plane, was the nearly empty third fuel tank—the center tank—with its modest fifty gallons.

Inside, the cabin was configured in typical 747 fashion. On either side, each row of first class had a window and aisle seat. Another pair occupied the space between the aisles. Up the spiral stair were eight more first-class seats. Several rows of business-class seats occupied the area just behind the main first-class cabin. In the main cabin, each row had four economy-class seats in its middle section and three seats on either side by the porthole windows. There were 433 seats in all.

One 747-100, exactly like Flight 800, had been converted for use as Air Force One to carry the president of the United States. Another in the series had been remodeled to carry the space shuttle on its back between launching destinations. Boeing had designed the 747 initially in competition for a military contract to provide the U.S. Air Force with a large transport plane; when it failed to win the contract, it decided to develop a commercial version instead. The 747-100 had been the first model of the line, hailed upon its debut on February 9, 1969, as the largest commercial plane in the world, and immediately nicknamed the "jumbo jet." More than one thousand of the planes had been manufactured between the line's introduction and the end of production in 1986. The safety record of the 747-100 and two succeeding 747 lines was one of the best in aviation history: 1.6 fatal accidents per million departures. Statistically, that meant Flight 800 had less than two chances in a million of a serious mishap. To be sure, the odds increased, if only infinitesimally, as the plane grew older, and every takeoff and landing aged a plane as changing air pressure expanded and contracted its metal body, straining its myriad rivets and steel panels. Nearly all of Boeing's 747-100s were still in commercial use, though some of the older ones had been quietly sold by U.S. airlines to developing nations. Number N93119, as it happened, had left the Boeing plant in Everett, Washington, on October 27, 1971.

Glistening in the twilight, Flight 800 veered east along the coast of Long Island's south shore. As it leveled off at 13,000 feet, the pilot announced that flight attendants were free to move about the cabin. It was Janet Christopher's routine to stand up and snap shut the safety-belt harness on her jump seat. She would walk over to the lockers near the galley, where she would remove her uniform jacket with her twenty-five-year pin on the lapel, and hang it up. Then she would bend over to get her apron from a bottom locker so that she could begin beverage and cocktail service for first-class passengers. She had a full house—twenty-nine passengers—and as usual, she wanted to get a head start on serving them.

In the cockpit, the pilots continued their banter with Boston air-traffic controllers. At 8:28:13 P.M., Boston Center advised: "TWA 800 you have traffic at one o'clock and, ah, seven miles southbound, a thousand foot above. He's a Beech 1900."

At 8:28:20 P.M., TWA responded: "TWA's, ah, 800 heavy, ah no contact." That meant the pilots had not yet seen the aircraft just off to the right, but within a moment, they radioed Boston to say they'd seen the plane and were easing off accordingly. On the busy Eastern Seaboard, one of the heaviest corridors in the world, planes often came within a thousand feet of each other in altitude at five or seven miles apart. As long as each was made aware of the other, there was no cause for concern. But in the cockpit, Captain Kevorkian did notice something a bit awry. "Look at that crazy fuel-flow indicator there on number four," he said of the number-four engine.

"See that," he repeated, apparently watching the needle on the dial jump. Later, the "crazy fuel-flow indicator" remark would provoke intense scrutiny among investigators, and perhaps indeed indicate a subtle, underlying problem. Among seasoned pilots, however, it was considered a momentary aberration and no cause for alarm. As a result, there was no follow-up to the remark from the pilots on Flight 800.

At 8:30:16 P.M., Boston air-traffic control gave the Flight 800 pilots instructions to climb to 15,000 feet. Snyder immediately acknowledged the controller's instructions.

"Climb thrust," Kevorkian added. "Climb to one five thousand."

"Power's set," Krick said. It was now 8:30:35 P.M.

The jumbo jet then rose at more than 400 MPH. As it did, Janet Christopher apparently switched on the coffee machine in the first-class galley.

At 8:31:12 P.M., the plane reached 13,760 feet. It was far enough from land that to a bystander on the ground it seemed to be a sliver of white and red glimmering in the final moments of sunlight as it steadily shrank in size toward the horizon. Its exact location was listed on radar as 40:39:39 north latitude, 72:38:47 west longitude.

Aboard Flight 800, everything seemed normal, but to Captain David McClain, who was piloting an East Winds Airlines commuter plane from

Boston, Massachusetts, to Trenton, New Jersey, the TWA jumbo jet rated a worried second look. McClain was leveling off his own plane at about 16,000 feet when he first spotted Flight 800 heading directly toward him from about twenty-five miles away. What caught McClain's eye was that the jet's landing lights appeared still to be on. Standard procedure called for them to be turned off at 10,000 feet. Also, the landing lights seemed brighter than usual, and not white but a brilliant yellow. He stared at the plane and noticed that the intense light seemed to be near the jet's number-two engine. Had an engine caught fire? But the plane seemed to be staying on course and trailing no smoke, so McClain dismissed the idea. Still, he leaned forward just a bit because the plane was far enough away that he couldn't see it clearly in the deepening dusk. He guessed it was an international flight by the way it was clinging to the coastline, following its easterly course.

After what seemed like two minutes but may have been less, McClain became uneasy again. He toggled his left landing light to attract the oncoming jet's attention as a motorist might warn an approaching car that its bright lights were on. By now, McClain guessed he was about fifteen miles from Flight 800 and perhaps two thousand feet above it. Almost as soon as he flickered his lights, Flight 800 exploded into a bright fireball before his eyes.

"What the hell was that?" McClain asked. His copilot, Vincent Fuschetti, had been looking down, reading his own plane's instruments. When he looked up, he saw the huge orange ball of flames.

"Call Center," he told McClain. He meant that McClain should notify Boston air-traffic control. "Say something. You've got to say something."

At 8:31:50 P.M., McClain radioed Boston Center, using his plane's air-traffic moniker, Stinger Bee. "We just saw an explosion out here. Stinger Bee Five Zero Seven."

The Boston controller who responded had not noticed anything amiss. "Stinger Bee Five Zero Seven. I'm sorry. I missed it. Ah, you're out of eighteen. Did you say something?"

"Ah, we just saw an explosion up ahead of us here. Somewhere about, about sixteen thousand feet or something like that. It just went down in the water."

In another commercial plane nearby, USAir Flight 217 from Charlotte, North Carolina, to Providence, Rhode Island, most passengers were dozing or reading at 8:31 P.M. But Dwight Brumley, a U.S. Navy electronic-warfare technician stationed at Pensacola, Florida, who was heading to a meeting in Providence, happened to look out his window, his attention drawn by the blinking lights of a small, propeller-driven airplane about five hundred feet below the USAir aircraft. The plane was traveling in a southwesterly direction. About ten seconds after the small plane had passed beneath Flight 217's path, Brumley saw a flarelike streak that looked, as he later put it, like a bright white light, or an unexploded fireball in the air. The flare was moving from Brumley's right to his left—in an east-northeasterly direction. The flare traveled for about three to four seconds, seemed to brighten in intensity for another two or three seconds, appeared to peak, then descend. This event took no more than ten seconds. Next, Brumley saw a small explosion in the area where he had last seen the flare. A second later, the small explosion became a large one. All this appeared to occur about three to four thousand feet below the USAir plane. The fireball mushroomed to about two hundred feet in diameter, then lengthened as it sank toward the water. Brumley actually saw it hit the water, then turned to summon a flight attendant.

"Did you see that, too?" said James Nugent, seated in the row behind Brumley.

Nugent said he could see the cabin lights inside the plane a moment before it erupted into a fireball. The plane seemed to stop in midair from the explosion "like a bus running into a stone wall."

"I'll bet it'll be on the news tonight," Brumley said.

———

At 8:31:12 P.M., just twelve minutes after takeoff, something in the vicinity of the center fuel tank set off a catastrophic explosion on board Flight 800. The force of the explosion knocked a gaping hole in the bottom of the fuselage and caused the forward section of the plane to buckle and crack. Within five seconds, a band of fuselage around the neck of the plane unpeeled like a safety strip around a medicine bottle, causing the forward section of the plane, about thirty-three feet of fuselage from the nose back toward the wing, to break away. The sudden loss of mass made the plane pitch up sharply, climb more than 3,000 feet, and bank to the left and then to the right as its engines used fuel already drawn from the tanks. At about 17,000 feet, without further fuel to propel them, the engines sputtered and stalled. At that point, the plane nosed over and began a high-speed dive to the ocean. About a mile from the water, the left wing broke off, releasing unused fuel that created a giant cascading fireball.

The cabin, within a fraction of a second of the explosion, was plunged into darkness as the plane's power cables were severed. At the same time, thousands of rivets that held the fuselage together shot through the plane like bullets, embedding themselves in passengers. Some passengers were also hit by heavy beams and by flying pieces of fuselage. Heads were cracked open, bodies torn apart. As the front of the plane fell away, passengers in the seats closest to the break were spilled into the air. Some of these were the passengers who would be found floating on the ocean's surface that night. First-class passengers and the cockpit crew seated in front of the break rode the nose section down to the water; they would be among those dragged to the seafloor. In the aft section of the plane, those remaining passengers not already killed by the force of the explosion or by flying debris were hit by a blast of 400-mile-per-hour air—three times the force of a Force 4 hurricane. Their bones were smashed, skin ripped away, and internal organs torn apart. The onrushing wind actually reduced the jet's speed from 400 to 200 MPH in an instant, snapping the necks of those aboard and killing any last survivors. The abrupt drop in speed, medical examiners said, caused many aboard to suffer an internal decapitation in which the skin holds the head on the shoulders, but the spinal cord, larynx, and other connecting tissues are severed. There was, the experts agreed, no time for screams. Hit by such force, a human body has only time for a last gasp of air before it dies.

In truth, no one would know for sure how long the passengers remained conscious, but the expert consensus would be that death or unconsciousness, for all aboard, came almost instantly after the initial explosion.

On Flight 800 human life was extinguished, but the chaos continued. Structural beams, the cabin's shattered interior, luggage, and seats whirled in the air as if in a tornado, battering bodies already dead. Yet for all the turmoil and loss of life aboard, analysis later conducted by the CIA at the request of the FBI would show that forty-nine seconds passed from the initial explosion to the plane's plunge into the ocean, a measurement made by comparing the clock inside the plane's cockpit voice recorder to that of a U.S. satellite. The cockpit clock stopped within a fraction of a second of the initial blast. Just forty-two seconds later, the satellite's infrared sensors detected a fireball in the sky and tracked its descent.

With flames streaming behind it, the plane pitched and then went into a dive. The fuselage spiraled as it fell, throwing off fiery chunks. Seats and luggage filled the air, as if the sky itself had exploded, scattering wreckage and remains for miles. The plane continued its fall at about five times faster than its normal descent. When it lost its left wing and erupted in a fireball, thousands of pounds of jet fuel spilled across the sea to create a coiling snake of fire that became the wall of flame that Ken Seebeck and his Coast Guard crew would see moments later.

From a Boston Center air-traffic control screen in Nashua, New Hampshire, that monitored all flights in the New England area and south to eastern Long Island, the crash was perceived as one blip becoming several blips at 8:31:12 P.M. The transponder aboard Flight 800, which sent the jet's identity and altitude to be monitored by air-traffic controllers, was cut off in that tenth of a second.

On the East Winds Airlines commuter plane, Captain McClain and his copilot, Fuschetti, were badly shaken. Their voices, played back later for investigators, would convey the horror of what they had just seen. Still, their message was not immediately clear to Boston air controllers juggling numerous flights at the time. Nine seconds after McClain called in the explosion, an Alitalia flight notified Boston Center of an explosion "just ahead of us." Fifteen seconds later, a Virgin Atlantic plane again alerted controllers: "Boston, Virgin Zero Zero Niner. I confirm that out of my nine o'clock position we just had an explosion. It looked like an explosion out there about five miles away, six miles away."

"Virgin Zero Zero Niner, I'm sorry your transmission was broken up. What'd you say?"

"At our nine o'clock position, sir, it looked like an explosion of some sort about maybe five or six miles out of my nine o'clock position."

The message registered at Boston Center at 8:32:49 P.M., yet the reply was surreally polite. "An explosion six miles out at your nine o'clock position. Thank you very much, sir."

At Boston Center controllers scanned their screens, looking for a signal from Flight 800. Instead they saw numerous blips later identified as pieces of the airplane as it broke up and fell through the sky. Air-traffic controllers notified the FAA.

At 8:32:56 P.M., a controller tried to get TWA Flight 800 on the radio: "TWA 800, Center." There was no reply.

"TWA 800, Center," the controller said again. No response.

At 8:33:09 P.M., Boston said: "TWA 800, if you hear Center, ident." The order was for Flight 800's pilots to press a button on their control panel that set off a transponder signal, which would light up on the radar screen, identifying their tail number and indicating their altitude. No signal came back.

At 8:33:17 P.M., Boston called out to McClain's commuter plane: "Stinger Bee Five Zero Seven. You reported an explosion. Is that correct, sir?"

At 8:33:21 P.M., McClain answered: "Yes, sir, about ah, ah, five miles at my eleven o'clock." A moment later he added, "We are directly over the site with that airplane or whatever it was that just exploded and went into the water."

Boston Center continued to radio for Flight 800 to answer.

"I think that was him," an unidentified pilot in the area said quietly over the radio to Boston air control. It was now 8:35:43 P.M.

"I think so," an air-traffic controller replied forlornly.

"God bless him," another unidentified pilot said over the radio transmission.

At 8:36:58 P.M., Boston Center called McClain to thank him for his report and to confirm that he had seen a splash in the water approximately twenty miles southwest of Hampton Bays.

"Ah, yes, sir," McClain answered. "It just blew up in the air. And then we saw two fireballs go down to the, to the water. And there was a big, small, ah, smoke form, ah, coming up from that. Also, there seemed to be a light. I thought it was a landing light and it was coming right at us at about, I don't know, fifteen thousand feet or something like that, and I pushed on my landing lights. Ah, you know, so I saw him and then it blew."

McClain looked down at the flaming wreckage on the ocean below as he passed back over the site. "God bless those people," he said.

———

Katie Hettler, who had hugged her older brother good-bye in the parking lot of the Montoursville high school on a bright blue midafternoon, was at her computer at about 10:00 P.M. with a television on in the background. Behind her, she heard something about a plane crash. She turned in her chair to hear a report that a TWA jet bound for Paris had crashed. "Mom, Rance's plane!" she screeched. "I think it crashed."

Gary Hettler quickly turned on the small television set in the kitchen, where he, Jackie, and Gary, Jr., were popping corn. "Jackie, what was Rance's flight number?" he demanded.

"Eight hundred."

"Oh my God."

Jackie screamed. Gary, Jr., started cursing and pounding the kitchen table with his fist.

"Katie, call Melissa, see what the Karschners know," Jackie said. Melissa, Amanda's younger sister, was in Katie's class at school.

With trembling fingers, Katie dialed the number.

"Katie, I can't talk to you," Melissa said, in a voice that Katie had never heard. Then Melissa hung up.

The television was on in the Karschner kitchen, too. Amanda's mother, Pam, was upstairs frantically looking for her daughter's flight itinerary.

"Okay, Pam, calm down, what's Mandy's flight number?" Dale Karschner asked. He was forcing himself to stay calm, to keep the family calm.

"Flight Eight hundred," Pam answered.

Dale felt his legs give way. With a moan, he slumped to the floor.

As calls began coming in to the Hettler and Karschner households, both mothers had the same reaction. Amid their tears and frantic fear, they went from room to room, grabbing framed family pictures. Childhood snapshots— bright happy eyes, proud smiles with missing front teeth, clothes that only a mother still recalled, photographs of classes, of athletic teams, of Rance in his football uniform with "84" on the jersey, of Amanda at a track high-jump event, prom pictures: Rance so upright and handsome in his tuxedo, Amanda resting her head gently on her father's shoulder.

Pam Karschner scooped up her pictures of Amanda, got in her car, and drove a quarter mile to the Hettler house. It was a strange impulse. Despite Amanda's recent crush on Rance, Pam barely knew the Hettlers and had never been inside their home. In the Hettlers' kitchen, shocked relatives and friends were gathering. Pam stepped over the Hettlers' old black Labrador retriever and asked where she could find Jackie. She was directed back to the den, where she found Jackie surrounded by pictures of Rance.

They were still young women—Pam was thirty-nine, Jackie just forty—and yet now they felt terribly old, heartbroken, and depleted. For more than two hours, they sat hugging the photographs and crying uncontrollably. Jackie, in shock, refused to believe that Rance was dead. Something terrible had happened, but Rance, as powerful and fit as he was, had to have survived and saved a few of the others—starting with Amanda.

As the mothers sat grieving, their families fielded call after call. In Montoursville, almost every house was lit up, almost every phone engaged. The crash of Flight 800 had torn the town's fabric as surely as if a giant knife had ripped it down the middle. Talking did nothing to heal the gash, but against such an unseen, awful fate, there seemed nothing else to do.

Or perhaps there *was* something they could do. By midnight, the mothers had decided: They would find their children. A quarter mile apart, in the middle of a July night, two families began packing up their utility vehicles for the five-hour drive to a town on Long Island's south fork that they had never heard of before that evening. In the midst of their preparations, someone thought to call the school.

By then, the principal and much of his staff were in their offices, dealing with the catastrophe. Other students and their families were calling in, too, wanting information, wanting to know what they could do to help, crying as they tried to talk. The Hettlers and Karschners learned that a bus had been chartered to carry members of the sixteen sundered families to Kennedy Airport in New York. Since neither the Hettlers nor the Karschners had any clear sense of how to get to East Moriches, taking the bus seemed a sensible idea.

At 4:00 A.M., the bus departed from the same school parking lot where another bus had begun its journey some twelve hours before, an impossibly long time ago. On the bus, Pam and Jackie sat together across the aisle from their husbands and daughters. But for a murmured word of comfort here and there or a moan of inexpressible sorrow, the bus was as dark and silent as a cave. The sound that Jackie focused on—the sound that she would remember for the rest of her life—was the loud thumping of the bus's many tires over the breaks, every hundred feet or so, it seemed, in the highway concrete. THUMP THUMP . . . THUMP THUMP . . . THUMP THUMP. So disoriented did Jackie feel, and by now so exhausted, that she wondered in the dark if that sound was the sound of her heart.

In a brownstone in the East Eighties in Manhattan, Heidi Snow had spent her early evening torn between giddy delight at Michel's marriage proposal and loneliness because she might not see him for weeks.

"I almost missed my flight because the car got stuck in traffic," Michel said when he called from the airport. Hearing his voice, she almost wished he *had* missed it.

"I'm at the same terminal where we came in from Florida," he said. "And, hey, I found the bathroom."

Heidi laughed. When they'd gotten off the plane from Florida, she'd had to go to the bathroom so badly she'd managed to hurry right by the one adjacent to the gate.

She remembered that flight for another reason. They were seated near one of the exit doors. She told Michel she never listened to the flight attendants as they gave safety instructions. "I don't even know where my flotation device is," she told Michel. He grabbed her hand and guided it beneath her seat. "Heidi, it's right here, feel it." He said his trip from Paris to New York had been a very rough ride. "Our plane did a dive or something. There was a man with his son seated next to me, and when the plane dived, the father grabbed his son, but, Heidi, I had no one to grab, and I was scared."

Now, from the pay phone by the gate, Michel told her to study hard for her stockbroker's exam. "They're boarding now," he said, and added, before he hung up, "I love you."

Dutifully, Heidi tried to study. She was still trying at about 9:30 P.M., when her mother called. "Heidi, did Michel actually leave tonight?" she asked.

When the news sank in, Heidi called TWA. The first person she reached said, "We can't release that information." Frantic, Heidi tried another TWA phone number and got a busy signal. Shaking, she went downstairs to the family from whom she rented her apartment. When they opened the door, they thought Heidi had been mugged. As soon as she explained, the husband of the family drove out to Kennedy Airport to see what he could learn. An hour or so later, he called from his car phone to say that Michel was a confirmed passenger on Flight 800. That was when Heidi called Michel's sister in Paris—at 3:00 A.M. Paris time—to tell her Michel was almost certainly dead. "I think it's best that you call your father," Heidi said.

In Houston, Joe Lychner was at home on the phone to a business associate when he heard the call-waiting beep. "Joe, did Pam and the girls get on that plane to Paris tonight?" It was his mother-in-law.

Stunned by the news, gasping for breath, Joe turned on CNN and called TWA in New York, only to reach the same useless recording that hundreds of other callers were getting. In an hour, nearly a dozen friends were gathered in his living room as he tried to grasp the fact that his wife and daughters were gone.

On a dark road in Connecticut, Larkyn Dwyer's mother took the final turns that would bring her to her cousin's house. Ann Dwyer was not, by nature, superstitious. And yet a nameless anxiety had taken hold of her as she watched

Larkyn board Flight 800. Vague as it was, the anxiety provoked strangely pre-scient behavior on Ann's part. She and her son, Kyle, left the terminal and got as far as the parking lot, but then, at Ann's insistence, returned to Gate 27. There was Flight 800, still tethered to the gate tunnel. Ann was told a luggage mix-up was causing a slight delay. Again, Ann and her son left. This time she got as far as the terminal's exit to the street before retracing her steps to Gate 27, where the big jet with Larkyn inside continued to wait. As she looked through the window at the plane, she remembered that Larkyn had whispered to her at the terminal that she was scared. Again, Ann and Kyle returned to the car. When she insisted on going back a third time, her son really thought his mother had lost her mind. "Hey, Mom, all right already!" Nevertheless, Ann watched the plane pull away from the gate. "Mom, I'm sure she'll be fine," Kyle said. "Don't worry. Let's go."

"Yes," Ann Dwyer said with a sigh. "We can go now, I guess."

No sooner had the headlights of Ann's Mercedes swung into her cousin's driveway than the front door opened. "Ann," the cousin said, her face drawn with fear. "Tell me what flight number Larkyn was on."

———

In a modest New England–style saltbox house in a small town in the Pocono Mountains, Charlie Christopher was listening to sportscaster Bob Costas nar-rate an Olympics preview from Atlanta. Across the bottom of the television crawled a bulletin about the crash of a TWA jumbo jet en route from JFK to Charles de Gaulle. Christopher gasped. For a moment he went numb. His son, Charles, working on a Boy Scout project on a nearby couch, was the first to speak. "That's Mom!" he screamed. "That's Mom!"

Christopher struggled to suppress the panic and start thinking clearly. His twenty-six years of government service—in the FBI and as a National Parks Service ranger before that—had taught him to keep calm in a crisis. Make care-ful judgments; don't act on impulses that can lead to stupid mistakes.

On a coffee table nearby lay a computer printout of TWA flights Janet had left behind when she was trying to get her husband and son on the same flight. The paper offered a nugget of hope. Two TWA flights to Paris had been sched-uled to leave Kennedy Airport fifteen minutes apart.

Christopher hurried to the kitchen-cabinet door where Janet kept emer-gency numbers for TWA and crew scheduling. He dialed one number and heard a recorded voice tell him the office was closed. The recording transferred him to another recorded voice that told him to leave a message. He slammed the phone down in a rage.

"Dad, let's go to Kennedy," Charles said to his father. "Let's just go there."

Christopher took a deep breath and told himself again to be calm. "We're not going to do anybody any good if we go anywhere. If Mom's hurt, and they take her to a hospital, the first thing she's going to do is call us. And if she can't reach us she'll feel worse off."

Christopher tried to think like an FBI agent responding to someone else's disaster. "Keep an even keel. Don't shoot unless fired upon. Don't panic," he kept saying to himself. He wanted to know which plane had gone down. He wanted to know if there were survivors. He needed a helicopter and a boat in case his wife was out there in the water. Who could get him the helicopter? Who could get him the information he needed? That was when he dialed Jim Kallstrom's home number and heard back from his old friend almost immediately, with the sound of Kallstrom's siren on the FDR Drive screaming in the background.

After Kallstrom hung up, Christopher thought of an airline agent in Minneapolis who'd worked with Janet at TWA but had since joined Northwest Airlines. As Christopher had hoped, the ticket agent still had access to TWA's passenger manifests on his home computer. He said he'd check to see which of the two Paris-bound flights Janet had been on. He would also call a TWA vice president at the St. Louis headquarters.

Minutes later, the ticket agent called back. He'd pulled up the TWA system, he reported, only a minute or two before TWA had shut down access to it. Still, he'd been able to confirm that the plane that went down was TWA Flight 800. "And yes," he whispered, "Janet was on it."

Christopher looked hard at his son and told him the news. As he hugged him, he thought, Janet was tough. If she died, it would probably be while she was saving somebody else. That was her biggest weakness, and in fact her biggest strength. He told Charles to pack a bag for Janet in case she'd been found alive and taken to a hospital. As the boy ran off, Christopher called Janet's sister, Lynn, in East Hampton, some thirty miles east of East Moriches. She'd been watching television with her family but assumed Janet was on her usual Friday–Sunday schedule. She and Janet were very close. They had just spent a week in Paris together. Christopher told his brother-in-law, Steve, to get his boat out to East Moriches. Steve had heard there were already too many private boats at the site, that they were hampering the rescue effort.

"But Janet is out there. Think of something."

The friend from Minneapolis called back with a phone number at TWA that would reach a human being, not a recording. Christopher told the woman who answered that his wife was on Flight 800.

"Well, I can't confirm that," the TWA employee said.

"I'm not playing a game with you. Let me tell you the names of the people in the Flight 800 crew tonight. I have a computer list," he said.

Still, the woman refused to give Christopher any information: whether the rescuers had found any survivors, and if so, where those survivors were. "I'm not qualified to answer those questions, sir." She spoke in a stiff, formal manner, as if reciting from a TWA legal manual on how to avoid saying anything of consequence that might be used against the airline in a court case.

"Look, I'm the husband of a flight attendant and I am an FBI agent!" Christopher blasted into the telephone. "Now knock off the bullshit. I'm not playing games! Let's get down to the real world. This is combat and there are real bullets flying. I want information and I want information *now!*"

"I can understand, sir. I want to help you, but we are not permitted to give out that information until it has been verified and formally released," the woman said.

Christopher left her with his name, his beeper number, his home telephone number, and the number for FBI headquarters in Manhattan.

He hung up the phone and saw his son standing in front of the television. Coverage of the crash had preempted all programs by now. Tears were streaming down his son's face. Christopher was desperate to comfort him, but couldn't think of anything to say.

Instead, as if in a dream, he called family members: Janet's parents in Indiana, his own mother in West Virginia. The calls were the hardest he'd ever made.

"I've been trying to call you but your line's been busy," said Christopher's mother. "I wanted to make sure Janet was safe at home."

"Mom, Janet was on the flight," he said.

At 10:40 P.M., an FBI car pulled into Christopher's driveway. Within a half hour, four more arrived. Watching television and making coffee fell outside the agents' usual duties, but they insisted on doing what they could, and to both the Christophers their company was comforting. When the time seemed right for Charlie and his son to go to Long Island, the agents said, Kallstrom would surely send a chopper. Meanwhile, the best service they could provide was to persuade Charlie to sit tight. Christopher wanted to be at the Command Post in Manhattan. He wanted information as it came in, and he wanted to help, however he could. Gently, the agents assured him he was helping by staying where he was until they all knew more. As news reports kept flashing across the television in the Christophers' living room, only two things seemed clear to the agents: The crash of TWA Flight 800 had been no accident, and Jim Kallstrom was the best imaginable guy to lead the FBI to the terrorists who had caused it.

CHAPTER 3

BRIGHT, WHITE LIGHT

At the crash site in the bright morning light of Thursday, July 18, debris bobbed amid thickening swells as far as the eye could see. The large chunk of TWA Flight 800's tail still sat oddly upright like a tombstone in the water. Small fires continued to burn on glistening fuel slicks. Still, the scene of violent destruction had subsided, along with the flames, so that it appeared almost placid. Most of the wreckage had sunk; the worst fires had burned out; the floating bodies had been retrieved. Through these ghostly waters, like soldiers searching for fallen comrades, the crew of the *Rude* (pronounced "Rudy"), a National Oceanographic and Atmospheric Administration vessel normally assigned the task of mapping the seafloor with sonar, trolled for bodies and debris 120 feet below.

In one sense, the crew of the *Rude* and the widening investigation of which it was a part were lucky. Had TWA Flight 800 gone down two or three miles farther offshore, it would have sunk beyond the continental shelf and settled onto an ocean bottom several hundred feet deep. The recovery effort would have been far more difficult, the chances of retrieving the plane's black boxes and other clues to the crash far more remote. As it was, a side-scan sonar device, which looked like a small missile, could be put over the *Rude*'s side and gently lowered by cable to the ocean floor. From there, it could transmit a digital outline of the floor as precise as that of any physical map. An outline of the wreckage could then provide essential guidance to the team of divers—drawn from the FBI and Suffolk and Nassau counties, New York State police, and the New York City police and fire departments—that was gathering at the Coast Guard station in East Moriches even now.

Yet the work was harder than it appeared. Distinguishing wreckage from rocks and other debris could prove tricky, and a growing chop complicated the process. Later that week, as the weather worsened, a ten-foot wave would nearly capsize the *Rude*. A computer graph of the sonar scanning would show the wave as a sharp spike, circled by a crew member and appended with the notation, "John threw up here." Across the top of the sheet someone else would write, "Welcome to the Seas of Hell." But on this morning, the seas were still reasonably calm, and at nine o'clock in the morning under a midsummer sun, the day was already a scorcher.

Ashore, without a sea wind to mitigate it, the heat was more intense. On the lawn of the Coast Guard station in East Moriches, hundreds of officials, rescue workers, and volunteers rested gratefully after their gruesome night in the shade of a huge white party tent, where they wolfed down sandwiches and coffee from a Red Cross canteen. In a vast media encampment a quarter mile up the lone road from the station, Dan Rather, Tom Brokaw, Joan Lunden, and other television personalities reclined in air-cooled Winnebago vans sent by national networks, while mere newspaper reporters were forced to sit in the hot sun, cooling themselves with Gatorade and water whenever the Red Cross van passed through. Kept from the station by a tight security cordon of Suffolk County police, a couple of journalists sought information between meager news briefings by using scanners to monitor officials' cell-phone conversations, and used what they overheard—such as the number of bodies recovered—in their hourly "stand-ups," microphones in hand as the cameras rolled.

Inside the Coast Guard station, unaware of the journalists, Jim Kallstrom sat at the desk Schiliro had appropriated for him, putting through one call after another over a "hard-line" phone, which the journalists could not monitor. He sat on the edge of his chair, as if ready to spring from it. In his office at 26 Federal Plaza, a cushion on his seat bore the permanent imprint of his backside at its outer edge, while the rest of it appeared never to have been sat upon. As always, he sat with his feet securely planted, like a football lineman in a crouch at the line, awaiting the snap of the ball. Any agent who had worked in Kallstrom's vicinity knew the boss's favorite expletives: "Moron!" and "Asshole!" dished out in equal measures, though usually after Kallstrom had slammed down the phone on the recipient of his ire. When a subordinate made a mistake, Kallstrom would cry, "I'm going to cut your balls off with a rusty hatchet!" Once, he used the line on the same agent too often. "But, Jim," observed Kallstrom's press coordinator, Joe Valiquette. "You did that to him last week."

So absorbed was Kallstrom in orchestrating this first full day of the investigation that he failed to notice a guardsman in a crisp uniform who stood staring at him with a perturbed expression, munching a powdered doughnut between sips of coffee from a Styrofoam cup. After several minutes, the guardsman turned on his heel and brusquely walked out the door. Only then did Kallstrom notice him. "What's with that guy?" he asked Pickard.

"He's the commander," Pickard said with a shrug. "You're at his desk."

Intensely focused, passionate about his work, and seasoned by a quarter century of FBI experience, Kallstrom was, at fifty-three, perfectly poised to head up what would soon prove the largest, most complex investigation in the FBI's history. Within the bureau, he was a legend: the pioneer of creative electronic surveillance devices and ingenious techniques that in the 1980s had enabled his special operations team to devastate the Mafia. In J. Edgar Hoover's waning years, the FBI had made a practice of nabbing low-level mobsters and claiming progress in the war on organized crime, but street thugs were soon replaced, while the bosses who ran the mob families remained free, their operations intact. To Kallstrom, that had seemed like Vietnam all over again: bureaucrats offering body counts as proof the war was being won when in fact it was being lost. The only hope he and a handful of other agents could see lay in tapping the bosses and indicting them under the new RICO laws—the Racketeer Influenced and Corrupt Organization Act— which held that the mob boss who murmured the order for a hit in some Brooklyn social club was as guilty as the "perp" who pulled the trigger. Unfortunately, the only surveillance tools available at the time were cars, binoculars, and cameras. Kallstrom changed all that, with extraordinary results. By 1995, when he was made head of the FBI's New York office, all five major Mafia families had lost their leaders and several other high-ranking members, some seventy-five important hoodlums in all. Meanwhile, family members had now begun to cooperate with prosecutors. The families still operated, but with street thugs in charge. The overarching enterprise of organized crime had been dismantled.

Since the early 1990s, Kallstrom had also helped direct the tapping of international terrorists and became intimately involved with the tracking of Sheik Omar Abdel-Rahman, Ramzi Yousef, and other terrorists. Though no evidence yet suggested as much, Kallstrom was among those who felt he might well be dealing now with another terrorist act. He was sorry that the Coast Guard commander had been forced to surrender his office for a short while, and appreciated the Coast Guard's help, but he had a lot of inquiries to set in motion—inquiries that just couldn't wait.

In fact, Kallstrom was grateful for *all* the help he could get, not only from the Coast Guard and local police but from the National Transportation Safety Board (NTSB), which by federal protocol would be the FBI's partner in the investigation, at least until evidence of a crime was firmly established, at which point the FBI would take complete charge. Any time now, Robert Francis, an NTSB vice chairman assigned to head the agency's "Go Team" for the Flight 800 crash, would be arriving from Washington. Despite the potential problems of a jointly directed investigation, Kallstrom was determined to make the alliance work—too much was at stake for interagency rivalry—and eager to add the NTSB's expertise to the FBI's own.

Certainly the NTSB could be helpful. Since its founding in 1967 as an independent government agency, it had worked to determine the cause of every major transportation accident in the United States, and usually succeeded. It was responsible for railroad, marine, highway, and pipeline safety, but its major realm was aviation. In the intervening three decades, some 100,000 civil aviation accidents had occurred in the United States, most of them involving small planes. The NTSB had investigated them all. Of the 200 major U.S. aviation accidents in that time, the NTSB's investigators, most of them engineers, had determined the causes of all but a few. Along with explanations, the NTSB made recommendations for greater public safety to the FAA, which had the sole power to order the aviation industry to implement the recommendations. It was the NTSB, for example, that had framed new standards in aviation to help avert icing, windshear, fire, midair collisions, runway overruns, and alcohol abuse by pilots and crew.

The key word in the agency's mandate was "accident." As long as the Flight 800 crash eluded explanation, both agencies would work the case simultaneously, but in the top echelons of both the NTSB and FBI, strong suspicions that a bomb or missile had downed the plane shaped differing attitudes from the start. Kallstrom and his fellow FBI agents were energized by the case, aware that they might soon bear sole responsibility for solving a hideous crime. The NTSB investigators, who also suspected that a crime had been committed, felt their role would be pro forma—and brief. Dr. Bernard Loeb, an aeronautical engineer and the NTSB's director of aviation safety, was so convinced a bomb had brought the plane down that he chose not to assign his best investigators to TWA Flight 800 that week. Besides, they were already immersed in three other commercial-airline disasters: two involving 737s in Pittsburgh and Colorado Springs, and the ValuJet crash in the Florida Everglades. Once he had the black boxes and the radar tapes for Flight 800, Loeb was sure they would indicate terrorism and the NTSB would be out of the picture.

Kallstrom had called Francis from the Manhattan Command Post shortly after midnight to introduce himself, and heard a cordial, well-bred voice on the line. Francis apologized for not flying up from Washington until morning; the FAA had informed him that none of its flight crews was properly rested. Francis was an experienced enough aviation official to know how critical the hours immediately after an accident could be, but there was nothing to be done. Instead, he would fly up at 5:00 A.M. to MacArthur Airport in Islip, Long Island, where, at Kallstrom's suggestion, an FBI helicopter would pick him up for the short hop to the Coast Guard station in East Moriches.

When the chopper set down in the station's parking lot at around 6:30 that morning, Kallstrom and Pickard came out to greet their counterparts. They saw a tall, patrician figure in an NTSB baseball hat, followed by three associates. Kallstrom walked over to a weathered but handsome man in his late fifties with friendly blue eyes and a handshake as firm as his own. From his phone talk with him, Kallstrom had recognized in Francis a fellow son of Massachusetts, but he could also see that he and Francis came from very different worlds.

"The rest of your team coming over by car?" Kallstrom asked.

Francis seemed surprised. "I want to see what the situation is first," he said. "We'll fly out as many investigators as we need."

Kallstrom and Pickard were surprised, but they tried not to show it. They'd expected hundreds of NTSB investigators to be swarming the area by day's end. Perhaps, thought Kallstrom, he didn't understand quite how the NTSB worked. Just how many investigators would Francis be likely to send when he'd viewed the site? Francis answered the question before it was asked.

"Anyway, we'll have more than NTSB here," he explained. "We'll get Boeing, Pratt Whitney, TWA, the mechanics union, the pilots' union. They'll all be part of our crash investigation."

Wait a minute, Pickard thought. Those are all parties that could be involved—responsible. At the least, they have their own interests. Where's the independence there?

Francis explained that safety board officials had already taken a critical first step. By federal protocol, the NTSB had to ask the Navy for help in salvaging wreckage from a plane crash over water. In Washington, Dr. Loeb had called the Navy's supervisor of salvage, Captain Chip McCord, who had agreed to send up salvage ships with cranes and sonar, manned by divers trained to retrieve military wreckage. In fact, the Navy had promised a wide array of vessels within forty-eight hours. As soon as the Navy began hauling up vital pieces—like the two black boxes containing tapes of the plane's flight instruments and pilot communications—the NTSB could begin sifting for clues to the crash: kicking tin, as they called it. Even now, NTSB investigators in Washington were assembling radar tapes of Flight 800 to begin studying the critical moments before and after the crash, but until there was wreckage to study here at East Moriches, Francis explained, there was no need for dozens of NTSB investigators to be sitting around.

As they spoke, ambulances were pulling away from the station. A few hours before, they had arrived with sirens screaming, ready to transport survivors to hospitals. Now they left quietly and empty.

"Why don't you and I grab a cup of coffee," Kallstrom suggested as he ushered Francis into the station and flashed Pickard a look. "I'll get you up to speed."

"Great!" Francis replied with a smile. Francis had just returned from several demanding weeks in the Florida Everglades where he had served as the NTSB's chief spokesperson in the ValuJet investigation. That one, as the NTSB suspected practically from the start, had turned out to be an accident with a clear cause: Oxygen tanks in a cargo hold had exploded. So the time had been well spent. With Flight 800, Francis was almost sure that a bomb or missile had taken Flight 800 out; so this was different. For this assignment, Francis had packed three blue button-down Oxford-cloth shirts, enough to last him until proof of terrorism or sabotage was established and the FBI could take over.

As the two men headed into the Coast Guard station, Kallstrom mentioned the FAA's disconcerting radar report with the mystery blip from Kennedy Airport. What did Francis make of it? Perhaps, the NTSB man allowed, the blip would be the investigation's first proof of terrorism. At the same time, he cautioned, large-scale radar could be as unreliable as radar detectors in cars. Radar stations, he explained, have been known to record returns from trucks, ships, sides of buildings, flocks of birds, radio towers, weather, and smoke, but these first reports were still intriguing. Obviously, Francis agreed, they should be kept confidential until other radar readings of Flight 800 from other locations could be correlated with the one from Kennedy.

Kallstrom told Francis the FBI had received numerous calls from eyewitnesses. "Nobody called and said, 'I shot down the plane,' but anyone with a brain thinks there's a chance this is terrorism. Whether it's 10 percent, 50 percent, or 90 percent is irrelevant. We have to investigate the hell out of it." Kallstrom then gave Francis a rundown on how the hundreds of FBI agents assigned to the investigation were being deployed. He explained how they were working in concert with the Coast Guard, the Suffolk County and state police, and other agencies. He also told him about the specialized FBI and law enforcement team of divers they'd put together. He hoped they could begin probing the water within a day. When there was nothing more to say for the moment about the crash and the investigation, Kallstrom turned the conversation in a more personal direction. "So where'd you grow up?" he asked as he got up to pour another cup of coffee from the coffeemaker in a corner of the room.

"Cohasset," Francis said.

"Cohasset!" Kallstrom said with a grin. "So you were one of those rich kids on the ocean."

Francis laughed.

"I'm from a little town called Millbury, near Worcester," Kallstrom said.

"Where did you go to school?"

"U. Mass at Amherst. You?"

"Close by," Francis said. "Williams."

"Close by, yeah."

Kallstrom had put himself through college by washing dishes and serving meals at a sorority house. He had a second job as a delivery boy for a florist. (He drove so fast even then that his deliveries often ended up strewn over the back of the van; as a result he became, out of necessity, a rather good floral arranger.) He knew better than to ask if Robert Talbot Francis II had worked his way through Williams. "Well, I guess we're both die-hard Bosox fans," he said of his beloved Boston Red Sox, "and we come from the same state. So we ought to be able to work together, right?"

"Yes, indeed."

Francis might be a blueblood, but he had earned his aviation expertise. Before joining the NTSB, he had worked with the FAA as the agency's congressional liaison; earlier, he had served as an administrative assistant to Representative Gerry Studds, a Massachusetts Democrat. Later, he spent nine years heading the FAA's Paris office; he was fluent in French.

Different as the two men obviously were, Kallstrom rather liked Francis. He could see the NTSB man was a diplomat, cool and clearheaded—that was good. An urbane fellow with friends in high places might not hurt. In fact, Francis was a close friend of Pamela Harriman, the powerful Washington hostess, whom he had met in Paris after her arrival as U.S. ambassador to France; he owed his latest job, in large part, to her sponsorship. Kallstrom knew this already—he wasn't without his sources—and was pleased to think that his new partner had ready access, as a result, to the highest circles of the Clinton administration. Kallstrom would need all the cards he could play.

In the commander's office that morning, Kallstrom and Francis forged an agreement that would carry them through the next year. They would appear jointly before reporters and make consistent statements. That way, they would try to control speculation about the cause of the crash. It was an important tactical decision, presenting the two agencies as equal partners to the world, even though the NTSB would be in charge, technically, until evidence of a crime appeared. If the agreement was in that sense a concession on Francis's part to Kallstrom, in another sense it was Kallstrom's concession to Francis. Despite its lead agency status and the imminent arrival of twenty-six investigators, the NTSB was overwhelmed by the FBI's attack on the case, with hundreds of agents already assigned and all means at its disposal. The inequity was almost comical.

At the same time, Kallstrom cautioned Francis that the NTSB and its investigators would have to treat every piece of retrieved debris as evidence. Items would be cataloged and a record kept of every set of hands through which they had passed to establish a chain of custody. Francis agreed, though he knew this would complicate his own investigation, as the NTSB and other accident investigators would be eager to examine the plane parts and to follow their own established procedures for conducting scientific analysis of wreckage. The men also agreed that, as a practical matter, the FBI would conduct all eyewitness interviews and set up a system to analyze potential evidence as it was recovered on the surface or from the ocean bottom. The FBI would play a major role as well in monitoring autopsies and identifying the victims. Meanwhile, the NTSB would set up its own system to scutinize plane parts after the FBI had done its job of checking for explosive residues or signs of a bomb or missile.

Terms of the partnership established, the men walked down to the dock and in the morning sun boarded a Coast Guard cutter to inspect the site together. With them was Coast Guard admiral John Linnon, who was still glowing with gratitude to Kallstrom for a simple gesture that had meant a lot. Earlier that morning, Kallstrom had found him in the parking lot, talking with his superior, Coast Guard commandant Robert Kramek. Linnon had arrived from Boston at 2:00 A.M. and felt he had the situation under control: On his orders, every Coast Guard vessel within a day's travel of the crash was on its way to help. The commandant had arrived just moments before from Washington. Linnon was pleased to see his superior, but worried that Kramek had come in part to see for himself if Linnon was up to the job. When the FBI chief came over, he gave Linnon a bear hug as if they were old buddies, though they had met only once before. Then Kallstrom told the commandant, "You know, this guy and I go back a long way. Everything is going to be okay with us, so don't you worry about a thing." The commandant visibly eased.

When the cutter reached the crash site, Kallstrom and Francis got their first close-up look at the awful mystery they were meant to resolve. Police and Coast Guard boats bobbed at the periphery of the debris to keep the curious away. Above the site, the *Rude* idled, its sonar scanner swaying 120 feet below. From the bridge of the cutter, Kallstrom and Francis waved to the weary workers and called out their thanks. Kallstrom felt almost presumptuous—who was he to thank them?—but he could see the men were pleased. Even if most of them had no idea yet who he and Francis were, they could guess these were the two in charge. In the face of such chaos and incomprehensible horror, the presence of leaders seemed to restore a welcome sense of order, if only symbolically.

Back on shore, Kallstrom found an FBI mobile command van waiting for him. The Coast Guard station's commander would be pleased, Kallstrom thought; he could have his desk back. As for Francis, he looked plainly envious.

The next day, Kallstrom and Pickard would see Francis outside the Coast Guard station waiting patiently on line to use a public phone.

"What are you doing?" Kallstrom asked. "Don't you have a cell phone?"

"I work for an agency that doesn't even own a car," Francis said.

"We have to fix that," Kallstrom said. "How can you run an investigation without the basic equipment?" He turned to Pickard. "Find this man a home, right away."

Pickard looked at Kallstrom dumbfounded. It was 5:00 P.M. on a Friday in the summer. Where in the world was he going to find a trailer now?

"Okay, boss," Pickard said, and left to begin his search. As he walked outside the Coast Guard station, he noticed a big trailer rolling slowly up the road, crunching gravel under its tires.

"Who gets that?" Pickard asked Schiliro.

"It's ours. I ordered two. We've got another on the way."

"Well, it just became Francis's new home," he said. "Get me the keys."
Pickard went back inside to tell Kallstrom and Francis.
Francis was speechless. Kallstrom just smiled.

On Thursday morning, in his own FBI van, Kallstrom checked in with Louis Freeh. The FBI director was in a high-level meeting, one of his senior executives told Kallstrom, and would have to call back. In passing, Kallstrom mentioned that the NTSB was holding a press conference that evening, and that the FBI would be participating.

"You think that's a good idea?" said the executive. "I mean, maybe the FBI should keep a low profile on this thing. We don't need to parade into some news conference."

Kallstrom felt his temper shoot up. "That's crazy," he exclaimed. "You have 230 people dead, many of them children, and I've got 700 agents working on this case, and the notion that we're going to sit here and not say anything, that's crazy. We have to tell people that we're doing everything humanly possible to find the answer to this."

"But policy is we don't talk about ongoing criminal cases," the executive retorted. "And we don't talk about evidence. That's based on criminal law."

"I know the rules of evidence," Kallstrom said. "You don't have to tell me. I don't plan to talk about evidence. What the public is asking—and, quite frankly, deserves to know—is what's going on, when are we going to get the bodies out of the ocean, how are we going to bring up the pieces of the plane, and how are we, the FBI, going to try to learn what happened? They'd also like to know if they're *safe*. All those questions have nothing to do with the evidence."

Kallstrom slammed the phone down and fumed. What a classic case, he thought, of carrying a sensible rule to such extremes that it makes no sense. You had to be more flexible. You had to think. And even in a bureaucracy as strict as the FBI, you had to *feel*.

Within the hour, Freeh called back, and Kallstrom told him about his dispute. "Jim, do whatever you think you need to do. You know the rules."

"Yes, sir, I do," Kallstrom replied.

From that point on, Kallstrom spoke to nobody at headquarters but Freeh, whom he briefed several times a day for the first weeks and at least once a day thereafter. Freeh always took the call, and to anyone sitting in his office when Kallstrom came on the line, Freeh radiated admiration for his ADIC. "You got it, Jimmy," he'd say. "I'm glad we've got you heading this crisis for us." Freeh had appreciated Kallstrom's decisiveness and ingenuity since the days they worked together in New York. As a federal prosecutor on what would come to be known as the Pizza Connection case, Freeh had come to him with a frustrating dilemma. He had a tip that a Sicilian overseer of the Pizza Connection drug ring had told a New York contact to call him at a certain time from a pay phone along a section of Queens Boulevard. Freeh's problem was that there were nearly one hundred phones along the wide boulevard. "I'll take care of it," Kallstrom said, and arranged to have every pay phone on Queens Boulevard shut off—except the one on which he had placed a court-ordered wiretap. After trying half a dozen inoperative phones, the Sicilian worked his way right to the one with Kallstrom's tap.

Now *that*, thought Freeh, was good work.

To the families gathered at the Ramada Inn at Kennedy Airport, a horrifying day was being made worse, if that was possible, by TWA's bureaucratic reaction to the crash. Amid the anxiety and confusion, what the families wanted above all else was confirmation that their loved ones had been on Flight 800. Driving that need was the desperate hope that a son or daughter or wife or husband had not been on the doomed flight after all but had been shunted instead onto some other international flight and was riding safely into Paris in a taxi, unaware as yet of the news. The airline claimed it was disseminating information from its manifest as quickly as it could. The FBI had received a tentative manifest from TWA and the FAA almost immediately, but the airline preferred not to release a full manifest to the public until it could be thoroughly checked. It had its reasons: To include names of passengers who had canceled out of the flight at the last minute would expose other families to needless trauma, and perhaps expose the airline to more liability than it might already be facing. On a night of delayed traffic, at least two TWA flights had failed to reach Kennedy Airport in time to make connections and add passengers to Flight 800—one from Los Angeles, another from Chicago. Yet perhaps some of those passengers had reached Kennedy by another airline and made Flight 800 after all. The airline wanted to check every ticket stub to be sure who had actually been on Flight 800.

The truth was that TWA was unprepared. Its chief executive officer, Jeffrey H. Erickson, was asleep in London when the crash occurred—1:30 A.M. London time—having spent the evening uncorking champagne to celebrate the best financial news TWA had heard in years. Little more than a decade before, corporate raider Carl Icahn had taken control of TWA in a hostile takeover, then slashed its workforce and sold off its most lucrative air routes for $550 million. Icahn had also pumped millions into TWA and would later say that he had saved the airline, but by 1992, TWA had gone into Chapter 11 bankruptcy. A year later, Icahn departed, leaving the airline's employees and its creditors to clean up the mess. Erickson and his chief public relations man, Mark Abels, had been toasting the airline's first profitable quarter in nearly a decade, and in particular a second-quarter return five times that of the same quarter the previous year. Both domestically and internationally, TWA's passenger loads were increasing dramatically.

Later, Erickson would be criticized for failing to stage a video news conference from England before flying back to New York. Yet had he done so, he might have done little to assuage the families' grief and confusion. Awkward and untelegenic, Erickson wore glasses that seemed too narrow for his wide face and kept his hair matted over his forehead like ABC News host Ted Koppel. When he finally surfaced before the glare of the television cameras in New York, Erickson said little, apparently on the advice of TWA lawyers, and answered few questions. While the impression may have been unfair, or at least unintentional, he came across as a bottom-line executive worried more about his company's image than the lives lost on Flight 800 and the desperate survivors. Had the head of TWA's Trauma Response Team been at his side to guide him, Erickson might have done somewhat better, but she was vacationing in California and did not return until late the next day.

For top management, but even more so for TWA pilots, flight attendants, reservation agents, and ground crews, the crash was both a shock and a devastating personal tragedy. Of the 230 who were killed, 53 were TWA employees, either on duty or traveling on their own time. Dozens of children had lost one or both parents. Many of the employees had started out together when TWA was like a close-knit family and had worked side by side for decades.

As the day wore on, the families' frustration turned to anger, and local politicians, including New York City mayor Rudolph Giuliani and New York governor George Pataki, were increasingly dismayed on their behalf. Why hadn't salvage crews gone to the crash site to bring up the rest of the plane and the 126 bodies buried within it? Where were the divers? What if, as one frenzied relative put it, some of the passengers were still alive within the cabin, trapped by debris, breathing the last of the cabin's pressurized air? Frazzled public relations men from TWA tried to reassure the families that swift measures were being taken, and law enforcement officials added what they could. Divers from the FBI and the police and fire departments were already gathering at the East Moriches Coast Guard station. Navy ships were on their way. Within a day or two, the officials declared, bodies would begin to be brought up and identified. Soon after that, surely, this awful vigil at the airport hotel could end, and the families, bearing their loved ones, could go home to grieve. But as news helicopters showed in almost hourly updates, the only activity at the crash site was the slow circling of Coast Guard and police vessels, harvesting chunks of debris off the surface.

That afternoon, Chief Engineer Patrick Keller of the Coast Guard told his weary crew of four to head their forty-four-foot boat to shore after fourteen hours of recovering bodies and debris. They had fished out quantities of mail and some personal belongings, and had spent the last two hours tediously gathering in yellow pieces of aircraft insulation. Suddenly, Keller noticed something odd. A small burgundy-colored box was bobbing in the green sea amid the bits of insulation and seat cushions. "Hey, let's take a look at that," he told his crew.

The boat angled close enough for the guardsmen to reach their gaff hooks out to the box, but the hooks were no help in pulling the small box up. Gingerly, the guardsmen lowered one of the crew headfirst over the side, holding him by his ankles. Each time the guardsman grabbed for the box, a wave snatched it away. Finally he got hold of it, and kept a tight grip on it as the others pulled him back up.

"Will you look at that?"

Inside sparkled a diamond engagement ring, the largest any of the guardsmen had ever seen.

Moments later, a Coast Guard boat with an Associated Press photographer on board pulled alongside. The crews of both boats showed what they had pulled in during the long day's search. It paled beside the ring, which Keller held out as the photographer clicked away. By the next day, the picture of Keller's sea-weathered hand holding the ring had been published around the world. Had it really been intended as an engagement ring? And whose was it?

To the victims' families waiting at the Ramada Inn, the ring, as much as an object could, dramatized the human tragedy of TWA Flight 800. Someone had died before he could present this ring to his future wife. But among the families at the hotel, no one had any idea who that someone might have been.

———

Shortly before noon, Kallstrom walked over to a meeting he and Francis had called at the East Moriches Coast Guard station. About one hundred people had crowded into an upstairs conference room. Kallstrom started by asking everyone to introduce himself. "Just say who you are and explain what you bring to the table."

Though most in the room had worked through the night, their usefulness had come to an end. The roll call included volunteer fire chiefs and ambulance crews, National Guard reserves and village traffic cops. Jim McMahon, superintendent of the New York State Police, and police officials from Nassau and Suffolk counties were there, ready to assist in any way possible. Kallstrom thanked them all and said the FBI would be coordinating the various law enforcement agencies for the criminal probe. He said the FBI would try to accommodate everybody.

Then Francis spoke. The NTSB vice chairman seemed much stiffer before a crowd than alone with Kallstrom. When Suffolk County executive Bob Gaffney, the top official in a county of nearly two million people, moved to ask a question, Francis replied in what seemed a patronizing tone, "And yoooo are?" Gaffney, a former FBI agent, dutifully responded with his name and title, then added, "And you arrrrre?" When someone else asked how the NTSB planned to handle a particular problem, Francis brushed it off, saying simply, "We're good at that." A moment later, Francis said he needed tight security for the investigation. "Well," snapped Suffolk County police commissioner Peter Cosgrove, "we're good at that."

Francis was badly misreading his audience. Suffolk County had one of the most sophisticated and largest police departments in the nation, larger than those of Boston, San Francisco, or Detroit, with nearly three thousand officers. Cosgrove felt his officers had done a remarkable job in securing the area within an hour of the crash. Yet this Washington stuffed shirt was speaking of his force as if they were bumpkins.

Francis's colleagues seemed equally tactless. Al Dickinson, chief investigator for the NTSB's probe, announced matter-of-factly that, "the nature of the job to be done here will quickly be shifting and many of you won't be needed anymore." Dickinson was talking to people who had been up all night pulling bodies out of the water as jet-fuel fumes scorched their lungs. Now they were being told to leave.

"Look, this is my goddamn county and you're not going to talk to me like that!" one Suffolk official told Dickinson, whose face reddened.

"Come on, we've been up all night," Kallstrom said. "I'm sure Al didn't mean anything by that. We've got to make some sense of all this, and we can't have hundreds of people doing the same thing. We've just got to organize ourselves."

The soothing words came too late. Gaffney stormed out of the room, followed by deputy county executive John Gallagher, Police Commissioner Cosgrove, and Suffolk County police chief Joe Monteith. "I'm pulling the county out of this whole mess," said the normally low-key Gaffney. "Who do these people think they are? No one is going to treat our people this way."

"Calm down, Bob," Monteith said to his boss.

"Don't tell me to calm down," Gaffney snapped.

By then, Kallstrom was at his side. "We really need you guys," he said. "You have to stay and help us."

After a few minutes of back-and-forth, Gaffney finally agreed. "Okay," he said grudgingly. "But we're just in it for the FBI."

As Kallstrom reentered the FBI van, he was met by a flurry of incoming calls from anxious politicians. "Senator D'Amato on line three," one agent called out. "Boss, the governor's on hold on line four," said another. Kallstrom did what he could to brief these and other officials, then slumped in his seat with a sigh. "Everyone wants to know what the hell's going on," he muttered to himself, "and I don't know shit."

He called in Schiliro and Pickard and told them bluntly, "This is chaos."

"Well, what do you think we need to do?"

"Let's slow down," Kallstrom said. "Let's set priorities. Let's do the basic things first. Let's build the foundation strong so that when you build the house, it's not going to cave in. Because if you build a weak foundation the first few days when everyone is panicked and everyone is running and screaming and yelling, you're screwed."

At least one problem had been solved. All morning, the FBI agents and Coast Guardsmen had wondered how journalists were getting updated body counts and other facts before they were announced. Fortunately, Joe Cantamessa, Kallstrom's old Mafia-busting pal and electronics wizard, had just arrived after driving all night from North Carolina. As his first assignment, he'd been asked by Kallstrom to plug the leaks.

Cantamessa had decided to take a stroll through the press camp—already dubbed Satellite City—to see what he could find. Short, trim, and bespectacled, with the lingo of a Brooklyn Romeo, he looked nothing like an FBI agent. But his smooth talk and nothing-is-impossible attitude had enabled him to place a tiny microphone in Mafia boss Paul Castellano's television set while bodyguards stood nearby. Posing as a television repairman to fix a set made fuzzy by Kallstrom and his crew, Cantamessa invited the two thugs to look over his shoulder "so you don't think I'm pulling anything funny here." With this same confident air, he was able to move through the press camp without attracting any notice. It took him only a minute or two to spot the receivers that radio and TV crews were apparently using to monitor cell-phone conversations from inside and around the Coast Guard station.

Kallstrom ordered an end to all cell phone use, both at the station and out at the crash site. At the station, AT&T had just arrived to install a bank of hard-line phones. For calls from the crash site, Cantamessa sent an FBI technician out to see how well a bureau walkie-talkie, using a secure, dedicated FBI channel, would work over ten miles of water. It worked just fine. From then on, an FBI agent with a secure radio was assigned to each boat at the crash site. The latest body counts thus traveled securely from the crash site to the Coast Guard station, then to families of the victims, and only afterward to the media and general public.

Kallstrom was especially worried about securing the crash site. The waters had been cleared of volunteer pleasure boaters, but now he widened the restricted area considerably. What if some boater, as a joke, dumped a missile launcher or evidence of a bomb for unsuspecting investigators to find months later? Kallstrom called for the area to be protected not only by Coast Guard vessels but aerial surveillance. If a rocket launcher did emerge from the water and ended up in court, a defense lawyer would surely ask how the FBI knew it had not been dropped there by an airborne prankster sometime after the explosion.

Soon, divers would begin sifting the depths for evidence of a genuine bomb or missile, but in pursuing the possibility that terrorism had downed TWA Flight 800, there was another piece of foundation that Kallstrom knew must be set. In the day-after news, accounts of missilelike streaks had proliferated. Kallstrom wanted agents to check out every one of these reports; he wanted other accounts to corroborate them, and he wanted them fast. The best eyewitness reports would be those obtained soonest, before time and the endless media coverage affected the memories of even the most well-meaning witnesses. In his first news conference, Kallstrom planned to announce a toll-free number for eyewitnesses to call. Already, hundreds of agents teamed with Suffolk police officers had fanned out through Suffolk County under the day-to-day command of two key players on the FBI–NYPD Joint Terrorism Task Force who were so dedicated and so good that they'd become legends among their peers.

FBI agent John Liguori and his partner Tom Corrigan, a New York City detective, were both in their mid-thirties and both experts in terrorism. For years they had tracked Sheik Omar Abdel-Rahman and his followers, gathering evidence that had just brought the sheik a life sentence—plus fifty years—for plotting to blow up New York's tunnels and bridges, the United Nations, and even FBI headquarters in Manhattan. Liguori and Corrigan had exposed the plot just as the sheik's followers were in a Queens garage, making explosives and preparing to set off their first bomb. Liguori and Corrigan knew each other so well that they could work an entire day side by side in the frenzied Command Post and communicate only with nods, grimaces, and hand gestures. Yet in character, they were contrasts. Liguori sat ramrod straight, his tie pulled tight, his jacket always on, his jet-black hair neatly combed. He talked only when he had something worth saying. Corrigan, whose thick, prematurely white hair made him look more seasoned than his thirty-eight years, had a quick grin and boisterous sense of humor. He never wore a tie if he could help it. His rumpled charm vanished, however, when he felt he was closing in on his prey. Then he would become so quiet that his colleagues on the squad would tease him. "Oh, don't bother Tommy today," they'd say. "He's working." So intensely would he work, and into such late hours, that he would sometimes fall asleep at the office, his head resting on piles of reports.

Liguori relied more on careful research, Corrigan on intuition. Together they made a perfect team to serve as the case agents for Flight 800. Usually, case agents made most of the decisions on an investigation. But Flight 800 was so sensitive that Pickard and Kallstrom were overseeing the direction. So for this one, Corrigan and Liguori reported directly to Neil Herman, the Joint Terrorism Task Force chief who had been investigating terrorist bombings for twenty-three years. He had the utmost respect of his troops. Herman, in turn, would report to George Andrew, the talented if impulsive assistant special agent in charge, who would pass the latest information up the chain to Pickard, who would then brief Kallstrom. It all sounded more bureaucratic than it was; in fact, it was the most direct way for the FBI's most seasoned terrorism experts to keep one another informed.

Within a day of the crash, the FBI had four eyewitnesses with military or piloting experience, or both. One was Dwight Brumley, the electronic-warfare officer who had viewed the explosion from a USAir commuter plane. On Friday, agents visited a Navy criminal investigative field office in Newport, Rhode Island, to find a crisply uniformed, well-spoken officer in his mid-forties ready and able to offer concise observations. At about 8:25 P.M. on July 17, Brumley recalled, he had been in seat 5-F—a window seat on the right-hand side—of USAir Flight 217 from Charlotte, North Carolina, to Providence, Rhode Island. Brumley described the prop plane that had first attracted his attention, and the flarelike white streak that appeared after the plane passed below. No red or orange traces appeared with the white light, he said in answer to the agents' questions, and no fire or smoke trailed behind it. Nor did any piece of the projectile, if indeed it was one, fall away as it rose in a northeasterly direction. It looked more like fireworks than a missile, racing skyward before bursting into a cascade of light and color. Brumley described how the object burst into a small explosion that quickly expanded into an oval fireball about 200 feet long. A second later, there was a second burst and a much larger explosion. Brumley figured his USAir flight was about 4,000 feet away from the second blast. As the fireball expanded and began plummeting out of the sky, Brumley's plane passed directly over it, at 21,000 feet, and the fireball vanished from view.

Brumley's knowledge of weapons and aircraft made him an ideal eyewitness, and the agents who interviewed him had no doubt he had viewed some aspect of Flight 800's explosion. For months afterward, Brumley's story haunted the agents as almost irrefutable evidence that some kind of missile had hit Flight 800. And yet, the most important details were absent. At no point, Brumley said, had he seen TWA Flight 800, so at no point had he seen the projectile hit the plane—or anything else. Nor could he say that the projectile was a missile. It had none of the telltale signs that he'd learned in his military training were typical of missiles. If it had been falling rather than ascending, Brumley might have thought it a shooting star or a meteor. It could have been a missile, but he couldn't be sure. James Nugent, the passenger sitting behind the weapons expert, had also witnessed the explosion, though his description was not as specific as Brumley's. As for the pilot of the USAir aircraft, he had been looking north and so saw no sign of the flare that Brumley described—or the explosions.

Then there was Captain David McClain, who had been flying the East Winds Airlines commuter plane from Boston to Trenton that passed close enough to Flight 800 for him to observe a bright light under its wing just prior to an explosion. Based on his description, and his credibility as a pilot, the FBI missile team surmised that what he may have seen was the rear end of a missile streaking toward the 747.

The most compelling accounts, however, came from the crew of an Air National Guard helicopter who were facing the explosion as it occurred. These were rescue pilots trained to be alert. Major Fritz Meyer of the Air National Guard told investigators that while at the controls of an HH-60 military helicopter, concluding routine air-rescue training maneuvers just off Westhampton with a National Guard C-140 cargo plane, he saw a flash of light heading in the same direction as Flight 800. But Meyer's impression was that the streak was not ascending toward the plane. Rather, it was like a "shooting star moving in a gradually descending arc over the top of the plane." He was sure he did not see it coming up from the ground, nor did he see a smoke trail. Meyer did not suggest he had seen a missile, but the FBI noticed that he did use the words "streak," "light," and "plane" in a single sentence.

Captain Chris Baur, seated next to Meyer in the helicopter when the sighting occurred, said he saw a track of light actually meet the plane, that he thought he saw a midair collision, and that two explosions followed. Perhaps, he said, the track of light was a flare. "Denis, is that pyro?" Baur asked Denis Richardson, the chopper's flight engineer, when he saw the two explosions. He was asking if the flash of light he'd seen was a flare. But Richardson was looking in another direction when the flash occurred and turned just in time to see the fireball. To investigators he could only confirm that Baur had asked the question.

As Liguori and Corrigan read through the transcripts of these eyewitness interviews, they became increasingly interested in the possibility that the jumbo jet had been hit by a land or sea-to-air missile, a presumption that raised a flurry of questions that the agents would have to pursue. How could terrorists smuggle a missile and launcher—heavy, unwieldy objects—into the United States? Why, if they managed to do so, would they plan to launch a missile sixty miles east of Kennedy Airport, when an ascending or descending plane was miles away, rather than plan a much closer-range attack nearer the airport? And if they had, would even the most sophisticated land-to-air missile have any chance of hitting a target eight or ten miles distant? One question, however, was easily answered: Powerful, shoulder-fired missiles did exist, and thanks to the United States, terrorists had them.

In the mid-1980s, during the Soviet Union's invasion of Afghanistan, the United States delivered thousands of Stinger missiles to the Afghan rebels known as the mujahideen. The missiles, also called MANPADs—for Man

Portable Air Defense System—were heat-seeking weapons to be used against Soviet HIND helicopters. Unquestionably, many had passed into the hands of terrorists. In fact, many of the mujahideen whom the United States had armed had later joined terrorist training camps in Lebanon's Bekaa Valley.

A fax from the State Department alerted agents at the Command Post to what could possibly be a more tangible link between the mujahideen, a group of Islamic warriors that emerged from the Afghan war, and the possible downing of Flight 800. The fax had appeared the previous morning—some nine hours before the crash—in the Cairo and Washington offices of *Al Hayat*, the largest Arab newspaper. On the day after the crash, a smattering of extreme political groups and anonymous callers and faxers had emerged to take credit for Flight 800, claiming to have downed it with a missile or bomb to publicize one cause or another, but this fax was the only claim that had come *before* the crash. Translated by the State Department from Arabic, the fax offered praise to Allah, railed against the Saudi family for arresting Islamic fundamentalists, then focused on the United States.

It seems that the blowing-up of the principal headquarters of the infidel American army in the Ullaya neighborhood of Riyadh which caused eighty crusaders to perish was not a good enough lesson for them to depart. Instead, their secretary of defense came to threaten the mujahideen to fight them if necessary. The response was swift and equal to the size of the defiance of the despicable secretary of the invaders, William Perry. Once again, the Movement for Islamic Change established its long arm and capabilities when it targeted the American pilots' compound in Al-Kobar. The explosion damaged six buildings and destroyed two of them completely. In addition, a number of buildings suffered various degrees of damage. Based on our information, they have suffered more than 300 dead and 600 wounded. We can decisively declare that all the targeted were Americans and what was reported in Saudi and the American media was disinformation and far from the truth. The mujahideen will deliver the ultimate response to the threats of the foolish American president. Everyone will be amazed as to the size of that response. Determining the time and the place is the hand of the Al-Mujahideen, and the invaders should be prepared to leave . . . dead or alive. Dawn is their departure time, isn't dawn near enough.

—The Movement for Islamic Change
—The Jihad Wing of the Arabian Peninsula

The fax might prove an idle provocation and its timing a mere coincidence, but for the moment, Corrigan and Liguori told Kallstrom that, based on their three years of intensive work tracking international terrorists, and an examination by terrorist experts, the fax seemed genuine.

Nothing would be said publicly about the fax either that day or in the days that followed, but within the Command Post, the possibility that a Middle Eastern terrorist group had downed Flight 800 now seemed more likely than ever.

————

Along the outlying roads and summer towns of this midsection of Long Island's south shore, many joggers, bicyclists, beach walkers, and porch sitters saw streaks, flashes, and an explosion: a fireworks, or so it initially seemed, curiously two weeks after the Fourth of July. Most of these civilians were as credible as the military eyewitnesses.

Ann DeCaro, an IRS employee, told the FBI on Friday that she had been walking laps around a high school track with her friend Betty Manzella, an employee of the Suffolk Board of Elections, in Mastic Beach near East Moriches when she noticed an object above the tree line. The object was ascending rapidly from left to right. At the tip was a very bright light with a bright yellowish-orange tail. She assumed it was fireworks, but then the clouds obscured the shape for a few seconds. To Manzella, the light appeared bright white with a dot of orange, like the top of a flare and a white smoke trail. Both women then saw a gigantic fireball. "Oh my God, people are dying," said Manzella to DeCaro. Manzella had just seen an aircraft because of the sun reflecting off it and assumed from the fireball in the sky that the plane had just exploded. "Oh no, that was fireworks," DeCaro told Manzella. Then Manzella felt and heard what appeared to be thunder. The women were so unnerved by what they had seen that they broke off their exercise routine and hurried home.

Another was Joseph Delgado, an elementary school principal in Westhampton who had been stretching beside the school before jogging when he saw a streak rising above the tree line, and called the FBI on the night of the crash. To the agents who rushed over to his home, Delgado provided further details that were startling. First, he had seen a bright white light with a reddish-pink aura around it. The light ascended from behind nearby trees in a "squiggly" pattern and shot straight up, increasing in velocity as it did. Delgado believed the object hit a second object in the sky that appeared stationary and seemed to glitter. He said he must have blinked because he didn't see the actual impact, but did see a "puff" or white flash following it. Next, he saw two balls of fire falling past trees on the horizon. He didn't hear anything, he added. The whole event took about seven seconds. The principal was responsible, well-spoken, and utterly sure of what he'd seen.

As reports of other sightings came in, Kallstrom considered whether to order his agents to canvass the area door-to-door. Even random observations might suddenly assume critical significance. A resident might have noticed an unfamiliar panel van parked Wednesday night on his street; a gas station attendant might remember fueling such a van and noticing that its driver seemed nervous. From such stray threads, pictures sometimes emerged. On the other hand, once word of an FBI canvass spread through the surrounding towns, crackpots might be encouraged to invent stories. Earlier in his career, Kallstrom had wondered how anyone could do that; he didn't wonder anymore. In a meeting with Pickard, Liguori, Corrigan, and others, he weighed the options for nearly twenty minutes, then said with a sigh, "I think we have to do it." Every interview of any consequence would be typed up as a so-called "302 report" and sent in to the Command Post. Over the next weeks, Liguori and Corrigan would sift through hundreds of them, usually in the evenings when the phones were quieter. Sometimes a detail would seem to jump out, and the investigators would eagerly pursue it. Other times, reading 302 reports was a lot like reading the phone book.

Most of the eyewitnesses interviewed in the first day or two said they saw a flare in the sky. That made sense. If a missile was involved, the burn of the propellant would possibly leave a trail of smoke or light. The color of what was visible from the ground would depend on the type of propellant used. The missile itself would probably not be visible to the naked eye, nor did anyone claim to see anything that might indicate a possible missile launching site. Also, only a few had seen the streak ascending. Most, in fact, had thought it might be descending or moving horizontally, and none seemed to have seen an object strike the aircraft. Baur, the Air National Guard pilot who saw Flight 800 explode, thought he might have, but he couldn't be sure.

Everyone who called the FBI about a possible missile sighting was taken seriously. First, agents asked general questions over the telephone. Then a team of two agents went to the home. If that was productive, missile experts were sent for a third interview. Most times they went with the witness to the scene of the sighting so the FBI could note the coordinates where the person was standing and how the flare moved across the sky. Some witnesses were quickly dismissed because they saw events in the wrong part of the sky or at the wrong time or because other facts proved impossible. But Kallstrom was taking nothing for granted. One woman from North Carolina claimed she had seen a missile in the sky over her home. FBI agents were sent to interview her anyway.

Agents were also sent to interview another woman in New Jersey after George Andrew, Pickard's deputy, saw her being interviewed on television. "Why haven't we talked to this woman?" an irritated Andrew asked agents in the Command Post. To the agents who then interviewed her, she sounded reasonable at first, but when she told the agents she had been at every historical event of the last century, either personally or spiritually, they quickly said their good-byes. "Okay," Andrew said, a bit embarrassed. "At least we checked it out."

Shortly after dawn on Friday, Corrigan sent a caravan of federal agents out to Manorville, a town near East Moriches, to follow up on one of the more intriguing 302 reports. A local resident had reported that he saw a flarelike object that appeared to have been fired from the nine-hole Pine Hills golf course just before the crash. The resident swore he'd seen a streak rise above the tree line, shooting up in the sky like a NASA rocket.

The sun was barely over the horizon when the agents pulled up along the fairway grass in their sedans. They emerged, all in dark suits, to begin pacing across the links in a wide phalanx, a car's length apart from one another, looking for telltale scorch marks or debris from a missile like a launcher or a tube. A caretaker, out early to groom the course for morning golfers, looked up in amazement. "What are you doing?" he called out.

"We're on federal business," an agent called back. "We'll be out of here in no time."

Two hours later, the agents had tramped across every green inch of the Pine Hills course and found no evidence. The course was pristine—except for the imprints of their shoes.

———

By early Thursday afternoon, the day after the crash, some seven hundred FBI agents were assigned to the TWA investigation. Many, under Liguori and Corrigan, were fanning out to canvass East Moriches and the surrounding towns. In these sleepy, middle-class summer communities where a fish sandwich could still be had for five dollars and an ear of hot buttered corn for a buck, the crash had already become strangely surreal, too far offshore to have been seen or heard by most residents, yet bringing hundreds of police cars, fire trucks, and ambulances that sped wailing to and from the East Moriches Coast Guard station as helicopters whirred overhead. Now the presence of the FBI agents, ostensibly on the trail of a hideous crime, made the tragedy seem even more alarming. The agents, with their FBI badges around their necks, were an odd sight along streets lined with antique and tackle shops, a newspaper store, a deli and a gas station, but not much else.

To the townspeople of Center and East Moriches, towns that seemed to meld into each other, the FBI agents appeared almost ubiquitous in those first days. In fact, only a small fraction of the seven hundred agents assigned to the investigation were in the area. Most had other leads to pursue, generated from the Command Post or at Kennedy Airport. For the strong foundation Kallstrom wanted to build, their work was as vital as any information being gathered in the vicinity of the crash.

These agents worked in teams of four to six, each team assigned to an aspect of the case. One worked on Flight 800's cargo and baggage. The FBI wanted to know how many pieces of luggage had been put in cargo holds, and tried to find out how many were carried aboard and stowed above seats or hung on suit racks. If a passenger came under suspicion, directly or indirectly, the FBI wanted to be able to pinpoint the location of his luggage on the plane, possibly to prove if it had contained a bomb. Of particular interest was the container of human corneas delivered to the cockpit just before takeoff. Putting medical cargo up front was standard procedure, especially when it contained human organs or tissue, but why had the corneas arrived so late, and why was the crew not alerted to it beforehand? They had been sent from a reputable eye surgeon, but could someone have placed a bomb in the container, either at the hospital or en route? Outlandish as the idea seemed, it suggested a chilling logic: So-called lifeguard cargo was not, as a rule, checked for explosives, nor did it undergo a metal-detector or visual search. Once put on a preapproved freight list, it went on board, as long as the people delivering it were preapproved vendors. To the FBI, this was hugely disconcerting. It rendered not only the corneas but the vials of HIV-contaminated blood highly suspect. It also led the agents to recommend to the FAA that security measures regarding lifeguard cargo be tightened across the board.

Dozens of other teams divided the manifest among them and embarked on the laborious work of background checks on every passenger and crew member. Eventually, agents would visit every victim's family, except for five who declined to be interviewed. Such painstaking care was expended not only on the manifest of Flight 800 but on that of the plane's westbound flight from Greece. By late Thursday, Kallstrom, through the State Department, was seeking approval from the Greek government to interview workers at Hellenikon Airport. Within days, agents would be sent to Florida, the Midwest, Texas, and Canada to interview Flight 881's passengers, including the 109 Bosnian refugees. Finding the Bosnians would prove a major challenge. Many lacked addresses or had given only forwarding addresses; most spoke little if any English, and nearly all of them had scattered throughout the country to take prearranged jobs. The dozen Greek merchant seamen on Flight 881 were no easier to find. Within two or three days, most had boarded various cargo ships destined for ports in Central and South America, but the agents tracked them all down.

At the Manhattan Command Post, agents scrutinized airline passenger lists for anything unusual. They checked court documents for divorce proceedings and legal disputes that may have involved the victims. They reviewed credit reports and employment records. They subpoenaed the fifty largest life insurance providers to find out if any of the 230 victims had life insurance policies; if so, who the beneficiaries were; and if the policies were large and/or recently purchased. They also wanted to know if anyone else had taken out insurance policies on any of the victims. Might any of the passengers have been targets of sabotage or saboteurs themselves?

Still other teams monitored every suspected cell of terrorists in the United States and worked with the CIA and the Defense Intelligence Agency to track, as best they could, the most virulent ones abroad. If any terrorists had brought down Flight 800, they would be boasting about it among themselves. It was bragging by John Gotti and his lieutenants about the shooting of Paul Castellano that had enabled Kallstrom and his "wires and pliers guys" to nail them with life prison terms; it was bragging by followers of the blind sheik that brought them down before they could carry out their plans to bomb New York landmarks. Whatever their nationality and brand of fanaticism, criminals in one sense were the same: All had sizable egos.

There was one line of inquiry best initiated not by the agents, but by the assistant director himself. In the midst of that frantic day after the crash, Kallstrom took a moment to go up to his twenty-eighth-floor private office and close the door behind him. From a fold in his wallet, he fished out an odd-looking black key with a square top. In the credenza behind his oversize walnut desk was the ivory-colored telephone he used to make classified calls to the highest levels of government. The "STU phone," as it was called, was formally known as a Secure Telephone Unit. A twist of the key inserted part of a code on the phone line. To complete the code, Kallstrom punched in his personal identification number. Now he could directly dial the director of the FBI, members of the cabinet, even the president himself, and have the call ring through to their own designated STU phones. Calls on a STU line were for matters of national security. Needless to say, a compelling advantage of the system was that STU calls could not be intercepted. The code scrambled conversation on the line if anyone tried to tap into it. This was a call that Kallstrom wanted to keep private, at least for now, even from Pickard and Schiliro.

He wanted the answer to a blunt question: Could a U.S. military plane, warship, or submarine have fired a missile at TWA Flight 800 by mistake? Had friendly fire killed 230 innocent people?

Kallstrom's call went straight to the office of General John Shalikashvili, the chairman of the Joint Chiefs of Staff. To expedite his response to STU calls, the general's own key was always inserted into the phone as soon as he arrived at his office. Now, when it rang, a senior aide pounced on it, punched in the general's own code number, and picked up the receiver to hear Kallstrom ask to speak with the chairman himself about the previous night's midair disaster.

After a warm exchange of greetings—the two had met several times before—Kallstrom came to the point. As part of its investigation, the FBI would have to consider the possibility that Flight 800 had been hit by a missile fired from a U.S. military ship or plane. As a courtesy, Kallstrom was giving General Shalikashvili advance notice that his agents would be calling all branches of the military to learn what assets had been in the area of the crash site the night before. The military would be expected to provide documentation to back up their responses, and cooperate with interviews as needed. "We have no reason to think that a misfire from the military took out the plane, but given the eyewitness reports of streaks of light in the sky, we need to cover all our bases," Kallstrom said. "I want to make sure we have the complete cooperation of everyone over at the Department of Defense."

"I understand," the general replied. "In fact, I've already asked my Joint Chiefs the very same thing. I've been told by the command authorities that there was nothing like that, Jim; no accidents, no friendly fire. But I understand why you have to look at every detail."

"We have to do a thorough investigation, that's all," Kallstrom said. "It may also serve to protect you against any allegations that may come out later."

"Jim, you have our full cooperation. Just let me know what you need." Shalikashvili replied. The general admired Kallstrom and knew he would take the investigation wherever it needed to go. In his own mind, he had already ruled out friendly fire. Shalikashvili knew that a missile exercise would never have been conducted ten miles off the coast of Long Island, which was thick with commercial air traffic. A missile exercise in that corridor would be as ill-advised—and unlikely—as artillery drills across Interstate 95.

The general did wonder if a missile had been fired by a terrorist. There was, after all, that Kennedy Airport radar tape from the FAA showing an unexplainable blip near the plane just before it crashed, which conceivably could have been a missile.

That morning, the general had met with members of the House National Security Committee and Intelligence Oversight Committee to discuss Flight 800 and the fatal bombing of the Khobar Towers military residence in Saudi Arabia and whether the two incidents could be related. Along with Richard Clarke, special assistant to the president on terrorism, and Tony Lake, the national security advisor, he was concerned that the Olympics in Atlanta might be the next target. They thought Kallstrom's worst fear might well prove true: The downing of Flight 800 could mean war if it was part of a state-sponsored campaign.

Before he left his private office, Kallstrom made another STU call to Louis Freeh to report his conversation with General Shalikashvili. That done, he could omit any mention of friendly fire in the teleconference scheduled for four o'clock to brief the FBI's senior ranks in Washington. As he headed down to the office conference room where the teleconference briefing was already set, he felt a wave of fatigue come over him. He had been up all night, and suspected that sleep was not on the agenda for the second night after the crash, either. Hunger was an easier need to fill: From his office refrigerator, he took a Diet Coke and then grabbed a fistful of pretzels from a jar on his secretary's desk. Sometime in the last twenty hours, he had eaten a sandwich, but he had no memory of what kind. He did remember the coffee and an apple he had been given at the Red Cross tent at the Coast Guard station.

Kallstrom found Pickard, George Andrew, and various other senior agents settled in the conference room, ready to talk into a microphone at the center of the table. He hated this stuff. He had spoken with Freeh three times that day already. Why waste time repeating the same news to a conference-call device hooked up to a room full of FBI bureaucrats in Washington? The reason, of course, was that the bureaucrats needed to feel in the loop; the point of the teleconference was to soothe their egos. Kallstrom led the briefing impatiently and then endured the predictable flood of questions, many of them irrelevant. When the bureaucrats asked for a teleconference briefing every day at 5:30 P.M. until further notice, Kallstrom rolled his eyes. As the meeting broke up, Kallstrom delegated the job to Pickard, who soon dubbed it "The Five-Thirty Follies." Before long, Freeh would be skipping them, too. He was getting his news directly from Kallstrom.

For the architect of this investigation—already the largest in FBI history—merely putting the foundation in place was not enough. Now Kallstrom had to explain it to a shaken American public in as much detail as he could without compromising his plans or violating federal rules of evidence.

Early Thursday evening in the parking lot of the Coast Guard station at East Moriches, still just a day after the crash, the rotors of Kallstrom's blue-and-white FBI helicopter began to turn. From the command van, a figure now familiar to hundreds of Coast Guardsmen, local police, and other investigators on-site but still relatively unknown outside the law enforcement fraternity appeared in a change of clothes for the short trip to his first national press conference. Before heading over to the helicopter, he walked onto the seawall to see if the boats had brought in more bodies or debris. There he saw dozens of agents visibly exhausted, perhaps even dulled by shock at what they'd seen the previous night. Kallstrom sought out George Gabriel and pulled him aside.

"Look," Kallstrom said as he stood on the lawn outside the station, "this obviously isn't going to end anytime soon. We're going to have to take care of our agents. Make sure they're getting sleep, and make sure they get counseling if they're stressed. It's easy with all the pressure right now to forget that these people are human beings. Don't forget to take care of the troops."

Gabriel's fishing trip with his son seemed weeks, not hours, in the past. Since taking those calls on the boat, he had worked without pause in such a state of high alert—and high adrenaline—that the notion of sleep, either for his agents or himself, had simply not occurred to him. But he conceded Kallstrom's point. From then on, he and the other FBI supervisors rotated agents in ten- to twelve-hour shifts. Soon, counselors were also brought in. Over the next days, Gabriel learned to recognize when they were needed. The agents didn't break down, but simply withdrew and became quiet, or refused to go home and insisted on working without a break. The images that haunted many of them, it turned out, were of the youngest victims, who reminded them of their own children.

In his chopper, Kallstrom flew from East Moriches to the Sheraton Hotel in Smithtown, about forty miles up island, for his first news conference. He arrived at about 7:00 P.M., an hour before the conference was scheduled, to meet with Francis and plan their joint remarks. Because the NTSB's command center and press office were at the Sheraton, the hotel had become a press site by default. Fortunately, there were no weddings or conventions scheduled for the banquet room, which could barely accommodate the hundreds of journalists and television cameramen who squeezed in. Kallstrom and Francis strode in to stand behind a wooden podium topped by dozens of microphones crudely taped together on a gooseneck.

Francis spoke first. In the monotone that would become his trademark, he spoke as if he were addressing a room full of experts on a topic with which they were already familiar. "I'll spend a little bit of time talking about how we're proceeding," Francis began, as several reporters grimaced. Clearly, he was *not* going to discuss how the plane might have exploded. "The highest priority remains the recovery of the victims in this accident," he concluded, "and that will continue to be the case." Then Kallstrom spoke.

"Good evening, everybody," he said. "Nothing is more important than the public safety and the national security"—raising the possibility for the first time that a terrorist act might have downed the plane brought reporters to attention.

The first question shouted by a reporter raised the missile issue.

"We have a lot of witnesses," Francis answered. "We're in the process of going through the witness statements." The NTSB vice chairman may have been more suited for his job than the FBI agents had imagined. He was managing to make the possibility of a missile attack seem boring.

Then Kallstrom responded: "Now obviously, we know a lot about the terrorism issues. We've all read about the cases. So we are here to see if and when we shift this investigation, if we shift it at all from where it's going now to somewhere else. But we are not ready to say that yet. The public should know that we are taking all the steps necessary. It may not be obvious. Most of what we do is not obvious to the public."

Kallstrom had disclosed no more than Francis had. He'd referred only in passing to the eyewitness accounts of flarelike streaks, and said nothing about the disturbing initial radar report from Kennedy Airport. But reporters noticed that he came across as a person, not a bureaucrat.

While Kallstrom and Francis were taking pains to be discreet, the public was hearing the first news of a more dramatic press conference held earlier in the day by two eyewitnesses at the New York Air National Guard base in Westhampton. Major Fritz Meyer spoke of seeing a streak of light before the plane exploded. Though he never mentioned the word "missile," the media mentioned it for him. Indignant, Meyer drove over to the Coast Guard station early Friday morning to clarify his remarks. "I have no idea what it was," he told reporters huddled around him. "People were saying it was coming up from the ground. I never said that." He made sure to note that in Vietnam, as a decorated helicopter pilot, he had dodged missiles himself. The press liked his John Wayne bravado. The FBI was less impressed. Agents soon learned that Baur, Meyer's copilot, felt Meyer was a show-off, and Meyer, in turn, resented Baur. Perhaps the conflicts in their reports—Meyer still thought the flare had come from one direction, while Baur was adamant that it came from another—were due more to mutual animus than clear recollection.

Meyer, Baur, and the other eyewitnesses would have been surprised to learn that many of the FBI agents, particularly those on Kallstrom's newly formed missile team, now strongly suspected that a missile had destroyed Flight 800. They found many of the accounts credible enough to warrant a second, even third interview, but they were also listening carefully to what they heard—and didn't hear. At the outset, the only witness who used the word "missile" was Ann DeCaro. But she described a "bottle rocket like a missile" in the context of her description of fireworks. No eyewitness claimed to have seen a missile. Instead, they, too, described fireworks or spoke of "flarelike lights" and "streaks in the sky." The agents were careful not to mention the word "missile" either, so as not to influence the eyewitnesses. A missile, they thought, might have seemed more apparent to some, if not to all of them. On the other hand, how likely was it for scores of clearheaded, responsible citizens to report a missilelike streak if the streak *wasn't* a missile? Would fireworks, say, or the vapor trail of a military plane prompt all these reports of something seemingly so unusual?

Along with these reports, agents were drawn to several accounts of a person in a dented green car on the shore, who on several evenings prior to July 17 had been seen pointing a long cylinder out his car window. A towel was draped over the cylinder, apparently to hide it. The witnesses reported that he had been parked at Smith Point Beach, the point on shore from which the shortest line could be drawn to the plane's midair explosion.

Based on those accounts, Schiliro directed agents to set up roadblocks in the area and ask random drivers if they, too, had seen the suspicious green car. Several recalled it clearly enough to suggest it might be an old Gremlin. With that lead, other agents began combing through motor vehicle records for the owners of Gremlins.

Meanwhile, at Kallstrom's instruction, an FBI team called local police departments in Connecticut, New Jersey, and New York, asking for any recent reports of stolen or abandoned boats. Soon enough, well over a dozen such boats were located, but no scorch marks or any suspicious debris were found.

By Friday, two days after the crash, agents had initiated hundreds of other boat-related FBI inquiries on the north and south shores of Long Island, New Jersey, Connecticut, and the Massachusetts coastline. Teams searched every local marina, looking for boats from which a missile may have been fired. They did their best to determine every boat that had been out on the water the night of July 17 and to interview the owners. They also checked all boats moored at Block Island, forty miles east of the tip of Long Island off the Rhode Island coast, and nearby Fishers' Island, as well as Nantucket and Martha's Vineyard, off Cape Cod.

Together with the Suffolk County police, the agents went so far as to review records of every vessel that had passed beneath the three drawbridges above the south shore of Long Island—at Quogue, Smith Point, and West Bay—during the three months before the explosion and several days after it, a task made possible because the bow numbers of every boat that passed under those bridges were recorded by the bridgekeepers so that monthly bills could be sent to the owners: Large boats were required to pay tolls. Over the next few weeks, the agents reviewed more than twenty thousand passages over a three-month period and examined another twenty thousand files on all vessels that passed through New York harbor in the month before and after the explosion. Finally, they checked Coast Guard files on all boats the Coast Guard had boarded on July 16, 17, and 18. So far, none of these vessels aroused undue suspicion.

There were, of course, other vessels in the water on July 17.

After his call to General Shalikashvili, Kallstrom mentioned to some of his senior agents the possibility that friendly fire could have brought down TWA 800. In fact, he had raised the possibility with Pickard when reports of streaks in the sky started coming in hours after the crash. He had no reason to believe this had happened, he cautioned, but by Thursday afternoon, the day after the crash, the FAA had supplied an interesting update. Its radar experts had concluded that the blue marks on the printout, the apparent "mystery blip" on the Kennedy Airport radar tape, were a computer glitch, one that had occurred when raw data were fed into the computer. The proof: computer techs identified the problem that caused it and no such "mystery blip" had appeared on other radar tapes of the crash site from other locations. However, the radar had disclosed the presence of a P-3 Orion, a U.S. Navy plane loaded with electronics, crossing the crash-site area almost directly above Flight 800 just as the jet exploded. Kallstrom was quiet for a moment when the report came in, remembering General Shalikashvili's solemn assurance that friendly fire had not downed Flight 800. "Let's talk to 'em," he said grimly.

An initial interview by agents late Thursday with the P-3 crew turned up nothing suspicious. The P-3 Orion, its crew explained, is a twin-engine propeller plane that hunts for submarines with sophisticated electronic gear. This one, under pilot Ray Ott, had departed from Brunswick, Maine, for Lakehurst,

New Jersey, where it was to run training maneuvers with a submarine about sixty miles off the New Jersey coast. Neither the pilot nor his crew had seen or heard the explosion of TWA Flight 800. This was, perhaps, less odd than it seemed: Though the P-3 Orion may have been no more than a mile away from the jet, it was flying at 22,000 feet, some 10,000 feet above TWA Flight 800, and headed south, away from the jet as it exploded below. When word of the crash came over the plane's radio, however, Ott turned the P-3 back to offer assistance. He descended to 1,500 feet over the crash site, which he said looked L-shaped to him, and radioed the Coast Guard to advise that the P-3 had life rafts, exposure suits, and six hours of fuel. He also said the P-3 could act as a communications platform in the sky if need be. "Tell me how we can help," he radioed. For thirty-five minutes, the P-3 circled the area, waiting for an advisory. Finally, the Coast Guard told the P-3's crew members that they would not be needed in the rescue, and they continued on their way.

The agents left satisfied that the P-3 crew was telling the truth, and that the submarine hunter's proximity to Flight 800 was a harmless coincidence. But as more and more witnesses throughout Thursday claimed to have seen a streak of light in the sky at the time of the explosion, the crew's failure to corroborate those reports began to appear odd. Why hadn't *they* seen a missile streak? And could they really have been so close to the plane at 8:31 P.M. and not heard or seen it explode?

"Maybe their mission was classified," Kallstrom mused to Pickard, "and they've been ordered not to cooperate."

"Or maybe these guys were screwing around someplace they shouldn't have been," Pickard said. "Is it conceivable they were playing games with the submarine and shot off a missile?"

So the agents conducted a second round of interviews with the crew on Friday morning, with the same results. The crew had seen nothing unusual in the sky, not even the explosion. This time, Captain Ott was testy under questioning. "Are you saying I'm lying?" he demanded. "Are you questioning my patriotism here?" Nonetheless, he appeared reluctant to give details of his plane's mission that night. He assured the agents there had been no armaments aboard, but his mission, he said, was classified, and until his superiors told him otherwise, that was how it would remain.

Kallstrom and Pickard were now convinced that the crew was stonewalling. At the least, the plane must have had sophisticated radar that would have registered the explosion and picked up the arc of a missile, if one had been fired, unless the P-3—or the submarine with which it was engaged in the exercise—had fired the missile itself and the radar log had been destroyed. Kallstrom was angry as he scanned the report of the second interview Friday afternoon. He told Pickard to find agents with military experience, preferably former P-3 Orion pilots, who might subject the crew to a more rigorous grilling.

Pickard had agents review computerized personnel files. They located a former F-14 Navy pilot, an Air Force Academy graduate who had flown F-111s in the Persian Gulf War, four former military pilots who had fired missiles or fended off missiles, and three computer analysts to make better sense of the P-3's radar record. For their third interview with the P-3 Orion's crew, the FBI would be loaded for bear.

Still angry, Kallstrom told his secretary, Kathy MacGowan, to get Admiral Flanagan on the phone immediately. William "Bud" Flanagan, chief of the Atlantic fleet for the Navy in Norfolk, Virginia, was the four-star admiral ultimately responsible for seeing that Navy vessels were dispatched to the crash site to help bring up wreckage. Flanagan was away from his office when Kallstrom's secretary placed the call. Instead, a rear admiral on his staff got on the line.

After an exchange of pleasantries, Kallstrom asked the rear admiral what could be done to get better information from the eight-person P-3 crew.

"They've given you all the information relevant to your search, sir," the rear admiral intoned. "Anything else is outside what you need to know."

"Wait a minute," Kallstrom said. "I understand that this crew was on a secret training mission with a submarine. If that's the case, we need all the details of that mission right away. Plus we need to talk to the submarine's crew."

"As I told you sir," the rear admiral said a bit stiffly, "we checked, and there is nothing more you need to know."

"Goddammit," Kallstrom shouted, "I'll call the Secretary of Defense if you don't clear that crew to talk fully right now. I want them lined up outside their aircraft ready to answer our questions. I want to know everything from when they took off to when they landed, from A to Z. If I don't, I will lock those assholes up."

As a rule, Kallstrom tried not to indulge in conspiracy theories. In his twenty-five years of government service, he'd seen little in the way of cover-ups beyond the occasional midlevel bureaucrat trying to hide his own mistakes. The men and women he knew in law enforcement were solid and true; they'd joined the FBI or the New York City police department more as a calling than a career. Kallstrom felt that military officers possessed the same standards and zeal. Still, this was *strange*. Did the Navy have something to hide? At the same time, Kallstrom knew he might be overreacting. He had just worked through his second night without sleep. Adrenaline and cup after cup of watery black coffee could do only so much to fend off his fatigue and keep his nerves from fraying. He'd shaved, showered, and put on fresh clothes again from the wardrobe he kept in his office for unexpected vigils like this, but his senior agents were beginning to look at him with real concern. It was Friday morning, more than thirty-six hours after the crash, and he still hadn't taken a break.

Kallstrom trusted General Shalikashvili implicitly, but he wanted all the help he could get. As it happened, one of the other Joint Chiefs of Staff was a friend: General Charles Krulak, the commandant of the U.S. Marines. The two men knew each other from the highly successful Marine Corps Law Enforcement Foundation, which Kallstrom and four other friends had formed a few years earlier to provide scholarships to children of Marines, FBI agents, and other federal and state law enforcement officers who died in the line of duty.

He put in a call to Krulak at the Pentagon. "General, can I count on you to be my point man on this?" Kallstrom asked. "When you go into the tank this morning"—the tank was the room at the Pentagon where the Joint Chiefs of Staff met to review battle plans and hold strategy sessions—"tell the others I need their help. I want to make absolutely sure that all the weapons systems, personnel, anyone who was remotely in the area, are accounted for. Nothing can be dismissed."

Krulak readily agreed, and spoke forcefully on his friend's behalf that day. "I know this guy Kallstrom. He is tough and thorough," Krulak told the other generals. "He is going to want answers, and we need to help him out."

The Joint Chiefs had already been assured along their individual chains of command that friendly fire did not play a role in the downing, but if Kallstrom wanted more detail from the branches of the military, they would cooperate. As a result, during their daily tank meetings the Joint Chiefs discussed Kallstrom's latest requests for documentation or for access for his agents to interview their officers.

A four-star general, the son of a three-star general, Krulak loved the Marine Corps and was pained even by the thought that any U.S. military personnel could engage in a friendly-fire cover-up, yet, like Kallstrom, he was determined to investigate the possibility no matter where that might lead.

At the Joint Chiefs' meetings, the latest leads on a possible bomb or missile, as well as missile capabilities, would also be discussed. If a terrorist or sovereign state was definitively linked to the crash of Flight 800, the Joint Chiefs would give the go-ahead to put the president's contingency plan into action. In the coming days, the Joint Chiefs would review the overall contingency plan and develop multiple options to send to the president, with specific provisions for any one of several enemy countries who could have sponsored a terrorist act against the United States.

Krulak strongly suspected terrorism. The bombing of the Marine barracks in Beirut in 1983, which killed 241 Marines without warning, immediately came to his mind. The night of the Flight 800 crash, he had sent an alert to all U.S. Marines guarding U.S. embassies, particularly in the Middle East, to don battle helmets and flak jackets, and to check every incoming visitor's identification, even if the person was familiar to them. "We want to raise the threat conditions" was how Krulak put it.

Kallstrom got off the phone confident that Krulak would enlist the help of the other military chiefs to get him the answers he needed.

Before heading to Long Island, he decided to pay a visit to a friend, John Cardinal O'Connor, the head of the Catholic archdiocese of New York. He could think of no one better to comfort the families and he knew all he'd have to do was ask. Also, he was troubled. He wondered if he had gone too far in the press conferences in showing his anger for this potential crime.

"Jim, I would hope anyone would be angry," Cardinal O'Connor said over coffee at his residence. "Good Lord, everyone in the United States, everyone in the world, should be outraged if this is an act of hate and terrorism. So don't you be afraid to let it show."

On the helicopter out to East Moriches, Kallstrom felt buoyed by his brief visit, and focused again on how much he needed the wreckage to get the answer to what had happened to this plane. He began to seethe about the starchy rear admiral. Why hadn't Admiral Flanagan called him back? Where were all the ships that Francis had assured him were on their way? When a call came from Attorney General Janet Reno, asking what she could do to help, Kallstrom said he was waiting for the Navy, and not happy about it. Reno told him to call her if he needed her to do anything—and for Kallstrom to get some sleep. When she rang off, Kallstrom decided to make more calls of his own.

Outside, a gray sky had given way to rain that beat down on the tin roof of Kallstrom's command van. Already, the rain, along with rising seas at the crash site, had forced a pause in the salvage of surface debris and further delayed the divers. By now, the salt water might be washing away any traces of an explosive from the plane. By now, too, any chance that a survivor might be in the water, clinging to a floating piece of wreckage, was gone. Over in the Ramada Inn, the families of the victims were awaiting word: of more bodies retrieved, of some explanation for the crash. Kallstrom, to his enormous frustration, had virtually nothing to tell them.

For the third time in two days, Kallstrom punched in a call to the Naval command office in Norfolk, Virginia. As before, when he asked how soon Navy support would arrive, a staff officer professed not to know.

"Well, that's just not goddamn good enough," Kallstrom exploded. "How many ships, how many divers, and when?"

"I'll try to find out, and if you want, you can call back in an hour or two," the staffer replied.

"I'm not in the mood for 'call back in an hour.' I need to know when this shit is coming up here on the goddamn phone now. This is not business as usual," Kallstrom shouted, and slammed down the phone. For a moment, he stared at the phone in brooding silence. Then he called a friend at the Pentagon, Admiral Jay Johnston, chief of naval operations. "I can't get a straight answer out of anyone," he exclaimed to one of Johnston's assistants.

"You need to talk to Admiral Bud Flanagan in Norfolk," the assistant advised. "He's in charge of our Atlantic fleet."

Great—a game of telephone tag that led back to where it had started. *Flanagan.* Kallstrom sighed. Why was this admiral making a hard job even harder? Kallstrom dialed again. This time, Admiral Flanagan was in his office.

"Why isn't the Navy here yet?" Kallstrom demanded. "Where's the heavy equipment we need to get the plane off the ocean floor? Where are the divers we need to get started?"

"Your first ship's coming tonight," Admiral Flanagan said. The *Pirouette,* stationed off New Jersey, was designed for deep-sea salvage operations, with a side-scan sonar device that could be lowered to the ocean's bottom and detect wreckage. Other ships would be forthcoming. "I give you my word, sir," said Flanagan, "they'll be under way soon."

Kallstrom could hear Flanagan's no-nonsense manner, and appreciated it, but was dismayed by what he heard. "Under way soon? Why aren't they here by now?"

Flanagan explained he was sending two high-tech salvage vessels carrying divers—the *Grasp* and the *Grapple.* The *Grasp* had just returned from a six-month mission to the Middle East. Leave had been canceled, and the ship would depart as soon as it could be reequipped for the recovery. That would take at least another seven hours, Flanagan said. As for the *Grapple,* its two engines had been removed weeks ago for repairs; as soon as one engine could be reinstalled, the ship would be on its way. With one engine, Flanagan added, the *Grapple* would move half as fast but still arrive faster than if they waited to restore both her engines. "We're probably looking at Monday afternoon for the *Grapple,* and maybe late Sunday for the *Grasp,*" Flanagan said. "Remember, it's a three-day steam to Long Island from Norfolk, Virginia."

Kallstrom was pleased to hear, at least, that Flanagan was sending every diver he had: more than 200 in all. "That's terrific, sir," he said. "I just want to make sure this stuff is coming as fast as is humanly possible. Is there anything else I should be requesting? Anything else you think I need?"

"No, Jim," Flanagan said gently. "We're sending you every asset we have available on the East Coast."

Kallstrom told Flanagan about his agents' unsatisfactory interviews with the crew of the P-3 Orion. Was there anything more he should know about the plane's movements on the evening of July 17, and the submarine with which it was engaged? Flanagan said he would see to it that the P-3's crew answered all of Kallstrom's questions about their classified mission in complete detail. He would see to it that the submarine crew cooperated with agents, too.

Kallstrom rang off reassured. He could hear the integrity in Flanagan's voice. He seemed like a real down-to-earth guy. Perhaps the admiral was surrounded by toadies who hadn't deemed Kallstrom's first messages worth passing up to their boss. But if the Navy came through as Flanagan promised, the remaining 126 bodies might be brought up within a week. That was less than ideal, but it was a schedule Kallstrom could accept. And if the Navy was as helpful as Flanagan indicated, perhaps Kallstrom could soon put his conspiracy theory to rest.

For now, the Coast Guard was filling in the breach. Under Admiral Linnon, whom Kallstrom had so strongly praised to his superior, eight large cutters were methodically sweeping the grid of 240 square miles established as the outlying area of investigation. The cutters closest to the crash site were picking up tons of debris. Abetted by some twenty smaller vessels and by the police boats and pleasure cruisers at the site on the night of the crash, the Coast Guard by Friday morning had collected more than sixteen thousand pounds of the plane: chunks of the wings and tail, insulation, seats, and so on. This figure didn't include passenger luggage and other belongings, which, like the plane debris, were brought to the Coast Guard station in East Moriches but logged in separately. The debris was not only logged in; its exact location was recorded by global positioning satellite instruments.

What to do with it all? By Friday morning, the four leaders, Kallstrom, Francis, Admiral Linnon, and Suffolk County police chief Joe Monteith, had worked out a plan. The debris was carefully logged in, then shipped back out from East Moriches to a large Coast Guard vessel called the *Juniper*, several miles offshore, where FBI bomb technicians, chemists, and metallurgists studied each piece. As they did, the *Juniper* ferried the debris to a Brooklyn pier, where workers loaded it onto National Guard trucks that could take it with police escort to the farming town of Calverton on the north shore of Long Island. On a map, the route made no sense: It traced almost a complete circle, or oblong really, from East Moriches into Brooklyn and then out again. As a practical matter, it was the only way to transport huge chunks of debris. Within a day, the *Juniper* would be supplanted by a brigade of smaller boats that ferried the debris to the Shinnecock Coast Guard station, from where it could be driven to Calverton directly.

At least once a day, a caravan of camouflaged Army trucks loaded with fresh wreckage would make its way through the small towns to Calverton so that every piece could be tested as soon as possible. Usually, the convoy proceeded without a hitch.

One day early on, though, the caravan was stopped by an official of the New York State Department of Environmental Conservation. Lewis Schiliro, who was accompanying the shipment to Calverton, inquired as to the delay. He was told firmly that there appeared to be hydraulic fluid and other chemicals spilling on the roadway, and that the official had the authority to stop anything presenting an environmental hazard. Schiliro beeped Kallstrom.

The FBI chief headed straight to the state's Emergency Preparedness Command Post in East Moriches. "You'd better get ahold of your guy down there and move him out of the way or we're going to run over him," Kallstrom bellowed at the official in charge. "We're not going to hold up this investigation for a couple of drops of leaking hydraulic fluid. Tell him to get a tissue and plug the leak up."

Kallstrom added: "If he doesn't begin moving those plane parts now, I will have him arrested for obstruction of justice. It's not like we're talking about some gushing oil well."

Within fifteen minutes, the procession of trucks began to move—on direct order from Governor Pataki.

From the start, the Calverton destination was nearly perfect for what Kallstrom had in mind. Joe Monteith, a gentle Irishman and a dedicated law enforcement professional who for years had had a close relationship with the FBI, had informed Kallstrom the day after the crash that a vast hangar once used by the Grumman corporation for building military aircraft stood vacant in Calverton, some twenty miles out of Moriches. Grumman had used the 100,000-square-foot space to construct several fighter planes concurrently, including the F-14 Tomcat. Since the early 1990s, however, the hangar had lain abandoned, the result of downsizing at Grumman after the Cold War. Chief Monteith assured Kallstrom that the hangar was more than large enough to accommodate all the wreckage from Flight 800. It was large enough, Monteith added half-humorously, that the FBI could reconstruct the whole plane there if Kallstrom chose.

Early Friday afternoon, after his heartening talk with Admiral Flanagan, Kallstrom flew over to Calverton in his chopper with Robert Francis and Tom Pickard. From outside, Calverton's three low-lying hangars were unprepossessing. Inside, they were ghostly, echoing spaces, so vast that the electricity to keep them lighted and functioning cost $5,000 a day.

"All that went on here . . ." Kallstrom said softly to the others as he walked around the massive hollow hangar, "all that effort to build those fighter planes to keep us free. And now it's being used for this." He meant the thirty-foot piece of Flight 800's charred right wing, which had already been brought to Calverton and was resting on the floor covered only with outdoor carpet to protect the expensive wood flooring and to keep evidence from being contaminated by past aircraft manufacturing use. Given the contribution it had made the first time around, the hangar felt to Kallstrom like a good-luck omen.

Already in the hangar, federal agents in fatigues and black T-shirts were preparing for a long and difficult operation. Yellow crime-scene tape was stretched around piles of smaller wreckage, most of it gathered from the ocean surface before the weather had turned bad. The wreckage was placed in vertical rows and cataloged by an FBI evidence response team. Then it was inspected by agents from the FBI, from the U.S. Bureau of Alcohol, Tobacco, and Firearms, and by Suffolk County police bomb technicians with bomb-sniffing dogs. Parts to be examined more closely were set aside in a holding room where agents could decide whether to send them to the FBI laboratory in Washington for more analysis. For on-site testing, an array of mobile field equipment was being set up in rooms off the hangar floor. It included sensitive mechanical sniffers that could distill fumes from debris, microscopes to examine metal, and X-ray units to see through thick fabrics for metal fragments and chemicals.

At Kallstrom's direction, the bureau's most talented explosives experts were either at the hangar already or on their way. Among them was Steve Burmeister, a chemist, who had a reputation for finding the tiniest crystal, trace, or drop that could provide the key to a crime. As head of the FBI laboratory's chemical unit, Burmeister had tied the Unabomber to three of his fatal mail bombs shortly after his capture by the FBI in May. He was also the agent who had linked Timothy McVeigh directly to the Oklahoma City bombing, after finding specks of explosive residue embedded in McVeigh's shirt. Also in the hangar was Tom Thurman, chief of the FBI lab's explosives unit. The forensic work of Thurman's team after the Pan Am Flight 103 crash had made him and his team famous in the law enforcement world. Drawing on an extraordinary memory for technical detail, Thurman had helped identify the circuit board of the bomb's timer from a tiny fragment, and recognized that it was identical to one found in an unexploded bomb seized in Togo two years before. The match had led Thurman and his team to an electronics firm in Zurich that had sold twenty of the timers to Libya; the FBI already knew that Libyan agents had checked a bag onto a flight that connected with Pan Am Flight 103. From that trail, the United States had been able to charge Libya with the crime and demand the Libyan agents be tried under U.N. sanctions.

At Calverton, the FBI specialists would be looking for deformations in metal that indicated a bomb explosion. These included "torturing," "feathering," or "pitting"—all distinct signatures left by high-velocity explosions. They would also be looking for evidence of a missile. A small missile, fired from a shoulder launcher, would create a hole about two to three feet in diameter. The metal around it would "petal," like a flower, and crater in a distinctive manner. It might also leave a very sooty scorch streak of at least twenty feet. A high-velocity missile—fired by a plane or warship—would actually cause less damage by passing through metal more quickly, but it would still leave a hole at least as wide as itself, and the edges of that hole would melt and resolidify, leaving evidence of tearing, melting, and cracking. At the same time, the damage it caused would be far greater and far easier to detect than that left by a shoulder-launched missile.

If either a bomb or missile had hit Flight 800, the FBI would almost certainly detect it—once they had the wreckage to study.

Later on Friday, Kallstrom flew out to the Coast Guard station in East Moriches again. The morning's storm had chased sonar mapping teams and recovery workers from the sea. Many were camped out on the station lawn or taking shelter under the big white tent set up by the Red Cross, where a canteen supplied meals and coffee. To divers and investigators who had served in the military, the U.S. Coast Guard station felt like an Army base, with the Red Cross canteen its twenty-four-hour mess hall. The wind from the dying storm was still stiff enough, Kallstrom noticed, to keep the station's American flag fully extended. It seemed a symbol, not just of freedom, but of the need to keep this investigation at full throttle. From this day forward, Kallstrom decided, until the investigation was done, the flag would not come down, and it would be lit at night, a constant reminder of the importance of the mission.

As he walked into Friday's 8:00 P.M. news conference at the Smithtown Sheraton, neatly dressed but now two nights and three days without sleep, Kallstrom knew that expectations ran dangerously higher than they had the day before. The press had spent time with the victims' families and heard bitter denunciations of TWA for failing even to call the victims' families to confirm each passenger's presence on the plane. At four o'clock that afternoon, New York City mayor Rudolph Giuliani had added his voice to their frustrations, telling the press that TWA's management had lied. The airline had told reporters that families were notified by noon the day before. "That is not correct. They are still looking into it," the mayor snapped. "A good practice to follow that I learned long ago is to tell the truth."

Above all, the journalists wanted a clear, definitive answer as to what had caused the crash, and they would have been less than honest if they denied that the answer they hoped to hear, both to make sense of the crash and to sensationalize the story, was that terrorists had blown up the plane.

"We're not here to declare this a terrorist event," Kallstrom announced bluntly from the podium. There simply wasn't any evidence as yet. "We have a lot that looks like mechanical and a lot that looks like criminal, but nothing that gets us to critical mass, that puts us over the top." He acknowledged the many eyewitness reports of light streaks in the sky; he announced the FBI's toll-free telephone number, as well as its Internet site, to solicit further accounts or information from anywhere in the world. "We will know what happened on that airplane whether it's twenty-four hours from now or a week from now," he said. "And," he added, "if it's a terrorist event, we will find out who the cowards are."

Kallstrom gave the journalists nothing new to report, but his obvious sincerity again impressed them. So did his obvious exhaustion.

After the news conference, Kallstrom took the helicopter back to headquarters in Manhattan. For several more hours, he was briefed by Pickard and members of the Terrorism Task Force at the Command Post on information being gathered by the hundreds of agents now on the case. To Kallstrom's relief, the foundation appeared to be solidly and securely in place.

Finally, at 2:30 A.M., Kallstrom and Pickard allowed themselves a break in a small, adjoining room with two scuffed leather sofas. On the FBI's new telephone hot line and Internet site, more eyewitness reports had come in to support the possibility of a missile attack and raise the chilling concern—one that Kallstrom had carefully avoided mentioning to the press for fear of panicking the public—that the terrorists might fire a second missile.

"I'm petrified," Pickard said to Kallstrom. "I'm almost half waiting for the phone to ring telling us we've got another airliner down. I don't know how we would handle it. Do you think we should order planes to be rerouted around Kennedy?"

"We still don't have one scintilla of proof that a missile was to blame," Kallstrom said with a sigh. "Let's not set off a panic. Let's just make sure everybody's awake at the airports."

In fact, much was being done without public notice. Air-traffic controllers at all major U.S. airports were on heightened alert. Pilots were being warned to report any unusual activity in the sky. Security measures, already tight for the Atlanta Olympics, had been tightened further. Agents at the Atlanta games were on full alert.

As likely as the missile theory now seemed, however, the doubts of some missile experts in Washington remained no less persuasive. "Why pick the Hamptons?" Kallstrom mused. "That's what I don't get."

"Access to open water?"

"Yeah, but there's plenty of water near Kennedy. And the plane is slower and lower on takeoff—a much easier target."

"Doesn't make sense."

"Nothing does, so far," Kallstrom replied. "No sense in any of this at all."

Kallstrom's body hurt. His mind felt like mush. He needed some sleep. Groaning, he lumbered up to his twenty-eighth-floor office, lay down on the hard-cushioned, royal blue couch against one wall, and fell asleep instantly. Two hours later, as he had ordered, the duty agent at the Command Post dialed his office and let the phone ring until Kallstrom answered it with a gruff "Kallstrom."

"Good morning, sir."

On this Saturday morning, the city sky was dark.

"What do we have?" Kallstrom asked.

"A new day," the duty agent said, "and not much more."

CHAPTER 4

READY FOR WAR

$\mathbf{K}$allstrom's chopper was waiting for him, rotors churning, out at the West Side helipad near 26 Federal Plaza when he arrived at about 7:00 A.M. with Pickard and the FBI press spokesman, Joe Valiquette. Valiquette was reluctant to ride anywhere with the FBI chief, in any vehicle, at any time, even if, as was the case this morning, the vehicle had a pilot who was not Kallstrom. Somehow, just having Kallstrom in the vehicle seemed to make the trip dangerous.

The chopper lifted off and headed out to East Moriches. Though he didn't yet know it, Kallstrom was starting a day that would prove the most emotionally draining of his FBI career. Valiquette, with a legal pad on his lap, sat in the rear beside his boss with his seat belt unfastened, while Pickard sat up with the pilot. About fifteen minutes into the trip, with the chopper high in the sky, the door beside Valiquette popped open and he felt himself being sucked out. Frantically, he clutched at air. In another instant, he would be free of the chopper. That was when he felt a yank from behind. *Kallstrom.* Grimly, the FBI man was holding Valiquette by his shirt until he could reach a big hand around his press aide's neck and pull him back onto his seat. In one continuous motion, Kallstrom reached over, pulled the door closed, and latched the lock.

"You—you saved my life," Valiquette managed, deathly pale.

"*Will you fasten your goddamned seat belt?*" Kallstrom bellowed.

While the ashen Valiquette buckled up and tried to recover his equilibrium, Kallstrom looked out his window, the close call already forgotten, studying the whitecaps far below. Friday's storm had blown over, but he could see that the seas were still too choppy for the FBI and police scuba divers to begin their work. That was his first frustration.

As soon as his chopper touched down at the East Moriches Coast Guard station, Kallstrom hurried in, accompanied by Pickard, to be updated by Schiliro.

Hundreds of agents were canvassing marinas, stopping drivers at roadblocks, and interviewing local residents who reported flarelike streaks in the sky at the time of the crash. The biggest investigation in FBI history was well under way, and the eyewitness reports continued to suggest that a terrorist-launched missile had provoked it. Perhaps the terrorists were still in the area; perhaps another plane was about to be targeted. The pressure was intense, the stakes awesome. A war might already have begun, for all the investigators knew. Yet no tangible clue had emerged. Meanwhile, no divers in the choppy water meant no bodies or wreckage retrieved. Because of the weather, the *Rude* had returned to refuel and had unloaded its side-scan sonar data to be analyzed and transferred to a digital map of the wreckage. The Navy's first salvage ship, the *Pirouette*, had arrived as scheduled the previous evening, but the weather had kept it, too, from working at the crash site. To Kallstrom, its presence only underscored the absence of other Navy ships and divers that ought, he felt, to have arrived by now, too. And where were the NTSB investigators that Francis had promised? If all that wasn't exasperating enough, a crackpot had breached security.

It had been quite a performance. Wearing a green U.S. Army Reserve flight suit with his name embossed on a leather name tag, "Lieutenant Colonel Williams" had arrived just hours after the crash and used his illuminated batons to direct takeoffs and landings of helicopters carrying Kallstrom and other officials. At one meeting at the Coast Guard station on Friday, he had let everyone know that he was in charge. "I'm running the landings and takeoffs, and if someone doesn't follow my instructions, I'll wave him off," the lieutenant colonel had declared. Police and FBI officials had duly agreed to tell their pilots to follow his directions.

Finally, on this Saturday after the crash, one of the Coast Guard pilots had raised two questions about the gung-ho traffic director. First, Williams had said he was with the U.S. Army Reserve—but the Army Reserve was in no other way represented at the site. Second, he was using hand signals used for planes on aircraft carriers, not for helicopters on land. Challenged on his credentials, Williams blustered, then quietly vanished.

Lieutenant Colonel Williams could be shrugged off, and security could be tightened, but the investigation needed more: more scientists, more resources, more progress, more results.

In the Coast Guard commander's office, Kallstrom placed a call to FBI headquarters in Washington to demand more phones, more computers, and other equipment to analyze evidence. Two supervisors on the other end of a conference call failed to grasp his urgency. They told him he would have to wait until Monday. Kallstrom's voice rose. "You don't know it yet, but we're at war." Outside the screen door, Pickard, Schiliro, and others looked up. Did he know something they didn't? "Gentlemen, let me explain," he boomed into the phone. "We have a lot of people working here. And I see a lot of people walking when they should be running."

His words echoed across the front lawn of the station, where the scent of death lingered over docks still stained with blood. Hauling out bodies and cataloging debris had sufficed for the night of the crash, perhaps even for a day or two after, but in the face of what still seemed a terrorist attack that had left no clues so far, simply being on duty wasn't enough anymore. The mystery had to be solved—fast. Nothing less than everyone's best effort would do. "People are walking when they should be running" became a motto for the rest of the investigation. It was printed and tacked on the wall at East Moriches. It was posted on ships. It was a constant reminder on a moving electronic sign at the Command Post in Manhattan. And from Pickard and Schiliro on down to the youngest agents, the pace picked up.

Yet for all the items on Kallstrom's checklist, he was increasingly troubled by the complaints filtering back to him from the families at the Ramada Inn. Of the 104 bodies retrieved the night of the crash and brought to the county morgue, only two had been positively identified. Grief stricken and unable to act, the families of the victims had grown desperate—and angry. For three days they had listened to stone-faced TWA lawyers and public relations men, airport officials, and government bureaucrats promising that the victims' remains would be identified and released any hour now, any day. And so far— nothing. Suffolk County's medical examiner, Dr. Charles Wetli, had been especially offensive to the families. The delay in making positive identifications suggested strongly that he was incompetent, or at least overwhelmed. His few pronouncements, direct or indirect, suggested a manner so clinical as to seem inhuman. One family member had heard that he was planning to come to the Ramada Inn equipped with a carousel of slides showing, in graphic detail, the physical condition of the bodies he was examining, so as to explain why the process was taking so long. The family member hid the extension cord, so if Wetli showed up with his slides, he would not be able to use the projector. Mayor Giuliani, who had denounced TWA the day before, stood with the families before television cameras on Saturday morning and publicly scolded Wetli for his arrogance and apparent incompetence.

Kallstrom told Pickard and Schiliro that he wanted to see for himself why progress at the morgue was so slow. Afterward, he would fly over to the Ramada Inn to reassure the families the FBI was doing all it could to help them.

"Gee, I don't know, Jim," said George Andrew, the agent who usually spoke his mind without hesitation. "Don't you think you have enough stress to deal with right now without that?" Pickard and Schiliro agreed but said nothing.

Kallstrom bridled a bit, but knew Andrew was trying to protect him. "George, this is a whole new ball game we're in," he said. "These people deserve to meet with me. They're the ones who've lost their loved ones. I need to tell them we're not going to let them down."

Before he left the trailer, a friend, Dick Torykian, called to urge Kallstrom not to do anything without getting sleep: "Just remember what Vince Lombardi said: 'Fatigue makes cowards of us all.' "

"Thanks," Kallstrom said. "But there're some promises I have to keep before I do."

Kallstrom had a personal reason for the trip to the morgue, too. For Charlie Christopher's sake, he'd promised to do all he could to see if Janet's body had been found.

On the helicopter ride to the morgue, Kallstrom thought about the last time he'd seen rows of dead bodies. They had been U.S. Marines, lying in the dirt of a makeshift morgue under a field tent in Vietnam. This time, he feared, would be worse. It would be civilians, not soldiers. There would be mothers, teenagers, and children. Kallstrom had two teenage daughters himself and knew how precious a child's life was; how powerful the bond between parent and child; how inconsolable, for the rest of his life, he would be if one of his daughters died. Nothing could be worse.

The short, energetic man with reddish, thinning hair and white lab coat who strode out to meet Kallstrom and Pickard seemed genial. Perhaps, thought Kallstrom, too genial. Dr. Charles Wetli had the brisk, self-satisfied air of a chemist in his laboratory checking an experiment. As they walked over to the morgue building, he cheerfully indicated the refrigerated trucks that stood outside, their motors running. The county morgue was not equipped for scores of bodies at once, Wetli explained, so until the ones inside were identified and moved on to funeral homes, the rest would have to wait out here—on ice.

Inside, Wetli took the agents through a series of rooms in which experts, most of them from the FBI with help from Suffolk County detectives, were analyzing bits of evidence. A fingerprint team was taking prints from bodies whose hands remained intact. In some cases only one hand, or just a few fingers, remained. For Wetli, the highest priority was to make each identification scientifically certain. That, as he explained to Kallstrom and Pickard, was why his office had delivered only two victim IDs so far. Even now, agents were going out to many of the victims' homes to lift prints from a glass or doorknob that could be used to match fingerprints from the unidentified bodies. They were instructed, too, to retrieve hair from combs, pillows, or clothing, and any possible residue of saliva—on a toothbrush or the chewed end of a pen—for DNA matching.

Dental records filled another small room. From victims whose jaws remained intact, X rays had been taken and matches were being made. In a third room, personal effects were stored: jewelry found on the deceased, cataloged by number, and in other files, photographs sent by the families, cataloged by name. When a positive match between number and name had been made, the identification would be added to the list and the personal effects sent back to the victim's family, along with the bodily remains. In yet another room, forensics experts were examining X rays of the bodies to see if bits of metal or other foreign material fragments might have come from a bomb or missile. In the last of the small rooms sat half a dozen dark-suited funeral directors, solemn as crows, who had volunteered to make arrangements for the dead once they were identified, acting as liaisons between hometown funeral homes and the Suffolk County morgue.

Then Wetli led the agents into the morgue's large, antiseptic, hospital-like examining room. He continued to talk as they entered, seemingly unaware of row after row of torn and broken bodies, some badly mutilated, that lay on cold steel gurneys. Some were covered with white sheets, but most were naked and exposed. To Wetli, clearly, the bodies were just work—a lot of work—to be done.

"The injuries we saw on the majority of people were consistent with instant loss of consciousness and instant death," he told Kallstrom and Pickard. "With that four-hundred-mile-an-hour wind, it was the ultimate whiplash. The head becomes separated from the spinal column and you sever at least the function of the brain stem. . . . Literally, your head is being pulled off your body," Wetli went on. "We call it an internal decapitation. A good many of the adults were found that way. A lot of the children were not found that way because they are more elastic than adults. . . ."

Kallstrom and Pickard had taken a deep breath before entering the room to prepare themselves. The scene was worse than either had imagined: more than fifty naked bodies, some of them mangled. Most were women; many were young girls. Their skin was chalky, their eyes gray from the sea. The stench of jet fuel and burned flesh filled the room. Pickard felt as if he'd been belted across the stomach with a baseball bat. He looked to Kallstrom for support but Kallstrom was no help.

"The vast majority were severely injured," Wetli went on. "We had a face in twenty-five pieces. The jaws were crushed. . . ."

On one of the first bodies they passed, Pickard noticed a wristwatch that still told correct time—11:43 A.M.

"But then, many bodies had relatively little damage," Wetli said. "I guess you would have to correlate where they were seated, maybe in the rear, or over the wing, or first class. I don't know yet if there's a pattern, but some were ejected unscathed."

Wetli pointed out that on many of the bodies, there appeared to be sprinklings of stage glitter. "It's the weirdest thing," he said. "It's everywhere. You open an eye and you see Mardi Gras glitter."

"It was in the cargo," Kallstrom managed. "Eight hundred pounds of it. Meant for some show or circus in Paris."

Kallstrom wiped perspiration from his forehead. Wetli glanced at him. As he'd anticipated, Kallstrom revealed the usual symptoms of law enforcement macho confronted by multiple corpses. As for Pickard, Wetli thought he might faint as his eyes darted from the clock on the wall to tile designs on the floor to the half-dozen technicians in green jumpsuits wheeling an X-ray machine down the rows. He tried to look at anything but the bodies.

"We've had big problems with the X-ray technicians," Wetli said, following Pickard's gaze. Dealing with so many bodies was testing their nerves. Before the identification process was done, Wetli would see no fewer than fifty technicians come and go. The dentists, Wetli added, were faring better, because most were part of a county dental response team set up six years earlier by a local dentist to deal with disasters such as this. "We had a dental assistant come in to look at some photographs," Wetli said, pointing to a bulletin board where snapshots provided by relatives of the victims were being posted to aid in the identification process. "She said, 'Oh wow, I saw those teeth the other night. . . .' " She rummaged around and came up with the file of a young girl whose body she had helped photograph and tag, as a volunteer, the night of the crash at the East Moriches Coast Guard station. "I remember she had the cutest overbite," the dental assistant said forlornly. In a moment, she had matched the snapshot of a happy, healthy girl with one of the bodies laid out at the morgue. Wetli was relieved to sign off on yet another positive identification.

"Generally, the children have been tough for the dentists," Wetli added. "Today's kids don't get cavities so much, so they don't have a lot of dental work. Makes it harder to match them up. . . ."

Kallstrom walked slowly past half a dozen technicians conducting an autopsy: probing, cutting, and sewing up a body with the detachment of tailors. Down another row, he found what he was looking for. Janet Christopher's face was intact. He swallowed hard. But when he lifted her hands to look for the rings that Charlie had described, he saw that her arms were badly broken. Charlie had told him that Janet, along with a simple gold wedding band, wore a 1971 Syracuse University class ring. She couldn't afford one when she graduated, but years later, Charlie had given her one as a birthday gift. "You'd think it was a ten-carat diamond ring," Charlie had told Kallstrom. "Roman candles could not have lit up her face that brightly." Charlie had also told Kallstrom that Janet wore a big Swatch watch with upside-down numbers and silly-looking hands. But Janet's fingers were swollen and scraped, and without rings. Her wrists were bare, too.

"I want to see the paperwork on that body," Kallstrom told the nearest morgue worker. He saw that Janet had been recovered from the surface at about two-thirty on the morning of the crash. He flipped to the list of personal effects and there they were: the Syracuse University ring, the gold wedding band, the Swatch watch. What more did Wetli's workers need to tell a frantic husband that his wife was really dead? Why did Charlie have to agonize through two days of uncertainty, tormented by visions of Janet freezing as she clung to debris in the inky water?

Kallstrom was not someone to pull rank to get special treatment for himself, but this was for Charlie—and for Janet. "I want that body autopsied right away," he told Wetli grimly. "I want you to do everything you can to get her home *as soon as possible.*"

In Wetli's office, Kallstrom and Pickard sat down heavily and tried to regain their equilibrium. Kallstrom was both shaken and angry. "It's obvious you have to get some help in here," he told Wetli, trying to keep his voice calm.

"Well, I think we're doing a good job," said Wetli, leaning across his desk. "You know, this isn't Hollywood. You can't just bring people in, pull down the sheet, and have them say, 'Yup, that's him.' We've got to rely on fingerprints or other positive proof that can stand up in probate court. And people don't understand that. They want everything done yesterday."

In fact, Wetli said, he appreciated the families' concerns, but the politicians irked him. Mayor Giuliani, New York senator D'Amato, and especially Governor Pataki were making Wetli and his staff the scapegoats for the families' frustration. And here was Pataki declaring Wetli would do it the governor's way—whatever that was. Fortunately, Wetli said, the law protected him from meddling politicians.

Wetli explained that on the day after the crash, his team had conducted twenty autopsies. The next day, they'd done forty. As soon as the families of those victims sent dental or fingerprint records, the victims could be positively identified. "We can't afford to make mistakes," Wetli said. "My marching orders are that there will be zero tolerance for mistakes. We're treating this as if we have 230 homicides on our hands."

"I know you're doing a good job," Kallstrom said, "but you have more than you can handle. We've got to get more people in here. A minimum of fifteen or twenty. It's just not working fast enough."

Wetli shrugged. To Kallstrom and Pickard, he seemed unable to grasp the enormity of the situation. Emotionally, too, he was limited. The tunnel vision that enabled him to work on damaged bodies also limited his sympathy for the agonized families waiting in an airport hotel. The system was working as he'd set it up. Why complicate it with a lot of new pathologists and technicians who would just divert him from the autopsies he was performing so carefully, one by one by one?

When they stepped outside, Pickard asked, "Did you see anything this bad in Vietnam?"

"Not this bad," Kallstrom said. "Bad, yes, but this was different. The kids. . . ." He pursed his lips, a gesture Pickard had come to recognize.

"I can't understand those doctors," Pickard said. "It's like just another day at the office for them."

"That's the business they're in," Kallstrom said. "The business of dead bodies. But when it's your mother, or father, or daughter, and they act like that, it makes you want to cut their throats."

Kallstrom knew how numb a man could become when death was all around him. When he'd come home from Vietnam, he told Pickard, "I didn't smile. Didn't laugh. It took months before I could feel happy or even cry. Human beings can only take so much."

Before he and Pickard left, Kallstrom made a point to seek out FBI agents assigned to the morgue building, to put his arm around each and say how much he appreciated the job they were all doing. Then the two men boarded the helicopter and headed west for the Ramada Inn to meet the families. They said nothing during the flight, except when Kallstrom leaned over to tell Pickard that he did not want agents assigned to the morgue for more than three days. "The fingerprint experts are okay, they're used to it, but no one else," he said. Hundreds of agents would put in three-day shifts on the grisly work at the morgue, examining bodies for evidence. The experience, brief as it was, would stay with them forever.

By the time Kallstrom and Pickard lifted off in their chopper from the Suffolk County morgue, agents under their command had logged more than one hundred accounts in the East Moriches area of a streaklike something seen in the sky just seconds before the blast. Eventually, the number of eyewitnesses corroborating that impression would grow to 270. Though none mentioned the word "missile," the missile theory, as agents were calling it, was growing more compelling by the hour. Kallstrom had asked John O'Neill, head of the FBI's counterterrorism unit in Washington, to assemble experts from every government agency that could offer data and insights on missiles and their capability. O'Neill tapped the Pentagon, the CIA, the State Department, the Defense Intelligence Agency, and the National Security Agency, among others. On Saturday afternoon, the experts convened at the FAA's Washington headquarters, where they could view radar tapes from Boston and New York air-traffic control showing Flight 800 just before and after the explosion. George Andrew, as Tom Pickard's deputy, flew down to brief the experts on what the FBI had found so far, and to see what technical help the FBI could get from them.

In a large conference room, Andrew, a former Navy fighter pilot, spent nearly two hours explaining what the FBI knew and sharing with the experts many of the most compelling eyewitness accounts. Throughout, he avoided any use of the word "missile." He wanted to see if these weapons analysts would conclude on their own that a missile had downed Flight 800. "Gentlemen," Andrew said after his briefing, "we need your guidance. I suspect by now you're thinking the same thing we're thinking. Missile, right?"

Nearly everyone in the room had reached that conclusion, and no, they told Andrew, it wasn't far-fetched. Of course, they wanted to analyze the wreckage and know more about the plane's speed and coordinates at the time of the crash. They agreed that while it was theoretically possible for a small, shoulder-fired missile to bring down a slowly ascending aircraft that had not yet reached 15,000 feet, this was pretty much approaching the outer limit of range for such a weapon, provided the missile was launched from a boat directly under the plane; the ten miles or so from shore to the plane's trajectory would be well beyond the missile's range, but a boat was certainly possible. It confirmed what missile experts at the Defense Department had preliminarily told Kallstrom the night of the crash.

Moreover, intelligence officers revealed that classified satellite imagery had disclosed a boat traveling up and down the Long Island coast from July 16 to July 19. This back-and-forth movement seemed odd: Fishing boats usually traveled in one direction, then back to port. The officers promised to work with Andrew to track down the boat's identity by examining satellite transmissions, so that agents could follow up.

Andrew asked if any U.S. weather or spy satellites might have recorded a larger ship or plane that might have fired a more sophisticated missile. Was there, on such imagery, a missilelike streak? The experts didn't know but promised to find out. Though Andrew said nothing of it at the meeting, what he had heard made more plausible another boat-launch scenario that had arrived the day before from foreign intelligence. A source in Iran had tipped off the FBI that followers of Sheik Omar Abdel-Rahman had downed Flight 800 with a missile in revenge for his incarceration. The terrorists, the informant added, had been aided by an Egyptian working for TWA in New York and by a worker at JFK. The two had provided operational intelligence about the aircraft, worked with two other terrorists who rented a boat with sophisticated radar, and fired the missile from its deck. The sheik and his network were being viewed by an increasing number of intelligence experts as the perpetrators of several incidents that previously had seemed unrelated. At his sentencing the previous January, the sheik had delivered a diatribe that appeared to encourage his followers, in carefully couched words, to terrorize the United States aggressively as revenge for his imprisonment. Soon thereafter, the Egyptian newspaper *Al Hayat* had received a fax warning that the United States would pay for the sheik's conviction. To the FBI, the sheik's followers appeared to have a motive and the means to down a commercial jet.

In Washington and New York, agents were pursuing yet another missile theory: that friendly fire had destroyed the plane. By raising the possibility himself on the night of the crash, Kallstrom had legitimized a route of inquiry that agents under his command might have hesitated to suggest themselves. Now the U.S. military, particularly the Navy, were as suspect as the sheik's followers until proven otherwise. Kallstrom wanted the coordinates of every military ship, submarine, and plane in the crash-site area the night of July 17 that might have had armaments capable of downing Flight 800. He also wanted to know if any missiles or other ordnance or explosive chemicals were missing from U.S. military stockpiles.

Tantalizing as the missile theory now appeared, hundreds of agents in New York were working to determine if the explosion was, instead, the result of a bomb. To most of Kallstrom's team, a bomb still seemed the likelier weapon. A clever terrorist could fashion one small and light enough to fit in a portable cassette player, as the Libyan bombers of Pan Am Flight 103 had done. The other lesson of Pan Am Flight 103 was how vulnerable commercial planes were to a new generation of bombs, devised entirely from plastics. Plastic explosives could pass unnoticed through airport metal detectors and were unlikely to alert a security guard watching an X-ray screen. A more sophisticated scanner that could detect even minute amounts of plastic explosives was available, but each machine cost $1 million. So far, the FAA had installed just three: one in San Francisco and two in Atlanta. At JFK, there were only older-model metal detectors.

A bomb built of plastics could be smuggled into the checked or carry-on luggage of a suicide bomber or an unsuspecting passenger. On international flights, passengers and their baggage had to travel together, a deterrence to bombers who preferred not to be killed by their handiwork, though not an insuperable one: In one instance, the unwitting pregnant girlfriend of a Palestinian terrorist had attempted to board a flight from London to Israel with a bomb in her luggage, timed to explode once the flight was airborne. A security agent at Heathrow foiled the scheme. For that matter, even a crude metal bomb might be stuffed into curbside luggage, which at JFK was often loaded directly onto a plane, even on international flights, without being put through X-ray machines. A bomb could be slipped into a food-tray slot or beverage cart by a terrorist working undercover in an airport commissary—or attached to a fuel tank by a bogus maintenance worker. Whatever its components and wherever it might have been placed, a bomb on Flight 800 might well have included an altimeter device to detonate when the plane reached a certain altitude. Was it significant that just before the explosion, Flight 800 had begun to climb to 15,000 feet? Had a bomb been set to detonate at, say, 13,700 feet?

By Saturday, hundreds of agents were interviewing everyone who had contact with the plane. They were studying JFK's security measures as well as TWA's contract suppliers and following up on several leads that suggested, directly or indirectly, that a bomb caused the crash.

The easiest leads to pursue were, statistically, the least likely to pan out. By Saturday, after an initial post-crash lull, dozens of fringe political groups and lonely crackpots had called or faxed the FBI to take responsibility for the bombing of Flight 800. In all, the FBI would log forty-nine of these. After the World Trade Center bombing, an unknown group identifying itself as the Fifth Battalion Liberation Front had claimed credit in a letter to *The New York Times*. The letter looked fake; it turned out to be real. But far more often, such claims are not genuine.

It was an odd business, taking unearned credit for a catastrophe, risking lengthy jail terms for a crime someone else had committed. Sometimes political radicals hoped to terrorize their enemies without actually having to plant a bomb, to broadcast their own political messages to the world and to avoid conviction because no hard evidence against them would be found. Crackpots had their own reasons, often inscrutable even to them. Usually, the FBI dismissed the more ludicrous of them after it checked out whatever scant information was provided and then placed their names on file. This time, Kallstrom wanted every claim checked out thoroughly, as if it held the key to the investigation.

One of the first claims had come at 2:45 A.M. on Thursday to a television station in Tampa, Florida. A man who sounded Middle Eastern announced, "If you have a tape recorder you better put it on now. I am a member of Islamic Jihad. The plane is the first of many things that will happen if Americans don't leave our people alone." Agents listened to the tape recording and reviewed their files and surveillance of suspected radicals in the Florida area, but the threat was worded so vaguely, with no follow-up clarification, that agents added it to a lengthening list of remote possibilities.

In a call to the Pillsbury company's corporate headquarters in Minneapolis, a "Paddy O'Reilly" declared that the Irish Republican Army was responsible for the bombing. The call was traced to an Irish bar, but the caller was never found. Another call came into TWA's headquarters in St. Louis, Missouri. The would-be bomber mentioned no political group or cause and offered no reason for having downed Flight 800, but did say he planned to blow up another TWA jet in midair within the next week. TWA officials contacted the FBI, which traced the call to the home of a man in the Midwest who allegedly made the threatening call, but nothing more came of it.

Other claims seemed more plausible. One described how an Iranian who worked for TWA in Athens had loaded Flight 881 with oxygen capsules filled with explosives. ValuJet's recent air disaster over the Everglades was the result of oxygen canisters that exploded in the cargo hold. The day after the crash a caller to the switchboard of Associated Newspapers in London said that Muslim fundamentalists had downed the plane to secure the release of fellow believers held in French jails; until the prisoners were released, all airlines flying to France risked having their planes blown up. Of the early claims, the most convincing remained the one that had come by fax—nine hours before the crash— written by hand in Arabic and faxed to the editorial offices of *Al Hayat* in Cairo and in Washington, D.C., with its reference to the June 25, 1996, bombing of the U.S. military barracks at Khobar Towers in Saudi Arabia that had killed nineteen U.S. service personnel, and its threat of another imminent attack.

Leads also came from calls to the FBI's hot line, from e-mail, and of course from interviews in the field. A particularly promising lead came from an FBI interview Friday at Kennedy Airport with a contract worker who had been aboard Flight 881 after passengers from Greece disembarked—but before the plane received passengers as Flight 800 to Paris. As the worker was changing the movie video for the next flight, he saw a man hurry back up the aisle to look for something in row 26 or 27. The worker said he watched the man squat on his knees so low under the seat that his head touched the floor. "Do you need some assistance?" the worker had asked. "No," the man had said, "I'm just looking for my mother-in-law's reading glasses." After a moment, the man stood up and left, as quickly as he'd come.

The worker thought it odd that a passenger would return to the cabin thirty minutes after the flight, unaccompanied by airline personnel. That the man looked Middle Eastern now seemed telling, too. Corrigan and Liguori agreed that this was suspicious activity, and reported it immediately to Pickard and Kallstrom. One detail in the worker's story startled the agents. As a fugitive in the Philippines after the World Trade Center bombing, Ramzi Yousef had tucked a small "test" bomb into a seat on row 26 of a Boeing 747 Philippines Airlines flight in December 1994—killing a Japanese businessman. In a 747, row 26 was situated directly over the center fuel tank.

The agents knew that Yousef had allies. Had one of them imitated Yousef's strategy and placed the bomb more strategically this time? Soon, the agents hoped, Flight 800's fuselage would be raised for intense scrutiny at Calverton. Meanwhile, every passenger and crew member on Flight 881 from Athens to New York was a potential suspect. So was anyone who had access to the plane either at Hellenikon or Kennedy Airport. And the number-one suspect now was a Middle Eastern–looking man who favored navy blue warm-up suits.

One by one, the passengers and crew from Flight 881 were located and asked, among other questions, whether they had returned to the plane for any reason. One man had. The man said that he, his wife, and his mother-in-law, all of whom lived in the Midwest, had been vacationing in Greece. Without any further prompting, he described returning to the plane about thirty minutes after disembarking to look for his mother-in-law's reading glasses, which she thought she had left on her seat—in row 26. He showed investigators the reading glasses; the mother-in-law verified his story, and added that she later found her glasses in her purse. As it happened, the man did not look Middle Eastern to the agents who interviewed him; he was a light-skinned American, but what mattered was that his story checked out.

The reading-glasses lead was an example of why Kallstrom did not disclose to the press much of what he had learned in those first days after the crash. Not only did agents have to pursue leads without tipping off possible suspects, they also had to protect a suspect's privacy until evidence of guilt could be firmly established. The tabloids would have run headlines that Friday about the Middle Easterner from the Midwest. News crews would have staked out his house, at the expense of his local reputation, all because of a well-intended tip that did not pan out. Meanwhile, the agents kept the midwesterner's name on their list of suspects.

If a bomb had indeed blown up Flight 800, more clues might emerge from the detective work being done—quietly so far, without disturbing the grieving families—on the ill-fated passengers and crew. Early on, an Algerian name on the passenger list interested agents. The passenger in question had registered for the flight simply as "Mr. Ferrat." It was a "Mr. Singh" who was suspected of the deadliest air bombing to date when he checked a suitcase aboard a Boeing 747 Air-India flight in June 1985, but did not board the plane himself. The bomb in that suitcase had split the plane apart off the coast of Ireland, killing all 329 people on board.

Unlike Mr. Singh, the passenger called Mr. Ferrat had boarded his doomed flight. He turned out to be a thirty-nine-year-old millionaire businessman named Mohamed Samir Ferrat, who owned residences and businesses in France, the Ivory Coast, Switzerland, and Maryland. He was traveling on a French passport and led a flamboyant lifestyle. Information from the State Department showed that he also traveled extensively to Beirut, Cyprus, and other areas of the Middle East where terrorist cells were active.

The FBI was particularly sensitive to passengers from Algeria, from where the militant Islamic Salvation Front, or FIS, had carried out plane hijackings and set off deadly bombs in Algeria and France to protest the disavowal of elections by the Algerian government, which feared an Islamic group was about to win. The group also opposed the French government's support of its former colony. The day before Flight 800 blew up, a leader of one of the militant factions was killed.

Soon after the crash, the investigators' hunch about Mr. Ferrat seemed borne out by a call from Dr. Wetli, at the Suffolk County morgue. Wetli reported the unusual condition of a certain male passenger whose spine had been blown out of his body with more force than even flying debris and 400-mile-per-hour winds in the cabin could have produced. Wetli wondered whether the passenger might have been seated near an exploding bomb.

Agents turned to Flight 800's passenger manifest, which included seat assignments. The mutilated man had been in first class. Seated on one side of him was a child—not, as it happened, Larkyn Dwyer—whom agents quickly dismissed as a suspect. Across the aisle was Mr. Ferrat.

The high-living Mr. Ferrat, whose body had not yet been found, hardly seemed to fit the profile of an Islamic suicide bomber, though he may have been secretly involved with a militant cause, for which he was ready to die. Or perhaps a device had been placed in his carry-on bags or luggage without his knowledge. Or maybe an impostor with fraudulent papers had boarded the plane in his name.

Soon thereafter, the CIA's Paris office sent a teletype that heightened interest in Mr. Ferrat. The CIA advised that he might have been a target of assassination by Algerian Muslims. The source of the information was apparently a Ferrat family friend who had told officials at the U.S. embassy in Paris that the wealthy executive might have given money to one Algerian group and been killed by another as retribution. An anonymous caller phoned the U.S. embassy in Algiers with an eerily similar report. A terrorist group called El Noure had targeted the passenger who called himself Ferrat but who was, in fact, an Algerian ex-member of a competing group called Bachir Hannaqui. The caller added that a similar incident would occur, possibly within the next three months. When asked why he was providing this information, the caller said simply, "I just wanted to warn you about what is to happen."

As agents pursued this lead, another piece of the puzzle fell into place. Recently, Ferrat had bought a new million-dollar life insurance policy on himself. In fact, he held several such policies totaling several million dollars, more than any other passenger on Flight 800.

———

Every interview for the case, whether it appeared to point to a missile or bomb as the cause of the crash, flowed back as a 302 report to the overburdened desks of Liguori and Corrigan at the Manhattan Command Post. Though both men had been out to East Moriches and done a few interviews themselves, the higher priority for each was to plow through the accumulating thousands of pages. They were the memory banks. On its own, a report might appear to mean nothing. Matched with another, it might assume significance. Liguori and Corrigan had to hope they saw the connections and put the pieces together. They were best positioned to keep investigators from pursuing questions already answered.

By the weekend, both men had put in sixteen- or seventeen-hour days. Finally, at Kallstrom's urging, they emerged from the squad room—unair-conditioned on weekends, as they'd discovered—to which they'd retreated with their reports three floors below the Command Post, and headed blearily home. For Liguori, that meant a thirty-minute drive to his home just outside of Manhattan to rejoin his wife and three children. Corrigan's own drive, in an unmarked police car, was to the nearby borough of Queens.

From his car phone, Corrigan called his office answering machine, leaving reminders for himself on what he needed to check upon his return. As he drove home, he started thinking about his father, a highly regarded former New York

City homicide detective, and how it was his mother who encouraged her four children to follow in his father's footsteps; each of them did. Then his thoughts turned to his wife, Colleen, and how he had dashed out the door on the night of the crash. Her first reaction to the crash and his immediate involvement with it was "Oh no, not again." He had barely completed the investigation of the blind sheik, which had kept him away from home days at a time for four years. The eldest of their three boys was four. Colleen had just taken a leave from her job as a legal secretary at Disney, and the Corrigans were in the midst of selling their house and packing to move to a larger one on Long Island. In addition, they were due to go upstate to Lake George, as they did every summer, for a family vacation. Rather than lose their deposit on the cottage, Colleen had agreed to go alone next week with the boys. Corrigan knew he could count on her, but this was pushing it.

Corrigan barreled through the doorway of their two-bedroom redbrick attached house, just across the East River, and forgot once again to keep the screen door from slamming behind him. Colleen's warm smile told him that this time he was forgiven. On the front porch, they shared a beer and talked over the events of the last few days. Corrigan apologized for messing up the family's plans and dumping everything in Colleen's lap—again. Colleen told him she understood. "Really, I do" she said. "Just go find whoever did this to these poor innocent people." Then Corrigan climbed wearily upstairs to sleep.

Four hours later, he was up again, showered and wearing a change of clothes, to head back to the Command Post. When he bid Colleen good-bye, he tried to hide his exuberance, but as soon as he was out the door, he felt like a boy headed off to a baseball game with his mitt tucked under his arm.

Not far from Corrigan's house, in the same sprawling borough of Queens, the helicopter carrying Kallstrom and Pickard from the Suffolk County morgue in Hauppauge touched down at a remote corner of Kennedy Airport. Then a car whisked them the short distance to the Ramada Inn where a posse of New York politicians hurried out to greet them. From their faces, Kallstrom might have assumed that a terrible virus had afflicted everyone inside. In a sense, it had.

The politicians' aides ushered Kallstrom and Pickard through the lobby, past scores of people in shock, many of them red-eyed from crying, to a guest room where Mayor Giuliani awaited them. "Jim," the mayor said in a somber voice, "it's so good to see you."

Giuliani and Kallstrom had known each other since the mayor's tenure as the U.S. Attorney in Manhattan in the 1980s. They'd worked together on several cases and liked each other. Usually, Giuliani looked brisk and upbeat. Now, to Kallstrom, he looked drained.

Giuliani had just met with the families for the third day in a row. His stern indictment of TWA for not responding sooner and his criticism of Dr. Wetli had relieved some of the tension among the survivors. With Giuliani they had found an ally. "I mean, I can't believe that guy," the mayor muttered to Kallstrom. Asked by the families why he couldn't shift his base of operations to a larger morgue so that bodies wouldn't have to be kept waiting outside in refrigerated trucks and more medical examiners could work on those inside, Wetli had said with breathtaking tactlessness: "One kitchen may be [better than] another kitchen. [But] you prefer to make your own gourmet meals in your own kitchen."

"Be prepared," Giuliani warned his old friend. "They're going to go after you. They want answers you haven't got yet."

From the bathroom sink in Guiliani's room, Kallstrom splashed cold water on his face and tried to rally for the meeting. In the mirror, he saw how pale and drawn he looked. His eyes were puffy. It had been four days since the crash, and he had slept a total of two hours. Memories of the morgue played through his mind. He was exhausted, and the two hours he'd spent on his couch Friday night had aggravated the back pain that had plagued him since a chopper crash in Vietnam.

Kallstrom could feel the anger and grief as soon as he appeared at the doorway of the Ramada's high-ceilinged ballroom. About one thousand weary people sat or stood in family clusters, many of them sobbing. Among them was Joe Lychner, who had flown in from Houston to bring back his wife and two little girls. So were Ron and Ann Dwyer, and Heidi Snow. The Hettlers and the Karschners stood together, a cluster apart from the other Montoursville families. Aurelie Becker sat with the arm of her husband, Walter, around her. The couple had flown in from St. Petersburg, Florida, carrying photos of their teenage daughter, Michelle, for the medical examiner. Before leaving, Michelle had called from the airport to tell her parents that she was going to Paris "for the party of my life." French, Italian, Greek, and Swedish families who had flown over from Europe were demanding translators for Kallstrom's prospective remarks. Among the French were Michel Breistroff's parents, Michel and Audrey, who stood far apart from Heidi Snow. To Heidi, their grief seemed also to imply a condemnation of her, as the American girl partly to blame for their son's death by luring him over to the United States to visit her. (In fact, the thought hadn't entered their minds. The Breistroffs knew that Michel had come over to attend a friend's graduation from Harvard and simply stayed on to see Heidi.)

Amid these fierce and roiling emotions, Kallstrom, in a blue blazer and khakis, with a tiny white ribbon on his lapel, a symbol of the victims, walked up to a single microphone atop a long metal pole in the front of the room. Pickard took a spot along the wall to his right, bone-weary and worried for his boss.

After a short introduction by a Red Cross worker, Kallstrom began by telling the families why the FBI was investigating the crash. He was there, he said, to learn whether the explosion was a crime. He said the bureau had no idea what brought the plane down, but that clues from the wreckage would probably reveal what happened to the plane. Not much wreckage had been retrieved yet, however. He said his first priority was to find the bodies still below, and then to bring the wreckage up from the bottom. For those reasons, he said, the Navy was en route. After promising that the FBI would assign as many agents as necessary to get the job done, Kallstrom opened the floor to questions.

"When are you going to start finding more bodies?" one woman shouted from the middle of the room. "I want my daughter's body back now."

"If this was terrorists, who did it?"

"Why don't you guys bring in submarines?" said a third. "They could be trapped down there."

Pickard, still nauseated from the morgue, sighed when he heard that. Mister, he thought, there is no submarine, no nothing, that is going to bring your loved one back.

The questions became testier, the voices louder.

"How could you let this happen?" one man demanded furiously.

"How could you let terrorists blow this plane up?"

"How could you *not know* these people were going to do this?"

Kallstrom answered each question as well as he could. "Sir, I understand your grief," he told one man, "but please know that we would never, ever, knowingly let anybody do anything like this. Of course we wouldn't. But if this is what happened, believe me we will work around the clock to find these people."

"But how could you let this happen?" the same questioner repeated.

Pickard was stunned by the attacks on Kallstrom, who had slept only two hours since the explosion and had just come from pushing the stubborn Dr. Wetli to expand his staff. Yet Kallstrom showed no defensiveness. He said nothing about himself or, for that matter, about his trip to the morgue. It was as if he understood that he had become a convenient target for rage at a horror that had, so far, no other human face.

Pickard managed to catch Kallstrom's eye, and ran his finger across his throat in a signal to "cut it." *Let's get out of here*, he mouthed sternly to Kallstrom. But Kallstrom waved him off, and continued.

As the barrage went on, a few people in the room began coming to Kallstrom's defense. Someone shouted, "Shut up and sit down," to the man who persisted in blaming Kallstrom for the disaster. At last the pace of questions slowed, and fury gave way to grief. Kallstrom felt he had achieved his objective. He wanted the families to know that the FBI was part of the solution, not part of the problem. In closing, he vowed he would not stop until he found the answer, and that he would tell the families whether the crash was criminal as soon as he reached "a high degree of certainty." And he added: "You will hear it from me before the press and the public hears it."

The crowd, which had viewed him with hostility when he began, now applauded, the nicest sound Kallstrom had heard in days. Out in the hallway, several families surrounded him to apologize for the angry questioner.

"No need to apologize," Kallstrom said. "And don't hold it against the gentleman. He just lost his family."

Kallstrom had reached the end of the long hallway when he heard a woman's urgent plea and turned around. "Mr. Kallstrom," she cried out. "Mr. Kallstrom, please."

In the nearly three days since her son had died, Jackie Hettler had gone from shock to rage to agonizing resignation that her powerful young athlete had not survived the crash of Flight 800. Sobbing, she told Kallstrom that Rance would have given anything to be able to hear him address the crowd so eloquently and frankly. With her husband at her side, Jackie explained to Kallstrom that ever since Rance was a child, he'd wanted to be an FBI agent. It wasn't an idle dream: In September, he'd planned to attend Boston's Northeastern University for its well-known criminal-justice program, then apply directly to the FBI. Jackie gave Kallstrom one of the pictures she'd brought: a strong, handsome, blond teenager with a confident gaze, happily certain of his calling. "Would it be possible," Jackie managed, "if I could have an FBI cap to bury with my son?"

Holding Rance's picture in his hand, Kallstrom said softly, "We'll get you a cap, all right. I'm sure your son would've made a great agent." As he hugged her, he noticed that he had crumpled the picture he was still holding. He left the hotel in tears.

"I'm glad that was you up there today and not me," Pickard told him as they ducked into a car that would take Kallstrom to the chopper and Pickard back to the Manhattan Command Post.

Kallstrom patted his friend on the back and gave him a strong one-arm hug. "Tommy, I'm glad you were with me."

Seated beside the pilot as the chopper rose up and east toward Smithtown for his next conference, Kallstrom looked at the small, creased photograph of Rance Hettler again before slipping it into his briefcase. He would tape it onto his computer, he decided, in his office at 26 Federal Plaza, a reminder of the lives lost, especially the children, on Flight 800.

———

Two hours later, at the podium of the Smithtown Sheraton's banquet room, Kallstrom realized that his mind was still with the victims' families. So he talked about what he'd seen and felt.

"I had a very emotional day," he said, his voice low and tired. "I've just left the families. I think it puts this tragedy in focus to visit with all of those people and see the unbelievable emotions they are going through. . . . The scope of the human tragedy that is before us here is not a pretty sight."

Kallstrom said some families had suggested the investigation had become a part-time effort because of concern that the Olympics in Atlanta might be marred by a terrorist act. "That's simply not true," Kallstrom said. "I tried to dissuade them of that. I told them that I was their advocate. I also told them that one of the people in the tragedy was a friend of mine, which I'm not going to go into here."

Kallstrom's voice cracked, and for a moment, he looked off, over the heads of the press corps to the darkness at the back of the room. Usually quick to exploit a silence with questions, the journalists sat respectfully—and curiously—still. What were they to make of an FBI official so unafraid to let his feelings show?

CHAPTER 5

A Body Slips Away

Sunday morning at about 5:45, Kallstrom got up from the sofa in his twenty-eighth-floor office and padded across the hall, shirtless and barefoot, to his private bathroom. It had a shower stall, so he could keep working around the clock as long as he felt it necessary. More clothes had come from home, brought by agents who lived near Kallstrom in Connecticut. In the days to come, he would fall into a routine of taking his clothes to a Chinese laundry two blocks from 26 Federal Plaza. Its proprietor would soon greet Kallstrom as a neighborhood regular.

Kallstrom had allowed himself another few hours of sleep, though not yet a trip home. He missed his wife and two daughters, but this was not the first time a case had kept him at the office around the clock. Not until the twelfth day after the crash would he rediscover the small luxury of sleeping in his own bed.

At this hour, in desolate downtown Manhattan, 26 Federal Plaza stood nearly dark but for a dull fluorescent band of light from the Command Post on the twenty-sixth floor. Showered and dressed, Kallstrom headed down to find Pickard and other agents in a twenty-fifth-floor conference room discussing a possible missile attack on TWA Flight 800.

On the walls of the "war room," the agents who constituted Kallstrom's "missile team" had tacked radar charts of all aircraft, commercial and military, known to be in the area of the explosion just before and after 8:31 P.M. on July 17. One agent was an F-14 pilot who had been fired on with rockets in the Persian Gulf War; others were weapons experts and computer analysts. In addition to the radar charts, they had pinned up maps of the East Moriches area and studded them with red, blue, green, and yellow pushpins to show where the eyewitnesses—now more than two hundred and counting—had stood when they saw a streak of light. Clamped to an easel were blueprints of the 747-100, sent overnight by Boeing's aircraft designers in Seattle. On the conference table sat several small models of a 747, purchased at a hobby shop and assembled by an agent who had stayed up all night to build them in time for this meeting. The glue he had used was not yet dry, and its smell was still noticeable. The parts of the plane already recovered were indicated on the models, but with the Navy salvage ships still not on hand, there were very few of those.

Kallstrom began by noting that nearly all the experts the FBI had consulted so far believed that if a missile had downed Flight 800, the odds were that it had been a shoulder-launched type. The radar maps showed no hostile fighter planes or warships in the area that could have fired a more sophisticated missile. Aside from the computer glitch on the Kennedy Airport radar tape, none of the radar tapes showed a missilelike projectile of any kind, either, but that hardly ruled out a shoulder-launch scenario. In fact, the lack of a streaking object might argue for it. As the experts noted, a shoulder-launched Stinger was so small and fast-moving that it might not show up on radar at all: Since each radar tower swept the sky in four- to twelve-second cycles, like an orbiting lighthouse beam, a Stinger could have reached its target between sweeps.

Of the shoulder-launched missiles that a terrorist might have used—the so-called Man Portable Air Defense Systems, better known as MANPADs—the American-made Stinger was the most commonly available on the international black market. Tens of thousands might be in the hands of militants, in the Middle East and elsewhere, who viewed the United States as an enemy. The Pentagon had designed obsolescence into the Stinger: After a few years, its launching device would fail, whether or not the weapon was used. But perhaps, Pickard noted dryly, terrorists had learned how to replace those parts.

A Stinger's range was 16,800 feet—about three miles—and the farther away its target the less likely the missile was to hit it. The missile would eventually detonate on its own and disintegrate. A Stinger's accuracy was affected by the angle of the shot: Aimed straight up, it would have considerably less chance of hitting a target at the limit of its range than it would if aimed at, say, a 45-degree angle. Yet TWA Flight 800 had exploded at an altitude of 13,700 feet. Certainly, that ruled out the scenario of a Stinger fired from the Long Island shore, eight or ten miles away from its target as well as three miles up in the sky. A Stinger would have had to be fired from a boat almost directly below the plane. Even then, though, the odds against hitting a plane flying at the altitude of Flight 800 were formidable.

Pickard and the missile team would soon learn that other kinds of MANPADs had greater ranges, making them more capable of reaching Flight 800. The Soviets had one known as the SA-14 and another called the SA-18; NATO had nicknamed them, respectively, the Gremlin and the Grouse. Both were surface-to-air heat-seeking missiles capable of being shoulder-launched or fired from a small vehicle or boat, each with a range of just over 18,000 feet.

They were distinguished by their proximity fuses, which enabled the missiles' high-fragmentation warheads to detonate within twenty meters of their targets rather than on impact; the short-distance explosion tended to cause more damage. Early heat-seeking missiles, such as the U.S.-made Redeye, were designed to seek the heat of an engine and thus probably would have had to be fired from behind the aircraft, while the Grouse, believed to be a copy of the U.S. Stinger, had the capability of being aimed at other parts of the airplane. Both the Grouse and the Gremlin had been commonly available on the black market in the aftermath of the Soviet Union breakup. Each, however, was a sophisticated weapon that required an operator trained in its use. Neither was designed to reach an altitude of more than two miles, and for the heat-seeking warhead on each to find the heat, it had to itself be cool. The battery-powered propellant had enough coolant to last only forty-five seconds after activation. In that time, the operator had to lock on his target for at least six seconds, then launch. Some of the Stinger-like missiles the FBI researched had targeting systems that emitted beeps of increasing volume as a target flew into range. When the sounds became clear and distinct, the shooter could lock on to his target and fire. The system increased the odds of a direct hit considerably. So did the shoulder-launched heat-seeking missiles, which, even if not perfectly aimed, might hit one of the four engines of a commercial jetliner or a nearly empty center fuel tank, with hot explosive vapors made volatile by the heat generated by the plane's air-conditioning units just beneath the tank. Perfectly fired, a heat-seeking MANPAD was what the U.S. military called a "fire-and-forget" missile: It would reach and destroy its target for sure. But that was a trickier business than "fire-and-forget" implied.

The missile team also studied another MANPAD missile, the French-made Mistral, which had a range of five miles and an altitude of two and a half miles, rendering it easily capable of hitting Flight 800. Mistrals had been sold to most European nations as well as to Egypt, Saudi Arabia, and Kuwait. The Mistral had its own electronic "seeker" in the warhead enabling it to change course if necessary in order to hit its target. But the distribution of Mistrals was thought to be tightly controlled—enough so that none were known to have reached the black market.

For more than a decade, intelligence agencies and terrorist experts had been concerned that MANPADs might be used to attack civilian airliners. In the early 1990s, a high-level State Department report had addressed the issue directly, citing growing evidence that terrorists, rebel militias, and even criminal enterprises had focused on the possibility, too. On the other hand, smuggling a MANPAD of any kind into the United States presented quite a challenge. Its launcher was a tube about four feet long and eighteen inches in diameter, with a missile about the size of a golf bag. Neither launcher nor missile could be disassembled into small parts and packed in suitcases—not that such parts would fail, in any event, to set off the most primitive airport metal detectors. So the possibility that such a weapon had been brought into the United States through U.S. Customs remained remote, though not inconceivable.

Still, if this had occurred, Kallstrom somberly wondered aloud, what would keep the missile launchers from trying again? "Push the missile theory as far as you can," he urged his missile team. "Know everything you can about it. Know what different missiles can and cannot do. Tell us what we should be looking for in the wreckage, what kind of signatures in the metal, and whether we should also be looking for missile components, missile launchers."

And Kallstrom added, "Find out for me just what a missile would do to a 747 jumbo jet."

The Washington experts whom George Andrew had seen the day before were compiling relevant information. So too, Pickard reported, were specialists in explosives, weapons, and missiles at the Naval Air Warfare Center, a sprawling complex in China Lake, California, and at Wright Patterson Air Force Base in Dayton. China Lake's resources were especially encouraging: more than 4,000 civilian and 1,000 military experts worked at the 1.1-million-acre site. "The guys at China Lake and Wright Pat have lots to say," Pickard said, but he admitted, "It's all a mystery to me. They're talking feet per second and effective range and this and that component. I don't know what the hell it's about."

"We need translators," Kallstrom agreed. Before the week was out, an agent named Steve Bonghart would become the liaison between law enforcement and the missile experts. A Naval Academy graduate and former F-14 fighter pilot, he would take the coefficients of energy, speed, and light, and turn them into English.

As he studied the models, Kallstrom again mentioned the possibility that friendly fire had downed Flight 800. He told Pickard he wanted a separate group of agents to focus exclusively on friendly fire, in conjunction with the missile team. What U.S. military planes and ships had been in the area? What maneuver was each engaged in at the time, and what armaments did each carry? What further information could U.S. spy satellites provide? By now, Kallstrom doubted that friendly fire had destroyed Flight 800, but as the head of an investigation already shaping up to be the most complex in the FBI's history, he would assume nothing, and demand hard proof before ruling out any suspect—even the military branches of his own government.

In the shoulder-launched missile scenario, the obvious first suspect was the boat that George Andrew had heard about in his Washington meeting. By Sunday, close analysis of the classified footage taken by a U.S. military satellite had identified it as a fishing trawler almost directly under Flight 800 when it exploded. From that footage, the FBI had managed to find the vessel, which was still trawling off the coast of Long Island. Unfortunately for the investigation, an early-Sunday-morning visit by agents confirmed that trawling was all the trawler *had* been doing since it left port. The captain and crew were local, and the boat bore no arms or scorch marks that might indicate a missile launch. Though agents would scrutinize the boat's legal documents and seek signed confirmation that it had left port when the captain claimed, it would soon be ruled out as a suspect. The captain and crew readily acknowledged having seen a fireball in the sky; fortunately for them, the boat had been a few miles from the crash site, far enough away to be safe from the wall of fire, spattering jet fuel, and even falling debris, too far even for anyone on board to have seen the plane go into the water.

Another boat-launch scenario materialized almost as soon as Kallstrom and Pickard arrived Sunday morning by helicopter at the East Moriches Coast Guard station. Admiral Linnon advised the agents that the Coast Guard had just received a tip over marine radio about two tugboats outside Moriches Bay. According to the tip, the tugs had arrived a few days earlier from the Middle East. Ken Maxwell, a large, very likable, intense agent whom Kallstrom would soon appoint to head daily operations at the Calverton hangar, happened to be at the station. Kallstrom told him to take four agents out with a Coast Guard patrol and board the tugs right away.

The agents buzzed out in a Coast Guard boat and found the tugs close by each other in the inlet off East Moriches. "This is the United States Coast Guard," a lieutenant called over a bullhorn as they drew alongside. "Prepare to receive a boarding party for inspection."

The boarding party motored over in an inflatable Zodiac, expecting to confront a crew of Middle Eastern terrorists. Instead, they found the tugs manned by young men from Alabama. The crews' employer was the Great Lakes Dredging Company, a world-famous outfit. The crew members readily acknowledged that they had returned from the Middle East a week before the Flight 800 disaster, where they had worked on a dredging project off Qatar in the Gulf of Oman. The trip had been routine, the crew said. So was their assignment in Moriches: to build up the storm-battered Westhampton Beach. A thorough, two-hour inspection of both tugs revealed nothing suspicious: no explosive chemicals or missile components, no stowaways, no scorch marks from a launch. Just a big pot of Irish stew simmering on the stove.

As Maxwell was climbing over the tug's railing to reboard the Zodiac below, he noticed scorch marks on the oily deck of a nearby barge. The agents sped over to board the suspicious vessel, but after an hour's inspection and interviews with the crew, including verification of all licenses and documents, Maxwell and the agents returned to the Coast Guard boat. The scorch marks and burns on the boat had resulted from a welding operation on board, not a missile launching. "All negative," Maxwell radioed Kallstrom.

By then, Kallstrom and Schiliro had seized the next tantalizing lead, phoned in by Suffolk County police. A woman in Hampton Bays was saying she had a picture of a missile in the sky taken at an outdoor party the night of the crash. To the two agents who knocked on her door moments later, Linda Kabot handed over a photograph she had taken on July 17 between 8:00 and 8:45 P.M. with a Minolta 35 mm camera and a zoom lens. In the foreground were several beaming guests outside on the deck of a waterfront restaurant called Dockers. The occasion was a fund-raiser for Kabot's boss, the planning commissioner of Southampton. The deck faced south, with a view of Shinnecock Bay, but Kabot had been facing north, with her back to the sea, when she took the picture. At the time, she had noticed nothing peculiar in the sky behind the guests, but when the picture came back from the developer the next day she saw a pencil-thin object in the background that looked like a missile.

The agents looked hard at the picture. Sure enough, there was a missilelike streak. Kabot was clearly a responsible citizen. She could hardly have doctored the photograph. The agents brought the picture back to the FBI trailer in East Moriches, where Kallstrom and Schiliro studied it together.

"It looks like it to me," Schiliro said. "What do you think?"

Kallstrom held it up to the light, handed it back to Schiliro, and said, "Let's get it analyzed. And let's talk to everyone who was at the restaurant for that party." Schiliro ordered the agents to get the negative from Kabot. With both negative and photo carefully in hand, the agents boarded the next shuttle flight to Washington to have it analyzed at the FBI's laboratory.

Soon enough, another Long Island resident, Heidi Krieger, gave the FBI a picture taken the night of the crash that appeared to show a slim, long object flying along the horizon just above land. But even more startling was the missile *video.*

Soon after the crash, a bartender mentioned to a local police officer that his cousin had been vacationing on Chesapeake Bay in Virginia when he spotted several burly men with shaved heads loading a missile onto the back of a truck. The cousin had a video camera with him and recorded the curious event. Only later did the timing of the sight seem suspicious to him: 5:00 P.M. on July 17.

The bartender's cousin gave his video to the agents, and at the Calverton hangar a number of the agents examined it. First they saw a man on a fishing boat with his wife. Then the scene shifted. "Hey, honey, look at the missile," the man said. What he saw on the shore were three men with shaved heads on the back of a flatbed truck. In the truck rested an orange cylindrical object at least eighteen feet long. To the agents, the object appeared to be a drone: a missile that contains no explosives because it is used in training exercises for fighter jets. Still, a drone is actually fired and can travel at two hundred miles an hour.

What if one used in a military exercise had happened to hit Flight 800 instead of its intended target?

Corrigan and Liguori dispatched agents to the Chesapeake Bay dock where the video was shot. They spoke to the son of the owner, who explained that he and his father had an agreement with the Navy, which routinely shot drones for missile practice. He and his father would go out by boat and tow the drones back to the commercial dock. There they would haul the drones out by crane, load them onto a flatbed truck, and return them to the Navy base. At first, the owner's son said he and his father had recovered no drones since May 10. But when the agents went back to the man who had shot the video he insisted the footage was taken on July 17. "I know when I was on vacation," he said. The agents returned to the dock and learned that the son of the dock owner had forgotten to record a drone recovery in the logbook on the evening of July 17. The drone had been launched at 3:48 P.M. and splashed down at 4:18 P.M., hours before the crash—and, of course, hundreds of miles away. Within a day, agents ruled out the Chesapeake drone, though the exercise raised the possibility that the Navy might have fired other drones closer to the crash site. The Navy said it had not. Agents conducted an exhaustive search, including checks at various military bases, inventory documentation of drones, and review of radar. Months later, they would conclude that the drone theory, at least, could be dismissed.

Soon, a second video surfaced that seemed to show a missile streaking through the sky off Long Island. However, it had been shot on July 12, five days before the crash. Could the video have captured a test-run launch? The local resident who called to report the suspicious streak in his footage was an air conditioner repairman who had decided to test his new video camera at dawn while working on the Smithtown Hospital roof. He wanted to shoot the sunrise but was distracted by a smoke plume rising slowly in the sky. He panned away for a moment but then came back to the plume, only to find it rising higher over Long Island Sound. "I guess this is a missile," he said on the videotape. He thought nothing of it at the time, but in the aftermath of the crash, he called the Manhattan Command Post. At first the man didn't want to surrender the tape to the agents who came to see him, because it included his son's first fishing trip. Only when they assured him he would get it back did he turn it over.

At the Command Post, task force members played the tape, stopping frame by frame to scrutinize the plume. Perhaps, some agents theorized, a terrorist was testing the best time of day and direction to launch a missile. The tape was turned over to missile experts at the Pentagon, some of whom agreed that the repairman might have captured the tail end of a missile streaking through the sky. Several experts from the Defense Intelligence Agency flew up from Washington to Long Island, where they asked the repairman to take them up to the roof where he'd shot his video, at the same time of day, and explain just what he'd done, step by step, frame by frame. It was another long shot, but who knew? It might just be the clue that led to a breakthrough.

———

To the victims' families, whether a missile had downed Flight 800 mattered far less than recovering their loved ones. By late Sunday, the undiplomatic Dr. Wetli had been forced to take on five additional pathologists and twenty more in support staff, including Dr. Michael Baden, the former New York City medical examiner who had served as a forensic expert on the O. J. Simpson defense team. The number of positive identifications had risen from two to thirty-six. Those bodies left the morgue by hearse, and their families checked out of the Ramada Inn to accompany them home. Some families lived close enough to Long Island that a hometown hearse could retrieve the body in Hauppauge. A funeral director from Montoursville, Pennsylvania, for example, made the drive to pick up Amanda Karschner's body. Others were driven to airports by Long Island funeral directors and put on planes home.

Charlie Christopher had spent the weekend at home in Pennsylvania with his son and a rotating posse of fellow FBI agents. Since the night of the crash, he had wanted to drive up to New York—not to sit in a hotel but to get out on the water and search for Janet. Gently but firmly, the agents, at Kallstrom's behest, had kept him from going, explaining that dozens of Coast Guard and police boats were patrolling the crash site and outlying waters, searching for bodies and debris.

"And survivors," Charlie would bristle.

Yes, they would say. The boats were looking for survivors, too. Meantime, Charlie should stay put, taking care of his son and letting the agents do everything else. Already, agents had cleaned the house, mowed the lawn, and gone out for groceries.

So he watched the television news reports, scoured the papers, fielded calls from friends—and hoped. Even on Friday, long after the time when experts on the effects of immersion had concluded no one could still be alive, Charlie clung to the hope that somehow Janet had pulled through. The rescuers would find her caught in an air pocket inside a piece of the plane at the ocean's bottom, or she would be spotted fifty miles offshore, floating on a piece of wing.

In the house, Janet seemed so alive. Flowers she had cut from her garden were in a vase, and her clothes were in the laundry hamper in the bathroom. Beside her computer lay the flight schedules she had consulted as she tried to get her family last-minute reservations on Flight 800. In the refrigerator were the meals she had cooked, each wrapped in plastic and marked by day, enough to see her husband and son through until her return.

On Saturday, Kallstrom had called Charlie to tell him he had seen Janet's body. He'd told him that her wedding band, watch, and Syracuse ring had been found on the body and that he would let Charlie know as soon as a positive identification was made. But from the questions Charlie asked, Kallstrom could tell that his old friend was still hoping a mistake had been made.

Early Sunday, FBI agents at the morgue told Pickard that Janet Christopher had been positively identified through fingerprints examined by the FBI Disaster Squad. Kallstrom was heading into a memorial service with New York's archbishop, John Cardinal O'Connor, at a TWA hangar at Kennedy Airport when Pickard beeped him and offered to call Charlie.

"Charlie, we found Janet's remains," Pickard said in the straightest delivery he could muster when Christopher came on the phone. "The Disaster Squad matched the prints."

"Nobody has her prints. That's impossible!" Charlie protested.

"No," said Pickard. "TWA took her prints when she first got hired. She had probably forgotten and that's why she didn't tell you. It's just one of those things, Charlie. We do have a fingerprint match."

Charlie said he was going to go up to the Hauppauge morgue himself to check the body.

"I'm not going to let you," Pickard said. "I don't want you to remember her that way."

"You can't stop me," Charlie said.

"Charlie, I'm telling those agents out there that you're not to leave."

On the other end of the line, there was a stunned, and hurt, silence.

On Sunday evening, when Kallstrom and Francis wearily convened their daily press conference, the reporters were excited. They wanted to know whether it was true that portable testing machines administered by the Bureau of Alcohol, Tobacco, and Firearms at the Calverton hangar had detected some residue of explosive chemicals on the underbelly of the thirty-foot chunk of wing brought over on Friday. Some newspapers quoting unidentified sources had reported the positive hit in their Sunday-morning editions. Kallstrom declined to confirm the findings, but did say that pieces of wreckage were being sent to the FBI lab in Washington for testing.

"Is that the piece the newspapers said has residue on it?" a reporter asked.

"I'm just not going to comment on the evidence," Kallstrom said.

"But it's the piece that you recovered Friday, right?" the reporter pressed.

Kallstrom paused before saying quietly, "I believe it was Friday." Reluctant to answer more questions on the subject, he started to leave the podium. That was when Francis stepped in.

"I think that my friend is getting a little uncomfortable talking about this, so I think we'll not talk about the specific pieces," Francis said. It was a small moment, but it made the partners more of a team, united against any attempts to categorize the crash before the facts were in.

That evening, the FBI laboratory in Washington completed a test on the wing that showed that no such residues were present, but the incident left a residue of its own. For weeks, Kallstrom would be told by his agents that they suspected ATF agents at the hangar were tipping off journalists about positive hits on their portable machines, apparently eager to get credit for beating the FBI to the discoveries. The seeming leaks—and the disloyalty that appeared to inspire them—would anger Kallstrom, who wondered why one or more of the ATF agents were such unwilling team players.

About a mile offshore that same evening, a newly arrived vessel, large and gray like a warship but with cranes at its bow and stern, idled amid the swells as several small boats set out from it to a spot marked on digital maps assembled by the NOAA boat *Rude*. One by one, the U.S. Navy divers in the boats pulled on their masks, adjusted their oxygen tanks and hoses, and fell gently into the dark sea.

The *Grasp* was the first of the two specially equipped Navy salvage ships that Admiral Flanagan had promised Kallstrom two days before. It had arrived when the admiral promised; the *Grapple*, with one of its two engines incapacitated, would arrive a day or two later. Like its sister ship, the *Grasp* had side-scan sonar. It also had a team of Navy divers. Among them was Lieutenant (j.g.) Stephane Blais, thirty-two years old, a three-year veteran of the *Grasp*.

Ordinarily, Blais and his fellow divers would dive only during the daylight hours, but as soon as they arrived that Sunday evening, Commander Bobbie Scholley, the Navy's diving supervisor for the operation, ordered them to look for bodies. Since sunlight penetrated only about forty feet beneath the surface, a nighttime dive to the seafloor was no different below from a daytime one. The divers carried powerful flashlights and wore helmet lights. The little robot ROV, or Remote Operated Vehicle, which accompanied them, could also beam light across the piles of seafloor wreckage they would soon encounter.

Ten feet from the bottom, sea life had kicked up a cloud of silt on the ocean floor. Blais and his partner, Mike Gallant, slowed for a soft landing to avoid stirring the silt even more. Even so, and with their lights to guide them, they could see only two or three feet ahead. Blais looked at his watch: twelve minutes' worth of air at the bottom before they'd have to head back up.

In the darkness, chunks of wreckage turned up so suddenly that the divers were barely able to avoid being caught by them. The dangers were all too obvious. Great webs of wire and cable, floating like seaweed, could snag a tank; jagged metal edges could slit an oxygen hose.

On this first trip down, the divers hoped mainly to familiarize themselves with the wreckage they would be exploring the next day, but as Blais and Gallant were about to head back up, Gallant spotted a man still strapped in his seat. The divers swam over and unlocked his safety belt to free him. To Blais, the man looked like a crash-test dummy in an automobile commercial.

The divers each grabbed an arm and began their steady ascent. Blais tried not to look at the body between them. When the divers broke surface, Blais fished out a body bag from his dive belt. Treading water, the two divers struggled to put the body into the bag, then handed him off to the crew of a waiting Suffolk County police boat. During the handoff, the zipper opened and the man slid into the water, out of sight, straight to the bottom.

Blais and the others looked at one another aghast. There was nothing to say, really. It had happened, that was all. In a day, or two, maybe they could find him again.

That night, after dinner, Blais climbed into his metal bunk bed and looked at the photographs of his wife and six-month-old son that he had taped to the wall. He wondered if the man's family was at the hotel, waiting for news of his recovery.

Then he turned away from the pictures and found himself sobbing into his pillow.

CHAPTER 6

BURDEN OF PROOF

By Sunday, the press conferences at the Smithtown Sheraton had assumed a sense of ritual. Kallstrom and Bob Francis of the NTSB stood together at the lectern, gave their daily update, and fielded questions from reporters. The public was following events of the crash so closely that CNN did not hide the fact that Kallstrom and Francis's daily televised news briefings were on its list of most-watched broadcasts. They were an odd couple: Francis the formal, dry pragmatist, Kallstrom the passionate, down-to-earth investigator. While Kallstrom enjoyed sparring with reporters, exuded confidence, and delivered his answers frankly and courteously, Francis at times appeared irritated by reporters, and gave restrained responses in his predictable monotone manner.

To the public, they seemed leaders of equal footing in the investigation, and in a sense they were, since their agencies were partners. With Francis, though, there was less than met the eye.

Francis occupied a unique position in the investigation. He was the public face of the NTSB for the Flight 800 investigation, and could make whatever public pronouncements he wished. Moreover, as one of eight NTSB vice chairmen, Francis could not be dictated to or removed by Chairman James Hall. As an assistant would tell one reporter, Bob Francis felt responsible only to the person who had appointed him: the president of the United States. But he held no decision-making power; that was in the hands of James Hall. In Washington, Hall and his aviation director, Bernard Loeb, had decreed that a handful of NTSB investigators sent up the day after the crash would suffice until wreckage was recovered, and that Al Dickinson would be the chief investigator for this probe, their man on the scene. Francis would get briefed by Dickinson so he could know what to say at the press conferences, but otherwise he was out of the loop.

So omnipresent did Francis seem that for weeks, Kallstrom and his senior agents remained unaware that Francis was a mere figurehead and had little input into how the NTSB proceeded with its work. Even then, however, Kallstrom considered Francis an integral part of the team the FBI chief had forged among the various agencies. Francis could, and did, act as an important liaison between the FBI and the Coast Guard, the Navy, and the Suffolk County Police Department. As off-putting and stiff as he might seem, Francis was as committed as anyone else to finding out the answer to the crash.

Personally, Kallstrom embraced Francis as an upstanding fellow, and in many ways he was. Seasoned by years of experience, clearheaded and intelligent, he had established a public image of dignity and diligence for the NTSB that would serve the safety board well. Television viewers liked Francis, too, and had begun sending him notes of support along with occasional care packages of cookies.

To reporters, however, Francis could be rudely dismissive. "Just because you have a loud voice doesn't mean you're going to get your question answered," he snapped at one reporter, turning his back to answer another questioner. The detail-minded aviation writers were especially frustrated. They felt that Francis was stonewalling them—failing to provide adequate technical information on the NTSB's portion of the investigation and its findings. Curiously, Hall and Loeb had had occasion to feel the same way: On the ValuJet investigation, Francis had actually given out *less* information, at a critical time, than the NTSB's top men wanted to disseminate.

After his initial tour of the crash site with Kallstrom and Admiral Linnon of the Coast Guard, Francis had gone to the Ramada Inn to talk to the families, where he was introduced by Hall's chief aide, Peter Goelz, whom Hall had sent to be the agency's liaison with them. Goelz was an astute, empathetic fellow who would soon earn the families' trust, and Francis's fluency in French was a great help with the Breistroffs and other French families who had flown over after the crash. Francis had also made a quick trip home to McLean, Virginia, to get more clothes. Three oxford shirts, he could already see, would not see him through the investigation—not when the FBI had so far failed to find evidence of wrongdoing in the crash that could eliminate the NTSB from further involvement.

At the instruction of Hall and Dr. Bernard Loeb, several investigators in those first days set about learning the 747's history and service record. A preliminary review showed everything was in order. All airworthiness directives issued by the FAA to correct various small problems with 747s had been met within the required time; the plane's maintenance records were clean, but the review had just begun. The NTSB team knew that a properly maintained aircraft could fly for decades. They also knew that a twenty-five-year-old plane in constant use could have problems.

"Constant use" was the key factor. The aviation industry measured a plane's age less by years flown than by the number of its takeoffs and landings. This was a more complex matter than it seemed. Certainly the strain on a plane as it lifted off was considerable. So was the effect its more than 180 tons had when it touched down. The real stress, though, came from pressurizing the cabin, which expanded the fuselage by an inch or so. The fuselage then contracted upon being depressurized after landing. This repeated inflation and deflation strained the rivets that held the fuselage together and weakened the aluminum skeleton. The 747 that had become Flight 800 had flown 93,303 hours—as many hours as a factory worker spent on the job from high school graduation to retirement. More tellingly, it had flown 16,869 cycles, or flights: nearly 17,000 expansions and contractions. It was a middle-aged plane growing old.

The NTSB investigators had learned that TWA had purchased the brand-new plane from Boeing on October 27, 1971, a year after the first 747-100s rolled off the assembly line. The plane saw four years of service without incident when, on December 15, 1975, during a national recession, TWA sold it to the Iranian air force. In a Boeing hangar in Everett, Washington, the plane was stripped down for use as a military transport. The beverage bar, in-flight movie projectors, and other amenities were removed; the TWA logos were taken off the tail and forward fuselage. The plane was then ferried to the Boeing Military Aircraft Co. in Wichita, Kansas, for more modifications, but these additional modifications were never performed. Instead, a year later, Iran sold the plane back to TWA without having taken physical possession of it. On March 2, 1977, it was returned to service by TWA.

Iran's role in the history of tail number N93119 stirred curiosity, but not for long. From 1975 to 1977, Iran was still under the iron rule of the Shah, one of America's staunchest, if less admirable, allies. Besides, two decades had passed since Iran's brief ownership of the plane.

Of far more interest, Iran had also bought N93118, the 747-100 that had come off Boeing's assembly line immediately before N93119. That jet had blown up in midair over Madrid on May 9, 1976, after being struck by lightning that exploded fuel vapors in the left-wing tank. The NTSB investigators examined reports of the crash of N93118 and analyzed other plane crashes in a search for telltale similarities to the fate of Flight 800.

Over the years, TWA had filed sixty-eight reports with the FAA of various problems with the plane. The citations included a tire blowout on takeoff in 1987, a loss of oil pressure in an engine a year later, a failure of the nose landing gear to retract after takeoff in 1989, and damaged wiring in a food cart causing it to smoke during a flight. These problems appeared insignificant to the investigators, who nevertheless looked more deeply into them.

The 747 was ambitiously designed by Boeing to be the workhorse of the industry, and while no one could be sure, the hope was that such a huge and expensive jet would last at least 20 years, or for 20,000 takeoffs, or 60,000 hours in the air. Over time, elaborate new maintenance and upgrade programs were devised to extend the plane's life, and by 1986, more than 1,000 Boeing engineers dedicated themselves solely to support of the in-service fleet. Teams of six Boeing engineers conducted heavy-maintenance checks periodically of each plane. As soon as signs of aging were found, service bulletins went from Boeing to the airlines, outlining modifications for all other 747s. Thus it was common for 747s to exceed this 60,000-hour life expectancy. About 380, or nearly half, of Boeing's initial, "classic" series of 747s—the 100, 200, and 300 series—were still in use after more than 60,000 hours and showed no unexpected signs of aging that might argue for grounding them.

Of the twenty or so industrywide service bulletins that Boeing had issued on its 747s, only one indicated a major problem. As the planes expanded and contracted from one flight cycle to the next, their internal frames, after thousands of cycles, had begun to crack. The cracks were so slight that workers relied on nicotine stains on the fuselage or fissures around the rivets to locate them. The stains were from cigarette smoke inside the pressurized cabin that escaped through the cracks. Generally, the cracks tended to begin just behind where the flight crew sat, on the upper deck above the nose.

That bulletin was issued in 1986. Within a few years, most 747s had been retrofitted to prevent cracking. Yet a decade after the directive, TWA had not yet addressed the potential problem on the plane that would end as Flight 800. Whether this contributed to the disaster was an open question. The odds were very much against it. Flight 800 had been inspected thoroughly at 13,000 and 16,000 cycles. Those inspections showed only minimal, almost infinitesimal, cracking in the worrisome area of the internal frame behind the cockpit. When that section of the plane was eventually brought up from the sea, it would show no signs of significant age-related cracking.

Still, the issue of Flight 800's age would linger over the investigation. If not cracks in the internal frame, had something *else* in an aging plane given way at 8:31 P.M. on July 17?

————

Already, NTSB investigators at the Calverton hangar were setting up processes to analyze debris. Meanwhile, in Washington, Loeb and his investigators were studying a growing number of radar reports. At first, they had to rely on computer printouts, but now they had magnetic tapes from which they could extract raw data, including the identification numbers of each plane in the area, and plot them on maps. They had wondered in the first days if a midair collision could have occurred between Flight 800 and another plane. But tapes showed conclusively that that had not happened. The tapes, which the FBI was studying too, had been gathered by the FAA from various commercial airports in the region, up and down the East Coast. In the following days, other radar data would be obtained by the FBI from a military radar site in Virginia, as well as from the Sikorsky helicopter company, in Bridgeport, Connecticut, which maintained its own extensive radar facility. In all, investigators examined radar data on Flight 800 from nine locations in five states.

By the end of July, investigators would be able to deduce from the radar that the nose had come off after the initial explosion, while the plane continued to ascend without it, as air rushed into the open cabin. The radar would also show Flight 800 first as a single blip, then as several blips when it exploded, so that investigators could track pieces to the different areas of the crash site and so help in the mapping for wreckage retrieval and the sequencing of the plane's breakup. Little else could be determined, however, once the aircraft exploded, because it lost the transponder signal that indicated its exact altitude.

In particular, the radar tapes offered no clues as to *why* Flight 800 had fallen out of the sky and revealed nothing that might indicate a missile approaching or hitting the jetliner (though the FBI knew that a shoulder-launched missile could have hit its target between four-second and twelve-second radar sweeps). On the initial radar maps, several aircraft flying in the immediate vicinity of Flight 800 minutes before the explosion had been plainly evident and already identified for the FBI. One was the P-3 Orion. Another was the USAir commuter plane from which Dwight Brumley had observed a flare-like streak, and the East Winds Airlines commuter plane whose pilot had observed the first explosion. There, too, was the National Guard helicopter captained by the self-possessed Major Fritz Meyer, as well as the C-140 cargo plane accompanying the helicopter in its training maneuver. So were the trawlers and tugs known to have been in the area, and the *Adak*, among other Coast Guard vessels, but nothing else.

"Track down every foreign satellite that has radar whirling up there," Kallstrom told George Andrew. "Find out if *they* captured anything." The FBI soon had access to all U.S. satellites, including the one that had picked up the fishing trawler. None revealed any unexpected or unidentifiable objects in the sky in the area of the crash. But this survey was not definitive: Some U.S. satellites tend to do their radar sweeps less often than land radar sites, as little as every hour or so over North America. A crucial blip might have appeared on any one of their tapes, but if it didn't, that hardly ruled out the possibility of a missile.

As the FBI broadened its search, even Russia was asked if any of its satellites might have revealed a missile or projectile in the crash-site area. Eventually, the Russians reported that nothing unusual had appeared. To make certain, Kallstrom also hired an independent radar expert to do his own exhaustive study of the FAA, private, and military tapes. The expert would pore over computer printouts and tapes for months and find nothing to indicate a missile. Further, the FBI's expert would note that the FAA's low-altitude collision avoidance alert system was operating and active at the time of the crash, and that this system was not tripped by targets on the radar screens of any of the nine radar sites.

Yet unrevealing as these radar studies appeared to be, how could the agents explain why 270 eyewitnesses were *sure* they had seen some sort of flarelike streak?

Meanwhile, as the NTSB workers proceeded at Calverton, a palpable excitement hung in the air. The answer might already be at the hangar, in a piece of wreckage that revealed a malfunction or terrorist act. More likely, the plane's black boxes would be found soon—they were designed to respond to underwater sonar with a readily identifiable "pinging" sound—and would help fill in the picture. In most of the air disasters it investigated, the NTSB found its key clues right there in the cockpit conversations between pilots and in the instrument-data recordings. Usually, when it did, an obvious mechanical cause presented itself, and the investigation was soon wrapped up. But this time, the NTSB investigators felt sure, the black boxes would show evidence of a missile or bomb.

As quickly as divers recovered wreckage, it was shipped to Calverton for analysis. As the trucks laden with the aircraft pieces crept through the narrow roads of the island's tree-lined communities, residents came out of their homes and shops to watch.

One day Tom Corrigan's wife, Colleen, was leaving the beach in Hampton Bays with their sons when she saw a caravan slowly emerging from the Shinnecock Inlet Coast Guard Station. The caravan turned north toward Calverton, the same direction she was headed, and she found herself following it, like a mourner in a funeral procession, for the next ten miles. Transfixed by the crushed and torn pieces of metal ahead of her, Colleen thought of the lives lost, of the horror of the deaths, but most of all of the effort her husband and his fellow task-force members were expending to find out the cause of the crash.

———

At an oceanfront memorial service Monday afternoon for the victims, Bob Francis and Peter Goelz, James Hall's chief advisor, sat on one side of Jim Kallstrom in the second row of white folding chairs. To the shocked and grieving families who constituted most of the crowd, it was consoling, at least, that the federal government cared enough to be there.

On Kallstrom's other side was a less likely figure: Lewis Schiliro, the earnest, reserved head of the investigation's Long Island operation. About an hour before the ceremony, out at the FBI command trailer, Kallstrom had told Schiliro he would be going to the service, and then startled his lieutenant by saying, "Come on, let's go together."

"Jim, I've got a million things going on here," Schiliro protested. "I don't need to be going to some memorial service."

This was the second time in two days that Kallstrom had surprised his loyal adjutant with a decision that seemed not exactly wrong, but very un-FBI. Urged on by several of his colleagues, Schiliro had suggested the day before that Kallstrom stop giving daily news conferences. What if evidence of a missile or bomb was found, but the FBI had no suspect? Then the man who overnight had come to personify the Bureau would go from hero to loser. Kallstrom had heard out his old friend, but held his ground. "I have a duty to tell people what's going on," he said. "If we do find evidence of terrorism, we have to say so. You can't keep that secret for a year while you look for the culprit.

"If we didn't find the culprit after two years," Kallstrom allowed, "people would probably ask, 'Why can't you guys find this coward?' But that's life. You can't *not* say things because you're afraid of what's waiting around the corner."

"But I'm not the only one who feels this way," Schiliro said. "Other agents and even some prosecutors in the U.S. Attorney's office—they're concerned. They think you're putting people's confidence in the FBI at risk. And a potential prosecution at risk, too."

"Well, they're wrong," Kallstrom retorted. "That's why I don't take public opinion polls in making my decisions. Unless you're on the ridgeline, like I am here, you can't make those decisions."

"Jimmy, I'm only trying to point out the pitfalls. I'm trying to save your hide."

"I know you are, Lew," Kallstrom said as he got up to leave. "I appreciate it."

Kallstrom was the first to say there were situations when the FBI should be silent—when privacy or security was involved, or when evidence might be compromised. But aspects of this investigation simply had to be shared with both the families and the public. As he rode in his helicopter back to Manhattan that day, he realized he was taking a risk. If you're going to be a maverick, he thought, you've always got to win. Lose once, and they'll execute you.

———

By the next day, typically, Kallstrom had forgotten his discussion with Schiliro, and now here he was, asking him to face the public too. "Come on, Lew, take a ride with me to the service," Kallstrom said. "It's just a few minutes away."

The agents took separate cars. In his own blue Crown Victoria, Schiliro followed his boss through the contiguous towns, doing his best not to let more than a block's distance widen between the two cars. Soon enough they reached Smith Point State Park Beach, a narrow strip of shoreline closest to where Flight 800 had gone down. More than one hundred white wooden folding chairs, all of them filled, were set up in front of a stage overlooking the ocean on a gray and chilly day. In a row of seats onstage sat governors George Pataki of New York and Tom Ridge of Pennsylvania, among others. The politicians spoke, a boys' choir sang "The Wind Beneath My Wings," and a priest and rabbi recited Psalm 23 together. Another priest said a prayer in French for the European families. Then mourners placed roses and mementos, including a teddy bear, into a small Coast Guard vessel, which carried them to the crash site for the crew to lower into the sea. Other mourners brought single long-stem roses, photographs, and letters addressed to their lost loved ones to the water's edge and tossed them into the surf. Some waded up to their knees into the sea.

These gestures were soothing, but the families were still desperate to know when more bodies would be recovered. They had begun to feel that the investigation was stalled. Several turned to fix Kallstrom, Schiliro, and Francis with anxious stares. Did the investigators have news they hadn't yet shared?

As the tributes went on, the beeper on Kallstrom's belt sounded. He squinted at the number that appeared: the command van. Bending over, he called in on his cell phone to hear that the U.S. Navy divers had just located the bulk of the wreckage on the ocean floor. From his second-row seat, he walked to the side of the stage and motioned Governor Pataki over to tell him the news. The Navy, he said, was ready to position a ship over the wreckage and begin diving for the bodies trapped below. When Pataki went to the microphone to pass on the news, interrupting the service, the family members, many of their faces swollen from crying, burst into applause.

Schiliro was concerned that he wasn't out at the Coast Guard station, coordinating agents to respond to the Navy's find. Yet to his surprise, he also felt he was where he belonged. He listened to Governor Ridge say, "We grieve for innocents lost," and describe how the Montoursville French Club students had organized bake sales, car washes, and other fund-raisers for months to pay for their Paris trip. Schiliro could picture the kids at work and thought of his own three children. He saw the pained expressions of the family members and realized, for the first time, how dependent they were on the investigators for solace. As seasoned an agent as he was, this was a responsibility he had never felt before. He vowed, as he sat there, to encourage his agents to stay in touch with the families over the next weeks or months, even when there wasn't the news to warrant it. Kallstrom was right, he realized: This was not just another FBI investigation.

When Schiliro returned to the FBI trailer, he learned that agents had executed a warrant to search the Queens apartment of one of the victims of Flight 800.

The FBI had been investigating this victim, a former New York City schoolteacher, ever since neighbors reported he had acted strangely just before his Paris trip. The man had been under serious psychiatric care, it turned out, and was considered suicidal. He was in his forties and had no immediate family—another danger sign. More disturbing still, the taxi driver who had taken him to JFK airport reported that the man had kept a tight hold on a beat-up suitcase bound with rope.

That afternoon, agents and explosives technicians with bomb-sniffing dogs broke into the man's apartment and stayed for hours searching it. He had saved piles of tattered newspaper clippings critical of his teachers' union. They were tacked to the walls and strewn around a messy apartment that was clearly home to a recluse. Had this man taken an explosive aboard the plane and carried out a suicide mission? The search turned up no evidence of explosives, no suicide note, or anything else to indicate a violent plan. Nevertheless, Schiliro and Kallstrom told agents to have the condition of the man's body checked and to find his luggage and test for any residue of explosives. But here, too, a promising lead seemed to be going nowhere.

———

The Navy divers' discovery of the bulk of the fuselage signaled progress at last. After four days of little or no news, the families, investigators, and journalists felt suddenly hopeful. The divers would bring the bodies up, find the bright orange boxes that contained the flight-data and cockpit-voice recorders, bring some closure to a tragedy, and in the process, perhaps solve the case.

Governor Pataki, whose bulletin at the memorial service had galvanized the mourners, was by now a familiar figure to them. In the days since the crash, he had seemed to shuttle almost hourly between the Coast Guard station and Satellite City, offering updates from the investigators as cameras filmed him against an ocean backdrop. His manner was reassuringly low-key, and while the political dividends were obvious, he seemed genuinely to want to help. That afternoon, however, he blundered. When someone connected with the divers suggested privately to him that as many as one hundred bodies might be found within the main fuselage, the governor left television and other news reporters with the impression that those bodies *had* been found—and would soon be brought up. "We're hopeful that because of what has happened on the floor today, an awful lot can happen on the surface tomorrow," Pataki concluded.

The truth was that no one had sighted one hundred bodies. For Kallstrom and Francis, Pataki had made an already difficult day worse, as journalists, the White House, and grieving families clamored for more information about news that wasn't true.

By now, both Kallstrom and Francis knew how easily leaks could raise false hopes and waste everyone's time. Kallstrom increasingly suspected that many of the leaks were coming from the Calverton hangar.

At the crash site, new developments could be carefully protected, as Kallstrom wanted them to be. The divers remained on their boats; news of their findings traveled back to the FBI trailer via the secure walkie-talkie network that Cantamessa had developed, or through the Coast Guard and police on the scene, whom Kallstrom trusted. But at Calverton, all kinds of experts were gathered, many of them civilian, including representatives of the Airline Pilots Association, TWA pilots, mechanics, and the like. The NTSB had made everyone working in the hangar sign nondisclosure pledges, but information still leaked. Among the likeliest suspects, fairly or not, were the ATF agents whose portable testing machines had come up with premature, positive hits on explosive chemical residues. When Kallstrom sent directives to threaten the workers in the hangar with criminal charges, subpoenas, even polygraph tests, the leaks mostly dried up, but the tension increased between the ATF and the FBI. Months after the crash, to Kallstrom's astonishment, the ATF would issue a report privately to the NTSB, declaring the crash was *not* a crime. How could the same agency that had apparently revealed its positive hits to the press, with their clear implication of a criminal act, arrive at the opposite conclusion just months later? Kallstrom assumed the ATF was trying to outdo the FBI: a strange, intramural struggle that had everything to do with self-image and nothing to do with the search for truth in a high-stakes investigation.

The Calverton workers in the hangar resented Kallstrom's threats and the implication of disloyalty. More keenly, they bridled at what seemed, to them, an insulting—and counterproductive—refusal on the FBI's part to share the information it was gathering. Usually, the NTSB investigators and engineers from the aircraft manufacturer analyzed recovered wreckage as soon as it came in and shared information freely with others who might help: the airline, the FAA, air-traffic controllers, mechanics, and others. In fact, the NTSB was mandated to do so with a specified list of parties to be involved in its accident investigations. This investigation was different. This time, at Kallstrom's orders, all arriving pieces of wreckage were examined and photographed first by FBI agents. The FBI's pictures were tightly controlled—none, for example, could be released to the media without Kallstrom's authorization—and no other photographs could be taken, not even by the NTSB. The FBI shared important information with the hierarchy of the NTSB, including Hall, Loeb, and Francis, but cautioned them not to release it publicly. The workers in the hangar felt increasingly out of the loop.

Most frustrating, the FBI shared interviews—of eyewitnesses, of airplane workers, and so forth—only after blacking out the names of the interviewees. This was to protect those interviewed—especially someone briefly under suspicion—from appearing in the press as a possible bomber. But to the NTSB investigators, the censorship was unprecedented, an exercise in one-upmanship. "We're the feds," the NTSB investigators would say to local authorities at the crash site. "Well, we're the bigger feds," one FBI agent declared to a local official who was complaining about the attitude of some at NTSB. "We've got more people, more equipment. And we've got the guns." The line was meant as a joke, and said in private, but it disclosed a growing rift.

In that first week, one NTSB engineer in the hangar was so offended by the FBI agent in charge that he confronted him. "This is not a goddamn building," he said of the plane pieces gathering on the hangar floor. "It's an airplane. I can put it back together for you. You can't! If you want to participate in this reconstruction, then take the halo off your head!" When the agent scoffed at him, the engineer told him, "Our badges to get into this hangar are as big as yours— and don't you forget it."

Within a week, the FBI agent was gone from the hangar. In his stead was Kenny Maxwell, an aggressive but more pragmatic team player. Maxwell, the former head of the Terrorism Task Force and, more recently, head of the FBI's satellite field office in Newburgh, New York, some forty miles up the Hudson, was big and broad-shouldered with fair skin that turned red so quickly when he was angry or excited that his agents nicknamed him "Thermostat." Balding, he wore wire-rimmed glasses and looked younger than his forty-nine years. So dedicated was he, his colleagues joked, that he could only have married a fellow FBI agent, since no one else would have put up with constant case talk over dinner. His wife, Vera, had spent a decade on the Terrorism Task Force in Manhattan.

The engineers soon came to appreciate Maxwell and Kallstrom more than their own chief investigator, Al Dickinson, who, they felt, was a mere figurehead manipulated from Washington. He was also a bureaucrat who went by the book. Once, when a talented engineer cut a corner to get the job done, Dickinson bawled him out in front of his colleagues. Dickinson, his audience quickly concluded, was in over his head. As for Francis, they simply felt he didn't care about them.

They noticed, for example, that Francis seldom attended the five o'clock meetings at the hangar to review the day's progress. Much later, when he learned the bad feeling his absence had caused, Francis was exasperated. Didn't the engineers know that he had to participate in news conferences with Kallstrom late every afternoon in Smithtown, more than an hour away in heavy summer traffic? Besides, he didn't need to participate. He received daily updates from Dickinson and visited the Navy ships for a detailed briefing from the NTSB, FBI, and Navy officials. Some engineers resented his absence anyway, and felt that when he did appear, he came across as cavalier. When he visited the hangar, he never took the time to chat with the workers, let alone thank them for doing a difficult job. And why, if he was the agency's front man, didn't he wear a tie? To the working investigators at Calverton, he seemed dressed for a Hamptons cocktail party or the U.S. Open. The FBI officials might not share all they knew with the NTSB investigators in the hangar, but for the most part they had their confidence.

The engineers from Boeing, Pratt & Whitney, and others whose companies made parts for the 747-100 were also disgruntled. Not only did they feel the FBI's heavy hand in the general atmosphere at Calverton, they were denied even the censored accounts of eyewitnesses and other interviewees which the FBI gave to the NTSB. How could they conduct their own accident investigation without such documents?

One Boeing investigator was particularly incensed by the FBI's refusal—unprecedented, in his experience—to share wreckage photos or to let the aircraft investigators take their own, though Boeing engineers were working around the clock, and he needed to forward photos to his colleagues at Boeing in Everett, Washington. Eventually, the FBI agreed to share its photos with Boeing and other parties, but only if they produced a "valid reason."

"What's with these people?" the frustrated investigator fumed on a conference call with the home office. "Don't they know we have the same goal?"

Maxwell appreciated their frustration, but like Kallstrom, he felt that Boeing and the others were there to support the FBI and the NTSB, not pursue their own investigation. In an accidental crash, the engineers at Boeing might be more involved from the start, but this was potentially a criminal investigation, and Boeing and the others had no need to know what the FBI was doing or the contents of its criminal investigation. Even the FBI's own agents operated on a "need to know" basis. Few, aside from an overseer like Maxwell, were privy to much more than their own pieces of the puzzle.

"I know you see yourselves as some kind of Dick Tracy detectives," Kallstrom told the engineers during an all-staff meeting at the hangar after Maxwell reported the tension over access, "but you are not here to share in a criminal investigation. You have no right to this FBI information—and you are never going to have it, so you better get used to it."

Protecting the privacy of suspects was not just FBI policy, Kallstrom added. It was mandated by the Constitution as well as by the Federal Rules of Evidence. "What if we share a lead on someone and that person turns out to be perfectly innocent?

"Believe me, we're not trying to be secretive out of arrogance—as if we know what happened here but don't want anyone else to know," Kallstrom added.

There was another reason for discretion, which Kallstrom chose not to mention. Boeing and the others had a built-in conflict of interest. Cautious and scientific as they might be, most of them clearly hoped the crash was the result of a bomb or missile, not some mechanical malfunction that might expose their company to civil suits and jeopardize all of its other 747-100 jets—if not its entire 747 fleet. Pratt & Whitney, TWA, the unions, even the FAA had their own interests and concerns. The various factions might not skew the truth deliberately, but Kallstrom had to be sure that the investigation remained objective.

On the other hand, the aviation experts knew that the FBI relied on them for information. A Boeing 747 consisted of some four million parts, each of them accounted for in blueprints, nearly every one numbered. Thus the engineers could reconstruct Flight 800 section by section with amazing accuracy. Without them, the FBI would be lost.

In the case of Flight 800, the engineers were helped by TWA's long-standing policy of affixing visible numbers to seats. Many other airlines put seat numbers overhead, on or beside their carry-on bins. In the aftermath of the disaster, TWA had come in for much criticism, but among the workers at the hangar, its seat-numbering policy won it a lot of praise.

The engineers at Calverton and in Boeing's 747 plant in Everett, Washington, hashed over dozens of possible scenarios. One theory was that weak spots in the nose section of the jet had resulted in the breakup in the sky. The directive from Boeing about fuselage cracks behind the cockpit suggested that Flight 800 might have succumbed to the stress of its last ascent. Another early theory was that one or more engines might have broken away from the jet as it ascended; Boeing knew there had been problems with the fuse pins that held the engines in place. The most compelling theory had not yet emerged but would soon: that Flight 800's center fuel tank had exploded, immediately cutting the plane's power and splitting the fuselage.

As Boeing's aeronautical engineers knew, the left-wing fuel tank of the 747-100 built immediately before N93119 had exploded in midair after a lightning strike in 1976. Could the tank's own vapors have become hot enough for lightning to ignite them? Could a tiny imperfection, perhaps one that crept into the production line only as long as it took to manufacture those two planes, be responsible for both explosions? Of more significance to investigators was the center-fuel-tank explosion that had occurred in 1990 on a Philippines Airlines 737 on the tarmac of Manila's airport, killing eight people. The cause of that crash had not been definitely proved.

Whatever its origin might be, a center-fuel-tank explosion became the possible cause that overshadowed the others. The engineers knew that the center fuel tank, which had a capacity of 13,000 gallons, had held only 50 gallons that night. That in itself was not unusual, but could the vapors in the nearly empty tank have exploded? Unlike gasoline, the kerosenelike jet fuel was itself not highly volatile. Nor were the vapors, though if they were hot enough, a spark, theoretically, might have ignited them.

The engineers theorized that such a spark could only have come from a bomb, a missile, or some other source outside the tank since the plane was designed so that all ignition sources were kept well away from the tanks. In the center fuel tank there were no electrical currents strong enough to ignite the fuel vapors even if they had somehow become hot enough—about 100 degrees—to explode.

Nevertheless, Boeing engineers decided to see how hot the vapors in a 747's center fuel tank could actually get. They conducted flight tests on a 747 jumbo jet in California's Mojave Desert, closely mimicking Flight 800's conditions. Since the air-conditioning units, beneath the thick metal underbelly of the tank, had been running at full blast on the tarmac during Flight 800's delay, they ran the air-conditioning units for an hour or longer before flight. The aircraft then took off with heat sensors installed in its fuel tanks. The engineers assumed the temperatures in the tanks could not reach the 100-degree flash point, since this danger had been well considered in the tank's design.

They were, as it turned out, wrong.

CHAPTER 7

A SUBMARINE SURFACES

Governor Pataki had overstated the case, but he was partly right. By late Monday, bodies were coming up not by the dozens but one by one by one, a macabre task for the divers.

Lieutenant (j.g.) Blais had slept fitfully Sunday night, but suited up Monday morning ready to bring bodies aboard before the day was out. From the deck of the *Grasp,* he and his fellow Navy divers climbed into Zodiacs and Boston Whalers and put-putted directly over what was to become known as Debris Field #1, a four-hundred-yard-square grid where most of the wreckage appeared to lie. Sonar had located the plane's other wing, all four engines, and the aft section of the cabin, all of which appeared to have traveled as a unit some 2.2 nautical miles after the initial explosion. Debris Field #2, 1.5 miles to the west of Debris Field #1, contained the nose of the plane, including the cockpit, and the first 70 feet of fuselage. Closest to Kennedy Airport was Debris Field #3, a sprawling area that appeared to contain the first pieces that had fallen from the plane while it was still aloft. Parts of the center fuel tank and the air-conditioning units beneath it would be found in Debris Field #3: clues that the explosion might have occurred in their immediate vicinity.

In his wet suit, Blais felt the chill of the water as he slipped into it: about 70 degrees at the surface, but a bone-chilling 50 degrees at the bottom. Blais and the other Navy divers had never retrieved jetliner wreckage and bodies before, but the FBI divers and the police and fire department divers—from Suffolk and Nassau counties, New York City and State—had pulled up bodies before: murder victims, suicide jumpers, storm casualties, and so on.

Down by the lamplit fuselage, Blais moved cautiously amid wires and jagged edges looking for bodies beneath the clouds of silt. He checked repeatedly to be sure that some jagged metal edge was not about to cut his oxygen hose or slice through his wet suit. Debris Field #1 was, the divers said, like a bed of razor blades. The wreckage itself was surreally colorful, covered in sparkling glitter like fairy dust over much of the wreckage. By now, the divers knew that a huge shipment of glitter had been packed in the cargo hold of Flight 800, but this only added to the strangeness of the scene.

Blais and his partner, Mike Gallant, and the other pairs of divers slowly brought up the bodies one by one, trying not to look at them as they did. The first body retrieved was a man, nude and undamaged, whose hair flowed behind him as he rose to the surface.

At the surface, the divers passed the man up to a waiting Navy crew in one of the rubber boats. The crew members worked the man into an unzipped body bag, a task complicated by the choppy ocean. The man's arms and legs flopped one way, then the other. From the deck of the *Grasp*, Navy officers and crew looked on transfixed, like highway commuters gaping at a hideous accident.

By the time the divers returned with the next body, the procedure had mercifully been changed to what it had been the previous night. A bag was passed down to them in the water. A rope was cinched under the victim's arms to prevent a reprise of the first night's mishap, and the divers then slid the body into the bag underwater. To the divers' horror, a couple of the bodies could not be put in bags because pieces of the plane were embedded in them. The divers were instructed by the FBI not to remove the pieces, which might help tell the story of why the plane had exploded. Instead, the bodies were hauled up just as they were, leaving a footlong rod in one victim's stomach, a curl of metal in another's neck.

By now, the Navy divers had been joined by the special New York FBI dive team that had spent its last weeks securing water-sports areas for the Atlanta Olympics. They were assigned to remain at the Olympics to assist in bomb sweeps in a large lake where events were being held, but when Flight 800 exploded, Kallstrom and Joe Cantamessa, the divers' immediate supervisor, ordered them to Long Island. They were needed to help bring up Flight 800 victims and wreckage as quickly as possible from the ocean bottom. At 1:20 in the morning on Sunday, July 28, a bomb would rock a crowded public park at the Olympics, killing one woman and injuring dozens, and law enforcement agents would wonder if Atlanta and TWA Flight 800 were linked terrorist acts. (Within days, however, agents were discounting that possibility, saying that the Atlanta weapon, a pipe bomb in a knapsack, appeared to be the work of an amateur.)

Eighteen months before Flight 800 went down, Kallstrom had sent the FBI divers to Colorado for special training in diving in heavy currents and rapids. The currents on the Atlantic bottom off Long Island, as it turned out, were treacherous too, especially after a big storm whipped them up; the divers were grateful for the special training. Yet in another way, the operation seemed easier than many they'd encountered. Bob Burkes, a forty-two-year-old member of the FBI team, was accustomed to diving in black water—the Delaware River, for example—where visibility was nil. He would feel his way like an awakened sleeper in a bedroom not his own, except the furniture he knocked into was sunken shopping carts, or metal barrels, or even automobiles. At least in the TWA investigation, the divers' visibility during a good day was fifteen feet.

Kallstrom took care of the divers—not just those from the FBI but all the law enforcement divers as well. He made sure they all got double tanks, with special regulators and miniature computers that warned them when they were underwater too long. He frequently admonished his own divers: No one should dive if they had any doubts about safety.

The FBI divers stayed in local motels but were often politely asked to leave on summer weekends, when owners could raise the rates. Burkes, put off by the smell of stale tobacco in the motel rooms, chose instead to set up a tent in the nearby desolate Pine Barrens, and endured the mosquitoes in return for peace, quiet, and clean air. Compared to a lot of his postings in the Marines, this felt almost luxurious. Burkes was an ascetic, contemplative man who liked being on his own. His duffel contained clean clothes, an alarm clock, and a flashlight for reading at night. On board the *Grasp*, he would spend time between dives watching with fascination the Navy's sonar equipment or helping investigators sift through the retrieved personal possessions. He was particularly struck by the passport of a blond TWA flight attendant. He recognized the face. He'd seen her in a *Time* magazine report on some of the victims. The off-duty flight attendant had died in the explosion, along with her two little adopted children from Scandinavia. Holding her passport, Burkes felt heartbroken. His own daughter was in kindergarten.

By afternoon, the *Grasp*'s crew dropped large anchors to help keep the ship in a tight moor where it would remain for as long as diving continued. A metal mesh platform, or "stage," as it was called, was rigged to allow "hard-hat" divers, whose oxygen lines were attached to massive tanks on board, to join in retrieving the bodies. Though tethered by their lines to the ship, they could spend as much as an hour on the seafloor, whereas scuba divers had to surface after fifteen minutes. Hard-hatting was unnerving and claustrophobic to all but a few highly trained divers. After suiting up and putting on their helmets with oxygen hoses attached, the hard-hatters stepped into the stage—it looked like a Parisian elevator—and closed its door after them. The stage was attached to the ship by heavy cables and lowered by a hydraulic winch. As the divers descended, the silhouette of the big ship vanished overhead in the surrounding darkness. The cage struck bottom hard enough to bounce slightly, stirring a cloud of silt and sand. The divers then stepped out, moving awkwardly in heavy boots like astronauts on the moon. A scuba diver had an extra hose and mouthpiece if something went wrong, and a partner nearby to share his own extra mouthpiece if needed, in what they called "scare air." A hard-hatter who sliced his hose on razor-sharp metal had to signal the ship to switch oxygen to an auxiliary hose. If that wasn't done quickly enough, he was a dead man.

As long as they took care to ascend slowly each time, the scuba divers could dive several times before taking a rest. Not the hard-hatters. After each of their longer dives, they had to spend an hour in a metal decompression chamber that looked like a gigantic, oblong clothes dryer on deck. In the silence, many could think only of the horror they had seen. Sitting there, they found themselves idly picking pieces of glitter from their hair, their eyelashes, their faces and hands, even under their fingernails. Later, during long, hot showers, they scrubbed themselves down, but specks of glitter remained. Before long, there were specks glinting everywhere aboard the *Grasp*.

Two Navy scuba divers had been down awhile, searching for bodies, when one noticed an odd flutter of color amid the brownish silt. He waved his partner over, and the two approached it slowly, moving their flippers, as plumes of oxygen bubbles spewed up from their mouthpieces. There, resting in the water a few inches above the seafloor, was a fully unfurled American flag. The divers positioned themselves at either end of the flag and began folding it in the proper fashion, square by square, then triangle by triangle. As one diver held the flag fully folded, the other saluted it. Then, slowly, they ascended.

"Sir, we know you said only bring up bodies, but we couldn't leave this down there," one of the divers said to the FBI agent supervising the dive when he pulled out his mouthpiece at the surface. Christopher Peet, the agent working with the two divers, leaned over the side of the Boston Whaler to take the flag. "You guys deserve a medal," he said as the divers went down again into the depths.

Peet put the flag up near the wheel for safekeeping. At first he kept it hidden, an instinctive reaction. A month earlier, as a member of the FBI's evidence response team at the site of the bombing of the U.S. military residence at Khobar Towers in Saudi Arabia, Peet had been clawing through debris for clues when he uncovered a small American flag. He picked it up, and found some blood on it. A superior had told him to put the flag back; there were concerns about biohazard contamination. Peet complied reluctantly. No one, he thought now, was going to return this flag to the sea.

That evening, at about six o'clock, Kallstrom was in his office in the FBI trailer, winding up a call from Congressman Henry Hyde, when Schiliro walked in on him. "Some guys want to see you," Schiliro said. "I know you're busy, but I think you ought to see them."

Kallstrom shrugged. "Send them in."

The two divers, accompanied by Peet, squeezed into an office barely large enough for a desk and two chairs. One of the divers was holding the American flag, still dripping water, folded in the military style. "We found this flag this morning down in the wreckage," the diver said. "We thought you might present it to Charlie Christopher on behalf of all the divers."

For a moment, Kallstrom was speechless. "You guys are absolute class," he managed. "I can't thank you enough."

He stared at the flag in his hands, and then looked up.

"When I find the appropriate time, I'll present this to Agent Christopher," he said. "You have my word."

———

Despite Kallstrom's admiration for the divers and his relief that the first of the bodies below were being brought up, he wanted a lot from the Navy that the Navy had failed, so far, to provide—starting with the list of all military assets in the crash-site area on the night of July 17. What the Navy *had* confirmed was the presence of assets the FBI already knew about: the P-3 Orion; the large ship *Adak*, which had helped in the retrieval of bodies and debris the first night; the Air National Guard HH-60 helicopter and C-140 cargo plane engaged in routine maneuvers; and various other helicopters that had converged on the crash site. That list could hardly be complete.

As he was waiting, Kallstrom learned that two flight attendants in a commercial jet bound for Kennedy Airport an hour before the crash of Flight 800 had seen what looked to them like a gray warship off the coast, steaming south. Kallstrom called Admiral Flanagan's office to learn that the USS *Normandy* had been approximately 181 miles south of the crash site, headed toward Norfolk, Virginia, when TWA Flight 800 went down. "Why didn't you tell us about the *Normandy?*" Kallstrom bellowed to the assistant on Flanagan's staff. "This is not some cat-and-mouse game here."

The Navy bureaucrat said that Kallstrom hadn't asked about the *Normandy*, so the Navy hadn't told him. What he'd asked for was a list of military assets in the immediate vicinity of Flight 800 on the night of July 17. The *Normandy*, which had not been in the immediate vicinity of the crash, was an Aegis cruiser, capable of carrying surface-to-air missiles, but these armaments had a range far less than 181 miles, the distance at which the ship had been situated from the crash site at the time of the explosion.

"The Navy seems to be having a little trouble understanding us," Kallstrom told Admiral Flanagan's office. "So let's make it simple. I want to know about every asset positioned within two hundred nautical miles of the crash-site area on July 17—period. And that includes assets that did not, supposedly, have armaments on board capable of hitting Flight 800. Just tell me about them all."

As soon as he got off the phone, Kallstrom asked Pickard to initiate a background check of the *Normandy*: its capabilities, its recent history, and any pertinent information on its crew that might indicate the possibility of reckless action. When the check was completed—and not before—Pickard would have agents pay the *Normandy* a visit.

Kallstrom was still stewing about the Navy's failure to get him a full list immediately when an astonishing report came in—not from the Navy but from a tugboat captain.

In the waters off Montauk, Long Island, at about midnight on the day of the crash, the tugboat captain had been startled to see the green starboard lights of a submarine surface briefly. In the dark, he could discern no lettering or numbers to indicate even that the sub belonged to the Navy; perhaps it belonged to a foreign power. The captain had years of experience in those waters and seemed, to the agents who interviewed him, a very sensible fellow.

Kallstrom was still waiting for his list on Monday, five days after the crash, when Admiral Edward Kristensen, assigned to oversee the salvage operation, arrived as a party of one at the wheel of a rental economy car, having flown up on a commercial flight to Islip's MacArthur Airport.

Blond and balding, Admiral Kristensen was surprisingly humble and self-effacing for a high officer in the U.S. armed forces. His friends called him "Froggy," because of his dead-on imitation of a cartoon character of the same name. He liked to say that he had served thirty of his fifty-four years in the U.S. Navy because he had forgotten to check out. The only reason he had become an admiral in charge of ships, he said, was that he had failed as a fighter pilot. On a routine exercise near Pensacola, Florida, his multimillion-dollar plane had malfunctioned, and Kristensen bailed out. His superiors were impressed with his split-second instincts, but less so with the loss of the plane. Kristensen was assigned to land duties and proved a wise and compassionate leader who rose steadily through the ranks.

"So what the hell was *that?*" Kallstrom asked when he'd described the tugboat captain's report.

"I understand your concern," said the admiral. "You should get everything you want to know."

By the end of the day, Kristensen had talked several times to Admiral Flanagan's office to expedite the list of naval assets in the crash-site area. The list had been held up awaiting clearance for classified information, but under Flanagan's orders, Kallstrom had already received the details on the submarine involved in maneuvers with the P-3 Orion. The USS *Trepang* had remained well offshore on the night of July 17, both to navigate more easily and to stay in restricted military waters at a safe distance from commercial ship traffic. It was eighty miles south of the crash site when Flight 800 went down, but it had carried armaments, including thirteen MK-48 torpedoes, which could be fired only through the water at an enemy submarine or ship. Like most other modern submarines, the *Trepang* did have "out of water capability," weapons that could be fired at targets above water, but those consisted of only two harpoon cruise missiles on the night of July 17. Intended to hit ships, not planes, the missiles' aerial range was just 1,300 feet, far less than the altitude of 13,700 feet at which Flight 800 had been flying at the time of the crash. Even so, Kallstrom dispatched agents to board the *Trepang*, interview the crew, and satisfy themselves that they were getting the straight story.

As Admiral Kristensen was waiting to hear about the sub the tugboat captain might have seen, he listened to Kallstrom complain about the slow pace of the Navy. Surely more boats and more divers could be sent to the crash site. Could the Navy provide small submarines to help guide the divers from below?

"Good suggestion," Kristensen said. "I thought of it myself before I flew up. Problem is that a large submarine can't be brought into water that's just 120 feet deep. Smaller ones can, but then side-scan sonar from the boats is knocked out: Two underwater conveyors of sound communication cannot operate simultaneously, any more than two radio stations can occupy the same wavelength. And divers can't go down from the boat while the subs are below—they might swim into the propellers."

The best way to proceed, Kristensen explained, was for the more than two hundred divers aboard the *Grasp* and *Grapple*, as well as from both boats' larger supply ship, the *Oak Hill*, to make as many dives as they could, directed by side-scan sonar. They could also use a handheld global positioning system that placed a small boat within two to three yards of the wreckage the sonar was seeing below. On the bottom, the divers would use a handheld sonar that the Navy used to detect underwater ordnance.

"Okay, Admiral," Kallstrom said with a sigh. "You know best."

By the end of the day, the sub sighted by the tugboat captain proved to be the USS *Albuquerque*, with nuclear weapon capability and a crew of 127—12 officers and 115 enlisted men. The sub had been cruising north, back to its base in New London, Connecticut, when it surfaced briefly off Montauk at midnight, as the tugboat captain had reported. The *Albuquerque* is a fast-attack submarine equipped to carry various kinds of missiles, including harpoons, fired from the surface at targets as much as 85 miles away, and Tomahawks, land-attack missiles with an astounding range of 870 nautical miles. Neither missile was designed to be fired at planes. A harpoon could rise only 1,300 feet above the water's surface, a Tomahawk just 1,200 feet. And on the night of July 17, the *Albuquerque* had carried neither missile. As with the *Trepang*, its only armaments were MK-48 torpedoes, of which it had ten.

The civilian reports were disconcerting, but now that Kallstrom made it clear that he wanted to identify all military assets within a 200-nautical-mile radius of the crash site, the Navy command layers finally responded.

They reported that the USS *Wyoming*, a brand-new nuclear submarine that had begun its maiden voyage on July 13 from New London, was gliding about 150 miles south of Long Island on the early evening of July 17, en route to a naval base in Georgia. Compared to the *Wyoming*, the *Trepang* and the *Albuquerque* were bathtub toys. The *Wyoming* carried Trident nuclear missiles with a range of thousands of miles that could wipe out entire cities. But if a Trident missile had hit a commercial jet, it would have obliterated it, leaving neither wings nor fuselage to retrieve from the ocean floor. There would be little left of Long Island, for that matter. "If a Trident had shot down Flight 800," one missile expert remarked to interviewing agents, "the FBI office in New York City would have ended up in Harvard Yard in Boston. People who know anything about those weapons know that such a missile could not be launched without the whole world knowing. We certainly would not be asking ourselves, I wonder what happened to Flight 800."

That was one reason to rule out an attack from the *Wyoming*. Another was that the submarine was carrying no nuclear weapons. Instead, it was hauling missile-shaped concrete slabs in its twenty-four silos as ballast on its maiden voyage. The 560-foot-long *Wyoming*'s four torpedo tubes were also empty. At the time of the crash, FBI agents confirmed, the *Wyoming*'s crew of 15 officers and 150 enlistees was conducting routine tests of its engines and similar mechanical functions.

The door was now opened by Flanagan for agents to conduct a third interview with the pilot and crew of the P-3 Orion, one that was worth their time.

Pilot Ott, the P-3's commander, now acknowledged what the agents had already determined about the plane's firepower. The P-3 Orion was capable of carrying air-to-air missiles, air-to-surface missiles, and anti-ship harpoon cruise missiles. Like the USS *Albuquerque*, it could also carry Tomahawk missiles. Fired from the air rather than the sea, a Tomahawk certainly could hit a plane, and was slim enough to be all but undetectable by radar as it approached its target. Infrared sensors that tracked incoming missiles by their heat were also thwarted by Tomahawks, whose turbofan engines, taking over after initial propulsion by a solid propellant, emitted little heat. The missile produced no fire tail. Moreover, the Tomahawk was almost invisible to the naked eye, so that the pilot of a target plane would be unlikely to see it before it hit. A Tomahawk missile certainly could have destroyed a commercial jet.

But a Tomahawk, as the crew explained, would have pulverized the plane. More to the point, the P-3 Orion had carried no Tomahawk missiles on the night of July 17. It had carried no armaments at all that night.

For its mission to find the USS *Trepang* off New Jersey and Delaware on the night of July 17, the P-3 carried only sonobuoys, harmless listening devices that the crew dropped into the water to find the *Trepang*'s coordinates. Also on board were a number of chaf flares, decoys that diverted heat-seeking missiles. The flares played no part in the exercise, and none were set off during the P-3's flight.

The P-3 had not yet located the *Trepang* when it passed over Flight 800 at 21,000 feet. The submarine hunter's own radar, along with radar from various bases on the Eastern Seaboard, confirmed that the P-3 was close to Flight 800 when the jet blew up, but not quite as close as the agents had initially assumed. The P-3 was about three miles away when the first explosion occurred, heading south of the jet, so none of its crew had observed the blast. However, as soon as the P-3 crew heard radio reports from other pilots in the area about a commercial plane going down, they called air-traffic control then circled back to help. The crew members had been appalled by what they saw and circled the crash site at 1,500 feet. This is when they advised the Coast Guard they had life rafts, exposure suits, and could serve as a communication platform, but after about a half hour of circling the area, the Coast Guard waved them off. They then flew on to complete their mission. In a quadrant designated for military maneuvers, 80 miles south of the crash site, the P-3 dropped 52 of its 84 sonobuoys, and found the *Trepang*. When they returned to Brunswick, Maine, at 2:00 A.M., the crew logged in the number of sonobuoys they had dropped. The log of this mission and the P-3's flight voice recorder were turned over to the FBI agents at the interview. There were no inconsistencies between Ott's report and the mission log, nor did any of the crew members offer conflicting details.

Ott and his crew told the agents that the P-3 had instruments to alert them if their plane was being locked on by a missile launcher, but at no time, as they flew over TWA Flight 800, did the instruments react. This was significant evidence against the missile theory: A terrorist in a boat planning to lock on to Flight 800 would likely have tested his launcher's lock-on capability with other planes passing by moments before Flight 800.

Ott also provided infrared images of the crash scene recorded by a system called Inerd. Agents looked to see if the Inerd's tape might reveal a terrorist's small boat, but the system used such a narrow scope to survey the ocean's surface that viewing Inerd tapes was like looking at the water through a straw. Compared to an AWACS plane, which could survey a wide area and detect objects as tiny as a nickel from miles above, the Inerd was of limited help.

All this was reassuring, but between the first and third P-3 Orion interviews, a troubling fact about the plane had been brought to light by FAA radar tapes. As the tapes revealed, the plane was flying on the night of July 17 with its transponder off. This was the onboard instrument that provided a plane's coordinates and identification to FAA radar. Did this mean that the plane was flying undetected on a secret mission? In the third interview, however, Ott explained that his crew had notified Boston's civilian air-traffic control of its flight plan before embarking, and advised that the P-3 had a faulty transponder that worked only intermittently. In response, Boston air-traffic control had rerouted the P-3, which is why it was flying over Flight 800, close to shore, where it could easily be tracked by primary radar. In reviewing the tapes, the FBI actually heard the P-3 notify air-traffic control of the broken transponder. Later, agents would study maintenance records that showed the transponder had been faulty for months. It was now obvious that the crew had not deliberately shut off the transponder on the night of July 17. Civilian air-traffic controllers on that night had seen the markings of an unidentified aircraft on their radar screens in the vicinity of Flight 800, but knew it was the P-3, as transcripts showed. At 8:20:04, the P-3 was advised by Boston Center ". . . to ah cut you right across the Kennedy departure track, and ah you have no transponder I need to leave you on airways until you get into the, until you get into the warning area." ". . . Roger, we understand we'll stay with the airways," the P-3 pilot responded.

The P-3 was also in communication with Navy air-traffic control who monitor military airspace out of a Virginia facility known as VaCape.

If the P-3 Orion was no longer under suspicion, neither were other Navy assets in the area. A large, classified, electronic map in the Naval command center of the Norfolk naval base showed the location of every Navy asset in the world. On the night of the crash, in fact, Admiral Flanagan had studied the lights in the vicinity of Flight 800 and satisfied himself that no American warship or submarine could have downed the plane. Now he supplied Kallstrom with charts and records to show the coordinates of every such asset in the 200-mile grid around the crash site, as Kallstrom had requested. At five, sometimes six command levels, FBI agents conducted interviews and obtained signed documentation certifying that each asset was what, and where, Flanagan said it was. Radar and satellite imagery confirmed the locations. Unless literally thousands of Navy officers and crewmen were collaborating in a massive cover-up of the real location of a ship or submarine that had fired a missile capable of taking down a jet off a populated area like Long Island, the sweep offered reassuring indications that no such tragic mistake had occurred.

As for the possibility that missiles or other ordnance had been stolen, the Navy, Air Force, Army, and Marines supplied impressively detailed inventories of missing arms, ammunition, and explosives. Many grenades, for example, were unaccounted for, as well as C-4 explosive chemicals, between 1991 and 1996. But no one had stolen missiles, missile launchers, or any other arms capable of bringing down a plane.

Though the Navy had been slow to awaken to the FBI's needs, nothing in the information it was producing now appeared inaccurate, misleading, or even vague. In the piles of documents that agents were still sifting through, only one small inconsistency had appeared.

When FBI agents visited New London to inspect the *Albuquerque* and interview the submarine's crew, they learned that one weapon had, in fact, been fired off Long Island the day before the crash. At 8:30 P.M. on July 16, the mighty sub had emerged from the ocean depths, bursting to the surface just before sunset. A Navy sharpshooter, along with several crew members, appeared on deck bearing the body of a retired crewman who had requested a burial at sea. The sharpshooter fired three rounds from his M-16 rifle into the salmon-colored sky. The crew members removed the American flag that covered a black body bag and gently slid their comrade into the sea.

All three rounds were reported by the crew and verified by the FBI.

CHAPTER 8

RAISE THE FLAG

Six days after the crash, Kallstrom began to feel better, at least about the salvage operation. Six more bodies had been raised and brought in to the Coast Guard station at East Moriches, then driven over to the morgue in Hauppauge, bringing the total to 110. With the reinforcements that Dr. Charles Wetli had reluctantly accepted, 77 victims had been identified. By the end of the week, Wetli said, he would likely be done with the rest of the bodies on hand.

This left 120 bodies still to be found, identified, and sent home. Within the Ramada Inn at Kennedy Airport, tears and anger had given way to grief and fatigue among most of the families who remained. Many found themselves envying the families who had already received the remains of their loved ones; the grim vigil of waiting for confirmation of a husband's or daughter's death was terrible.

Joe Lychner, for one, had heard on Monday that his wife, Pam, had been identified; his daughter Katie was identified the next day. They both had been found on the water the night of the crash. His other daughter, Shannon, remained missing, so Lychner insisted that Pam and Katie be kept in the Suffolk County morgue's refrigerated trucks until his family could be buried at the same time, together. Already, the medical examiner had called to report that the two bodies were deteriorating. But Lychner refused to accept them until Shannon was found, too. If he was forced to sign a release, he would have Pam and Katie cremated and their ashes spread over the crash site so Shannon would not be alone.

Jackie Hettler and Pam Karschner, mothers of Rance and Amanda, had hardly known each other a week before. Now they spent nearly all their waking hours together, at times grieving on twin beds in a darkened room as they waited for news. They took their meals with the Montoursville families in a special conference room; the other families, by now a group of nearly one thousand people, ate numbly in the hotel's capacious ballroom, each family with its own designated TWA grief counselor hovering nearby. Ann Dwyer, mother of eleven-year-old Larkyn, remained in her room with her husband, Ron, taking an occasional call from friends in Arizona who phoned to console her, but who sometimes needed her to comfort them. Joe Lychner was too consumed with grief to make any calls, certainly not for his new job. He had no thought beyond retrieving the body of his other daughter. Yet because he was such a commanding presence—as articulate as he was attractive—Lychner found the families gravitating toward him as a sort of spokesperson. When the families began talking about seeing the crash site for themselves, Lychner, Ron Dwyer, and Michel Breistroff's sister Catherine served as representatives aboard a Coast Guard helicopter that circled the site and then landed at the East Moriches Coast Guard station, where they were given a tour of the makeshift morgue facilities. They grimly questioned Ken Burgess, the station's vibrant new head who days before had replaced the cantankerous commander, before returning to the Ramada, reassured that the Coast Guard and other authorities were doing all they could. Later, however, Ron Dwyer, among a few others, would come to wonder if a massive cover-up had been perpetrated.

As for Charlie Christopher, he remained at home, accompanied by his fellow agents. With the news that Janet's body had been positively identified and would be driven on Tuesday to the local funeral home, Charlie sagged. But then on Monday morning he got up early, as usual, and began taking care of business—the business of burying his wife.

With his son, Charlie drove over to the simple Salem United Church of Christ and arranged for a Saturday service. Then he took Charles out to the adjoining graveyard. "Dad, this is too far from home," Charles said. "I want a place I can ride to on my bike."

On her six-mile daily walk, Charlie recalled, Janet passed a pretty little cemetery not far from home. She had mentioned that its caretaker tended it nearly every day; she waved to him as she passed, and he waved back. Charlie found the caretaker, just as Janet had said, in the cemetery behind the white clapboard United Lutheran Church near their house. "You know my wife," Charlie said stiffly.

"Excuse me?"

Charlie explained about Janet's walks.

"Oh, of course." The caretaker brightened. "I saw her just last week."

When Charlie explained that his wife had died, the caretaker put a gentle hand on the younger man's arm. "You find any place here you like," he said. "I'll take good care of her."

With his son, Charlie chose a sunny, isolated plot on a little hill that would be easily visible from the road when he drove by. They returned that afternoon with a compass to pinpoint the right southern exposure so that the flowers, which Janet loved to grow in her garden, would get enough sun. The next day, with two fellow agents but without his son, he drove over to the funeral home to see Janet.

"I'm sorry, Mr. Christopher," the funeral director said. "It's just not right for you to view the body."

"I don't give a damn," Charlie said. "I'm going to see her because she's my wife, I love her, and she's the mother of my son, and that's the way it's going to be."

Embarrassed, the director explained that a fax had arrived from a California funeral company hired by TWA that apparently ordered local funeral directors not to let families view the victims' bodies.

"Forget the fax," Charlie said firmly.

"Okay," the director said with a shrug. "Let me prepare her."

Janet had arrived at the funeral home in a crude metal casket furnished by TWA. By the time Charlie returned with the agents on Wednesday for the private viewing, the director had lifted her onto a gurney, then covered her black plastic body bag with a sheet. When the director ushered him into the room, Charlie could see her face, covered with heavy makeup, and her hands, but that was all.

"You sure you want to do this, Charlie?" one of the agents whispered.

"I'm sure," Charlie said.

The agents and the funeral director left the room as Charlie gently patted Janet's arm. He saw her swollen face and a big gash on the right side of her head. He pulled back the sheet to see the black plastic sack fitted with elastic around her ankles and wrists. For some reason, he checked her feet to see that her toes were intact. They were. So were her fingers, though when he felt for her arms under the plastic, he realized both arms were broken, as were her legs, and that her back was broken, too. Some of the damage, Charlie knew, had been done during the autopsy at Hauppauge. Charlie had tried to prevent this, but New York State law required an autopsy before a body could be transferred for burial to another state. But Charlie could see that this was really Janet. He had to do that, not so much to confirm the identification as to confront, and absorb, the physical reality of her death.

Outside, Charlie told the funeral director that he wanted Janet to be wearing her favorite dress at the funeral. The dress was red with gold buttons. The agents offered to bring it over for him, but Christopher got it himself, along with a favorite Hermès scarf of Janet's to cover the back of her head, and a large TWA scarf to put in her hands.

That evening—Wednesday, July 24, one week after the crash—Charlie went to see his son, Charles, presented with the Order of the Arrow for his leadership and camping skills, a rare honor in scouting for a twelve-year-old. As he watched the ceremony, Charlie thought of Janet's love for her son and how she had changed her flight schedule to be present for the ceremony tonight.

———

The victims' bodies were being retrieved, identifications confirmed, funeral arrangements made, but one week after the explosion, investigators were no closer to solving the mystery of why Flight 800 had fallen out of the sky. None of the positive hits for explosive chemicals made on wreckage by the ATF or FBI's portable field machines had held up to closer scrutiny at the FBI's lab in Washington, nor had evidence of mechanical malfunction yet appeared. The black boxes containing the cockpit voice recorder and flight-data recorder—the likeliest keys—continued to elude divers, who scanned the wreckage for them with listening devices to hear the pinging noises they emitted.

Finally on that Wednesday, July 24, a hard-hat diver in Debris Field #1 actually stepped on the silt-covered corner of one of the boxes and exposed its bright orange casing. At about the same time, a nearby ROV, the small robot with its underwater video camera, beamed the first hazy image of the boxes onto a monitoring screen on board the *Grasp*. The Navy crew and investigators watching the screen let out a loud cheer as others hurried over to see. There they were in their bright orange casings, the size of shoe boxes, partially buried beneath sand, muck, and wreckage, which explained why their signals had gone undetected for several days.

When divers brought them up, the boxes were only slightly damaged. Agents on the *Grasp* quickly notified their superiors of the find on the secure-line walkie-talkies. Moments later, Kallstrom was on his way by helicopter from the Command Post in lower Manhattan. Robert Francis, just finishing dinner with a handful of reporters at the Smithtown Sheraton, rushed back to the Coast Guard station by car. The tapes had to be handled delicately. To preserve them out of seawater, they had to be placed quickly into coolers filled with freshwater. Meanwhile, a chain of custody had to be established should the FBI find grounds for a criminal prosecution. An agent named Bob Knapp was assigned to sit by them on their flight by Coast Guard Falcon aircraft to Washington's National Airport.

Among the NTSB investigators there at two in the morning to meet the plane was John Clark, a highly regarded aeronautical engineer whose close study of the radar tapes had helped prove that the mysterious blip on the tape from Kennedy Airport was not a missile but a computer glitch. The group drove straight to the NTSB's lab, where Dr. Bernard Loeb was waiting for them. The two orange boxes, designed not to crack or shatter during a crash, were then cut open to extricate the unit in each box that held the tape.

The tape felt damp, Clark noticed. That was good. If it had dried out, it might have started to crack. To wash off its sea salt, Clark dumped the tape into a small plastic tank of distilled water. Keeping it submerged, Clark then unwound the tape from its casing spool and threaded it onto a spool that could be slipped onto the NTSB's recorder, taking care not to twist it as he did. As the others watched, he removed the tape from the tank and manually guided it through the tape deck to extract the water from it. To dry it further, he patted it with gauze soaked in cleaning fluid. Now the investigators had a tape they could play back, duplicating it as they did.

The sound came through two sets of headphones. Clark and Loeb were the first to listen. The others stared at them, rapt, as they reacted to what they heard. Finally Loeb took his earphones off. "There is just a little noise at the end," he announced, "and then the tape just stops." The split-second sound, Dr. Loeb added, was almost identical to the one heard on the cockpit voice recorder of Pan Am Flight 103 when the bomb exploded in its cargo hold.

News of that final brief sound on Flight 800's recorders was made public by Kallstrom and Francis that evening. They urged the media not to jump to conclusions. Unless and until supporting evidence was found, there was no more reason to believe a bomb or missile had downed the plane than before the black boxes were found. Talking to reporters in a hallway after the news conference, Kallstrom added that he, for one, hoped the sound burst indicated a mechanical problem, not a crime. "The worst thing for our country is if this is a terrorist act," he said somberly. "As horrendous as it is, it would be better if this was an accident."

Privately, he suspected the sharp crack on the tapes did indicate a missile or bomb. But why TWA Flight 800? He had begun to wonder if TWA might be a symbol, to an Islamic terrorist, of American capitalism, like Coca-Cola or Chevrolet. Or had a shooter intended to hit another plane? Flight 800 had taken off only after an hour's delay and flown over Long Island at about the time a TWA flight bound for Tel Aviv was scheduled to pass that point. Perhaps the terrorists had meant to blow up the Tel Aviv flight. In fact, the Tel Aviv flight had been on the runway, about to take off, when word of Flight 800's crash reached the air-traffic control tower at Kennedy. At the FAA's urgent order, the flight was pulled back seconds before its scheduled takeoff. The flight's luggage and cargo were removed and checked. Only hours later did the flight, with its shaken passengers, finally leave Kennedy Airport.

At least Kallstrom had the list he had demanded, of every asset within a two-hundred-mile grid of the downed plane. Along with the assets he knew about—the P-3 Orion, the *Adak*, the USS *Normandy*; the Navy submarines *Albuquerque, Wyoming,* and *Trepang;* the Air National Guard Black Hawk HH-60 helicopter and C-130 cargo plane—were a KC-135 Air National Guard cargo plane flying at the time of the crash from McGuire Air Force Base to Mindenhall, England, and a C-141 cargo plane flying from Dover Air Force Base in Delaware to Vandenberg Air Base near Santa Barbara, California. The KC-135 had been twenty-five miles east of the crash site; the C-141 had been forty miles northwest. A third cargo plane, a KC-10, also had been in the air but even farther away. Clearly, none of these three newly disclosed military planes had flown near enough to Flight 800 to fire at it. None, more to the point, had had anything to fire.

In addition to knowing every asset in the area, Kallstrom had wanted a general understanding of how the military interacts in the air with commercial traffic. Through access granted by Admiral Flanagan, FBI agents learned that specific quadrants, each beginning twelve miles offshore and stretching seaward for hundreds of miles but extending upward from the ocean's surface to an altitude of only six thousand feet, are set aside for exclusive use by the Department of Defense. Otherwise, civilian air-traffic controllers oversee the airspace. Once a day, the FAA communicates with the military about the latter's plans, if any, for the quadrants over the next twenty-four hours. Mostly, the military uses this air highway to transport troops and supplies to ships at sea. Occasionally, it uses the areas for reconnaissance exercises. Deep within those areas are small restricted boxes of airspace where military ships are also permitted to conduct live firing exercises with small weapons or artillery. The restricted boxed areas are used primarily for naval artillery practice as gunners calibrate their five-inch-diameter guns. The military quadrants closest to the crash site, the agents learned, are known as Whiskey areas: W-105, W-106, and W-107. These, like other coastal quadrants, begin twelve miles offshore. But the live firing zone, or Pac area, closest to the crash site is eighty-six miles to the southeast. The area is hardly a secret: Commercial and pleasure boaters are constantly warned over marine radio and on nautical and aviation maps to stay clear of it.

On the day of the crash, the agents learned, the airspace defined by W-105, -106, and -107 was open to commercial air traffic. So was the Pac area. No military exercises, in other words, were scheduled to take place in those areas. In fact, no missiles had been fired in the Pac area for at least a two-year period preceding the Flight 800 explosion, the FBI verified through confidential communiqués and interviews. The Navy had originally planned to conduct a nonfiring training exercise in the Pac area on the morning of July 17, 1996, but the exercise had been canceled, with the FAA notified at 11:15 A.M. of the cancelation. In any event, Flight 800 had never come close to any of the Whiskey areas, let alone the Pac area. It had flown out on a common commercial sky highway known as "Bette" to pilots.

At the same time, Kallstrom had not yet ruled out friendly fire as a possibility, despite the assurances of General Shalikashvili, Admiral Flanagan, General Krulak, and others, as well as the ongoing investigation of military assets in the crash-site area. He believed the generals and admirals were men of enormous integrity, and he was sure that the officers he had sent his agents to interview were telling the truth, but perhaps they were unaware of a terrible mistake. Were officers down the chain of command engaging in some sort of cover-up?

———

As investigators analyzed the black boxes in Washington and the accumulating wreckage in the Calverton hangar, another major thrust of the investigation continued in a squad room on the twenty-third floor of the New York FBI headquarters. There, Liguori and Corrigan had sifted all weekend through piles of 302 reports and assigned agents to track new leads. As they finished one pile of reports, a larger pile would arrive. It was a losing battle. By Monday, the two could hardly be seen behind their desks.

That Monday, Liguori and Corrigan headed over to the TWA terminal at Kennedy Airport to see for themselves how security might have been breached. They wanted to know who had access to Flight 800, starting with the workers servicing the aircraft. They also wanted to learn everything they could about a Boeing 747 jumbo jetliner, especially the best hiding places for a bomb. A TWA security guard led them onto an empty 747 scheduled to depart that night, then left them alone to explore. When he was out of earshot, Liguori whistled softly. "This is some big bird." Neither agent had ever flown on a 747 before.

They wandered up and down the aisles, sitting in coach for a minute, then in first class, then in the upstairs lounge and adjoining cockpit. Corrigan took notes and drew some diagrams on a legal pad, marking "X" at various nooks that might house a bomb. The agents opened and closed overhead bins and looked beneath the seats and in the seat pockets. They checked the food galleys, lavatories, and flight attendants' jump seats. Corrigan found one hiding place, below the nose, large enough to house a family of four. After nearly two hours in a hot, stuffy, unair-conditioned plane, the agents were now prepared to understand the blueprints that Boeing had sent.

Meanwhile, agents assigned to the FBI's office at Kennedy Airport had arranged for airport and TWA employees to demonstrate what happens to an airplane when it arrives and before it departs. The mechanics, food-service workers, baggage handlers, cleaners, security, and others were asked to re-create every action they had taken, as far as they could remember, as they prepared Flight 800 for departure on July 17, 1996. If a worker had left his post to smoke a cigarette or call a girlfriend, the agents wanted to know about it. This wasn't about blame, the agents emphasized. It was about trying to learn the truth.

A bit sheepishly, the fuelers unscrewed the caps covering the wing tanks, yanked long hoses from large spools on the fuel-pumper trucks, and inserted the nozzles as if they were actually fueling the plane. One of the fuelers confessed that on the night of the crash, he had filled one of the tanks of Flight 800, finished his shift soon after, then taken the Van Wyck Expressway home.

En route, he'd heard the first reports of the crash on his Port Authority radio and felt almost paralyzed with guilt and fear. Had he done something wrong? Was it his fault that 230 people had just gone down in the Atlantic Ocean? Sweating, he drove back to Kennedy, punched in at his station, and went out to his fuel truck to see if there was something wrong with the Jet-A fuel in its tank—perhaps some water had gotten into the plane's fuel lines—but he saw there were no bubbles to indicate the presence of even the slightest droplets of condensation.

As he was finishing that test, barely more than an hour after the crash, FBI agents sent by Pickard and Kallstrom had arrived at the hangar. They questioned the fueler and other workers, and then ordered the fuel truck impounded so that it could be tested for contamination or sabotage. The fueler stayed by his truck before it was taken away, going over in his mind every step he'd taken to fill the tanks of Flight 800. No, he had concluded shakily, he did everything right, and yet the plane had still gone down. Relieved but still miserable, he drove home.

Another fueler reported that on at least three occasions beginning on July 9, he had noticed a fuel-flap cover missing on N93119—the plane that would be Flight 800 on July 17. More intriguing, TWA had ordered fuelers to fill two of the plane's four reserve tanks with 1,000 less pounds than usual: 2,400 pounds in each tank, rather than 3,400. These reserve tanks were tiny compared to the plane's three main tanks, but the fueler suspected that TWA had filled the reserves with less fuel to avoid visual detection of a serious leak in one of them. He himself had felt a few drops of fuel on the back of his neck from the reserve tank of this same plane earlier in the day, before it went to Greece. Since Jet-A fuel stings the skin, he was sure that what landed on his neck had not been water. The leak would have been in the upper part of a reserve tank, the fueler theorized, so that filling the tank only partway would keep the fuel from seeping out. But a reserve tank might have leaked nonetheless, and this may have been the fuel that caught fire and led to the explosion.

All this was noted and reviewed at the Command Post by agents who forwarded the information immediately to the safety board investigators. Meanwhile, Corrigan and Liguori watched as the food-service staff lifted the passengers' meals by hydraulic elevator to the jet's forward galley. They accompanied the contract employee who changed the movie video that night—the one who had seen the suspicious-looking "Middle Eastern type" who looked for his mother-in-law's reading glasses. They followed the cargo and luggage loaders, and the United States Postal Service workers, who had dropped off a large duffel of mail. They watched TWA employees at Gate 27, who removed stubs from the tickets as passengers filed into the jetway. Finally, a pilot reconstructed Captain Kevorkian's entire routine, step by step, prior to takeoff.

Corrigan and Liguori then stood at an airport entry gate watching TWA employees arrive for their workday. Unaware that they were being observed, the employees swiped their plastic identification cards through a magnetic slot that unlocked the heavy door leading to their work area. A blaring alarm would sound, the agents had been told, if anyone tried to tamper with the door or open it without an authorized swipe card.

But the agents noticed that not every worker used his card. A worker might hold the door open for someone who came after him. There was no electronic control on how many people could walk through on one "swipe." This bothered the agents. There would be no evidence, not even a scribbled entry in a visitors' log, to indicate that an unauthorized person had entered the most secure area of Kennedy Airport. If a familiar but unauthorized visitor could enter, perhaps the task force's latest suspect was the terrorist they sought.

The tip had come two days after the crash, when an anonymous caller phoned the U.S. embassy in Athens and suggested that an Egyptian who worked for TWA and had access to the aircraft might have planted a bomb on Flight 800. Task force investigators learned that the Egyptian had worked as a mechanic for TWA for thirteen years. He was single, in his thirties, and a Muslim who had attended the same Brooklyn mosque as several followers of Sheik Omar Abdel-Rahman. His coworkers had told agents that he was angry and arrogant.

The agents chose not to contact the worker himself. After all, if he had a role in the bombing and thought he had gotten away with it, he might lead the task force to his fellow plotters. Nor did the agents tell any of the Egyptian's TWA coworkers that they considered him a suspect. The last thing they needed was to create the impression that the FBI suspected all devout Muslims of terrorism. Instead, they began a quiet investigation. They examined his background, learned what he did on his days off, who his friends were, even that he had rented a video days before the crash. The agents watched the movie video for possible clues. If he hadn't planted a bomb himself, perhaps he had given access to the plane to a confederate. The FBI ran credit-card inquiries, looked into his background, and put him under surveillance. The Egyptian suspect had no idea that he was being monitored.

By the time Corrigan and Liguori completed their airport reenactment, they believed that as many as 250 people might have come in contact with the plane before it took off. The assessment stunned Herman and Pickard, who assumed the total would be a dozen or fewer. The task of investigating all the flight personnel was monumental. No less disconcerting was the reaction of the NTSB in Washington, which waved off the aberrations spotted by the agents as routine. Leaking fuel from a reserve tank? Happened all the time; it was clearly a matter of no consequence on Flight 800. Missing fuel-tank caps? Not a problem. To Corrigan, the NTSB's apparent lack of concern reminded him of his own reaction when his wife reported that the car sounded not quite right. "It's fine, don't worry about it," Corrigan would say impatiently. What does my wife know about cars? But the next day, the car would break down.

As Liguori and Corrigan were conducting their study of workers and security, other Terrorism Task Force investigators examined the call records of every pay telephone in the vicinity of Gate 27 from the time Flight 881 arrived from Greece until an hour after it departed as Flight 800. Perhaps a terrorist was watching the gate to be sure the plane flew as scheduled and called a co-conspirator to make his report. Or perhaps the co-conspirator was sitting in a boat off Long Island, readying his missile. The numbers called from those telephones were checked against FBI databases of known or suspected terrorists. Calls to Long Island and to cell phones were also checked out.

By the end of that first week after the crash, the agents were familiar figures at the TWA terminal, but for all the hours they were putting in, their only progress was in eliminating leads. Moreover, the investigators were still unsure whether the crash was even a crime, which meant that they had to look in several directions at once: disgruntled employees, nooks where a bomb could be hidden, various missile types.

After a day at Kennedy Airport, Corrigan got into the car with his partner for the drive back to lower Manhattan.

"I think it was a bomb. What do you think?" Liguori asked.

"I don't know. Could be a missile," Corrigan said.

"Great," Liguori said. "Just great."

In the absence of a strong clue from Kennedy, the agents were counting on NTSB investigators to find something in the black boxes. Their emergence from the sea late on Wednesday, July 24, had also provided the media with another dramatic photo-op, and expectations that the story on the definitive cause of the crash would be wrapped up, with a dramatic climax, perhaps by the end of the week. Already, the black boxes had acquired political ramifications as well.

That Wednesday, the families held a news conference outside the Ramada Inn at Kennedy. Bluntly and bitterly, they criticized government officials for treating them like children. They said they were angry at the slow pace of the investigation and lack of communication. They also complained that despite the recovery of 114 bodies, including three that day, the investigators' priority was raising wreckage. "We don't care about the black boxes," said Max Dadi, brother of the French country guitarist Marcel Dadi. "We don't care who did this. I just want my brother's body back."

Joe Lychner added that his wife and daughter Katie had been recovered, but he was still waiting for the body of his ten-year-old daughter, Shannon. He said he resented the sanitized briefings officials were giving the families. "We've lost everything," Lychner said. "They don't need to spare our feelings." Moved by the families' outcry and alarmed by the slow rate at which bodies were being found, President Clinton decided after viewing a newscast of the families to fly up to see them.

Meanwhile, work was going faster at Dr. Wetli's Suffolk County morgue—work that strained the nerves of the FBI agents assigned there. The morgue workers made X rays and performed autopsies; the FBI agents searched the bodies for fragments of a bomb or missile. It was grueling work.

Also studying the bodies was Dr. Dennis Shanahan, a consultant for the NTSB, who arrived at the morgue four days after the crash to see if the injuries of the passengers might offer clues to a mechanical cause of the crash. Shanahan was a pilot, physician, surgeon, and engineer. For most of his twenty-six years in the Army, he had conducted aircraft-accident investigations and research to learn how to prevent future injuries. At the time of the Flight 800 explosion, he had been serving as commanding officer of the U.S. Army Air Medical Research Laboratory at Fort Rucker, Alabama.

Recognizing his expertise, Kallstrom soon hired Shanahan to help the FBI agents at the morgue determine if the victims' bodies showed evidence of a bomb or missile. Shanahan began by correlating victims' injuries and causes of death with aircraft cabin and structural damage. He was not surprised to learn that 99 bodies had been found floating on the surface of the ocean after the explosion; with the nose having broken off, the fuselage would have spilled many of those bodies out. What interested Shanahan more was that 45 of those bodies had occupied seats in rows 17 through 28, directly above the center fuel tank, which corroborated the emerging theory at Calverton that the center fuel tank had exploded. As it did—if it did—many of the passengers, by now unconscious or dead, would have been sucked down through the blown-open fuselage.

Some of the floating bodies had serious burns, but these appeared to be the result of fires on the water's surface. Why the bodies in rows 17 through 28 had not incurred bad burns from the pressurized center fuel tank explosion as well was, for the moment, a mystery.

Most significant, none of the bodies Shanahan was examining showed the fragmentation that would have resulted from an explosive. An explosive would have left powder, discoloration, and material embedded in the bodies. But there was none.

————

President Clinton had been scheduled to fly to Atlanta on Thursday to make an appearance at the Olympics. Instead, he delayed that trip and flew to Kennedy to meet with the families. He also wanted to get a personal report on the investigation from its leaders.

Kallstrom and Francis arrived about forty-five minutes before the president at the Port Authority conference room designated for the meeting. Secretary of Transportation Federico Peña; members of the National Security Council; two assistant attorneys general from the Justice Department; and Kitty Higgins, the White House liaison with the FBI and NTSB had already taken their seats at the room's horseshoe-shaped table. The president of TWA, Jeffrey Erickson, was also on hand, seemingly in shock.

Clinton, accompanied by the first lady, walked in and greeted each person in the room. It was the first time Kallstrom had met him.

Francis, casually dressed, without a necktie even for this meeting with the president, spoke first about what the NTSB had learned from the black boxes. The previous night, the safety board's Clark and Loeb had begun to create a computerized image of the recordings, which they could enhance, slow down, and spread out on a computer screen. They had compared them to other sound images gleaned from the black boxes of prior plane crashes. The human ear cannot distinguish between the sound of an explosion from a bomb and a fuel-air explosion, Francis explained, but investigators can see the difference on a computer screen. The digitized sound of a bomb produces a sharp spike, while a fuel-air explosion occurs more slowly and presents a sloping line.

The brief sound—more like a click than a loud crack—was indeed like the one heard on the cockpit voice recorder of Pan Am Flight 103, when a plastic explosive ripped through the plane's forward cargo container over Lockerbie. The click heard on Pan Am Flight 103, investigators concluded, was the sound of the bomb exploding. On an oscilloscope, the Lockerbie click produced a sharp spike, indicating a high-frequency explosion. The click from Flight 800's recorder caused a spike, too. Almost certainly, the spike meant an explosion, but whether the explosion was high-frequency—i.e., the result of a bomb or missile—or lower-frequency, suggesting a fuel-air explosion, was so far impossible to tell, especially with a new generation of plastic explosives that might cause a different spike. Moreover, the spike would be affected by where the explosion occurred on the plane, relative to the location of the recorder's microphone. For all the computers and oscilloscopes at their command, the difference in spikes was so subtle and affected by so many variables as to be indecipherable.

To NTSB investigators, the strongest similarity between the Lockerbie and Flight 800 voice recorders was what *wasn't* heard: any indication from the cockpit crew before the explosion that there was a problem. With almost any mechanical problem, from engine failure to fire, a pilot would have had time, at least, to shout "Mayday." Even on the doomed ValuJet flight, when oxygen canisters had exploded in the cargo hold, the pilots had time to react. Instead, on Flight 800, the cockpit voice recorder revealed routine conversation—and then that split-second burst of sound, after which the tape went dead.

A further indication of a bomb or missile was that the other black box—the flight-data recorder—showed that no instruments malfunctioned before the tape went dead. It did show, however, that many electrically powered devices stopped at almost exactly the same instant, highly unusual if the cause had been mechanical. In fact, the NTSB would determine that both recorders went silent within a quarter second of each other. Later, they would learn that the captain's clock displayed 0031.30; the first officer's clock displayed 0031.20. Since each clock is set independently and powered by a battery in the cockpit, this was further proof that all electrical systems had stopped virtually at the same instant. Only a catastrophic event would have cut off the voice recorder and flight-data recorder in less than a split second.

So a bomb or missile explosion was likely but hardly certain, and so far, the radar maps the NTSB had studied from stations as far-ranging as Nashua, New Hampshire, and Norfolk, Virginia, added nothing to the picture. As everyone in the room was by now aware, the anomaly on the Kennedy Airport radar tape from the night of the crash had turned out to be the computer glitch that the FAA had suspected it was, a failure of the computers' software. The proof was that none of the other tapes showed such a glitch; it was remotely possible that a small Stinger missile could have failed to show up on radar as they made their four- and twelve-second sweeps. But it was almost inconceivable that a plane would not appear on all the radar. All the tapes were consistent in recording planes and helicopters that the NTSB knew were in the crash-site area— including the P-3 Orion that had initially raised Kallstrom's suspicions.

When Francis had concluded his remarks, Kallstrom told the president what the FBI had done in pursuit of the missile and bomb theories. He talked about the 270 eyewitnesses whose accounts had been recorded; he said witnesses were still coming forward and that they were all being taken very seriously.

The president wanted to know what the witnesses had seen.

"Some people saw things ascending," Kallstrom explained. "Others saw them descend or go across the sky. It's too early, Mr. President, to draw any conclusions from what they saw."

Clinton also asked about the families. He wanted everyone present to know he considered them a priority, and he wanted them to receive the remains of their loved ones as quickly as possible.

At the end of the meeting, Clinton shook hands with both Francis and Kallstrom, and with his back to everyone else offered a personal thanks. "You're doing a fabulous job in a tremendously stressful situation," he said. "Take care of yourselves. We're all behind you. If there is anything you need, just ask for it."

Press secretary Mike McCurry appeared at the entrance of the room to walk the president and the first lady out to their waiting motorcade. As the president was saying his other good-byes, McCurry sidled over to Kallstrom. "Take it from someone who does this all the time," said the press secretary, whose reputation for grace under pressure would be tested keenly in the months to come, "you're doing one hell of a job."

Outside, the president and first lady ran the inevitable gauntlet of reporters and television crews, but when they arrived by motorcade at the Ramada Inn, the media were kept outside. The Clintons were escorted to the same large ballroom where Kallstrom had managed to comfort most of the families the previous Saturday, but after five more days in the hotel with little news and 116 bodies still unrecovered, the families were more ragged than ever.

For Heidi Snow, whose engagement to French hockey star Michel Breistroff had begun and ended on the night of the crash, the meeting was an extraordinary event. To see the president up close was impressive enough; but then, when he shook her hand, he stunned her by greeting her by her first name. Perhaps someone told him her name, she thought. Heidi had brought a picture of Michel and showed it to him. Shyly, she asked him if he would like to have it. "I would love to," he said. Then he asked how she was doing. Heidi shrugged tearfully. Clinton hugged her and then held her hands.

The president's meeting with the families was scheduled to last forty-five minutes. It went on for hours. One by one, Clinton talked with each person in the room, about their lost sons and daughters and husbands and wives. A story that especially touched him was the one told by a warm, vivacious woman named Ann Carven: Paula's mother and Jay's grandmother. Mrs. Carven gave the president a small photograph of Jay and said that not long before, her nine-year-old grandson had been chosen at school to appear in a television commercial for a local politician. He was to play a young Bill Clinton. Knowing no more than that, Jay's mother brought him to the studio and sat in the darkness behind the cameras as Jay was seated on a chair and given his lines, typed up on a page, to memorize. In the script, an unseen questioner asked, "How much is one hundred plus five hundred?"

The answer Jay was to read was "seven hundred."

"But that's not correct," Jay said, taken aback.

"Well, that's the point," the director said. "In the commercial, Bill Clinton is wrong. It's a Republican commercial."

"I won't say that," Jay declared. "I love the president." And with that, he walked off the set.

Later, Clinton repeated this story to his aides and to Mrs. Clinton, but it wasn't the only story he remembered from that day.

Joe Lychner planned to give the president a list of demands. The families wanted Clinton to force the investigators to find all the bodies before worrying further about retrieving evidence, and they wanted the bodies identified faster. At the meeting, he was appalled to see many of the family members asking the president for autographs or posing for pictures with him, but the president's opening remarks had been so effective, and his lingering presence so impressive, that Lychner kept his list in his pocket. He assumed the president would do what he could; this was not, perhaps, a time for petitions.

Gary Hettler waited among a group of family members for the president to make his way over. Jackie, his wife, had gone back to Pennsylvania for the day to be with Pam Karschner at Amanda's funeral. "My son was planning to vote for you in November," Hettler told Clinton. "It would have been his first vote."

While the president spoke with the families, the first lady met in a nearby room with many of the hundreds of volunteers—from the Red Cross and other organizations—who had been at the Coast Guard station in East Moriches. That meeting, too, went on far longer than scheduled. After some four hours, Richard Clarke, the president's national security advisor on terrorism, decided to leave for Washington without bidding the president and first lady good-bye. He went into a small room secured for White House staff to retrieve the attaché case he'd left there, and saw Mrs. Clinton alone, seated at a table, her eyes closed, praying.

At La Guardia Airport, Clarke found an unusually long line at the ticket counter, long enough to keep him from catching the next shuttle, and wondered if he should elbow his way to the front and explain who he was. Surely the ticket agents would let him board in the interest of national security. Instead, with a sigh, he waited his turn.

When he got to the front of the line, he demanded, "What's going on here?" The ticket agent told him that the president had just announced new security measures. "I am sorry, sir," she said, "but it's taking time to check photo IDs."

Clarke felt suddenly sheepish. He'd caused his own delay. He was the one who had written the new regulations, which not only required photo IDs but also forbade cars to park near airport terminals and called for all cargo to be inspected. All carry-on luggage was to be searched, too, and more random searches conducted.

Clarke fished around in his pocket for his photo ID, thinking, if a terrorist can't produce a fake ID he should try another line of work.

Finally, he found his White House identification badge. The ticket agent looked at Clarke with a bewildered expression. Clarke shrugged, then took his badge back and hurried aboard the shuttle.

Even as those measures were being put in place, other more expensive ways to beef up security were being drawn up in Washington and presented as a wish list to White House chief of staff Leon Panetta. "Looks good," Panetta said when the wish-list of each pertinent agency was submitted by Clarke at a staff meeting. "How much will it cost?" The measures would cost $1 billion, a lot even by Washington standards. Panetta absorbed the figure silently, then wrote it down on his yellow legal pad. "We'll do it as an emergency supplemental," he said. "We'll go to Congress next week." Within two weeks, Congress would appropriate $1.2 billion. The FBI would hire more agents and analysts to focus on terrorism. So would the CIA. A high-level group would be convened to make air-safety proposals—more bomb-sniffing dogs, more sophisticated machines to scan cargo and luggage, and better training for airport security personnel monitoring X-ray machines—and be given the money to implement them.

All these were tangible, lasting ways in which the crash of TWA Flight 800 would affect the country. The intangible ways would take longer to gauge but, in the end, seem just as indelible.

————

In Montoursville that Thursday, hundreds of people crowded into a church to mourn for Amanda Karschner, among the first of the sixteen teenagers and five adults from Montoursville to be buried. Ribbons of blue and gold, the colors of Montoursville High School, hung throughout the community, from lampposts, car antennas, and store windows.

Janet Christopher's funeral was held two days later at a white-trimmed brownstone church near her home.

Notice of the service had been sent to every FBI bureau and station in the world, along with a request from Director Louis Freeh for agents to assist the members of Janet Christopher's family traveling to the services from as far away as Hawaii. In a hotel in nearby Strasburg, the FBI reserved a floor of rooms. At Charlie's home, various agents trimmed the lawn, cleaned up the kitchen, and prepared food for guests after the service.

Charlie had arranged for the funeral to begin at 1:00 P.M., not a minute earlier or later: Janet had prized promptness. When he arrived in a limousine behind the hearse, he was stunned to find hundreds of federal agents in formation along the path leading to the church. Along with Janet's parents and four sisters, dozens of her fellow flight attendants were there in uniform. So was Charles's Boy Scout troop. Some six hundred people remained outside while another three hundred filled the pews.

Charlie faltered starting up the church steps as the reality of Janet's death hit him so sharply he could hardly breathe. He stood for a moment. His son reached back and took his hand. "Come on, Dad," Charles said gently. The two climbed the steps together.

The most poignant tribute came from Jim Kallstrom, who talked about how long he'd known Janet and Charlie, how much he'd admired her. He read something about how a ship leaves a port, growing slowly smaller and smaller as it nears the horizon, until it gradually disappears. But at the same time that it seems to be vanishing from its point of departure, it's growing larger and more vivid to someone on the opposite shore, where Janet was standing now.

Kallstrom then told the congregation about the Navy divers who found an American flag amid the wreckage and presented it to him in East Moriches a few days earlier, asking that it be presented to Charlie and his son. Carrying it still folded in a military triangle, he walked with it to the pew where the Christophers sat. When he stood in front of them, he raised the flag as a priest might raise a chalice and said softly, "This flag is still wet with the waters of the Atlantic off the coast of East Moriches, and still has the sand from the bottom where the plane came to rest." He held it above him as sand and glitter fell to the church floor.

"Thank you," Christopher said softly as he stood to receive the flag. In a spontaneous gesture, everyone in the church stood and applauded. Then, to "The Battle Hymn of the Republic," Janet's favorite, the crowd filed out of the church to form a procession that took ninety minutes to make the three-mile trip to the cemetery.

Later, Charlie could see that Kallstrom was restless to get back to Manhattan, two hours away.

"I want to help you find out who did this," Charlie said as he walked Kallstrom to his car. "If you decide you're going to drain that ocean, I'll be the first guy there with my pump."

"I know, I know," Kallstrom said. "You're the best."

Christopher hugged his boss hard. "So are you."

———

Kallstrom drove alone back to New York, trying in the silent car to piece new findings together in a way that made sense. His thoughts kept drifting to Janet Christopher and to the funeral arrangements being made for other victims. He pulled into the East Moriches Coast Guard station as the sun had nearly set, and walked down to the edge of the water. It was ten days since the plane had gone down, and still there was no known cause. He felt impelled by the victims' deaths to find the truth. But the bond he shared with Charlie Christopher—and, by extension, with Janet—haunted him especially. No one outside the FBI could appreciate what that bond meant, and how an agent would do anything, even put himself in the line of fire, to help a fellow agent. The other fraternity that felt as tightly knit was the Marine Corps, and so perhaps it was more than a chance meeting that had led Kallstrom, as a young Marine captain just home from Vietnam, to the FBI academy in Quantico, Virginia, in February 1970. One night at the bachelor officers' club at Camp Lejeune, Kallstrom had found himself sharing a couple of beers with a military-looking fellow in civilian dress. "What outfit are you in, anyway?" Kallstrom asked.

"My outfit's the FBI," the man said. He was, as it happened, one of two agents in the FBI's Jacksonville bureau. The agent told Kallstrom that the FBI had decided to hire a thousand agents with money from an anticrime bill recently passed by Congress. Applying to the FBI had never entered Kallstrom's mind, but by the end of the evening, he was intrigued. The more the agent talked about it, the more the FBI seemed like the Marines without the uniform.

During the three-month program at the FBI academy, Kallstrom had weathered vigorous physical training (a cakewalk compared to the Marines' Hill Trail), along with endless lessons about the Constitution, federal laws, and the jurisdiction of the FBI. He became expert in handguns, and was issued a Smith & Wesson .38 revolver. Kallstrom would wear it every day of the TWA Flight 800 investigation, strapped to his waist or lower leg. He learned, too, that the bond among FBI agents was as strong as that among Marines.

After a short stint in Baltimore, Kallstrom had been transferred to New York: the FBI's biggest and most exciting office, where organized crime was often the top priority. There, Kallstrom came to figure out that surveillance was the way to loosen organized crime's grip on society.

The challenge was to create smaller and more sophisticated listening devices—and to work up a crack team of surveillance agents who kept pressure on the same Mafia targets, crime after crime, year after year, until they assembled enough evidence to arrest them. For that, a new head of the New York office proved crucial. Neil Welch had headed divisions in Buffalo, Detroit, and Philadelphia. In each, he had left behind a Special Operations Bureau dedicated to surveillance of organized crime. One day soon after his arrival in New York in 1978, he had summoned Kallstrom to his office, told him to sit down, and proceeded to ignore him, opening a newspaper in front of his face and reading it intently. Kallstrom fidgeted in his chair for several moments, then spoke up. "Excuse me, Mr. Welch," he said. "You called me up here. I thought you wanted me for something. If you don't, I've got a lot of things to do."

Welch put down his newspaper, leaned over his desk, and looked Kallstrom right in the eye. "Yes, I do want you for something," he said with a smile. "And I guess I've got the right guy."

That was the FBI at its best, Kallstrom felt: Welch was dedicated, but maverick enough to challenge the rules if changing them could make the bureau better. Welch wanted a strong leader to head his new Special Operations Bureau, and Kallstrom had passed his "newspaper test." Kallstrom and the crew he assembled dealt New York's five Cosa Nostra families devastating blows in the 1980s—planting tiny microphones and cameras where no one had ever dared—and, in doing so, helped make Kallstrom's big reputation. Among agents on that special team working for him, the bond was stronger, and more intense, than any of its agents could have expressed in words. One of those agents had been Charlie Christopher.

Now Charlie needed Kallstrom's help. To his profound frustration, Kallstrom wasn't sure how to provide it.

CHAPTER 9

WITH HIM ALL THE WAY

"**H**ey, boss, guess what?" Joe Cantamessa exclaimed from a phone at the FBI's command trailer in East Moriches. "They found the eyes."

In the days after the crash, Kallstrom had wondered if the cooler of corneas hand-carried into the cockpit of Flight 800 ninety minutes before takeoff had contained a bomb. Apparently, no one had put the cooler through a metal detector or X-ray machine. No one had even opened it. Amid the array of security precautions that airports had learned to take, lifeguard cargo was exempt on the naive assumption that medical cargo must be benign. Even Kallstrom could not imagine an eye surgeon or nurse plotting to bomb a plane, but a terrorist might have intercepted the container en route to Flight 800. A cockpit explosion would almost certainly kill the crew, or at least destroy the controls. It would also explain why the pilots sent no distress signal, why the black-box recordings cut off so abruptly, and why the nose of the plane had separated from the fuselage.

"What does it look like?" Kallstrom demanded. He was at his desk at 26 Federal Plaza.

"Jim, I gotta tell you, it's hardly damaged," Cantamessa said ruefully. "It's unbelievable. The lid cracked and pushed in a bit, but that's about it."

"Are you sure it's the right container?" Pickard asked from an extension line.

"Yeah," Cantamessa said. "You faxed me the picture, and I know exactly what we're looking for."

Kallstrom grimaced. "Are you looking at it right now?" he asked.

"I'm standing in front of it. As I talk to you I am staring right at it," Cantamessa said. "It's not a suspect piece."

Eight days after the crash, the container was only the latest in a lengthening list of discarded hunches. One of the earliest had been the shipment of HIV-infected blood intended for the Viral Oncology Research Laboratory in Paris. Like the corneas, the blood had arrived on board in a cooler as lifeguard cargo, exempt from security checks. Unlike the corneas, the blood had been placed in the rear cargo hold. In the first hours after the crash, fears of free-floating vials of contaminated blood had led the Coast Guard to warn boat volunteers over the marine radio, but the entire Styrofoam container had been found floating before dawn, well-marked and only slightly damaged, and had been hauled in by an anonymous volunteer.

At the Command Post in lower Manhattan, agents were still checking out the sources and destinations of other commercial cargo on Flight 800, then sending more 302 reports to Corrigan and Liguori, who prioritized leads and dispatched agents to track them down. Was there anything suspicious about that shipment of live turtles? Or the bowling-alley parts, the denim jeans, the cash registers? So far, the answer was no. Other agents were checking carry-on passenger luggage. So far, nothing had turned up.

Physical evidence was everything—but as of July 25, more than 95 percent of it still lay 120 feet deep. To help in the salvage operation, Captain McCord had directed the *Grasp* and *Grapple* to bring along various kinds of sonar. With the side-scan sonar already in use by the crew of the *Rude*, the *Grasp* and the *Grapple* would drag a yellow, torpedo-like device, about eight feet long, along the seafloor. At first it would be used to map the debris fields. Then it assisted in finding wreckage pieces. Its high-resolution sonar could detect hard surfaces—metal in particular—and supply a "paper trace" to record the contours of its "hits" as spikes on an electronic graph. To detect bodies, McCord ordered up laser-line scanners—similar in shape and application to side-scan sonar—as well as a number of small underwater robots called ROVs (remote-operated vehicles). Cameras aboard the ROVs could relay to crewmen on board the *Grasp* and *Grapple* on monitors what the ROVs were seeing as the lights played over the ocean floor. The robots, operated by crewmen on deck, had arms to retrieve small pieces of debris weighing up to fifteen pounds, which they put into buckets that were then pulled up to the surface. McCord had also brought up from Norfolk the *Deep Drone*, a vastly larger and more sophisticated ROV about the size of a minivan that could retrieve two-hundred-pound pieces as it scanned for bodies and assisted the divers.

That Thursday, eight days after the crash, ROV sonar located two of the plane's four engines, each thirteen feet long and weighing 8,800 pounds. To divers, the engines seemed to be intact though scorched, and crushed in spots from hitting the water. Nothing seemed to have exploded.

By July 28, the Navy's second salvage ship, the *Grapple*, arrived and anchored right over Debris Field #2, where the front of the plane had come to rest. One of the first objects lifted in that wreckage area was the plane's nose landing gear, which was so mangled that one investigator told a couple of reporters that it appeared to have been hit by a bomb. Francis batted down the idea. "It looks to me like it was in a big accident," he said at a news conference.

Nonetheless, some investigators would continue to suspect a bomb had been affixed to the plane's landing gear and pulled up into the nose-wheel well after takeoff. When the two nose-wheel tires came up still inflated, that theory would also die.

Though the cockpit continued to elude diving teams, investigators at Calverton noticed that other parts of the plane's forward section were coming from debris fields closer to Kennedy Airport, not from the field to the east where the bulk of the plane had come to rest. That was their first indication that the forward section might have detached in midair before the rest of the plane broke apart. What, other than a bomb or missile, could have made the nose do that? Lime-green pieces of the center fuel tank, also found in these western-most debris fields, provided further evidence that the tank had exploded. The pieces were scorched and melted, twisted and torn. Some had "petaled" out, as the investigators put it, like a flower coming into bloom. The air-conditioning units that sit underneath the center tank were found in the field closest to Kennedy Airport. Painstakingly, investigators recorded the latitude and longitude at which each piece had been found. With any luck, the relative positions of the pieces would reveal the sequence in which the explosion had occurred.

Once the side-scan sonar mapping in the days after the crash had revealed the three main fields of debris on the seafloor, pieces from each were color-coded: red for Debris Field #3, closest to Kennedy Airport, yellow for the central Debris Field #2, and green for the easternmost Debris Field #1. The notations would eventually fill fifteen three-inch-thick binders and be recorded in a vast computer database in a process that would grind on twenty-four hours a day, seven days a week, with two teams of investigators working twelve-hour shifts each.

As pieces from Debris Fields #3 and #2 came in, the speculation that week among agents as well as many Boeing engineers and NTSB investigators under Al Dickinson was that a bomb had been placed in the front cargo hold. The wreckage pieces didn't yet suggest that, but the front hold seemed the likeliest place. The Libyan terrorists who downed Pan Am Flight 103 had chosen the front cargo hold. So had the bombers of a French airliner over Niger, Africa, in September 1989 that killed all 171 people aboard. But no hard evidence of a bomb on Flight 800 had yet been found. In his daily news conferences, Kall-strom emphasized that no indications of a crime had been found and at the same time refused to rule out that a bomb or missile *may* have downed the plane. It was a delicate distinction not always observed by a press—and pub-lic—eager for answers.

Kallstrom, perhaps more than any of his senior agents, was sensitive to the other balance that had to be kept in the FBI's public pronouncements—

between the search for evidence and the effort to find the remaining bodies. One was vital to the nation's security, the other more important to a very large group of grieving family members. The divers were essential to both.

From the beginning, Kallstrom had understood he depended on the Navy for the salvage operation. When Admiral Kristensen had arrived five days after the crash, Kallstrom had left all salvage decisions to him, gratified to find him so sensible and unpretentious. Still, Kallstrom was the one who had brought in divers from Suffolk, Nassau, New York State, and New York City police and fire departments, as well as his own FBI divers. And at least one FBI agent was stationed on each boat. Soon, even the Navy divers had begun looking to Kallstrom as their leader.

Many of the divers, for example, began the operation with single-tank scuba gear, which gave them only enough air to spend a few minutes of each dive on the seafloor, but Kallstrom got them double-tank units as well as computerized regulators to warn them when they were staying down too long. At East Moriches, he had a helicopter pad built big enough for the Navy's CH 46. If a diver was hurt below or suffering from the bends, the CH 46 could get him to a hospital emergency room in minutes. Repeatedly, Kallstrom and Cantamessa warned the divers to avoid risks.

Nonetheless, the divers faced an ordeal—especially on the *Grasp* and the *Grapple*, where they were allowed four hours of sleep in rotating shifts and spent the remaining twenty hours of each day either diving or preparing to go down again. The Navy divers were tired after their salvage operation in the Mediterranean. But with the devastated families in mind, they stayed on duty almost around the clock. Eventually, some spent a night or two ashore in local motels, but only on weeknights. On weekends, the motels needed the rooms for premium-paying summer guests.

By Tuesday, July 31, two weeks after the crash, 67 of the 126 bodies on the ocean floor had been brought up. All but 6 of the 171 bodies accounted for had been identified at Dr. Wetli's fully staffed Suffolk County morgue, aided by dental and fingerprint records assembled from nearly every victim's family. Wetli had also sought help from the Armed Services Institute of Pathology to use DNA testing, a process that also helped the FBI determine if anyone on the plane was not whom he or she had claimed to be. On this basis, the FBI could conclude that no one had boarded Flight 800 using a false name.

Joe Lychner's other daughter, Shannon, was found on July 28, eleven days after the crash and, as it happened, his wedding anniversary. He had the three bodies flown to Chicago to be buried in Pam's family plot. For Ron and Ann Dwyer, the vigil lasted ten days. When word came, they arranged to have Larkyn's body taken to the Adirondacks, where she had enjoyed her last days, and cremated in a service near the Dwyers' vacation house. And then there was Rance Hettler.

In the eight days since Jackie Hettler had approached Kallstrom after his meeting with the families at the Ramada Inn, two FBI agents had been dispatched to assist her and her family at the hotel, just as agents had been assigned to help Charlie Christopher. Kallstrom felt the bureau had lost one of its own: Rance had simply been too young to serve. Soon after Rance's body was identified, Kallstrom invited the Hettlers to his Manhattan office, where he interrupted a meeting to greet them. Then he asked them upstairs to his private office.

There the Hettlers found Pickard and a dozen other agents assembled for a makeshift ceremony. Taped to the front of Kallstrom's computer, they saw the small picture of Rance that Jackie had given the FBI boss a week before. From his desk, Kallstrom pulled out an FBI baseball cap and slowly handed it to Rance's mother. Then he presented the Hettlers with what looked like a small black book. Inside was a gold badge with the blue FBI emblem, and official credentials for Rance, including a snapshot, making him an honorary agent of the FBI. Kallstrom told the Hettlers of the FBI tradition of framing the credentials of an agent who retires or who dies in the line of duty. The tradition, he said, would be observed in this case, too.

The following day, Rance was buried wearing the FBI hat.

———

On Friday, August 2, a huge find loomed on the sonar screen on the *Grapple*, positioned over Debris Field #2.

What the sonar screen showed was the curved windshield of the cockpit, which presumably lay near the plane's controls. For two days, divers combed the immediate area, until they located a web of twisted metal six feet high and eleven feet wide, entangled in endless strands of wiring. At first, they weren't sure what they had. Then they saw the body of Captain Kevorkian still strapped in his seat. Nearby, strapped into a jump seat, sat Richard Campbell, the plane's instructor–flight engineer. When the officers had been pried loose and raised to the surface in body bags, divers wrapped the cockpit with five-inch-wide nylon straps tied to the hook of an onboard crane, which raised the massive hulk in one slow maneuver. The assumption was that this wreckage might reveal why the plane's main electrical cables, leading to and from the cockpit, had been suddenly disabled, cutting off the black boxes located near the tail, and preventing the pilots from making a Mayday call after the explosion. The dials and controls might also suggest problems that had arisen before the explosion— Loeb and the safety board investigators were especially intrigued by the cockpit remark, minutes before the crash, about a "crazy fuel-flow indicator." The cockpit wreckage might also show whether a bomb had been placed within or near it.

Analysis of the cockpit controls would take weeks. Still, their retrieval was promising enough that FBI agents and bomb experts gathered on the docks at Shinnecock Inlet to await its arrival. Transported to Calverton by flatbed truck, the control instruments, amid a great tangle of wires, were hoisted up and into the hangar by a giant crane. Many of the investigators broke into applause at the achievement of hauling this mass of twisted and shredded metal, still dripping wet, off the ocean floor.

The cockpit with the pilot's seat dangling beneath it was suspended by the ceiling crane high above the floor and positioned for lowering. Then, as the technicians watched, a small, shining object fell from the wreckage and bounced onto the hangar floor. It was the captain's wings pin. Startled, the workers fell silent.

Pickard was present for this surreal spectacle and reported the cockpit's arrival immediately to Kallstrom, who was in his car heading to the Manhattan Command Post.

"What does it look like?" Kallstrom asked. "Does it look like a bomb was in there?"

"Jim, I can't even describe it," Pickard said. "It looks like jumbled-up wires, millions of miles of wires. It doesn't even come close to looking like a cockpit. It looks like a big plate of spaghetti."

"But does it look like a bomb was inside?" Kallstrom shouted.

"I don't know, Jim," Pickard said with a sigh.

"Well, what do the bomb techs say?"

"They don't know yet either."

When Pickard hung up, he thought Kallstrom must be saying to himself, "What a bunch of morons I have working for me."

By the end of the day, the technicians had pried apart the wiry mass and located the instrument panel. Many of the dials were knocked out of the panel and connected only by thin wiring. Yet they seemed undamaged. Their glass faces were still intact.

"Could these dials have survived if the bomb was in the cockpit?" Pickard asked one of the bomb technicians.

The technician shook his head. "An explosion would have blown the glass out all over the place," he said.

Like the corneas and the nose-wheel well, the cockpit yielded no immediate evidence of an explosion. But why the cables were severed and the dials not cracked, and why the pilots had no time to send a distress signal, no one could say.

On August 11, the last of four luggage bins was found on the ocean floor. The first three had shown no evidence of high-explosives damage. The fourth held last-minute luggage, including bags taken from the passenger cabin by flight attendants because they were too big to fit beneath a seat or in an overhead bin. Divers had been told to make its recovery a priority.

Pulled from the sea by crane, the last luggage bin hung in the air like a giant Dumpster, its door opened wide. As it was let down gently on the *Grapple*'s deck, FBI agents and safety board investigators could see that it had been ripped apart and assumed it had been damaged by a bomb blast. Steve Burmeister, the FBI's chief chemist, was up from Washington at the Calverton hangar that day and helicoptered over to East Moriches where he motored out to the *Grapple* in an inflatable raft. He examined the bin for surface "signatures"—blackening and darkening, for example—that might indicate a bomb. He found none. The bin was mangled, but its damage, he concluded, resulted from the crash, not a bomb.

Back at the hangar, Burmeister and other investigators returned glumly to their analysis of the center fuel tank, whose metal parts retrieved so far continued to indicate strongly that the explosion—whatever its cause—had occurred there. When a bomb explodes, its fragments or fibers tend to melt into adjacent metal. The investigators were looking for such evidence, though so far they had found none. Most bombs explode in all directions at once, creating a sphere of impact, so that metal surfaces within a 360-degree circumference will show recognizable patterns: cratering and pitting, microscopic streaking, as well as feathering and flowering. But there were no signs of this, either. A bomb would also leave particular soot patterns on metal. Yet for all the microscopes, jeweler's loupes, and magnifying glasses the investigators used to discern these signatures, they saw none.

At the same time, the experts were aware of a new generation of exotic explosive devices, such as shape bombs, that explode directionally, not spherically, so that they can be positioned to do the most possible damage. On Flight 800, a terrorist might have managed to wedge a shape bomb into his seat so that it pointed downward into the center fuel tank. These bombs, too, left certain kinds of pitting and cratering in the metal they disfigured, but their damage was confined to smaller areas of metal, possibly no wider than four inches, which would make the hunt more difficult. During the long, painstaking days at Calverton, metallurgists and explosives experts searched for these signs, too, wondering if some clever terrorist had created an entirely new kind of explosive, perhaps a liquid placed in fuel, whose "signature" would be even subtler—or undetectable.

Kallstrom appreciated what the experts were up against, but as the wreckage piled up, he decided he needed more specialists. If it were possible, he would have moved the entire FBI laboratory from Washington to Calverton. Instead, he asked Pickard to have Washington send up four more of its top explosives experts.

"No way," said the lab supervisor when Pickard called. "This is the first I've heard about it, and anyway they're needed here. We've got Khobar, the Unabomber, and Oakbomb." ("Oakbomb" was FBI vernacular for the Oklahoma City bombing.) "I can't spare these guys. You tell Kallstrom he's not running the FBI."

"Well, get ready for a call from Director Freeh's office," Pickard said, more bemused than irked.

A few minutes later, the lab supervisor called Pickard back. "Those agents Kallstrom had requested? They'll be on the six o'clock shuttle to New York."

Most of the workers in the hangar appreciated Kallstrom's commitment to the investigation—and to them. One notable exception was William Tobin, a veteran FBI metallurgist. To him, Kallstrom seemed overly aggressive and unwilling to accept his expert opinion. Tobin, a fellow ex-Marine, recognized Kallstrom's confident Marine stride, but felt Kallstrom lacked the scientific knowledge to justify it in this investigation. Tobin had worked thirty-five years in the FBI's criminal laboratory in Washington and had analyzed metal from hundreds of bomb blasts. He knew the damage a blast made, not just in its immediate vicinity but ten or twenty feet away. Though divers had salvaged only a small percentage of Flight 800's pieces so far, Tobin felt he'd seen enough to know that neither a bomb nor missile had downed the plane. He was certain that this midair explosion was the result of an accident, and the longer Kallstrom chose not to say so publicly, the more money and time he would be wasting on a needless criminal investigation.

Tobin restrained himself from approaching Kallstrom directly, but he complained frequently to Kenny Maxwell, the FBI's supervisor at Calverton, declaring that every piece of wreckage he saw confirmed his views. Then, in August, he was summoned to a meeting of investigators chaired by Kallstrom at 26 Federal Plaza. Tobin looked forward to it.

Sitting quietly among twenty or so seasoned investigators, Tobin listened to Kallstrom's overview of what the investigation had accomplished and what it needed to do. When Kallstrom invited comments, Tobin declared, "Mr. Kallstrom, it's quite clear that a missile did not take down this plane."

Kallstrom and the others were stunned. Kenny Maxwell grimaced. "And how do you know that, Tobin?" Kallstrom asked, with an edge that Pickard, Corrigan, and a few other close colleagues had learned to recognize as a danger sign.

"If there was evidence of a bomb or missile, we would have found it by now," Tobin said coolly. "We're just wasting our time if we keep studying the wreckage."

As the only FBI forensic metallurgist at Calverton, Tobin possessed an authority that no one in the room could challenge, but common sense suggested that a bomb or missile could have penetrated any part of the plane and caused only localized damage. With a mere 10 percent of the plane brought up, how could Tobin make such a judgment?

Kallstrom thought Tobin was looking for an easy way out. Perhaps he was a quitter who wanted to go home to Washington. "With ten percent of the plane up, how can you possibly give me that recommendation?" he said, now showing his anger. "That's preposterous."

Tobin continued, oblivious to the others' amazement. Finally, Kallstrom cut him off. "Tobin, let me ask you this. Just how many planes shot with missiles have you investigated in your life?"

"None."

"Then where do you get off telling me there is no missile," Kallstrom said. "What are you basing that on?"

"It's my expert opinion," Tobin said. "I know what I am talking about."

"I'm not in the business of speculation," Kallstrom stated. "I'm in the business of goddamn evidence. We cannot stop looking until we find the last piece of that plane. So go back out there and keep looking, understand?"

After the meeting, several agents approached Kallstrom independently to ask whether they could trust Tobin's judgment any longer. "The man obviously knows his technical stuff," Kallstrom told them. "Let's give him a chance to change his attitude."

The next day, Joe Cantamessa, Kallstrom's smooth-talking technical genius, irritated his boss, too, but unlike Tobin, he didn't do so deliberately.

When Kallstrom called from Washington to say he had been delayed at a briefing on Capitol Hill, Cantamessa was delighted to stand in for him at the news conference later that afternoon. The agent greeted the press with his usual cockiness, read the remarks Kallstrom had asked him to relay, then invited questions. He was surprised by how little the reporters knew about the procedures the FBI followed in testing for explosive residues. Earnestly, and in considerable detail, Cantamessa enlightened them, mentioning, as he did, that initial positive tests made by the field machines in the hangar on a few pieces had subsequently proven negative in Washington tests. For days, reporters had been trying to get such information, since a positive test would indicate a crime.

Afterward, Cantamessa sauntered over to the FBI's skilled spokesman, Joe Valiquette, who was a master at sound bites but whose reputation for revealing little or nothing to reporters had earned him the nickname Joey Leaks. To almost every press inquiry, Valiquette's reply was "The FBI does not discuss the status of any investigation, if in fact there is one going on." This kept misinformation from trickling out, though it did nothing to encourage the good feelings toward the FBI that Kallstrom was promoting.

"How'd it go?" Cantamessa asked.

"Go?" Valiquette echoed. "You talked about the evidence!"

Cantamessa looked dumbfounded. "But there is no evidence. The lab tests were all negative. There is no evidence to talk about."

Tight-lipped, Valiquette explained that test results, negative or positive, were part of the evidence, and evidence was never discussed, period. Moments later, Kallstrom called to ask Valiquette how the conference had turned out. "That's the last news conference Cantamessa does!" Kallstrom shouted. Word of Kallstrom's fury quickly filtered among the agents, and Cantamessa got the predictable deep freeze. Then in a few days, it was over, and the warmth returned.

Kallstrom himself had also suffered an embarrassment that day. He and FBI director Louis Freeh had gone together to catch a shuttle flight from New York to Washington for the congressional briefing on the crash. The ticket agent took Kallstrom's FBI identification without looking up. Then, recognizing the face in the photograph, she extended her arm.

"Thank you for all the work you've done," she gushed. "We're so proud of you. It's such an honor to meet you."

Kallstrom was caught off guard. "Oh, thank you," he mumbled.

As the other ticket agents abandoned their posts to shake his hand, too, Kallstrom blushed. Freeh stepped up to the counter. The ticket agent looked at Freeh's FBI photo ID.

"Oh, are you with him?" the ticket agent asked, indicating Kallstrom.

"Yeah, I'm with him," Freeh said with a grin. "I'm with him all the way."

———

As more and more pieces of the center fuel tank revealed scorching, burning, and twisting, the possibility that the tank had exploded seemed increasingly likely. That in itself amazed investigators: Center fuel tanks just don't explode, any more than 747s just fall out of the sky. But the evidence was strong enough that on August 7, Loeb and his safety board investigators decided to reconstruct the entire tank. It would take weeks, if not months, of continued dives to the ocean bottom to bring up all the wreckage associated with the tank, but this was at last a tangible goal. Whether or not it would prove what had downed Flight 800 was another question. Even if the center fuel tank *had* blown up, investigators would not necessarily know if its blast had been the initial one or a reaction to some other blast elsewhere on the plane. The reconstruction of the tank might show signs that a bomb or a missile set off the tank. If a mechanical malfunction had made the tank explode, the reconstruction almost certainly would show that, too.

As the tedious job began, Corrigan and Liguori drove out again to Kennedy Airport to learn about center fuel tanks on Boeing 747-100s. From under a parked plane, they looked up in awe at a huge metal rectangle, twenty-five by forty-five feet, about the size of a one-car garage. For their inspection, the tank was empty. They reached it by climbing a portable, hydraulic staircase to the front cargo hold, then walking into the tank through an open access door. A team of TWA workers showed them how the door was secured by nearly one hundred bolts.

"How long would it take to unscrew those bolts, put a bomb in, and screw them back again?" Corrigan asked.

"Inconceivable," the workers said.

"Let's give it a try," Liguori said.

It took five hours.

Flight 800 had started its last day at Kennedy, flew from Kennedy to Hellenikon Airport for a three-hour layover, and returned to Kennedy, where it sat from 5:00 to 8:00 P.M. before taxiing out to take off from runway 22-R. The chances that a terrorist could plant a bomb inside the center fuel tank during any of those layovers by unscrewing the one hundred bolts and screwing them back on—never mind how unlikely it would be that he could do this without being challenged—were, as the workers had said, inconceivable. Even a maintenance worker doing it for a terrorist friend would be observed.

"All right," Corrigan said when the job was done. "Now show us what happens when workers go to the tank for routine servicing."

To clean or repair the tanks, as the workers demonstrated, they first drain them completely of fuel. Even then, the lingering fumes force them to work in the tank with oxygen masks. One mechanic told Corrigan and Liguori that a few days before, he had entered a drained fuel tank without a mask. In less than a minute, he staggered and nearly vomited on the tarmac. For two days afterward, he told them, he had an excruciating headache. No one, he said, could survive in that tank much longer without an oxygen mask.

It seemed clear that a bomb could not have been planted inside the center fuel tank, but the agents knew the plane well enough by now to know that near the center fuel tank were various nooks into which a bomb might have been lodged so as to cause the tank to explode. Pointed downward from a seat in rows 19 through 30, a shape charge, designed to explode in a given direction, would have ripped directly into Flight 800's center fuel tank, but evidence of such an explosion would have to await the reconstruction at Calverton.

For the missile team working out of the twenty-fifth-floor war room at 26 Federal Plaza, the center fuel tank had also begun to gain significance. A terrorist might have targeted the center fuel tank with a heat-seeking, shoulder-launched missile or friendly fire from a U.S. warplane or ship might have hit it. Of the military assets that Kallstrom and the FBI now knew about from the Navy, the USS *Normandy* was not a likely suspect, since it was too far away from Flight 800 at the time of the crash to be within range of it. At the same time, the ship had a significant surface-to-air capability and needed to be checked out.

Corrigan learned that the *Normandy*, an Aegis combat cruiser, had been commissioned six years earlier and had already seen action. In December

1990, the ship had joined Allied forces in the Persian Gulf, making it the first U.S. warship since 1945 to see combat on her maiden cruise. During the Gulf War, the *Normandy* fired twenty-six Tomahawk cruise missiles. Five years later, it had launched another thirteen Tomahawks against hostile air-defense command and control sites in northern Bosnia-Herzegovina. Two days after the missile attack, a truce was signed.

On July 16, 1996, the *Normandy* had been loaded with ammunition at Earle, New Jersey, for a normal training exercise with other Navy ships in waters south of its home port in Norfolk, Virginia. The ship's logs indicated that at 9:02 A.M., the *Normandy* had departed the naval weapons station at Earle and headed toward Norfolk. When Flight 800 exploded on July 17 at 8:31 P.M., the ship was 181 miles southwest of the crash site, at latitude 37 degrees, 32.8 minutes north, longitude 74 degrees, 0.92 minutes west, off the Manasquan Inlet in New Jersey.

The FBI verified the precise location of the *Normandy* by military logs, radar maps, and satellite data. Pickard sent agents to the weapons station in Earle to get the serial numbers of all weapons that had been loaded aboard it. These were faxed over a secure line to the Manhattan Command Post. On the day he paid the *Normandy* a visit with special agent Kimberly Thompson, Corrigan carried those serial numbers and other confidential files in his briefcase.

Lying at rest at the naval base in Norfolk, the ship was even larger than Corrigan had imagined. Well over five hundred feet long, it had elaborate radar systems and missile silos. In the officers' quarters, the agents were introduced to an affable, stocky man in a crisp, tan uniform with a baseball cap that bore the name of the ship in gold lettering. Captain Frank Dimasi, forty-six, looked to Corrigan more like the commander of a detective squad than the captain of a large cruiser, but his casual manner belied his successful quarter-century career: Within a year, Dimasi would be promoted to the staff of the Joint Chiefs in Washington.

Dimasi told the agents that absolutely nothing was fired from the *Normandy* on the night of the crash: no missiles, no weapons of any kind. The captain said that a misfire from the *Normandy* was simply impossible. He had been aboard ship the night of July 17 and had heard or seen nothing unusual. A misfire, he emphasized, would have been very unusual. Not only the captain but every man and woman aboard would have heard what sounded like a freight train at full throttle. Besides, firing a missile required several officers and seamen working in concert to execute a complex series of steps. A drunken sailor firing a missile for fun, or a terrorist coming aboard, or a crew member making an honest mistake were impossible scenarios. Still, Dismasi understood that the agents had to see for themselves. His orders from Admiral Flanagan were to answer whatever questions they asked.

Over the next two days, Corrigan and Thompson interviewed Dimasi, his officers, and scores of enlisted personnel. The agents had free run of the ship and could buttonhole any one of the four hundred crew members as they made their rounds, but every report they heard about the night of July 17 was the same. No one had seen the crash—understandably, since they were 181 miles away—or anything in the sky besides stars. No one had noticed anything amiss on board. And no missiles, they all said, had been fired from the *Normandy* that night.

Corrigan wanted to get a feel for how hard it would be to keep a missile-firing secret or to cover up a firing if there had been one. He inspected the crew's bunks, dining areas, and workstations. He roamed the ship from top to bottom and studied the ship's navigation and communications systems. He and Thompson were briefed by Dimasi's weapons staff about the types of missiles that the ship carried. Corrigan already knew what he was about to hear, but he wanted to hear it from the crew all the same.

The *Normandy*, he and Thompson knew, could fire three kinds of missiles: the Tomahawk, the SM-2, and the ASROC, an antisubmarine rocket. From their study of the P-3 Orion and the three submarines in the crash-site area, the agents knew that Tomahawks could be discounted out of hand. Designed to be fired laterally, not from surface to air, the Tomahawk could reach a maximum height of 1,200 feet, and so could not have hit TWA Flight 800. Besides, the *Normandy* had carried no Tomahawks on its mid-July trip to Norfolk. The ASROC was a torpedo of devastating effectiveness—normally the *Normandy* carried thirty-six—but it was an underwater weapon. That left the SM-2, which was capable of taking out a plane.

Designed for use against missiles and aircraft as well as ships, the radar-guided SM-2 could reach an altitude of 90,000 feet at high speeds and be set to explode 30 feet away from its target, sending shrapnel-like continuous rods whirling into a plane's fuselage to inflict maximum damage. Once an SM-2 locked on to its target, there was no escape.

On its mid-July trip, the *Normandy* had had eight SM-2 missiles on board. Five were armed with proximity fuses and high explosives. The others were duds—training missiles without warheads. Unfortunately for the missile theory, the SM-2's range was between 45 and 90 miles, far short of the 181 miles that lay between the *Normandy* and Flight 800. Moreover, as the agents discovered, the SM-2 had none of the flarelike characteristics that so many eyewitnesses had observed: no bright white light or plume. Soon after launch, it shed its ignition source and was radar-guided. To an observer on the ground, as well as to the pilot of the targeted plane, the SM-2 was invisible.

Dimasi and his weapons officers explained that each of the missile types aboard the *Normandy* could be fired only after a series of complicated steps, safeguards, and cross-checks to prevent an accidental or unauthorized misfire. "You don't just hit a button and a missile goes off," Dimasi said. "It's not like,

'Oops, I pushed the wrong button.' " Even in the midst of battle, Dimasi said, "the double checks and triple checks are coordinated, to prevent a lone wolf from getting on board and launching these missiles."

To fire a missile, the captain and his weapons officer, standing in different locations, used induplicable keys—in tandem—to activate the missile mechanism. Then special computer codes had to be entered. At that point, two other crew members at the launching station entered their own classified identification numbers. Only then could the launching process begin. Before the missiles were actually launched, every crew member had to be notified. This was more than just protocol. The decks had to be cleared so that when a silo hatch opened on deck, no one was hurt.

As for the on-deck guns, they were .54 caliber, intended for use primarily against ships or low-flying aircraft targets. Fired laterally, they had a range of more than twelve nautical miles. When the guns were aimed upward, in antiaircraft mode, their range diminished to four nautical miles. Had the *Normandy* been situated directly under Flight 800, that range would have seemed significant. At a distance of 181 miles, it excluded another possibility.

Corrigan and Thompson climbed down into the missile silos to see for themselves. With flashlights, they checked the serial numbers on the missiles and compared them to the numbers on their clipboarded lists. Both agents were struck by the great size of the missiles they saw: an SM-2, for example, was 14 feet long and weighed more than 1,300 pounds. Each missile was girded in a lead seal that was removed only when the missile was set to be fired. Every seal on every missile aboard the *Normandy* was intact.

On deck, Corrigan and Thompson inspected each of the ship's 122 vertical missile launch bays: 61 at the stern, 61 at the bow. They found all the bays empty, consistent with inventory records. They also inspected the silos of the eight antiship harpoon missiles, launched from a pad at the rear of the ship, and studied the torpedo chutes. They even inspected two Gatling guns that could fire about 1,000 rounds per minute at a range of about 10 miles. Then they compared the serial numbers of the SM-2s and other weaponry with their documents from the weapons station at Earle, to be sure that all the numbers matched. All the serial numbers matched. Nothing was expended; nothing was missing.

Corrigan and Thompson then asked the captain for the ship's logs, as well as a list of any crew members who had been transferred from the *Normandy* since mid-July, to make sure no one had been shipped off to be kept quiet. This last was an explicit direction from Kallstrom.

The agents studied log entries back to the launching of missiles in Bosnia in September 1995. They compared them with log entries for the day of the Flight 800 explosion, to see if entries for missile-firing might have been entered and then erased. There was no sign of that. Indeed, nothing in the log for weeks prior to and following July 17, 1996, appeared unusual.

To Corrigan, one of the most convincing arguments against the *Normandy*'s involvement in the Flight 800 crash came not from his study of weapons systems and security codes but from a human happenstance. On July 17, in addition to its crew, the *Normandy* carried two children and four adult civilians, family members of the crew who were allowed on board as guests of the captain. Corrigan doubted that the captain would have allowed the crew's family on board on the night of a secret missile test. Yeah right, he thought, I can just hear him saying: Hey, bring the kids tonight for the big show.

Corrigan could tell that the crew thought the FBI's probe of their ship was an insult to their loyalty and patriotism. Gently, the agents tried to explain that every possibility had to be covered, no matter how remote. One might unlock the mystery: In the meantime, a thousand others would prove dead ends. By the time they left, Corrigan and Thompson knew the *Normandy* was one of those dead ends.

As Pickard and the missile team pursued the possibility of friendly fire, they also looked at the many ways a missile could have been launched by an enemy state or terrorist cell.

The experts at China Lake and Wright Patterson Air Force Base were more accustomed to studying the effects of missiles on fighter jets, and although there was plenty of data on what damage missiles do to the fuselage of a fighter jet, experts were not sure if a missile would leave a similar signature on a jumbo jetliner. They had nothing with which to compare the fuselage of Flight 800. But if the history of missile attacks on commercial jets was shorter, it was no more sanguine. Between 1978 and 1993, missiles had downed twenty-five commercial planes worldwide. Though some of these planes had managed to make emergency landings, many had not, and more than six hundred people, in all, had died. Most of these incidents had occurred in third-world countries or in breakaway states of the Soviet Union, where no follow-up investigations had been conducted and no evidence recovered or stored, so they were of almost no help in clarifying whether a missile had downed Flight 800.

The team's best bet, the experts advised, was to study the kinds of missiles known to exist—both in government hands and on the black market—and try to correlate their capacities to the known facts of the crash. In essence, there were three kinds: the ICBM, the SM-2, and the MANPAD, or shoulder-launched missile, of which the Stinger was an example. The ICBM had been eliminated right off: As all experts assured the team, an ICBM would have destroyed most of Long Island along with the plane. The SM-2, as Corrigan had confirmed for himself, was designed to be fired from the silo of a warship like the *Normandy*, not from a fighter plane, and certainly not from a terrorist's fishing trawler. As all commercial, military, and satellite radar had confirmed, no warship of the necessary size, either from the United States or any other power, had been situated remotely within the SM-2's ninety-mile maximum range on the night of July 17.

That left the shoulder-launched MANPADs, the likeliest suspects from the first. Most worrisomely, MANPADs of almost every kind were heat-seeking missiles, designed to strike a plane's engines. Since a 747 generates sixteen times the heat of a fighter jet, and moves much more slowly, it would be a much easier MANPAD target, theoretically. The hottest spot on a 747, however, might not be the engines that a MANPAD was meant to hit. It might be the area just beneath its center fuel tank, particularly if the air-conditioning units that sit underneath the tank had been running long enough to cook the vapors inside the tank, making them ripe for a spark or auto-ignition.

Specifically, the FBI's missile team had determined that if the missile launcher was standing west of the plane and shot at its rear, a heat-seeking missile would have targeted one of the plane's four engines—a less likely prospect, given the moderate damage to the two engines so far recovered. But if a shooter had stood in a boat east of the plane, the same heat-seeking missile might instead have targeted the center fuel tank, especially since Flight 800 was in a climb with its underbelly exposed when the plane blew up.

As a precaution, the FBI determined that no U.S. armed forces were conducting clandestine exercises with Stingers or any other MANPADs. Elite fighting units like the U.S. Navy Seals, the U.S. Army's Delta Force, and the U.S. Marines' Reconnaissance Unit used MANPADs in certain war environments and might conceivably have employed them in training exercises. All of these units were contacted; all denied having conducted any exercises on Long Island or off its coast on the night of July 17. Furthermore, no MANPADs were fired by any of these units anywhere within the United States on the night of the crash. Nonetheless, agents refused to take the denials at face value and, with Kallstrom opening the door through General Krulak and the other members of the Joint Chiefs, interviewed all command levels; scrutinized training logs, deployment, and other background information; then reinterviewed the units until they were satisfied that no MANPAD could possibly have been fired by U.S. forces, and that no cover-up of such a launching could have occurred.

No such checks, of course, could be made of terrorist cells or hostile foreign powers.

At the Command Post, around midnight when the phones died down, Kallstrom and Pickard would talk over the investigation and the latest missile files from the experts at the Navy's China Lake, the Army's Redstone Arsenal, or Wright Patterson Air Force Base and reach the same conclusions. A MANPAD did have the range to hit a plane 13,700 feet in the air if fired from directly below, and the list of possible sources for such a weapon was as long as they cared to make it. Since the breakup of the Soviet Union, MANPADs had fallen into the hands of nationalist rebels, international terrorists, even major-league narcotics traffickers. The arsenals of China, Poland, and Czechoslovakia, among others, had also been vulnerable to theft in the last several years, and their weapons had landed on the black market in the Middle East.

Still, even for a missile fired from a boat directly beneath it, the plane had been high enough to present a formidable challenge. Kallstrom, a sharpshooter in the Marines and the FBI, made his own analogy to a handgun's range. At twenty yards, a crack marksman had a fair chance of hitting his target; at seventy-five yards, his chances lessened considerably, though a bullet theoretically could still hit the target. Firing a missile—even a heat-seeking missile—at Flight 800 from a tripod or shoulder launcher aboard a boat was like shooting a handgun at seventy-five yards.

Aside from the slim odds of success with firing a shoulder-launched missile from a boat—and the stranger choice, as Kallstrom had noted soon after the crash, of launching such an attack so far from Kennedy Airport, when the plane was that much higher in the sky—there was another wrinkle in the missile-from-a-boat scenario. Any terrorist would have to know that if he launched his missile from beneath the plane, and his missile managed to hit its high-flying target, huge flaming chunks of the plane were more than likely to fall on his head.

The attack, in other words, would likely have become a suicide mission.

In fact, Kallstrom had thought of that within a day of the crash. FBI agents had checked with local hospital emergency rooms to see if patients with severe burn injuries had been treated. They had checked with local police departments to determine if any suspicious-seeming bodies had been found and made sure no unaccounted-for bodies were found in the plane wreckage. No suspicious patients or corpses or victims had been found.

———

At the crash site, divers were told to look carefully for any wreckage that might prove to be missile debris. They were also told to look for the remains of the boat from which the missile might have been launched, and the bodies of the terrorists who might have been aboard. At the Calverton hangar, missile experts searched the wreckage for telltale holes. With a missile there would be massive outside penetration and a signature similar to that of a bomb. FBI agents, mostly from the missile team, along with warhead specialists from the Pentagon spent days on their hands and knees on the hangar floor, scrutinizing small pieces, even sifting particles swept up from the hangar floor through sandbox screens for any indication of a detonated missile. Once, they thought they hit pay dirt. A ball bearing emerged that seemed to be made of titanium, perhaps from a missile base, but the laboratory found it to be stainless steel.

As investigators sifted for tangible evidence, members of the FBI–NYPD Joint Terrorism Task Force spent their days sifting through the obvious international suspects. They had found a choice few who fit the criteria better than others. Perhaps, by learning what those suspects had been doing lately, the agents might link them to Flight 800.

CHAPTER 10

THE NEW COLD WAR

Until shortly after 9:00 P.M. on November 5, 1990, international terrorism had seemed a remote possibility to most Americans. Occasionally, U.S. citizens abroad were caught up in it, notably when they were held hostage in Iran in 1979, or in the bombing of Pan Am Flight 103 in 1988, and the hijacking of the *Achille Lauro*. For the most part, terrorists aimed to destabilize their own governments, whether in Northern Ireland, Italy, or the Middle East. Then on November 5, 1990, Brooklyn-born Meir Kahane, founder of the militant Jewish Defense League, was slain in a Manhattan hotel after making a speech, and a new, Middle Eastern brand of terrorism made its American debut.

At the time, the shooting seemed an isolated incident. Later, FBI agents would learn that Kahane's assailant belonged to a network of Middle Eastern terrorists also responsible for the World Trade Center bombing, numerous attacks overseas, at least one plane bombing, and various other plots thwarted literally in the nick of time. With that hindsight and a far clearer sense of how the network operated, the FBI investigation of TWA Flight 800 would be driven from the start by the suspicion that the terrorist network had struck again.

As Kahane slumped to the floor of the New York Marriott Eastside Hotel, dying from a shot to the neck, a thirty-five-year-old Egyptian named El Sayyid Nosair pushed his way frantically out of the ballroom. When a bystander got in his way, Nosair shot him in the leg with his .357 magnum. Outside, he ran several blocks, then tried to hijack a cab, only to be drawn into a shoot-out with a postal police officer who wounded him. Yet despite what prosecutors called an "overwhelming weight of evidence," including the fact that witnesses saw him holding his gun, a state jury found the itinerant Egyptian not guilty of Kahane's killing on the grounds that no one had actually witnessed him pulling the trigger, among other things. Nosair was convicted, nevertheless, of illegal gun possession, assault, and commandeering a taxi at gunpoint, and sentenced to twenty-two years in prison. (Later, a federal jury did find Nosair guilty of conspiracy in connection with the killing.) Outside the courtroom, Kahane's supporters howled with indignation at the outcome as a crowd of Nosair supporters, nearly all of them Middle Eastern, countered with defiant shouts of their own.

At the trial, New York City police had concluded Nosair acted on his own, for lack of evidence to the contrary. But the FBI was intrigued and hired an Egyptian named Emad Salem to infiltrate the ranks of Nosair's supporters. Within weeks, Salem was able to give the FBI the name of a blind Egyptian sheik named Omar Abdel-Rahman.

The details on Abdel-Rahman were sketchy. A few months before the Kahane killing, the sheik had arrived in Brooklyn from Cairo, where he was known as a dangerous radical. Though he had been on a United States "watch list" for years of incendiary rhetoric and possible involvement in violence against the secular Egyptian government, he managed to obtain a visitor's visa. (U.S. government officials later blamed his entry on a computer error.) The agents soon learned that he had been preaching his fiercely militant version of Islam at the al-Farouq mosque on Atlantic Avenue in Brooklyn, which Nosair attended regularly. Unless the sheik advocated specific violence against the U.S. government, he had a right to free speech, and the sheik had not yet done that. As far as Kahane's shooting was concerned, the sheik had flown to London to participate in a conference a week before the murder and returned ten days afterward. The FBI's informant was able to turn up no evidence of complicity in the killing, but the sheik bore watching, as did Nosair.

In jail, Nosair was visited by Mohammed Salameh, a young Islamic fundamentalist and follower of the sheik. The FBI's informer, Emad Salem, befriended some of Nosair's friends whom he saw regularly at the al-Farouq mosque. By November 1991, he was introduced to the sheik himself. When Salem, a burly man, told him he was ashamed of having served in the Egyptian army and asked what sacrifice he could offer to make amends, the sheik suggested he kill Egyptian president Hosni Mubarak. Nothing less than murder was appropriate, the sheik said, because Mubarak presided over a blasphemous government which ignored Shari'ia, the strict Islamic law by which, for example, the punishment for adultery by an unmarried man or woman was one hundred lashes, and by a married person, death. Killing Mubarak might also help the sheik realize his ultimate goal of returning to Egypt to become its stern spiritual leader. Two years later, at a hearing for political asylum, the sheik would be asked if any government met his standards for Islamic correctness. No, he would say, not even Iran, whose ruling Muslims were Shi'ites, traditional adversaries of the Sunnis, to which the sheik belonged.

As he grew closer to the sheik's inner circle, Salem heard vague details of a plot to place bombs in various Jewish centers around New York. But then, in

July 1992, Salem and his FBI handlers had a falling out. Salem refused to risk wearing a wire and felt the plot was not important enough for him to jeopardize his life by testifying in open court. For their part, the FBI agents were irked that Salem, a braggart by nature, had failed a lie-detector test. Seven months later, when the World Trade Center was rocked by a 1,200-pound bomb, the agents who had handled Salem were horrified. If they had coaxed their informant into continuing his surveillance, even without a wire, could they have averted the disaster?

In fact, Salem had never met or heard of Ramzi Yousef, the bomb's creator. But within five days of the blast, the FBI traced the identification number found on an axle discovered in the blast rubble to a rented van that had held the bomb. The van had been rented by Mohammed Salameh, the young fundamentalist who had visited El Sayyid Nosair in prison after the Meir Kahane shooting and who also attended the sheik's fiery sermons at a mosque in Jersey City, New Jersey, where the sheik had moved and where Salameh lived. Salameh's roommate, as agents soon learned, was a fellow sympathizer named Ramzi Yousef. Salem and his FBI handlers had been just one degree of separation away from him.

The FBI now knew that the Kahane shooting and the World Trade Center bombing were not isolated incidents, that the perpetrators comprised at least a loose network, and that the network aspired to do more than assassinate a Jewish radical here or there.

Its target appeared to be the United States itself.

To the radical Muslim followers of Sheik Omar Abdel-Rahman, destroying the United States made perfect sense. Through the economic boom of the 1980s, America had extended its influence around the world, not just in the reach of its financial institutions but, more blatantly and offensively to the sheik and his fellow radicals, in the spread of its secular culture. Whether in the perceived heresy of Salman Rushdie's *The Satanic Verses* or the material temptations of *Dallas* and other television dramas, the spread of pornography or the sprawl of Disney and the rest of Hollywood's heathens, American culture appeared to threaten Muslim values. Nowhere in Islam's writings does God condone the killing of innocent people who happen to live by other faiths or values, but to radical Muslims, any means justifies the end of destroying infidel cultures. Against the military might of the superpowers, terrorism was their weapon.

This new breed of international terrorists made the Mafia, Kallstrom's top priority for more than a decade, look almost quaint. Kallstrom and his legendary special-operations team had spent the eighties tapping mobsters who would tell you, if you asked, that they loved the United States and would never want it harmed—as long as they could quietly pursue their illegal businesses within it. Snagging them had carried risks, to be sure, but occasionally, Mafia surveillance had its comic moments. Underboss Dominic "Donnie Shacks"

Montemarano had seemed invulnerable to a wiretap, conducting business as he did within his Brooklyn "Maniac Club," ringed by a high, chain-link fence, and patrolled at night by snarling rottweilers—until one of Kallstrom's agents, Lou Vernazza, hit on the plan of feeding them meatballs laced with laxatives and sleeping powder. Within an hour, the dogs had staggered inside, relieved themselves everywhere, and passed out, enabling the agents to enter the club by its back door and, stepping carefully, plant their bugs. To penetrate Genovese family boss Anthony "Fat Tony" Salerno's brick-walled Palma Boys Club in East Harlem, Kallstrom had agents dress in standard-issue sanitation department jumpsuits and drive up to the club at 3:00 A.M. in six city garbage trucks; while the agents made a fearsome racket, banging garbage cans against the trucks' threshers, other agents drilled through the brick to plant their taps. Then they ran a wire through the club's basement, so rat-infested that Kallstrom kicked a large rodent away from the leg of an agent. ("Let's hope it's not rabid," Kallstrom joked as he inspected the agent's bleeding bite mark. The agent, white-faced, was too appalled to respond.) Gambino boss John Gotti had felt safe conducting business in an elderly Italian woman's apartment above the Ravenite Social Club on Mulberry Street in Manhattan's Little Italy, unaware that Kallstrom's agents had broken in one night to tuck a tiny mike into a sofa, and a state-of-the-art fish-eye lens the size of a sewing needle for closed-circuit television monitoring. As the agents listened via the microphone in the couch where Gotti sat, they could hear the great don moving around beside it, slapping a fleshy ringed hand on his leg or clearing his throat as he bragged about illegal schemes and murders, including the rubout of rival boss Paul Castellano. In all three cases, the taps led to long prison sentences.

Mobsters were cold-blooded killers who preyed on society by controlling criminal enterprises driven by greed and power that affected just about everyone. Yet dangerous as they were, they rarely killed innocent bystanders. For international terrorists, of course, that was the whole point.

Ramzi Yousef, architect of the network's most spectacular hit to date, would later tell the FBI agents who arrested him that he watched the World Trade Center blast from Canal Street, a few blocks away, with keen disappointment. He and a confederate named Eyad Ismoil had driven the van into the parking garage, lighted a seven-minute fuse on the bomb, then raced up to the street in another vehicle, terrified when a truck in front of them stopped for a full two minutes at the garage exit. The bombers had underestimated the strength of the building's construction. They had placed the van next to a support pillar, and the bomb had obliterated it as planned, creating a huge crater, but the building's support structure was strong enough to keep the tower from toppling. Yousef had anticipated watching one of the towers fall against the other, taking both down and killing 250,000 people, numbers which, he would later tell investigators, would convince Americans that they were at war. But the building stood, and amid the many who were injured, only six people died. Chagrined, Yousef hurried back to the tiny apartment in Jersey City he shared with Salameh, packed his belongings, and flew that evening to Pakistan where his appalling mission had begun. Investigators suspected that the date of the bombing was chosen for a religious reason, but Yousef would admit that he'd picked it because it was at the end of the month and he'd run out of cash for the next month's rent.

When Yousef was arrested nearly two years later, he would offer tantalizing if unreliable clues about what had provoked his terrorist acts. "I have friends and relatives who were killed in Palestine by the Israeli army," he would explain through his lawyer.

Yousef would say he was born in Kuwait, on April 27, 1967, of a Palestinian mother and Pakistani father, and brought up in Pakistan, where he began to nurse fierce anti-U.S. sentiments along with his hatred of Israel. He was extremely smart—the FBI's explosives technicians would declare him a genius for the brilliant simplicity of his bomb designs—and trained in computer-enhanced electrical engineering in West Glamorgan, Wales. He was also facile enough with languages to be fluent in Urdu, the main Pakistani language; Arabic; and English. Yousef appears to have stood out as a recruit in the Afghans' guerrilla war against the Soviet Union in the 1980s, mastering the mechanics of bomb building at a training camp near the Pakistan-Afghanistan border. Apparently, the camp got the explosives for its recruits from Al-Dawat University, which had been founded by a militant Muslim named Abdul Rab Rasool Sayyaf. The United States knew about Sayyaf, but condoned his actions because the camp-trained terrorists, at that point, applied their skills against the Soviet army. With the Soviets' retreat, however, the victorious rebel army splintered. The mujahideen, whom the United States had backed, assumed power and alienated a more fundamentalist faction, which was based in the camps, and of which Yousef was a member. In addition, young terrorists like Yousef focused their animus against the world's other superpower. If one could be so easily vanquished, they reasoned, why not crush the other while they were at it?

Whether Yousef was assigned by camp superiors to bomb the World Trade Center or seized on the notion himself remains unclear. So do his connections to the sheik, though his use of confederates who were among the sheik's followers, including Mohammad Salameh, shows that he was, at least, within the same loose network. What *is* known is that he arrived well trained at New York's Kennedy Airport from Peshawar, Pakistan, on September 1, 1992. At U.S. Customs, he presented an Iraqi passport and asked for political asylum. As was customary at the time, he was released until he could receive a hearing on his asylum request. All he had to do was leave his passport with customs and provide an address where he could be found in the interim. Customs would forward the information to the Immigration and Naturalization Service.

Letting Yousef pass freely out of Kennedy Airport seems a colossal gaffe in retrospect, but at the time there was no procedural reason to detain him. He had committed no crime and was bringing nothing illegal into the country with him. America's ongoing hostilities with Iraq meant that Iraqis could not obtain visitors' visas, but victims of any repressive regime had the right to apply for political asylum. An astute customs agent did grow suspicious when another passenger on the flight, a Palestinian named Ahmad Ajaj, presented an obviously forged Swedish passport, and then noticed that Yousef and Ajaj both showed identification cards from the same community center in Afghanistan. They claimed not to know each other, though for the first leg of the trip the two had sat next to each other in first-class seats—an expensive luxury for residents of a community center. When officials went through Ajaj's baggage, they found bombing manuals and videotapes, including one that showed dramatic scenes from a Hollywood movie in which terrorists blow up a U.S. embassy. They arrested Ajaj on the spot on a false-passport charge. Later, FBI agents would learn that Yousef had put together the passport for Ajaj on their flight, merely pasting Ajaj's photo over someone else's picture. Yousef, memorably dressed in a wild, pink-flowered, Hawaiian-style shirt and sandals, would have been detained too, but the customs agent's superior informed her that the detention cell at Kennedy Airport could hold only one more person. Reluctantly, the agent told Yousef to come back later for more questioning. "Sure!" he said, and sauntered out.

Later, after the World Trade Center bombing, the FBI uncovered numerous phone calls from Ajaj in jail to Yousef's New Jersey apartment. Yousef had wanted his bombing manuals back, and Ajaj was trying to return them through his lawyers. When agents dusted Ajaj's passport and bombing manuals, they found Yousef's fingerprints everywhere, especially on a page that contained instructions for building a urea-nitrate-based bomb such as the one set off in the garage beneath the World Trade Center. By then, of course, Yousef would be long gone, and the damage done.

From Kennedy Airport, Yousef made straight for Jersey City, New Jersey, and the apartment of Mohammed Salameh. Over the next six months, he busied himself preparing the bomb he hoped would topple the twin towers. Later, his fingerprints would be found in the apartment, on explosive materials, and in a shed where chemicals were stored and the bomb partially constructed.

Just days before the bombing, Yousef went to the Pakistani consulate in New York and claimed he had lost his passport. Somehow, he finagled a new one in the name of Abdul Basit. He also bought a one-way plane ticket to travel on February 26 to Karachi, Pakistan, and ultimately to the desolate area of western Pakistan called Baluchistan, where a band of fellow terrorists awaited him. Though the World Trade Center bombing failed to meet his expectations, Yousef's getaway, within hours of the blast, went off without a hitch.

Back in the United States, not all of Yousef's co-conspirators fared as well. The other van driver, Eyad Ismoil, managed to escape the country, but Mohammed Salameh returned to Jersey City so destitute that six days after the bombing he tried to retrieve the $400 deposit on the Ryder van that he had reported stolen. It was a costly move, since federal agents had already located the van's identification number on the charred axle found just outside the bomb crater. When Salameh arrived at the Ryder office, he was greeted by FBI agents dressed in Ryder uniforms and wired with hidden recording devices. Salameh got his $400, then left as other FBI agents, including Charlie Christopher, waited outside in a car to see whether an associate would pick him up. When none did, the FBI car slowly followed Salameh as he hurried along the street to catch a bus. Just as he was about to board, two agents in plain clothes sprinted down the sidewalk and went for him. Salameh bolted toward Christopher, who emerged from an unmarked car in a navy jacket with bright yellow FBI letters across it. "FBI! Save me!" Salameh cried. "They're trying to mug me!" To Salameh's astonishment, Christopher grabbed him and slapped handcuffs on his wrists. Salameh had only one comment as he was hustled into the car. "You're wrinkling my shirt," he said.

Within weeks, two of Yousef's other co-conspirators, Nidal Ayyad and Mahmoud Abouhalima, were arrested, and the hapless Ahmad Ajaj, back in jail after a brief release, was linked to the crime as a co-conspirator. Along with Mohammed Salameh, they were put on trial in September 1993, where they faced a team of prosecutors led by the U.S. Attorney in Manhattan, Mary Jo White, whose ferocious dedication to putting terrorists behind bars had already made her a national star in law enforcement. Found guilty of conspiring to bomb the World Trade Center, each of the defendants was sentenced to 240 years in prison.

Yousef was gone, but his passport pictures and video footage of him from a surveillance camera at his local New Jersey bank, as well as fingerprints in the Jersey City apartment, were soon posted in every FBI and CIA office around the world. The FBI also engaged in a bit of creative advertising, printing Yousef's visage, along with details of his crime and a plea for information, on hundreds of thousands of colorful matchbook covers that were then distributed by the U.S. State Department throughout the Muslim world. Perhaps someone would be led to turn in the World Trade Center bomber—if not out of virtue, then for the $2 million price tag on his head.

Despite these measures, Yousef managed to elude detection. Later, agents would deduce that as he passed through Afghanistan, he stopped at a site to which the blind sheik made a call at the time from the United States. Agents would also learn that Yousef and Salameh had dined with the sheik at his New Jersey apartment two weeks before the World Trade Center bombing, but no proof of direct collusion between the two men could be established. Eventually,

Yousef settled in the Philippine capital of Manila, in room 603 of the Josefa apartments on the Quirino Highway, several hundred feet from the home of the Vatican's ambassador to the Philippines. When Pope John Paul II visited the Philippines, he stayed with the ambassador. Later, Yousef boasted that the Pope had been one of his next targets. On a table in apartment 603, police found a picture of the Pope, a reminder of work not yet done. Next to it was a map tracing the Pope's route on his most recent visit.

Yousef's more immediate plan, however, was to target America again by bombing twelve U.S. commercial jets in Asian airspace, all within forty-eight hours.

As a first test, Yousef and a confederate, Wali Khan Amin Shah, created a small bomb using a Casio watch and nine-volt batteries, among other store-bought ingredients. On December 1, 1994, they put it under a seat in a Manila movie theater, where it exploded, causing several injuries though no fatalities.

Yousef's second test was the small bomb put aboard a Philippines Airlines jet on December 11, 1994—the one investigators would be reminded of when the "Middle Easterner" looking for his mother-in-law's reading glasses on Flight 800 became a suspect. The flight he chose began in Manila and made a brief stopover elsewhere in the Philippines before heading on to Japan. The stopover was key. Yousef bought himself a ticket for the whole flight. As soon as the seat-belt sign was turned off, he went into the lavatory and, within minutes, assembled a bomb out of batteries, a Casio watch, wires, and nitroglycerin, which Yousef had secreted in a contact-lens-solution bottle. When he emerged from the bathroom, he returned not to his assigned seat but to one a few rows away—26K, over the plane's center fuel tank. He slipped his small bomb under the seat cushion, then disembarked when the plane made its first stop. Shortly after the plane resumed its flight, the bomb went off, killing the unfortunate businessman who happened to board at the stopover and was assigned seat 26K. Once again, Yousef was disappointed: He had hoped the bomb would destroy the plane. His mistake, he realized, was in not placing the bomb closer to the outer skin of the fuselage, so as to cause enough structural damage that the plane would be unable to land.

Yousef's bomb was so cunningly simple, and so different from the huge load of explosives used on the World Trade Center, that investigators had no reason to think he might be the Philippines Airlines bomber. The tipoff came on January 6, 1995, when he accidentally started a small fire in his rented room while mixing explosive chemicals. As thick smoke billowed from the apartment, alarmed neighbors called the fire and police departments. Rather than risk detection, Yousef fled, boarding the first flight to Pakistan. His roommate and compatriot, Abdul Hakim Murad, ran out of the apartment with Yousef, but was ordered back by Yousef to retrieve incriminating computer disks. When Murad returned to the apartment, he found the police. Murad explained that

he and his just-departed roommate had been setting off firecrackers to celebrate the New Year, but when the police searched the apartment they found
explosive chemicals. Later, when they scrolled through Yousef's laptop computer, they found his blueprint for bombing the American jumbo jets. Amazed,
the police called the FBI.

FBI agents soon realized that the multi-jet-bomb scheme had been worked
out to the last detail. In each case, terrorists would do as Yousef had done on his
Philippines Airlines flight: Book a seat on a flight that had a stopover, plant the
bomb on the first leg of the trip, and disembark during the stopover. The terrorists were to assemble their bombs in the planes' washrooms, as Yousef had
done, from nitroglycerin stored in contact-lens-cleaner containers. The nitroglycerin would be wired to Casio digital watches, modified as timing devices
powered by batteries taken from radios. The makeshift bombs would be placed
above the washrooms' ceiling tiles, or in rows of seats close to the one Yousef
had chosen for his Philippines Airlines exercise. When the terrorists disembarked and the planes had resumed their flights, they would explode en route
to cities including Los Angeles and San Francisco. In the apartment, the FBI
actually found several of the bombs fully or partially constructed.

Jittery that other bombs might be stored elsewhere by terrorists who were
about to put them to use, the agents notified the FAA, which immediately
grounded all U.S. planes in the Philippines, Singapore, and other Asian locations. Pilots and flight attendants aboard planes already in the air were directed
to check ceiling tiles in the restrooms and overhead bins. For weeks afterward,
passengers were not allowed to board U.S. airplanes in that region if they had
containers of liquid in their hand luggage. No vials of nitroglycerin were found,
but hundreds of bottles of perfume and aftershave were taken from irritated
passengers to whom the airport security workers, by strict FBI policy, could
offer no explanation.

Yousef had slipped away, but this time he made the mistake of returning to
Pakistan. By now, CIA and FBI investigators had infiltrated some of the country's terrorist cells, where word of the $2 million price tag on Yousef's head had
penetrated. In early February, a twenty-five-year-old South African student at
the University of Islamabad named Ishtiaque Parker walked into the U.S.
embassy with a riveting tip. Parker was a militant radical himself and had been
drawn into Yousef's plot to bomb the dozen American jumbo jetliners, but the
prospect of $2 million and a new life for his family—he had a wife and two-
year-old son—appealed to him more than becoming an international fugitive.
Parker had also had second thoughts about blowing up jets. He told authorities
Yousef was in town but would be leaving for Afghanistan in forty-eight hours.
The following day when Parker returned, an FBI agent at the embassy
promised him that he would get the $2 million reward if his help led to Yousef's
capture. The young radical then revealed that he had a date to meet Yousef for

coffee. As authorities watched from a distance, Yousef strolled around a corner, took a seat beside Parker, and ordered a coffee as casually as if he were on a break from his office job. For that little rendezvous, Parker would receive $2 million as promised, in payments over time, from the U.S. government.

In Washington, it was midafternoon on Sunday, February 7, 1995. Richard Clarke, President Clinton's special assistant on terrorism, was in his White House office when a classified telex from Islamabad arrived announcing that Yousef had been found. Immediately, he called FBI headquarters, expecting to find a lowly agent on weekend duty in the counterterrorism division. "O'Neill," came a crisp voice over the line. John O'Neill, the newly appointed head of the unit, had driven all night from Chicago straight to his new office to hang pictures, read memos, and get up to speed for his first day on the job on Monday. Clarke relayed the news from Islamabad. O'Neill called Tom Pickard, who in turn immediately called Kallstrom and Mary Jo White, the U.S. Attorney in Manhattan. Along with one of her deputies, Patrick Fitzgerald, a top terrorism expert, White raced over to the New York FBI Command Post. A team to bring Yousef back to the United States was quickly assembled and sent to board a military plane at Andrews Air Force Base outside Washington. The team included members of the FBI and its SWAT team, the U.S. Secret Service, the State Department, a hostage-rescue squad, and medical and communications people. Two FBI agents who had spent their last two years hunting Yousef were also on board.

Sunday night in Islamabad, a team of FBI agents and Pakistani police descended on a cheap hotel in downtown Islamabad, where Yousef was holed up in a $30-a-night room. Yousef was astonished when Brad Corbett of the FBI identified himself. In two hours, he would have been on a bus to Afghanistan, over the border and once again gone. Instead, he was handcuffed and fingerprinted. Still wet, the prints were faxed to Washington, where they could be compared to those found in Salameh's apartment and on Ajaj's bombing manuals; the FBI did not want to bring back the wrong man. When the match was confirmed, Yousef was taken by the Pakistani police in an entourage of unmarked police vehicles, their sirens silent and revolving lights off, to the Islamabad airport.

By now, the American team had arrived and was waiting on the tarmac. For the return flight, the high-tech military plane that had brought them could be refueled in the air by a companion aircraft. That was critical. No one wanted to risk a refueling stop en route from Pakistan to New York. Touching down in even a friendly country with first-class security would present legal issues. At London's Heathrow Airport, for example, British authorities might be compelled by law to require an extradition hearing to allow the legal removal of the prisoner to stand trial in the United States. Moreover, Yousef might seek asylum wherever the plane landed first. His chances of getting it in the jurisdiction of the Southern District of New York, where Mary Jo White and her team of prosecutors had assembled mountains of evidence against Yousef and his colleagues, were nil. Round-trip, the special flight would cost $11 million, the most money ever spent to bring a fugitive back to the United States.

Blindfolded and in handcuffs, Yousef was taken across the tarmac to the plane and hustled aboard. He was not told where he was going. His blindfold was removed once he was secured to his seat with a belly chain and with leg irons on his feet. He was, however, allowed to talk. With the agents' word that his remarks would not be taped, Yousef, to their surprise, talked at length, even after he was apprised of his constitutional right to remain silent.

Proudly, defiantly, Yousef acknowledged his role in the World Trade Center bombing as well as in the Manila bombings. He talked of his plans to destroy the U.S. jets—headed from Asia to airports in Honolulu, San Francisco, Los Angeles, and New York—and to assassinate the Pope. Unlike the four defendants already found guilty in the World Trade Center bombing, Yousef displayed no religious motivation. He had political reasons, he said, for his U.S. targets: America's aid to Israel helped Israelis torture, murder, and deport Palestinians, and thus justified his acts of war in response. But politics had nothing to do with the murder of the Japanese businessman in Manila, or with the Pope's planned assassination. The agents agreed that Yousef was drawn to terrorism more for the thrill of it, by the intellectual challenge of building his bombs, and by the notoriety he'd received for detonating them. He said that he wanted to write a book about his exploits and drew a diagram of the World Trade Center bomb, though he realized, as he was completing it, that it might be used against him, so he tore it up and swallowed the pieces.

Over the ocean, the dramatic refueling took place, permitting the flight to continue without touching down. Every half hour, an agent would get up from the seat next to Yousef and casually walk to the rear of the aircraft. Out of Yousef's view, he would scribble notes of what he could remember of Yousef's conversation. Oblivious, Yousef talked on. He told the agents about sitting on a park bench in Jersey City within an hour of the bombing, looking with frustration across the Hudson River at the darkened but still-standing World Trade Center towers. He talked of going to Manila and making more bombs there. Often, in the weeks since the fire in his Manila apartment had put them back on his trail, the agents had wondered why Yousef had not retired from terrorism and gone to start a new life in Peshawar, or perhaps Iraq. Now they knew: It was Yousef's ego. He loved his celebrity and wanted more.

When the plane landed at Stewart Air Force Base in Newburgh, New York, amid tight security, Yousef, still handcuffed, was blindfolded again and led from the plane in an orange jumpsuit to a waiting FBI helicopter with Lewis Schiliro and members of the FBI SWAT team aboard. The chopper flew him directly to

26 Federal Plaza in downtown Manhattan, where he would be processed, then hustled to the nearby Metropolitan Correctional Center, where he would be locked up to await trial. Just before landing, the helicopter pilot made a point of circling the World Trade Center. An agent yanked down Yousef's blindfold and pushed his face toward the window. "You see?" the agent said. "They're still standing." Yousef snickered. "They wouldn't be," he said, "if I'd had more money and time."

Six months later, the last of Yousef's known Jersey City confederates in the World Trade Center bombing was brought back from Jordan to stand trial with Yousef. Eyad Mahmoud Ismoil Najim, the actual driver of the bomb-laden Ryder van, had flown the day after the crime to Jordan, where he had grown up and which he considered his home. There he had remained a free man until the late spring of 1995, when at the request of FBI director Louis Freeh, he was picked up and detained on these matters by Jordanian authorities in compliance with a U.S. warrant for his arrest. That should have made the job of bringing him back a routine matter. But for Tom Pickard, who was then head of the New York National Security Division, the handoff of Ismoil became as tricky, in its way, as the arrest of Ramzi Yousef.

Before Pickard and members of the FBI–NYPD Joint Terrorism Task Force could leave for Jordan, FBI director Louis Freeh had to persuade the U.S. State Department to negotiate a new extradition treaty with Jordan, expressly to retrieve Ismoil. Because of King Hussein's efforts to help facilitate Middle East peace talks over the years, Jordan was beset by many political factions, some fiercely anti-American. Surrendering a Jordanian to the United States, even a suspected terrorist, would not be easy. Though the treaty was finally signed, Pickard and his team chose not to provoke factional hostility by making their arrival known. Instead, their jet touched down at 2:00 A.M. at the military airport in Amman. While the rest of the team stayed on board, Pickard disembarked and was led to a car that took him to an unair-conditioned bunker at the end of another runway. Inside sat a scowling Jordanian general in full dress uniform with rows of medals on his chest. "Just what do you have on this young man Ismoil?" the general demanded.

From an attaché case, Pickard withdrew documents that summarized an investigation of thousands of hours by the Terrorism Task Force into Ismoil's involvement in the World Trade Center bombing. "Your government has these papers already," Pickard said politely.

The general scanned them in silence. "I don't believe they're accurate," he said at last. "I've talked to the young man and he says these charges are not true."

"General, officials in your government above my level and your level have already reached an accord in this matter," Pickard said evenly. "It is not for us to decide. It is for us to carry out the agreement."

For several more minutes, the general debated the issue. Finally Pickard said, "General, the fact is I am not leaving without him."

After a long minute, the general shrugged. "Are you going to handcuff the young man?" he asked.

Pickard felt his breath come back. "General, I will follow whatever the custom is in your country."

"I've seen prisoners in America covered by hoods," the general said. "I don't want him covered by a hood."

"Whatever you prefer," Pickard said. Where did the general get this idea about hoods, he wondered? But he saw no point in asking.

"Well, let's go meet the young man now," the general said. "I will ask him whether or not he wants to go with you."

Two steps forward, one step back, Pickard thought, but what was his choice? "Let's see what he says."

The general led Pickard into another room, where Ismoil stood with several other men. Pickard recognized him immediately. "Mr. Pickard is from the FBI," the general said, as if introducing two strangers at a cocktail party. Instinctively, Pickard held out his hand. Why am I shaking the hand of a terrorist? he thought. But diplomacy was clearly the better part of law enforcement in this strange exercise.

"You don't have to go with him if you don't want to," the general told Ismoil.

But Ismoil had told a Jordanian court that he wanted to go to the United States to prove his innocence. He nodded toward Pickard and said in a soft voice, "No, I'll go with him."

The general drove Pickard and Ismoil to the waiting U.S. jet as Pickard whispered into his walkie-talkie, telling his team that he had Ismoil with him. "We are coming up to the plane now. No one come outside. Keep everything quiet, understand?" Ismoil climbed the metal stairs with Pickard behind him. In the cabin, with the door closed, agents seized and strip-searched him.

"Let's get the hell out of here," Pickard yelled over the roar of the engines. But as the plane taxied into position for takeoff, a tank rolled up to block its path. The control tower told the pilot he did not have permission to take off. Thirty minutes of tense radio communication among Pickard, the tower, and the powers that be followed, with the tank's machine gun pointed directly at the cockpit. Not until the vehicle actually rolled away did Pickard feel that the plane could leave with Ismoil aboard.

As the plane lifted up over the air base, Pickard called Kallstrom at the New York Command Post. "We're wheels up out of Jordan with the package," Pickard said. "We're on our way home."

"Good job, Tommy," came the familiar voice with its reassuring Boston accent. "See you on the other end."

———

Whether or not the sheik had helped orchestrate the World Trade Center bombing, he seemed linked to each of the six defendants finally rounded up, and clearly merited closer scrutiny. Fortunately, three days after the bombing, the FBI's ex-informant, Emad Salem, returned to duty. The World Trade Center bombing had horrified him. If the network was capable of this, what might its next target be? Like most informants, Salem had mixed motives: Later, he would be paid $1 million for his services, but in the case the FBI began to build now against the sheik and fourteen others, Salem was the key.

In the three years since the sheik had piqued the FBI's interest, a detailed file on his earlier life had been assembled with the help of Egyptian authorities. The FBI knew that Omar Abdel-Rahman had been born in Daqahliya province in Egypt's Nile delta, and blinded by diabetes at the age of ten. From then on he had studied Islam almost constantly, earning degrees at Cairo University's School of Theology and Cairo's Al-Azhar University. By 1965, he was preaching an exceedingly stern version of Islam, and excoriating the country's secular politicians. His first arrest came in 1969 for preaching against then-president Gamal Abdel Nasser. The following year, he was imprisoned for eight months for urging his followers not to pray for Nasser after his death.

More than two decades later, when he sought to persuade a U.S. immigration judge to let him remain in the country, the blind sheik testified that he had been tortured repeatedly during that eight-month prison sentence. If true, the abuse only hardened his views. Through the 1970s, he was returned to jail several times for seditious speech. Then, in 1981, he served a three-year term on charges that he issued a fatwa, or holy decree, for the murder of President Anwar Sadat. To the immigration judge, the sheik denied the charges. A letter submitted by the U.S. State Department at the hearing attested, to the contrary, that "with respect to the assassination of Anwar Sadat, president of Egypt, it has been established beyond any doubt that in August 1981, about two months before Sadat's assassination, this applicant issued a fatwa, or theological ruling making an act lawful under Islamic teaching, to Sadat's assassins in which it was stated that the killing of Sadat was justified in the name of God."

In fact, the sheik was arrested and tried for complicity in the killing, but acquitted by an Egyptian judge who determined that the sheik had been tortured while in detention, so that his statements could not be used against him.

The sheik by now had a huge following of believers ardent enough to act on one fatwa for violence after another in the 1980s and early 1990s, including the knifing of thirteen youths at a mosque in Assiut in July 1988. The sheik also was blamed for encouraging the demolition of twenty-two businesses owned by Coptic Christians in the town of Sanoures on Easter 1990; the March 1991 killing of a young Christian for allegedly proselytizing; the fatal beatings on May 31, 1991, of two Copts, one a pharmacist and the other a teacher, because they had participated in a family-planning campaign for Muslim women; and, most spectacularly, the June 8, 1990, assassination of human-rights activist and People's Assembly speaker Rifaat el-Mahgoub, along with five of his companions. In all, the U.S. State Department blamed hundreds of murders on the sheik's fanatical followers.

The fatwas for the last of those incidents, including the murder of el-Mahgoub, were issued by long-distance telephone. In April 1990, under house arrest in Egypt, the sheik had wangled an exit visa to Saudi Arabia for a religious pilgrimage. He never returned. Instead, two months later, he slipped into the United States thanks to the computer error at the U.S. embassy in Khartoum that allowed him a visitor's visa to begin a new life as an expatriate. In the aftermath of the Kahane killing that fall, he became a target of an FBI investigation, but without evidence to implicate him, agents could only watch as the sheik applied for, and received, permanent residency in the United States that winter.

Despite the sheik's legal status, the FBI came to feel that he had better be deported—fast. He was continuing to issue fatwas for violence in Egypt, and the FBI's informer Emad Salem was reporting details of a pipe-bomb plot to be carried out at Jewish locations in Manhattan. By now, Corrigan, Liguori, and agent Chris Voss were in charge of surveilling the sheik as part of a broader effort they called Terr-Stop. They contacted the Department of Immigration and Naturalization Services, which found two misrepresentations in the sheik's application for residency. He listed only one wife, though he had three, including an American. He had also declined to mention a 1987 arrest and conviction in Egypt for saying he was not a member of a political organization when he was, in fact, a member of an Islamic group. In March 1992, based on those inaccuracies, the INS rescinded the sheik's permanent residency status—his "green card." However, he could file for political asylum, and did so three months later. That was the application that obliged him to answer questions about his political past before a U.S. immigration judge in Newark, New Jersey, and that brought forth the stern letter from the U.S. State Department, contradicting the sheik's account point by point. The sheik, as a result, was denied asylum in March 1993, shortly after the World Trade Center bombing. The federal government chose at that time not to draw up charges that he had been involved in the bombing—the evidence was too scant—and reasoned that trying to detain him would be too expensive, given the sheik's poor health. Had the sheik chosen to leave the country at that point, he could have done so freely. Instead, he appealed his ruling, while conspiring to set off bombs in the country that had treated him so generously.

With the quick arrest of Mohammed Salameh outside the Ryder van rental office in Jersey City, New Jersey, Corrigan and Liguori were now almost certain that the sheik, to whom Salameh was so close, had some involvement with the World Trade Center bombing. If he had exhorted the six suspects who carried out the crime, he was as guilty—and as dangerous—as they were.

The hapless Salameh, though he was uncooperative and adamantly denied his guilt, provided invaluable help to the agents in filling out the picture. His vanished roommate, Ramzi Yousef, was an obvious suspect. Also, the investigators found Salameh's address book when they searched his apartment. It contained the names and addresses of various other members of the network. One was a cousin of El Sayyid Nosair, the original suspect in the Meir Kahane killing. On March 4, 1993, Corrigan was a member of the FBI team that swooped down with a search warrant on Ibrahim El-Gabrowny, another of Nosair's cousins, at his Park Slope apartment in Brooklyn. The visit cost Corrigan a hard elbow to the jaw.

Apparently, El-Gabrowny saw the team converging on his building and walked quickly toward the agents with his hands in his pockets. Corrigan identified himself as a police officer. When El-Gabrowny refused to put his hands against the nearest wall, Corrigan and another terrorist task force member forced him to do so. At this point, Corrigan felt a rectangular object in El-Gabrowny's breast pocket which he thought might be plastic explosives. When he tried to remove the object, El-Gabrowny struck him. Furious, Corrigan and the other agent wrestled El-Gabrowny to the sidewalk and handcuffed him. The object turned out to be a yellow envelope containing forged passports for him in various names and a forged driver's license for his cousin Nosair. The false documents earned him twenty-five years, the assault on Corrigan another twenty-two years in addition to twenty years for conspiracy.

The conspiracy charge would not be based, in fact, on the World Trade Center bombing, in which El-Gabrowny appeared to have played no part. It grew out of another plot Corrigan and Liguori were investigating as they and other terrorist task force members were picking up additional World Trade Center suspects and trying to track Ramzi Yousef. This plot led directly to the sheik.

With their key informant back in place in the sheik's inner circle, Corrigan and Liguori learned in March 1993 that the sheik had gone beyond casually suggesting to Salem that he assassinate Egyptian president Mubarak. A week before the president was to visit New York City, the sheik had issued a fatwa to two confederates, Siddig Ali and Abdo Haggag, to assassinate him as he arrived at the Waldorf-Astoria Hotel in midtown Manhattan. The FBI persuaded Mubarak to change his plans at the last minute and go to Washington instead of New York, frustrating the plot.

The agents could have arrested the sheik that month. Salem had enough conversations on tape of the Mubarak plot to make a persuasive court case, but because no actual attempt had been made on Mubarak's life, the conspirators might have been acquitted, or given sentences milder than the FBI wanted.

In May 1993, Emad Salem told the FBI that the sheik and his followers were now planning to blow up a number of major New York structures, including the United Nations, FBI headquarters at 26 Federal Plaza, the Holland and Lincoln tunnels, and the George Washington Bridge. To build the bombs, Salem steered the sheik's followers to a Queens garage rigged with FBI cameras and microphones—a trap set up by Joe Cantamessa, with help from Kallstrom, who at the time was head of the new research and engineering facility at the FBI compound at Quantico, Virginia, where he was directing the development of James Bond–style tiny cameras and microphones to snag terrorists and other criminals in what soon came to be known as "the house that Jimmy built." On June 24, 1993, the bomb builders were filmed and recorded mixing explosives. The entire ring, including the sheik, was charged with seditious conspiracy in a plot to "levy a war of urban terrorism against the United States." Along with his latest bombing plot, the sheik was charged with complicity in the Kahane killing and in the plot to assassinate President Mubarak. Asked to explain his actions in a first court appearance, he said piously, "All I know is that I have nothing to do with this case other than that I am a cleric who prayed in a mosque. I did not speak. I did not give orders. I have nothing to do with anything."

At a trial in which the sheik was charged with fourteen codefendants, Salem provided devastating evidence to counter the sheik's protestations of innocence. Prior to the trial, when they realized that Salem had been an informer, two of the sheik's codefendants chose to plead to lesser counts and become government witnesses. One, Siddig Ibrahim Siddig Ali, the technical mastermind of the bridge-and-tunnel bombing plot, was spirited away with Salem after the trial into the government witness protection program; the third witness, Abdo Mohammed Haggag, was remanded to jail. Seven of the other defendants received prison terms of twenty-five to thirty-five years. The sheik, already an old man, received life in prison with no chance of parole. At his sentencing, he again denied any role in the various plots ascribed to him, then added ominously that as a result of the sentencing, he could "no longer control things that may happen."

To Corrigan and Liguori, those words echoed seven months later in the aftermath of TWA Flight 800. Could the sheik's veiled threats have provoked his followers to retaliate? Did he relay a fatwa from his prison hospital in Springfield, Missouri, urging them directly to blow up a commercial jetliner? The agents were sure he could have done so.

No less likely a suspect was Ramzi Yousef, despite his own incarceration in a federal penitentiary. Yousef's trial for the Philippines Airlines bombing, and for the plot to blow up twelve U.S. jumbo jets, had begun May 29, just six weeks before TWA Flight 800 exploded in midair. Two other defendants were charged in the crimes. Did Yousef have other followers who had downed Flight 800 in a bid to force the United States to release the three defendants? Though no credible claim from a follower of Yousef materialized, the FBI would spend more than a year investigating Yousef's network.

On September 5, 1996, the three defendants were found guilty, and Yousef was sentenced to life for killing the Japanese businessman on the Philippines Airlines flight. In July 1997, Yousef went on trial again, this time for the World Trade Center bombing. His codefendant was Eyad Ismoil, the Ryder van driver who had escaped after the bombing but was captured in Jordan in July 1995. The two were given the same sentences as their four co-conspirators: 240 years in prison for each.

———

The sheik and Ramzi Yousef were two of three chief suspects on the night of the crash. These names were known to the press, who inquired about them at news conferences on the following days. The third name, and the likeliest suspect, was not known at that time to the public and not mentioned by Kallstrom or any other suspect whom the FBI was investigating. But at the Command Post in Manhattan, this third suspect was the one most strongly felt to have had the means, as well as the motive, to down Flight 800.

His name was Osama bin-Laden.

Two summers later, when U.S. embassies in Kenya and Tanzania were destroyed by powerful bombs in trucks parked nearby, most Americans would hear bin-Laden's name for the first time. President Clinton would accuse the wealthy Saudi radical of masterminding the atrocities and order the United States to retaliate by firing missiles at an apparent conclave of bin-Laden's confederates in Afghanistan, as well as at a Sudanese factory thought to be a bin-Laden–sponsored weapons manufacturer. But even before the downing of TWA Flight 800, the FBI and CIA, as well as the president's national security advisor, Tony Lake, and the president's special assistant on terrorism, Richard Clarke, suspected that bin-Laden was a serious threat to American security.

From various intelligence sources, court documents and affidavits, a portrait had emerged of bin-Laden as a wealthy, intense young man whose Islamic fundamentalism had led him to political activity and, eventually, to international terrorism. As one of fifty-two children born to the various wives of a Saudi construction magnate, Osama bin-Laden had shown no early signs of the radicalism that would later possess him. He attended Le Rosey, the Swiss boarding school of the international elite, then dropped out of college in Saudi Arabia to join the Afghan struggle against Moscow shortly after Soviet troops invaded Afghanistan in December 1979. He then returned to Saudi Arabia to participate in his father's construction business, and soon proved himself a shrewd capitalist in his own right, building tanneries and other businesses to parlay his inheritance into a major fortune estimated at $350 million.

By the early 1980s, bin-Laden apparently had begun allocating funds to help the mujahideen of Afghanistan fend off their Soviet aggressors. He supplied the rebels with arms, including shoulder-launched Stinger missiles, serving as a middleman between them and his ally of convenience, the United States. The United States, in turn, found bin-Laden a useful agent in this last pitched battle against what President Reagan called the "Evil Empire." When demoralized Soviet troops finally withdrew from Afghanistan in February 1989, the victors began to pursue a different agenda. The Afghan war had taught them that if one of the world's two superpowers could be humbled by a guerrilla war, perhaps the other one, equally blasphemous to the Muslim radicals in the refugee camps along the Afghan-Pakistani border, was as vulnerable.

That year, according to court affidavits, bin-Laden formed a group called al Qaeda ("the Base"), dedicated to overthrowing all Western governments, particularly the United States and Israel, and, for good measure, all governments in Muslim countries judged to be less than Islamically pure. Its council met on either side of the Afghan-Pakistani border to plot terrorist operations, and its fatwa committee drafted its own stern interpretation of Islamic law, to which bin-Laden's followers strictly adhered. Atheists and other nonbelievers were to be lashed and imprisoned; thieves were to lose various limbs, and adulterers would be stoned to death.

Not until the Persian Gulf War, however, did the U.S. government become aware that it had a virulent new enemy. Bin-Laden was incensed when Saudi Arabia welcomed U.S. troops to "holy" soil to fight Iraq and suggested that Saudi Arabia instead adopt a purely defensive strategy. He offered to use his family's bulldozers to build a barrier to exclude Iraqi troops. When his tone turned threatening, Saudi Arabia revoked bin-Laden's citizenship and froze those of his assets that remained in Saudi banks. By then, the FBI was on to him.

In 1992, bin-Laden moved his residence and financial empire across the Red Sea to the Sudan's fundamentalist dictatorship. That was when he appeared to start ordering his followers to murder Americans and attack U.S. facilities worldwide, starting with U.S. forces stationed on the Saudi peninsula and in nearby African states. In Somalia, bin-Laden's followers trained tribesmen opposed to U.N. intervention. At the same time, he set up terrorist training camps throughout the Middle East and scoured the black market for components to produce nuclear and chemical weapons.

Whether bin-Laden was working with followers of the sheik or Ramzi Yousef remained unclear. Like the sheik, bin-Laden gave frequent, fiery speeches to attract sympathizers; by the mid-1990s, each had his own following throughout the Muslim world. There was no evidence that bin-Laden had helped fund Yousef's attack on the World Trade Center or the sheik's plot to blow up bridges and buildings in New York, but in the wake of Yousef's arrest, the FBI discovered that apparently bin-Laden had encouraged Yousef in his effort to blow up the twelve U.S. jets, and speculated that bin-Laden's brother-in-law may have helped finance the venture. When Yousef fled his smoking apartment in Manila, bin-Laden may have facilitated his journey to Pakistan. Moreover, the hotel where Yousef was captured was apparently used by Afghan war veterans operating on bin-Laden's instructions.

Yet to Tony Lake, Clinton's national security advisor, bin-Laden remained a peripheral figure until the bombing of a U.S. Army barracks in Riyadh, Saudi Arabia, in November 1995, which killed five soldiers. Communiqués faxed to the Egyptian newspaper *Al Hayat* at the time of the bombing appeared to implicate bin-Laden in the crime. With urging from the White House, the CIA set up a task force in Virginia with the FBI to track bin-Laden's activities. Nearly three years later, the bin-Laden station would provide crucial information to agents after the U.S. embassy bombings in Kenya and Tanzania, enabling them to trace the first suspects back to bin-Laden almost immediately. But in June 1996, when a bomb exploded at the Khobar Towers building in Saudi Arabia, killing nineteen U.S. military personnel, task-force investigators were unable to link bin-Laden specifically to the crime. Privately, bin-Laden took credit for the Khobar bombing, and for some time investigators took him at his word. As a result, when TWA exploded three weeks later, they suspected that the plane crash might have been the latest strike in his campaign. Only much later did investigators come to believe that bin-Laden had been bragging about Khobar without cause.

On the night of the TWA Flight 800 crash, Lake and his deputy Richard Clarke at the White House, as well as investigators at the FBI's New York Command Post, immediately put bin-Laden on their short list of suspects, along with the sheik's and Ramzi Yousef's comrades. Bin-Laden could have learned from Yousef how to carry out the plan to blow up a dozen U.S. jets in forty-eight hours. Or he could have allied his fractious Sunni rebels with the Shi'ite Muslims who comprised Iran's militant Hezbollah. In the months before Khobar, a flurry of meetings in Iran had appeared to signal preparations for an important terrorist event. In turn, Iran's own surveillance of various U.S. embassies in the Middle East was stepped up. What if Riyadh and Khobar were bin-Laden's first strikes, and TWA Flight 800 his third? What if the bombing of the Atlanta Olympics on July 27, 1996—ten days after the TWA crash—was his fourth?

To the FBI investigators at the Command Post and terrorist experts, certain words and phrases in the fax sent to the *Al Hayat* news organization hours before the explosion of TWA Flight 800 echoed those in faxes received before the bombings of Riyadh and Khobar. To them, the faxes appeared to be powerful indications that a campaign of orchestrated terrorism had begun, and that the sheik, Yousef, bin-Laden, or some combination of the three were behind it.

The White House's contingency plan only underscored the gravity of what they appeared to face. It was this prospect, as much as the loss of 230 lives aboard a commercial jet, which within forty-eight hours provoked the most comprehensive investigation in FBI history.

On August 23, 1996, bin-Laden issued a directive entitled "Message from Osama bin-Muhammad bin-Laden to his Muslim Brothers in the Whole World and Especially in the Arabian Peninsula: Declaration of Jihad Against the Americans Occupying the Land of the Two Holy Mosques; Expel the Heretics from the Arabian Peninsula and from the Hindu Kush Mountains in Afghanistan." The declaration said that efforts should be pooled to kill Americans, and that more Muslims should be encouraged to join the jihad against the American "enemy."

The declaration made no mention of TWA Flight 800, and intelligence sources of the CIA, FBI, and intelligence agencies from various friendly governments consulted after the crash later confirmed that bin-Laden had not taken credit for the crash in conversations with friends or associates. But a declaration of war was enough for the United States to put prompt pressure on Sudan to freeze his assets there and expel him.

Poorer on paper, but with hundreds of millions of dollars squirreled away in secret bank accounts around the world, bin-Laden and his lieutenants moved that September to caves high in the Afghan mountains. From there, two summers later, bin-Laden would coordinate the bombings of the U.S. embassies in Kenya and Tanzania and provoke a military response that would involve some elements—only a few—of the U.S. contingency plan that would have been launched if TWA Flight 800 had proven to be state-sponsored terrorism.

Despite the arrests of Sheik Abdel-Rahman, Ramzi Yousef, and a score of others, the Islamic terrorist network appeared to have grown by the summer of 1996 and, to judge by bin-Laden's declaration of war, appeared even more determined to destroy the United States than it had been six years before, when Meir Kahane had been killed. Still, there were other terrorist groups—some from the Middle East, some based in Europe—no less capable of downing a U.S. jet, and probably no less eager to do so, that the FBI had to check out. Unfortunately, the FBI may have been hindered in this regard by the legacy of budget cuts imposed by CIA director Stansfield Turner during the Carter administration. As a result, many CIA covert operations worldwide in areas viewed by some officials at the time as increasingly safe, including the Middle East, were terminated. Two decades later, the cutbacks still appeared to account for a vacuum of useful intelligence in the volatile Middle East.

Was this why the FBI had not heard more from the Middle East in the weeks after the crash? Kallstrom and the Terrorism Task Force could not be sure if it was because Flight 800 was not a terrorist act, or if they were still feeling the effects of the gutting. However, not long after the crash, the FBI office at the London embassy received a call from a credit-claimer who identified himself as a member of an Iranian group. The call intrigued investigators, because the group had participated, just weeks before the crash, in a conclave of terrorists in Teheran. Among others at the Teheran meeting was Ahmed Jabril, leader of the Popular Front for the Liberation of Palestine (PFLP)—General Command, an organization known to favor airplane bombings. Five altimeter bombs were seized in October 1988 during a raid on a farm in Germany where the PFLP had been housed. Jabril was arrested and jailed for illegal possession of these devices.

Another call had come into the London FBI office about the 15 May Organization, a Palestinian terrorist group that chose airplane bombs to carry out their terror business. In the 1980s, the group, named for the date Israel had gained nationhood, had staged a series of successful attacks, including the bombing on August 11, 1982, of a Pan Am 747 en route from Tokyo to Honolulu. One passenger, a sixteen-year-old boy, was blown out of his seat and bled to death before the plane could land. Two weeks later, another 15 May plane-bomb plot failed when the explosive was discovered in a small bag aboard another Pan Am jet that had just arrived in Rio de Janeiro from Miami. When the FBI tracked down one of the conspirators and persuaded him to become an informant, agents were able to thwart a campaign of terror intended to blow up a dozen planes over a five-year period by getting to each of the bombs before they detonated. But in 1982, 15 May struck again, bombing a TWA flight from Rome to Athens and killing, among others, four American passengers, including a woman and her young daughter who were sucked out of the hole made by the bomb. Mohammed Rashid, one of the group's most powerful and clever operatives, was arrested later that year and sentenced to eighteen years in connection with that bombing. Rashid was released on December 16, 1995. Had he resumed his campaign with TWA Flight 800? Investigators were drawn especially to an earlier plot that targeted a jet bound for Greece from the Middle East using an altimeter bomb.

FBI investigators wondered if the 15 May Organization, or perhaps the PFLP, had planted an altimeter bomb on TWA Flight 800, timed to detonate when the plane reached a certain altitude, since TWA was climbing when it exploded.

As agents sifted through Rashid's movements since his release from prison, a rash of other calls and faxes pointed to even more esoteric suspects. "This is the Islamic Federation of God," one fax declared. "We started with your planes, we will not stop there. We will blow up your trains until we are recognized." The same day—July 24—the Hungarian National Police relayed a threat that Russian organized crime figures in New York would attack a second airplane by the next day, assisted by a Russian pilot who flew regularly out of Kennedy Airport, and the daughter of a Russian-born flight attendant. No such attack occurred, nor was any evidence found of imminent Russian mob maneuvers against American planes. On July 29, a New Zealand journalist received an anonymous call from a "quite lucid" caller who said that Israel's security agency, the Mossad, was responsible for downing TWA Flight 800 as well as the recent bombing in Dhahran. The purpose of these bombings, the caller said, was to destroy the Middle East peace process. Prime Minister Netanyahu, the caller added, was unaware of these "black operations."

Another lead abruptly fizzled, though not before seeming, briefly, to be the key to the mystery.

Two weeks after the crash, divers hauled up a badly damaged male nude body bearing a gold ring with the initials SF. The ring matched a description by family members of the ring worn by the thirty-nine-year-old Algerian businessman, Samir Ferrat, the multimillionaire bachelor whose nationality, as well as his recent trips to Beirut and Cyprus where terrorist cells operated, had drawn investigators from the start.

That the body was too damaged to be readily identified further raised suspicions. Could the body be that of an imposter, a terrorist on a suicide mission, using Ferrat's name and wearing his ring? Credit-card companies had notified the FBI that in the days after the crash, someone had charged purchases on Ferrat's credit cards. Had Ferrat collaborated in a bombing plot, and was he now blithely out on a shopping spree? Or could he have been kidnapped and perhaps killed by terrorists now using his credit cards?

A DNA analysis, however, was matched with a sample drawn from Ferrat's mother. Ferrat had been seated in first class, well forward of the center fuel tank, and his body showed no evidence of proximity to the blast. His carry-on luggage and checked baggage were found relatively undamaged; none of the bags revealed evidence of explosive materials. As for the credit cards, they had been used, agents confirmed, by a family member.

Though Ferrat remained on a list of suspects for some weeks longer, further checking filled in the portrait of a man who, far from engaging in suspicious activity, had led a distinguished career. He had flown to the United States to be with his mother, in Johns Hopkins Hospital in Baltimore with a terminal illness, and was returning home to his fiancée in France when he died.

At about the same time Ferrat's body was being brought up from the ocean bottom, the FBI agents had another reason to think that they had at last made a breakthrough. A man named Victor Bruno admitted that he was a member of the group that had put the bomb on TWA Flight 800. Several details in Bruno's account fit the FBI's working theories at the time. He said, for example, that he had been paid by Iranians to put a bomb aboard a TWA plane at the Detroit airport. This fit with indications that Hezbollah, the Iranian militant group, might have been implicated in a bomb plot that downed TWA Flight 800; Detroit was a center of terrorist activity. Bruno had contacted the Secret Service on the evening of August 1, and a posse of Secret Service agents escorted him downtown to the FBI Command Post. So compelling was his story that Sergeant Jack Casey, a hard-boiled New York City police officer and supervisor on the FBI–NYPD Joint Terrorism Task Force, awakened Corrigan with a call to his home at 2:30 A.M. "Tommy, I think we got it," Casey told Corrigan. "You'd better get your ass in here, this looks good."

As it happened, Victor Bruno was a deaf-mute. Several federal agents, one of whom knew sign language, held him in a back room for hours of questioning. The more he communicated, the more convinced the agents became.

Bruno's story began with a chance meeting he had with a group of Iranians, of whom he gave a detailed description, and relayed how they had given him a suitcase to put on an international flight originating at the Detroit airport on the morning of July 17. The FBI maintained surveillance on terrorist cells there at the time, and was aware of the activity. In fact, a possible Detroit terrorist-cell connection was one of the scenarios investigators had considered in a meeting with Pickard and Kallstrom the previous day. Bruno said he was to be paid $50,000 for his errand the very next morning at a meeting with the Iranians at a diner near Kennedy Airport.

The agents knew that all luggage for an international flight had to be checked by a passenger booked through for the entire flight, but Bruno may have managed, as he said he did, to get off in New York without having his bomb-laden suitcase yanked by security from the rest of the flight. Mistakes happen. Pickard, who had also hummed into the office at 3:00 A.M., thought the story fit so well that the case might be wrapped up by noon, with the Iranians in custody. Excitedly, he dispatched surveillance and SWAT teams to the diner to set up for the morning meeting and payoff. By about 7:30 A.M., Pickard was about to go upstairs to Kallstrom and tell him they had their man. That was when Casey walked over to Corrigan by the coffeemaker in the Command Post and said, "Ya know, Tommy, I've been thinking about this guy."

"Yeah?" Corrigan said.

"I was stabbed by a deaf-mute named Victor Bruno seventeen years ago when I was arresting him," Casey said. He showed Corrigan the scar he had across his forehead. "I looked at this guy hard and he's not familiar. But I don't know."

"Boss, just how many deaf-mutes named Victor Bruno could possibly be running around this country?"

"Don't be a wiseass," Casey shot back.

Just then, an agent appeared, breathless, from the room where Bruno was being questioned. "Call 911," the agent said. "This guy is foaming at the mouth."

Bruno's medication, as it turned out, was wearing off just as the agents received the results of a fingerprint check on him. He was a resident patient at the psychiatric ward of Bellevue Hospital in New York.

Pickard sighed. "Are you absolutely sure there's no truth to his story?" he asked the crestfallen agents who had grilled Bruno.

"This guy is certifiably nuts," an agent said. "Now he's claiming he helped us out with Lincoln's assassination."

A policeman was called to escort Bruno back to Bellevue, but apparently dropped him off at the front entrance without handing him over to a doctor inside. At about noon, Pickard heard sirens squealing outside the FBI building. Just then, Corrigan popped his head in Pickard's office door. "Hey, boss, remember that guy Bruno from this morning?"

"Don't remind me," Pickard said wearily. "Kallstrom was about to call Washington and tell them we might have broken the case. They'd still be laughing at us."

"Well, I think they're going to be laughing at us anyway. Bruno's on our roof. And he's about to jump off."

In fact, Bruno was swinging out from the roof on a wire as crowds on the sidewalk watched. Talking down a suicidal deaf-mute was no easy task. Bruno could barely read lips, he was so jangled. The agent fluent in sign language who had spent all night communicating with Bruno was sent up on the roof to start a finger-flying communication that lasted for hours, until Bruno was finally induced to come down.

Ten days later, the Terrorism Task Force received an urgent call from the FBI office in London. The London agents had just spent several hours interviewing a man who claimed to have put a bomb on TWA Flight 800. Corrigan took the call.

"This is a hot one," the agent told Corrigan, who quickly yelled over for Liguori to join him on the phone line. "Yeah? Tell me everything."

"It's a little strange," the agent relayed. "The guy's a deaf-mute. But very persuasive. His name is Victor Bruno."

"*Victor Bruno?* Oh, no," Corrigan and Liguori said.

Bruno had slipped out of Bellevue, hopped a flight to London, and made straight for the FBI office.

From then on, whenever a lead looked suspiciously promising, someone in the Command Post would cry out, "Victor Bruno," adding a little levity to the otherwise somber investigation.

Perhaps, thought agents in the wake of the Bruno debacle, this investigation was fated to lurch from one dead end to another. The next, no doubt, was the news on August 8 from FBI lab technicians at the Calverton hangar. Using portable machines on pieces of double-edged tape on a three-foot section of flooring, the technicians had found traces of two chemicals used in plastic explosives. Everyone knew from the several times that such traces had been found over the preceding three weeks that the field machines were fallible, but then came the results from Washington.

At 5:30 P.M. on August 8, as he was disembarking from his helicopter at the West Thirtieth Street helipad in Manhattan, Kallstrom got a beep from Kenny Maxwell, his agent in charge at the hangar. Maxwell had just gotten a call from the FBI's chief chemist in Washington. The tape had been run through sophisticated testing equipment.

The traces were real.

CHAPTER 11

Dog Days of Summer

At the Calverton hangar, as each piece of wreckage was logged in, photographed, and identified, it was given to bomb-sniffing German shepherds trained to sit down when they smelled even microscopic traces of explosive residues. On August 7, the dogs were walked up and down a three-foot section of flooring from the coach cabin. Still attached to the floor panel was double-edged tape to hold the carpeting in place. At first, the dogs were confused by the stench of brackish seawater and dead fish, which would grow more intense as days went by, but finally they seated themselves beside it. The floor panel, including its double-sided tape, was tested by the portable machines and drew positive hits for traces of chemicals used in explosives—hits that were now confirmed in Washington.

"What did they find?" Kallstrom demanded. He was talking on a heliport pay phone, a hard line that scanners couldn't listen in on.

"PETN and RDX," Maxwell told him.

"Where?"

"On the two-sided tape that holds the carpet down, on row 25 or 26."

Seat 26K was the one Yousef had chosen for his test-run bomb on the Philippines Airlines plane. It was in the midsection, over the center fuel tank, which investigators now felt was the site of an explosion.

Kallstrom hung up and rang Steve Burmeister, the chief chemist at the FBI. Burmeister had found and analyzed crucial evidence for many high-profile bombing cases, including Pan Am Flight 103 over Lockerbie, Scotland; the World Trade Center; and, most recently, Oklahoma City. Since the Flight 800 crash, he had shuttled between Calverton and Washington, often bringing small, promising pieces of wreckage with him to test at the Washington lab. The day before, he had brought the carpet tape to his lab.

"How much did you find?" Kallstrom wanted to know.

"Minute traces," Burmeister said. "Very minute traces. But PETN and RDX in any amount is pretty intriguing."

PETN, as Kallstrom knew, is pentaerythritol tetranitrate. A chemical explosive devised by the military, it had become an ingredient of choice for terrorists because it could be mixed with other chemicals to form the puttylike, more powerful plastic explosive called SEMTEX. The compound called RDX—research development explosive—had also been devised by the military and was first used on Soviet soldiers in Afghanistan. It, too, is an ingredient of SEMTEX. Properly fabricated, SEMTEX looks and feels like putty and can be molded into an unobtrusive shape—say, as the inner lining of an attaché case or carry-on bag. Because it has no metal parts or recognizable shapes, SEMTEX can pass undetected through metal scanners and X-ray machines. On Pan Am Flight 103, it was the explosive that had been placed in a portable radio–cassette player carried in a piece of checked luggage that ripped through the luggage bin and the fuselage of the plane. PETN, he knew, was also used in missile warheads.

"Where does this get us?" Kallstrom asked.

"Not where we'd like to be," Burmeister said with a sigh. "All we've got is chemicals. We don't have any collateral evidence on any of the wreckage yet." For all the investigators knew, some absentminded chemist with traces of PETN on his shoes might have come aboard the plane as a paying passenger weeks before the crash.

From the secure phone in his Crown Victoria, Kallstrom called Louis Freeh to give him the news. Freeh was interested, but wary.

"This just doesn't do it, Jim."

Kallstrom agreed that more of the plane had to be found to see evidence of blast damage. So far, no such evidence had been found.

The find did dispel one fear that had haunted Kallstrom from the start: that all chemical residues would be washed away by salt water within hours or days of the crash. No one had been able to say exactly how long such residues might survive underwater. Probably they would be washed away quickly from metal, but this latest find showed that traces remained far longer on absorbent fabrics—not just carpeting, but seat cushions or insulation. If a bomb had exploded on Flight 800, more residue would almost certainly be found on wreckage still to be retrieved. But despite Kristensen's round-the-clock dive operation, and the great many twisted chunks of metal on the hangar floor at Calverton, only 15 percent of the plane had been brought up so far. Of that 15 percent, only the one bit of carpet tape had yielded traces of explosives.

When Kallstrom returned to his twenty-eighth-floor office, he told Pickard: "Something important has happened. Get up here right away."

Pickard stopped at George Andrew's office on the way to the elevator and told him to hang up the phone, that Kallstrom had something important.

"We've got to find all the pieces around this floorboard," Kallstrom told the agents when he'd given them the news. "The divers should focus on that. I want every inch of carpeting in that area." On Boeing's detailed chart of the 747-100, every piece of floorboard was numbered. The board in question was panel 121. With the big sonar robot *Deep Drone* scanning the wreckage nearly every hour, the divers might soon be able to bring up all the floor panels adjacent to 121, and some of the carpeting as well. "Keep this quiet," Kallstrom added. "Until we know what this is about, the last thing we want is the media finding out about it and jumping to conclusions."

Kallstrom would have preferred to keep news of the discovery to a small circle of FBI agents and lab scientists, but he had to share it with the NTSB. He called NTSB chairman Jim Hall in Washington and told him that explosive traces had been found. Adhering to his need-to-know policy, he refrained from telling Hall where they were found. "We don't know what all this means, Jim," he said. "The reason it's there is probably criminal, but we're still analyzing it."

Hall asked if there was anything he could do.

"No, Jim, thanks," Kallstrom said. "But listen, this is a very close hold," meaning that Hall should handle the revelation on a strict need-to-know basis.

"I understand," Hall said in a deep Tennessee drawl. In his own way, Hall was an admirable public servant. He believed in leading his organization with dignity, working through the system and reaching reasoned compromises when intramural disputes arose. At the same time, like most high Washington officials, he had larger ambitions. He was said to want to run for governor of Tennessee. For him, the traces were good news. They meant the cause was almost certainly criminal, so that the NTSB would no longer be responsible for Flight 800—no longer overwhelmed by an investigation that was preventing it from addressing a host of other large aviation accidents, including an ongoing investigation of the ValuJet crash as well as the crashes in Pittsburgh and Colorado Springs. Without saying why, Hall called Al Dickinson, his chief investigator on the scene at Calverton, to tell him to establish a protocol for turning the investigation over to the FBI, should the need arise.

Kallstrom next called Robert Francis and repeated the need for secrecy. By now, Kallstrom knew Francis could be trusted and had grown to like him. Playfully, he liked to needle him about his elitist tastes. One day, heading out to the *Grasp* with Admirals Flanagan and Linnon, Francis talked about learning to fly during his college days. "Yeah—and for graduation, your daddy bought you a Gulfstream, right?" Kallstrom said. Everyone laughed, including Francis. In the weeks since the crash, Francis had taken a lot of heat from Hall and Dr. Loeb, the NTSB's director of aviation safety, for not consulting with them on the public statements he made. Ron Schleede, Loeb's deputy, had gone so far as to warn Kenny Maxwell that Bob Francis did not have any say over the direction of the safety board's investigation. "If Francis agrees to do something with the FBI," declared Schleede, "he has to run it by us first."

Kallstrom liked Francis all the more for that.

Both men knew, without having to say so, how close the FBI seemed to be to declaring the investigation a criminal matter, and that the NTSB would no longer act as the lead agency in that event. But as much as he felt, privately, that the crash looked like a crime, and as much as he wanted sole authority if it was a crime, Kallstrom knew he'd need help from the NTSB. The FBI couldn't put together broken planes or determine how a piece of wreckage got twisted in a certain way, and the NTSB experts would be needed in court to testify on technical matters.

The next morning at 6:45, Kallstrom called a meeting in the conference room down the hall from his office on the twenty-eighth floor of all his senior staff, key members of the terrorist task force, bomb technicians, and Steve Burmeister, who had flown up from Washington. "What I am about to tell you is to be kept secret," Kallstrom said. Word had spread fast overnight among the investigators, and privately they were galvanized by the news, but they tried to appear surprised when Kallstrom told them about the traces. "Remember, we've only got traces," he stressed. "I know some of you are thinking this is definitely a bomb, but we just don't know. We don't have any blast damage, and without that this could be worthless." But he was energized and so were the others. They were, as Pickard put it later, thinking "criminal" like never before, "If this leaks out to the media and I find out who did it," Kallstrom warned, "I'll cut your balls off with a rusty hatchet."

As Liguori and Corrigan walked down the hallway, Liguori saw his partner was lagging behind. "Why are you walking so slow?"

"I'm just trying to imagine," Corrigan said, "what it would be like to walk without balls."

———

At Calverton, Kenny Maxwell directed agents to set aside a separate hangar for Flight 800's carpeting, which was also comprised of numbered pieces. Using charts from Boeing, the agents could lay out the carpet squares looking for tears, shredding, or burns that might indicate bomb damage. They also examined the seats recovered so far in those areas, and looked again at the passengers assigned to them, as Dr. Wetli's staff at the Suffolk County morgue along with agents reexamined injuries and X rays, looking for bomb fragments. Each piece of wreckage was sniffed by the dogs. If a dog "hit on" a fragment of carpeting, flooring, or fuselage, it was sent to the portable testing machines, one of which belonged to the FBI, the other to Alcohol, Tobacco, and Firearms, some of whose agents continued to nurse a private rivalry with the FBI. If one of the portable field machines registered positive, the piece in question would be sent down to Washington—either to the FBI lab or the ATF lab. Kallstrom overheard some debate on where each piece should go and was agitated. "You guys are like a bunch of twelve-year-old boys showing off your biceps," he said. "This isn't about whose equipment is better, it's about finding the right answer, together."

By mid-August, divers had come up with the very piece of carpet that had rested above floor panel 121 and its telltale tape. The carpet showed no sign of damage. Nonetheless, the adjacent carpet squares and floor panels were sent to the Washington FBI lab, where none tested positive for explosive-chemicals residue or showed signs of bomb damage. A few suspect pieces were also flown to laboratories in England. Kallstrom and Freeh wanted independent confirmation of the findings, so that no defense attorneys would be able to question the credibility of the FBI lab tests if Flight 800 did turn out to be a crime.

Two days after the traces were found, Jim Hall came up to Calverton to inspect the progress. During a meeting, he surprised Kallstrom by raising the possibility of withdrawing the NTSB from its lead-agency position and turning over the investigation to the FBI. "Isn't there enough to say this is criminal now?" Hall asked. He seemed eager to be rid of the investigation.

"Definitely not," Kallstrom said. He explained the need to find hard evidence of the bomb's effects: the pitting or scarring of metal, for example, or certain teethlike tears. "And just think what happens if the NTSB announces it's handing over the investigation to the FBI," Kallstrom said. "Reporters know that means a criminal investigation. They ask how we know. We say explosive traces. They ask for details, what kind of bomb, where it was set, or was it a missile—all that. We say we don't know. We look stupid, and we may be wrong. What if the traces turn out to be from something else altogether?

"It's kind of like you hit this incredible fly ball," Kallstrom said of the positive find on traces, "and everybody in the stadium thinks it's going out of the ballpark, but an outfielder backs up against the wall, jumps up, and catches the son of a bitch. It's a good hit, but it's not a home run."

Though Hall seemed ready to have the FBI announce that a crime had been committed, hoping to extricate the NTSB from the investigation, William Tobin, the outspoken FBI metallurgist, was eager to buttonhole Kallstrom at the hangar and declare that in his expert opinion, the traces meant nothing: The cause was still clearly mechanical.

Tobin wanted another opportunity to educate the FBI chief. He wanted to show Kallstrom why the metal fragments were incompatible with a high explosive, for example; why the flowering damage to the metal was caused by the impact of the fuselage hitting the ocean surface, not from a missile or bomb. He knew Kallstrom would bristle at another such challenge, but Tobin believed he had a duty to perform, and he seemed to revel in being a lone wolf. When he heard that explosive chemicals were found on the wreckage, he was sure that Kallstrom would soon announce that the traces indicated a criminal act.

"Look, you've got to tell the American people that a missile did not take down this plane," Tobin declared.

Kallstrom's eyes narrowed. "I'm not trying to make this a missile," he said. "I'm not trying to make this a bomb. But I sure as hell want to make this the absolute truth.

"Tobin, you may be very right that there is no evidence in the 15 percent we've recovered so far. But how can you be saying this when we haven't got the rest of the plane yet?"

"If there was evidence, we'd have seen it," Tobin insisted. "You don't need any more of the plane. That's the whole point of metallurgical analysis. You analyze pieces; they tell the story. The story here is very clear: no bomb, no missile."

"Tobin, get off your lazy ass and keep looking," Kallstrom said, his face turning red. "And when you find something that doesn't look right, let me know and I'll have a real explosives expert come look at it. What do you want to do—fold your tent and go home? You tired? You miss your mommy?"

The two men stood toe-to-toe, Kallstrom towering over Tobin. Then Kallstrom lowered his voice slightly and said in stern, measured words, "Get your bony ass back in there and do your goddamn job. Keep looking. Look. Look. Look. Look. Look. Look. And when we get all of the plane in here and still don't see anything, then I'll stand up and say this was not a crime."

Tobin was as angry as Kallstrom. That day, he called his immediate superior in Washington, Dr. Randy Murch, one of the laboratory's deputy assistant directors, for whom he had great respect. He complained that Kallstrom was forcing him to continue to look for evidence of a bomb or missile that would never be found. He wanted to go on record with the FBI's lawyers that Kallstrom was pushing the missile theory without justification. He wanted a congressional hearing.

Murch had put up with Tobin's stubbornness before. The man was, after all, a forensic expert in how metals behave under stress. But Tobin seemed to think he was the most important person in the FBI probe. Had he forgotten that in science there was no room for hunches or opinions, that nothing substituted for proof? Was Tobin possibly overstressed, in need of a rest?

"Bill," Murch said, adopting the soothing voice of a doctor with an hysteric, "it's too early in the investigation to reach conclusions. This is how we are going to solve it. You are going to get back to work and do what Kallstrom says, continue to look for evidence. You are supposed to be conducting an objective scientific investigation up there."

Tobin muttered that was all he was trying to do and hung up, but Murch's message failed to keep him from sounding off to anyone who would listen. Two weeks later, as reports trickled back to him, Kallstrom decided enough was enough. He called down to the FBI lab and spoke to Murch, who had once worked for Kallstrom in New York. "Randy, I want this guy Tobin removed from the investigation. He obviously doesn't want to continue to investigate. It could very well be that Tobin is right. But you know, and I know, that that won't be clear until we have more of the plane up. This guy is unprofessional. And it's frankly outrageous that a guy who is saying these things is working for the FBI. I want him off the case."

Kallstrom told Kenny Maxwell to expect a new metallurgist—an FBI rookie, but one with a doctorate degree in material science. The NTSB had metallurgists of its own, and there were numerous military explosives experts at China Lake and the Pentagon. The FBI, too, had explosives experts in the hangar. In addition, Kallstrom sought an independent view from one of the best metallurgists in the country, a man who had just retired from Alcoa. Kallstrom hired him to examine the wreckage to determine whether the evidence indicated that a bomb or missile had taken down the plane. The Alcoa metallurgist would spend months on the task.

Kallstrom thought he had heard the last of Tobin, but he was wrong. Seemingly bitter and vengeful, Tobin would stir up trouble—and with his FBI experience to lend his accusations heft, he would do that pretty well.

Kallstrom was cautious about saying that Flight 800 was an accident; he was also cautious about saying that it was a crime. Days later came a twist that showed why. Neil Herman, the meticulously thorough head of the FBI–NYPD Joint Terrorism Task Force, was the one who first observed that the U.S. military occasionally chartered commercial planes. What if Flight 800 had been used to transport troops, and a soldier's boot had been contaminated by traces of PETN and RDX? "Absolutely," Kallstrom agreed. "Let's check it out." On August 13, TWA was asked to comb its records for any such charter of #N93119—and found one. Three months before the crash, on April 2 and 3, 1996, the plane had been used by Hunter Army Base in Georgia to transfer three hundred troops to the Persian Gulf for joint training exercises with other military branches.

This was not good news for the investigation. If a soldier's boot had left chemical traces, the agents would be no closer to determining whether a crime had caused the crash. If chemical traces from a terrorist's bomb or missile were subsequently found, a benign source of PETN and RDX would complicate the prosecution of anyone charged with the crime. A smart defense lawyer could ask how the FBI knew that those other traces weren't also left by soldiers' boots. At the Command Post that day, the mood was subdued.

From the FBI's office in Atlanta, agents visited Hunter Army Base to learn that among the troops who had ridden on #N93119 were eight explosive-ordnance technicians. But every soldier had been issued new boots, shoes, and uniforms just before the flight, and none of this gear had come into contact with chemicals of any kind. No explosives had been brought on board, only rifles and handguns locked in a safe and placed in the cargo hold. Moreover, the EOD technicians had not touched any live explosives for at least seven days prior to the trip.

The FBI called TWA again. Was the airline sure that no *other* charters to the military of plane #N93119 had taken place prior to April 1996? TWA was certain, and added that any military charters prior to 1992 would be irrelevant: The aircraft had undergone a complete interior overhaul in that year, with new seats, carpeting, curtains, and the like.

The mystery deepened on August 14 with the discovery of nitroglycerin traces on a piece of the forward galley. Agents had targeted the food carts as a likely haven for a bomb. If a portable radio–cassette player could contain the bomb that blew up Pan Am Flight 103, what would keep a terrorist from planting a bomb within one of the four-foot-high food carts? When Corrigan and Liguori studied the plane's preflight preparations, they felt that the catering process was a vulnerable point. A terrorist might have taken a job with TWA's caterer and slipped a bomb into an empty food tray slot, or a worker transporting the food to the plane could have fastened a bomb to the bottom of the wheeled food cart. The possibilities were numerous and unnerving.

The nitroglycerin traces complicated the puzzle. Ramzi Yousef had used nitroglycerin as an ingredient in his Philippines Airlines bomb, smuggling it aboard in a contact-lens-solution bottle. But a bomb made with PETN and RDX would not normally employ nitroglycerin. The two findings suggested different explosives designs. Nitroglycerin, a favorite of safecrackers, was also an ingredient in medicine used in small, potent quantities to increase blood flow to the heart and thus lower blood pressure. Perhaps a passenger had his blood pressure medicine with him, and it had somehow been flung into the galley.

As agents sought passengers on Flight 800's manifest who might have had heart trouble, Louis Freeh asked Kallstrom to fly down to meet with Attorney General Reno and her staff about the findings. The attorney general had been apprised of the first positive hits as soon as they were confirmed, and she had passed the word on to the White House, but a more detailed briefing was clearly in order.

Kallstrom flew down to Washington on August 22 and spoke in the attorney general's office to a group that included Jamie Gorelick, the deputy attorney general, and several high-ranking Justice Department officials, as well as Louis Freeh. Kallstrom emphasized, at the start and again at the end of his talk, that the residues did *not* prove a bomb or missile had hit Flight 800. Until blast damage was found, the investigators had nothing more than very intriguing leads. "It's like making a cake," Kallstrom said, indulging his love of metaphors. "You have flour, but you have no eggs, no butter, no icing. It's not a cake yet. It's only part of a cake. Until you have all the ingredients, you don't have a cake."

On the shuttle back to New York, Kallstrom was pleased that everyone in the attorney general's office seemed to understand what the residues meant and didn't mean. As he emerged from the plane at La Guardia's Marine Air Terminal, he heard his beeper, and hustled out to his car.

"You won't believe this," said Jim Margolin, the FBI press aide to Joe Valiquette in the New York office. "I just got a call from a *New York Times* reporter. They've got the residue story and they're running it in tomorrow's paper."

Kallstrom was stunned. Could there be any doubt that someone in Reno's office had leaked the news? This was unbelievable. For just over two weeks, the secret had held within a fairly large need-to-know circle: the FBI's director, Louis Freeh; dozens of FBI agents from Pickard and Schiliro on down; the FBI's lab scientists in Washington; and the top officials of NTSB. Now, within an hour of bringing the attorney general's staff into the loop, it was blown. Conceivably, an investigator at the hangar might have leaked, though Kenny Maxwell had done his best to restrict the information to a select few. Or perhaps someone already in the loop leaked, but the timing was suspicious.

"I told him I could neither confirm nor deny," Margolin went on. "But he kept saying this was proof of a bomb or missile, and he was going with it. He said he knows you were in Washington today and that you were probably getting ready to make an announcement that this is a bomb. Maybe you ought to talk to him."

Kallstrom called the *New York Times* reporter from his car phone as he was leaving the airport. The reporter said he had it from sources that the FBI lab had confirmed the PETN on the plane. Wasn't this proof that a bomb had taken down the plane?

Grimly, Kallstrom confirmed off the record that traces had been found, but cautioned that they might not indicate a bomb, and so a story alleging that the FBI had evidence of a bomb would not be merely premature—it might be wrong.

The reporter was unpersuaded. So were the editors of the *Times* whom Kallstrom called next. To publish the story would be to rush to judgment, he advised. Kallstrom knew it would do nothing to change the course of the investigation, but a story on the front page of *The New York Times* would lead to chaos to which he would have to respond. The story would unnecessarily alarm the public, and it would confuse the victims' families, who would think the FBI had been holding out on them, when all it was trying to do was pin down the facts before publicizing them. But the editors had made a decision: Tangible evidence that suggested a plastic explosive as the cause of Flight 800's crash was front-page news. They had a responsibility, as they observed, to inform the public.

The headline in the next morning's edition was electrifying. PRIME EVIDENCE FOUND THAT DEVICE EXPLODED IN CABIN OF FLIGHT 800. The story not only reported that traces of PETN had been found, but observed that "the discovery meets the FBI's previously stated standard for declaring that the plane was brought down by a criminal act." It stated further that senior investigators were not ready to declare the crash a criminal act in part because they did not yet know whether the explosion was caused by a bomb or missile.

That day, Kallstrom, Margolin, and several other senior law enforcement officials fielded hundreds of calls: from victims' families and their lawyers outraged that they should be "the last to know"; from reporters at other publications, furious the *Times* had scooped them; from high government officials irked not to be in the loop; and more. To all, they reiterated what they'd told *The New York Times*. Later that day at a news conference, Kallstrom read a prepared statement confirming the discovery of the chemical traces but stating that it was premature to assume an explosive was responsible. There would have to be additional proof, such as explosive shock waves in salvaged metal, he told reporters. The *Times*, undeterred, ran a follow-up story the next day, quoting Kallstrom, then describing an unnamed senior law enforcement official as having "laughed out loud" at the suggestion that traces of plastic explosives might have been left on the plane in some benign fashion.

Generally Kallstrom admired reporters and actually enjoyed the give-and-take with them. To him they were, with a few exceptions, "a force for good in this country." He couldn't understand why so many government and law enforcement officials refused to talk to reporters and then complained about the accuracy of their stories. In his own experience, reporters had usually gone the extra mile to get their facts straight and present their stories fairly. Besides, they were going to run a story whether or not they had his cooperation. "It's like the sausage business," he told agents. "They are going to make sausage every day. If you want to be part of the ingredients, then talk to them." But even when a well-intentioned reporter published a misbegotten story that made the FBI's work more difficult, quoting unnamed "workers in the hangar," Kallstrom only muttered something about rusty hatchets.

But these traces were unexplainable. In the five weeks since the crash, Kallstrom had been exhausted, exhilarated, angry, and grief stricken. Now, unable to clarify the seemingly obvious, he was frustrated. For a man so driven to find the truth, that was the worst of all.

———

There were moments in those last days of August when Pickard wondered if a bomber as diabolical as Ramzi Yousef had set out not merely to blow up

Flight 800 but to scatter false clues to bedevil the investigators in its aftermath. On August 28, another positive hit of RDX was found, a minuscule trace on a canvas curtain in the rear cargo hold of the plane. That no more PETN or RDX had been located in the vicinity of the first hit was maddening enough. How could grains of the chemicals, constituting no more than 10 percent of a salt packet from Burger King, be found in isolation? How could the floor panels adjacent to panel 121 not contain more—much more—of the stuff if it had exploded in a bomb? Why was there no visible explosive damage to the metal or other pieces where the traces were found? And how else, if not from a bomb, would explosive residue have become ingrained in the carpet tape? The minute traces of RDX in the rear cargo hold were seemingly too far from the first traces to be part of the same bomb—if there was a bomb. All but the last-minute passenger luggage was placed in the forward cargo hold. The rear hold contained mostly freight; the canvas curtain containing the new trace of RDX served as a space divider. It was certainly possible that someone could have put a bomb back there: The eight hundred pounds of glitter, for example, had been in the rear cargo hold, and who could say that a SEMTEX bomb had not been tucked within one of those boxes? But then, surely more traces would have emerged from the same area. So far, none had.

"If it looks like we have an explosion in the center fuel tank area, and we've isolated rows 14 to 28 as the possible location for the bomb, then this other RDX in the rear can't be a bomb, too," Pickard said to Kallstrom in a moment of exasperation in Kallstrom's office.

"How about multiple bombs?" Kallstrom mused.

Pickard swallowed hard. "Multiple bombs?" He hadn't thought of that. "But how do you detonate multiple bombs on a single plane?"

"That's for you to figure out."

Pickard thought a minute more and then shook his head. "Hell, no one's that good. They were lucky to get one off, if that's what they did."

"How about the vent system? Could the traces have been transported by it from one end of the plane to the other?"

"Yeah, well. . . . We'll check that out, too," Pickard said with a sigh.

Later, alone again, Kallstrom stood by the huge picture window of his office looking out. Sometimes he stood there for long minutes at a time, as if the answer was out there in the sweeping uptown view that extended as far as the George Washington Bridge, the Empire State Building, and the East River. His eyes settled on the United Nations building, among whose numbers were nations known to sponsor terrorism.

————

On September 6, the dogs sat down again, this time beside pieces of flooring directly above the center-fuel-tank area. The portable field testers registered positive, the Washington lab confirmed, and yet the mystery of the traces seemed no clearer. Again these were trace elements. Kallstrom spoke obsessively now of a "eureka" piece that would tell the tale; he even used the term in his daily news conferences, but this latest find offered no more tangible clues than its predecessors had. Then, after six weeks of positive hits and negative leads, the mystery unraveled.

Back in mid-August, the FBI had asked an official of the FAA based at Kennedy Airport if live explosives were ever used to help train bomb-sniffing dogs on an aircraft. In less than an hour, the answer had come back. Yes, the FAA did use live explosives for that purpose, but only on the tarmac, never aboard planes.

Later in August, Kallstrom told George Andrew to ask the FAA again if live explosives had ever been used, even once, on commercial aircraft to train bomb-sniffing dogs. Could the FAA make a thorough check this time? A few hours later, an FAA official assigned to the hangar gave the FBI a different answer. Often, local police forces did use live ordnance on commercial planes to train bomb-sniffing dogs. The FAA's office of security had no idea, however, which planes had been used for the tests. It recorded only the *flight* numbers of the planes used, not their *tail* numbers. The San Diego police, for example, would be granted permission to use TWA Flight 606 at the San Diego airport in the hours before it was to fly on a certain day, but the actual plane designated as Flight 606 might be different from day to day. As for the records of such testing, they were kept not by the airlines, or on the planes used, but at the airports where the tests were conducted.

The agents at the Command Post were staggered. They had checked the complete service record for #N93119 and found no dog-testing records. Now, with that casual admission from the FAA, the field of inquiry had broadened dramatically. The entire flight history of #N93119 had to be tracked back to 1992, when the plane had been overhauled and its interior refurbished. The FAA had to find out which airport the plane had touched down at every day of those last four years, how long it had remained there, and what flight number had been assigned to the plane. From all of those airports, records had to be obtained of when, if ever, dog-training tests had been held on planes, and when, if ever, #N93119 had been one of the planes used. The police departments that had conducted those tests had to be consulted as well. The FBI agents were dismayed that the FAA had not done this investigation on its own initiative, especially since its security office was aware that chemical traces had been found on Flight 800. What was wrong with these people?

On September 20, after three weeks of combing through records, the FAA notified the FBI that the plane with the tail number #N93119 had been at the Lambert–St. Louis International Airport in St. Louis, Missouri, on June 10, 1996, five weeks prior to the crash and, while parked at Gate 50, had been used for a bomb-testing exercise with a police dog between 10:45 and 11:30 A.M. The officer who had conducted the test was St. Louis airport police officer Herman Burnett.

The next morning, Corrigan sent Agent Jim Van Rhein, a thirty-year veteran of the FBI based in the St. Louis office, to the airport to interview Burnett. "You bet," Burnett said when Van Rhein asked him if he had used PETN, RDX, or nitroglycerin in his test that morning. "Used gunpowder, too. We keep all that stuff at a storage facility at the airport, makes it real convenient."

On the morning of June 10, Burnett had subjected Carlo, a German shepherd police dog, to an impressive gamut of olfactory challenges for his police-dog certification. Leaving Carlo in his police cruiser on the tarmac outside the gate, Burnett loaded the plane with enough plastic explosives to blow the airport sky-high: five pounds of SEMTEX, or C-4, comprised of PETN, RDX, nitroglycerin, and gunpowder; five one-pound sticks of ammonia dynamite; eight small containers of TNT; and various other substances. Then he had put the containers on a food cart in one of the galleys, wheeled the cart around the plane, and distributed the chemicals in different locations, all carefully noted. On a seat in the second row of first class, he unscrewed a cap of smokeless gunpowder and placed the can on its side; some of the powder, Burnett acknowledged to Van Rhein, might have spilled out in the process. In a magazine pouch behind a seat in row 10 of the main cabin, he placed one of his containers of C-4; another was placed in row 26, near floorboard 121. Then Carlo was fetched, and set loose in the cabin. Within minutes, he found all the chemicals. Burnett was pleased. "Carlo," he said, "you have just passed your certification test to be a bomb dog. Congratulations." As a reward, Burnett gave Carlo a "Kong" toy, collected all his explosive-chemical containers, and left the plane. "And some of the other containers, could they have spilled, too?" Van Rhein asked.

"Yeah, I could have spilled more than just a little," Burnett reflected. "The packages were old and cracked, and we hadn't used them in a while, so more than usual might have come out."

"How could these guys in St. Louis see us talking about explosive chemical traces on national television and not call the FBI to say they had tested a dog on a TWA plane?" Kallstrom asked Pickard. "What morons." In a news conference that day, he observed that no amount of chemical traces would be enough now for the investigators to conclude a bomb had exploded on Flight 800. Metallurgical evidence would have to be found—even if the bomber turned himself in. Yet the Carlo caper would not diminish the possibility that a bomb or missile had downed the jet. "If this is a bomb, there has to be a eureka piece. We have not stopped looking for it," Kallstrom said, noting that in Pan Am Flight 103 the eureka piece that showed blast damage was the size of a football. Privately, he was coming to feel that in order to do that, the investigators at Calverton might have to do more than finish the ongoing reconstruction of the center fuel tank.

They might have to reconstruct the whole plane.

A day after the dog fiasco, Kallstrom and his senior investigators were in his office considering their next steps. They were depressed.

"Hey, I just heard the NYPD flew one of its bomb dogs out to St. Louis to interview Carlo," Corrigan said. "At least Carlo hasn't been lawyered up yet. He's willing to be questioned.

"In fact," Corrigan added, "I heard at one point during the interview our dog just put his paws up to his face and told Carlo, 'You're a disgrace to the entire K-9 community. You oughta have your badge pulled.' "

There was a dead silence in the room. Kallstrom and the others looked at Corrigan as if he had been hallucinating. Then Kallstrom let out a huge laugh, and the others joined in.

CHAPTER 12

COEFFICIENT OF FRICTION

Throughout the weeks that chemical traces had tantalized the investigators, the press, and the public, most of Kallstrom's seven hundred agents on the investigation had worked persistently to run down the myriad other leads that had accrued. Many of those had come from residents of East Moriches and the surrounding area. Suspicious activity by odd-looking characters, photographs and videos that appeared to show clues to, or traces of, a missile on the night of the crash—all were painstakingly checked out.

None survived serious scrutiny.

An early fizzle was the tip from several local residents about a man in a battered green car, possibly a Gremlin, who parked on successive evenings at Smith Point Beach State Park and appeared to be pointing a small cannon out his window. By finding someone in the Smithtown area who knew vaguely where the suspect lived, and then doing a tristate motor-vehicle trace, the FBI found him. His "cannon" was a large video camera. He had been photographing sunsets, and so had partially covered the camera with a towel to keep excess light out. He showed the camera and its long zoom lens to FBI agents, who saw how the lens might be taken for a cannon. They could see, too, how the car might be taken for a Gremlin. But in this respect, too, the locals were mistaken. The freelance movie cameraman's car was a 1964 four-door Plymouth sedan.

The videotape of a missile "drone" being loaded onto a flatbed truck in Virginia had finally been dismissed after much rechecking. So too was the video taken some days before the crash by a repairman on the rooftop of Smithtown Hospital. This was the video that appeared to show a missile in flight—perhaps a test run for Flight 800. On closer analysis by missile experts at the FBI's Washington labs and at the Defense Intelligence Agency, it turned out to be a fighter jet.

The Kabot snapshot taken at a Republican fund-raiser, perhaps the most promising of the local leads, also turned out to be a bust. After two weeks, analysis by the FBI and CIA concluded that Kabot's camera was facing north-northeast. The TWA explosion occurred in a south-southwesterly direction, almost directly behind Mrs. Kabot when she took the picture. The investigators also concluded that the image was not a missile because it had only two of the three necessary signatures of a missile: a white dot that would signify a burning propellant, and a dark streak that would be the missile itself. It was missing the exhaust trail that would follow the missile. There were, as it happened, many planes in the air at the time the Kabot picture was taken. Radar showed about eight or nine had flown through that area at about the same altitude of the object in the picture. Almost certainly, the streak in Kabot's snapshot was from one of them.

As for Heidi Krieger's photograph of a seeming missile, it was analyzed microscopically at the FBI headquarters in Washington, where investigators literally wiped away the "missile" during a conventional cleaning of the film. It was just a speck of dirt.

The 270 eyewitness accounts of a missile streak were, to be sure, compelling individually, far more so in the aggregate. Many FBI agents felt—and would continue to feel long afterward—that the sheer number of them was powerful persuasion that a missile had hit the plane. Yet at the Command Post, the missile team under Tom Pickard found problems with nearly all the accounts. Some of the witnesses appeared to have been looking away from the explosion when it occurred. Only about a dozen had been standing in the right place at the right time, looking in the general direction from which a missile would have had to come. But none of those witnesses mentioned the word "missile" in their initial interviews—other than Ann DeCaro, who, though she would later say that she had used the "m-word," used "bottle-rocket type of missile" to describe what she said was a fireworks display. Some eyewitnesses used the word days or weeks later, when they were reinterviewed, by which time talk of a missile had saturated the airwaves. The accounts of eyewitnesses seeing flarelike streaks were all taken seriously by the FBI, and yet the more agents tried to figure out what people saw, the more confounding it became. Because they put the "streaks of light" in dozens of different locations, mathematical efforts to pinpoint the missile's trajectory based on the accounts made their task very difficult.

Even the eyewitness accounts offered by the Air National Guardsmen conflicted on many key points. By their descriptions, their helicopter would have been situated behind and below a missile. Thus they would only have seen the bright white light that emanated from the missile's rear. Yet Captain Baur had thought he saw a flarelike object with a brilliant red flame streaking from east to west. The red flare, he said, hit another object, ending its trajectory as if it had hit a wall. He thought perhaps he'd seen two small single-engine planes collide. Major Meyer, sitting next to Baur, thought he'd seen something "like a shooting star" moving from west to east, in the opposite direction from Baur's red flare. The streak, he said, then descended in a gentle curve toward the top of the plane. Richardson, the third guardsman in the helicopter, had seen neither a missilelike flare nor the explosion itself.

Though their helicopter carried no armaments more powerful than machine guns as a rule, through much of August the guardsmen were considered suspects as well as eyewitnesses. The possibility of a friendly-fire missile had put every U.S. military vessel, plane, and submarine under initial suspicion, but the guardsmen had moved higher on the list with the tip to the Manhattan Command Post that some of them had met secretly, before their initial FBI interviews, to be sure their stories were consistent.

"Find out if we have a problem with these guys," Pickard told Corrigan following the call on the crew's secret meeting. "Maybe these weekend warriors rigged something onto their Black Hawk and shot it off. Could they have set off a flare that hit this plane? I don't know how those things work."

In the helicopter out to Westhampton Air National Guard Base, Corrigan thought about the possibility of friendly fire. He believed that if a military accident was responsible, that information should be made public within twenty-four hours of the disaster. Longer than that, in his mind, would be a cover-up, an unforgivable crime. And if people were now covering up the deaths of 230 people, Corrigan knew one thing for sure: He and Liguori and the rest of the Terrorism Task Force would have no problem handcuffing them, and Kallstrom would probably grab them before anyone else had the chance.

Corrigan and FBI agent Joe Fanning first interviewed Baur, who was a pilot for U.S. Customs and practiced search-and-rescue missions for the Air National Guard on his days off, then Meyer and Richardson. The crew members volunteered that they had gotten together six days after the crash at the house of a major in the Air National Guard, who also happened to be a hypnotist. When asked, the guardsmen were happy to discuss the hypnosis session. In fact, they were thrilled to have done it, and felt it stimulated their memories. At the end, said Baur, they all felt so good they stood up and high-fived one another. They even videotaped the session and turned the tapes over to the FBI.

Corrigan admonished Baur to lay off the hypnosis, and not to read anything, in the press or elsewhere, about missiles. If TWA Flight 800 was a crime, he said, Baur could be an important witness, testifying that he saw something hit the aircraft. Any new information he gathered since the crash would taint that testimony.

Meyer came off as an even less useful witness than he had appeared to be in the initial days after the crash. He described what he had seen in such melodramatic terms that his story seemed greatly overdrawn. Baur's manner was similarly self-important, but his story was at least consistent and more credible. Of the three, Denis Richardson seemed the most credible. A paratrooper in Vietnam, he was nearly in tears as he recalled his frustration that the Coast Guard, in the initial minutes after the explosion, would not take the coordinates from him of where the wreckage had plunged into the water. He said he knew it would slow the recovery of the victims' bodies. He convinced the investigators, at least, that nobody on board the helicopter had anything to do with the explosion itself. As important, when the investigators went on to examine the helicopter, they saw that nothing on board had been modified.

"Boss, their stories square away," Corrigan told Pickard on the phone after the interviews. "No way they're faking it."

Another friendly-fire possibility had been eliminated, but the guardsmen seemed so sure of what they had seen that their accounts only strengthened suspicions that *something* had been shot at the plane. Haunted by the possibility, the missile team worked literally around the clock with experts from China Lake and the Pentagon, developing plausible scenarios for how a missile could have transformed Flight 800 into a fireball. Amid piles of graphs and charts, jargon and calculus, there were fascinating possibilities, though none as yet more persuasive than the supposition voiced the night of the crash: that a shoulder-launched missile fired from a boat beneath the plane could have hit it. Nothing definitive could be determined without physical evidence, and as more wreckage emerged daily from the crash site, the continuing absence of any obvious damage that might indicate a missile left Kallstrom's team deeply frustrated.

The various Terrorism Task Force teams pursuing leads on a bomb, rather than a missile, had no more luck. Of the passengers on Flight 800—from the start, a promising course of inquiry—none appeared to have bought large insurance policies that might suggest a homicide or suicide. The FBI had subpoenaed the country's fifty largest insurance companies for information about policies held by any of the 230 people aboard the plane, but this inquiry came up dry.

A crime of passion? A love triangle gone wrong? Twelve days after the crash, a bizarre incident led agents to suspect such a scenario. New York mayor Rudolph Giuliani had visited a Brooklyn funeral home to pay respects to Joanne Griffith, a TWA flight attendant from New York who had died in the disaster. The mayor caused a stir among the three dozen or so mourners, some of whom walked over to shake his hand. For about twenty minutes, Giuliani offered his condolences to the victim's mother, her relatives, and her colleagues, then turned to leave. As he walked into the hallway, he encountered a fistfight between two men: Griffith's boyfriend, Vincent Moore, and her estranged husband, Jerry Griffith. Giuliani moved to the side as the men shouted and shoved each other, until one of them stormed out the door.

Griffith had already attracted the FBI's interest. Other TWA flight attendants had reported that Griffith's new boyfriend was a flamboyant character who hung around Kennedy Airport pretending he was a pilot with lots of money. One attendant told the FBI that the boyfriend had given Griffith a new flight bag the day before she boarded Flight 800. Could the bag have contained a bomb? Agents also learned that Griffith had met Moore on an airport employee shuttle bus at Kennedy Airport the previous April. He was wearing a pilot's uniform, sources recalled: a white shirt with epaulets, a clip-on black tie, and a captain's cap with a silver wing pin. He had talked about his motorcycle, his sports car, and his family's successful business in Barbados. Griffith bought the whole picture, and after a quick romance, the couple was married in Las Vegas on May 26—just seven weeks before the crash.

Vincent Moore told agents who came calling that he was, in fact, a limousine driver, and had never claimed to be a pilot. Agents were told that he and Griffith had married, and that he was the beneficiary of Griffith's life insurance policy. After further investigation, agents learned that the marriage was invalid, because while Griffith had filed her divorce papers from her previous husband, a final divorce decree was not due to be issued until July 19. And while she may have intended to make Moore her beneficiary, Griffith had not yet mailed in a change-of-beneficiary form when she boarded Flight 800. The form was found in her dresser drawer, unsigned. That was apparently one reason Moore and Jerry Griffith had come to blows in the funeral parlor.

Though he appeared an unlikely bomber, Moore was clearly a flamboyant character. Investigators were told he had been married several times, within a month of the crash would be engaged to marry again, and had even had the temerity to call TWA after the crash to inquire whether he could use his late bride's travel vouchers. And so, to the FBI, he remained a suspect for some time. Eventually, the flight bag he gave Griffith was hauled up by divers and found to have sustained no unusual damage—the clothes inside it were not even torn—and so the "pilot" was shifted to the lengthening list of former suspects.

In their background checks on passengers, agents had looked above all for indications that a passenger might have been involved, knowingly or not, with terrorists, but none of the passengers aboard Flight 800 appeared to have had relationships with suspected terrorists. Aside from Mr. Ferrat, the Algerian whom careful examination had shown to be an honorable businessman, no passengers or crew appeared to be suspect terrorists.

Another of the more promising early leads had been the Muslim employee of TWA at Kennedy Airport who came under suspicion based on two anonymous tips in Athens received two weeks apart, and whom his coworkers had spoken of disparagingly to investigators. On closer examination, the agents learned that the employee had been out of town the night of July 17. The few phone calls he had made prior to the explosion were innocent. In the days after the crash, investigators followed him when he was off duty as he went into video stores and grocery markets and found no grounds for suspicion. Then, just as the Terrorism Task Force was removing his name from its list of top suspects, the employee and his supervisor quarreled and the worker was fired. Was it possible that the man, who had worked for TWA for many years, had staged an argument to give himself an alibi for slipping away from the scene of his crime? But the employee continued to live in the apartment where he had resided for some time, and did nothing further to arouse suspicion. Investigators concluded that his arrogant manner may have irritated someone enough to submit the anonymous tips in Athens. Quietly, he was dropped from the list, having had no inkling that he was ever of interest to the FBI.

As leads continued to be scratched off the list, so did a theoretical cause Kallstrom's missile team had checked out, remote as it had seemed: electromagnetic interference, perhaps from a military plane or vessel.

EMI was a danger invoked every time a commercial plane prepared to take off and passengers were told to turn off electronic devices such as laptop computers or cellular telephones until the plane was safely at a cruising altitude. The chances of low-level EMI from such personal devices interfering with the plane's navigation instruments or other controls were so slim that the FAA had no way to define them. Indeed, no clear-cut case of onboard EMI from a personal device had ever been recorded. Essentially, the rule had been adopted as a necessary precaution if even an infinitesimal risk existed, especially given the rise in the use of high-tech electronic devices and gadgets.

Theoretically, higher fields of EMI from outside a plane might interfere with a plane's instruments, causing a misreading or a malfunction. These fields might come from a stationary ground source, such as a radar tower, or a moving source, such as another plane. Over the last decade or so, several kinds of new military jets and vessels had been equipped with sophisticated and powerful electronic controls. Conceivably, these might generate enough EMI to disrupt another plane or vessel. Several Navy Black Hawk helicopters, themselves laden with sophisticated electronics, had gone into unexplained tailspins for which EMI from another source might have been responsible. Studies by NASA and the U.S. Air Force had reached no firm conclusions, but the threat was regarded seriously enough for the Navy to spend $175 million retrofitting its entire fleet of Black Hawks with EMI shielding. The Pentagon went so far as to spend $35 million on a subsequent study of EMI—a study that remains classified to protect against deliberate EMI interference by a foreign power. Conceivably, a military asset using powerful electronics might be capable of causing a commercial plane to crash. But, as the FBI agents appreciated at the outset of their study, EMI had never been listed as a cause or contributing factor in any commercial plane crash anywhere in the world.

The FBI considered the possibility of interference by both kinds of external EMI sources: ground sources, principally radar stations along TWA Flight 800's route, and the panoply of military assets in the crash site area, every one of which had been examined thoroughly by agents for friendly fire. Presumably, no scenario of either type would involve criminal intent, and so, strictly speaking, the FBI was stretching its mandate to consider EMI at all. But perhaps a field of EMI generated accidentally by a military plane or vessel had led to a cover-up. That certainly *would* be criminal. As it turned out, agents found no asset that even had the kind of equipment that could have generated a dangerous level of EMI.

The P-3 Orion, for example, was a submarine tracker operating only standard equipment. Another version of the P-3, called the P-3C, was equipped with extra electronic devices for intelligence missions, while a third version, called the EP-3, was actually designed for electronic warfare. But the P-3 Orion that had been in the vicinity of Flight 800 was not one of these two modified kinds. It had no special electronics that could have emitted electromagnetic fields any greater than those generated by the instruments and radar of other 747s taking off and landing at Kennedy Airport.

Similarly, the Black Hawk helicopter used on a training mission for the Air National Guard on the night of July 17, 1996, was found to be equipped only with standard electronic gear. So was its partner in the routine exercise, the C-130 plane. The Coast Guard boat, the *Adak,* had surface radar operating but no sophisticated radar-jamming equipment that might have caused EMI; such very expensive hardware was simply not needed in the *Adak*'s patrols for illegal fishermen, drug traffickers, and immigrants. In fact, agents concluded, the strongest source of electromagnetic interference encountered by Flight 800 would have been from the Kennedy Airport radar tower.

As a remote but not inconceivable prospect, the bureau also considered whether a U.S. military asset, foreign nation, or freelance terrorist could have directed a *Star Wars*–like beam of EMI at the plane—a "death ray," in effect. The U.S. military does have electromagnetic weapons, lasers, and weapons systems that could have interfered with the plane's instruments or set off a spark that may have caused an explosion. But no such weapons, the FBI found, had been aboard any military plane or vessel anywhere near the crash-site area. And there was no suspicion that a laser from a weapon set off Flight 800's onboard explosion.

Like static electricity, EMI was a tantalizing theory because it was impossible to disprove: It left no signature traces. But it remained low on the list of possible causes, both because no source of powerful EMI could be discerned in the crash-site area and, as important, because the plane's instruments, as recorded by the flight data recorder, showed no aberrations other than the "crazy fuel-flow indicator" that other pilots had found to be typical of 747s in general and the plane that would become Flight 800 in particular. And the plane had not acted erratically—if it had, that would have been the strongest indication that EMI was occurring. The pilots, as a result, had not radioed the tower to say they were losing control, as they almost certainly would have done in an EMI scenario.

In marginalizing EMI as a possible cause, common sense played a part as well. Planes fly along the east coast of Long Island, to and from the New York airports, many times an hour, twenty-four hours a day. None has ever reported an instance of EMI. No ground source of electromagnetism in the area is remotely as powerful as the towers of midtown Manhattan, which bristle with high-frequency radio antennas. And no plane has ever crashed over Manhattan.

As each day's haul of wreckage failed to disclose conclusive evidence of a bomb or missile, both Kallstrom and Pickard wondered if the impossible had happened after all. "747s don't just fall out of the sky," Jim Hall had said on the night of the crash, but perhaps this one had. Despite the extraordinary performance record of Boeing's most successful commercial jetliner, a mechanical malfunction might have downed this particular plane. More and more, Kallstrom believed the answer would emerge from the Calverton hangar. "The plane is going to talk to us," he kept saying. "It's going to tell us what happened."

In fact, answers were emerging every day from the hangar, proving that one or another scenario had *not* occurred.

By early September, for example, the plane's four engines had been hauled up by crane from the ocean bottom and transported to the hangar. They were in remarkably good shape, considering what they'd been through. Though they were somewhat charred and many parts were shredded, torn, or bent, none were damaged in ways that suggested a bomb or missile. While the blades were badly damaged, none appeared to have been destroyed: If a heat-seeking missile had targeted an engine, it would have demolished the blades first. At the hangar, the engines were reconstructed by Pratt & Whitney engineers, who explained exactly how each engine fell: which plummeted straight down, which fell at an angle. Nothing in any of the engines suggested a mechanical failure. Nor could a case be made that a fuse pin had snapped, so that an engine broke away from the fuselage and caused an explosion. Several fuse pins were in good enough shape to be used again.

As the center fuel tank began to emerge from pieces brought up daily from the ocean bottom, the Boeing engineers and NTSB investigators became increasingly certain that it had exploded. Yet even if true, this raised more questions than it answered. Center fuel tanks didn't *do* that, any more than

747s fell out of the sky. No one could find a manual on aircraft failure analysis that even discussed the possibility of an electrical or chemical failure in a center fuel tank. If one did explode, the investigators realized, the result would be massive destruction; they knew that from the Philippines Airlines 737 whose center tank had exploded on the ground. But whether the center fuel tank was the first explosion or a subsequent one, and what, in either case, had made it blow up, remained unclear.

The engineers knew that a tank explosion would start with combustible fuel vapors. The fuel itself—Jet-A fuel, as it was called—was not nearly as flammable as regular gasoline and could not, on its own, explode. The center tank on Flight 800 was almost empty, so that fuel vapors certainly had arisen, but that was normal. For the vapors to explode they would have to reach at least 100 degrees Fahrenheit. But how? Clearly, the air-conditioning units under the tank were the likeliest suspect, but jets idled on hot runways around the world every day, their air-conditioning units cranked up, and didn't explode. A spark or hot enough surface had to ignite the vapors once they heated to above 100 degrees; science strongly suggested the vapors could not explode on their own until they reached 400 degrees Fahrenheit. As investigators analyzed each of the lime-green pieces before attaching them to their mock-up of the center fuel tank, they found no rationale for the scenario, only a better understanding of how the explosion had proceeded once it occurred.

The outward petaling of metal on its right front side suggested the explosion had gone in that direction. Its forward wall had blown into the adjacent front cargo hold, then pushed the plane's keel beam—its spine—down. That, in turn, tore the fuselage from its bottom up to the porthole windows, causing the nose of the plane to break off. John Clark, a veteran safety board investigator, would monitor tests that concluded, to investigators' surprise, that the final, split-second "tick" noise heard on Flight 800's cockpit voice recorder was probably vibration coming through the structure and fuselage as the plane began to break up, not the sound of the actual explosion. As he explained, sound travels through structure ten times faster than it travels through air. The sound of the explosion itself, which travels through air, probably arrived at the microphone a fraction of a second later, but by then the cables leading to the recorders had been cut, so no further noise was recorded. Unfortunately for the investigators, this sequence of events would be the same whether the center fuel tank had blown up from a fuel-air explosion—a mechanical malfunction—or from a bomb or missile.

Why the center fuel tank had exploded was no clearer for the reconstruction. No chemical traces were found on any of the tank parts retrieved as yet, no pitting and scarring of metal in enough amounts to indicate a bomb or missile, and no large holes in the tank wreckage that would indicate a clear pathway of a missile. Yet maddeningly, there was no way to rule out a missile or bomb. There were so many gaping holes, slits, punctures, and penetrations in the center-fuel-tank pieces in the hangar, so many unexplained twists, bends, and tears, and so many pieces not yet salvaged, that the mystery only deepened as the analysis wore on.

Among the FBI investigators at the hangar and the missile experts at China Lake, the Defense Intelligence Agency, and numerous other military facilities, national laboratories, and private missile manufacturers, a fierce debate broke out. Some theorized that a missile could have disintegrated if it penetrated the center fuel tank and was caught in a massive explosion, leaving no sign of its existence. Or perhaps a missile could have exploded outside the plane, sending fiery fragments into the center fuel tank and causing it to explode, without even touching the plane. Others theorized that a missile could have penetrated the fuselage, set off the tank, and vaporized inside the plane's cabin. The United States and the Russians had designed missiles that would do just that, leaving little or no evidence behind. Others argued that even a vaporizing missile would leave some evidence behind. Its energy would be transferred, likely in the form of what experts called a "spawl," which behaves like a fragment, and would grow larger as it traveled through the aircraft, creating bigger and bigger holes in its path. There was no sign of a spawl or, for that matter, a "frag"— fragments of material blown up by a bomb that become airborne—on any part of the interior of the aircraft or the surface of the center fuel tank or embedded in the victims. The debate would rage on for months.

Could the center fuel tank have exploded from a mechanical malfunction, as most of the accident investigators were coming to feel? As accident investigators explored theories on how the vapors could have become volatile and what could have sparked these volatile vapors causing the tank to blow up, FBI agents were scrutinizing the plane's recent service record for answers.

Airport workers interviewed by the FBI had said that they had reported fuel leaks on several occasions, leaks which the NTSB called routine. But to the FBI, that history was interesting. The most recent spate of fueling problems dated to April 8. The first had been reported not by a TWA worker but by a passenger, who claimed in a call to the Command Post after the crash that his TWA flight on a 747 from Montego Bay, Jamaica, to Boston had been delayed for four hours because of refueling difficulties. The plane, it turned out, was #N93119. Maintenance records showed that an electrical short had apparently caused problems in the opening and closing of a fuel door, but the door had been fixed, and the plane refueled successfully.

On April 21, May 23, and June 4, more refueling problems had dogged #N93119, and each time adjustments were made and the refueling was successfully completed. A week after the April 21 refueling problem, the tanks were filled with fuel only after workers jiggled a switch that changed the power control from manual to automatic and back—meaning that the plane would not, for some reason, accept fuel by automatic feed, so that one of its fuel latches had to be lifted, and the fueling done by hand. But the significance of this, if any, was unclear.

In June, a maintenance worker had to change a circuit breaker to override an automatic shutdown safety device, designed to prevent overfueling, so that fuel could be loaded into the plane's wing tanks. Ten days before the disaster, the plane's fueling valves had shut down completely so that the wing tanks could not be filled. The valves reopened when workers drained an accompanying tank. Then, on July 11, a food-service worker reported that he saw fuel leaking from the plane. Most alarming was the report from the worker who had been hit with several stinging drops of jet fuel just before Flight 800's last departure. Once again, the fueling valves had been shut down. This time, mechanics pulled a circuit breaker to finish refueling Flight 800.

Then there was the comment made by the flight engineer on Flight 800 just two minutes before the plane exploded. "Look at that crazy fuel-flow indicator on number four," he had said. To the FBI agents' surprise, however, the NTSB dismissed the fueling problems, and the pilot's remark about a "crazy fuel-flow indicator," as routine and unimportant.

If that was commonplace, Kallstrom mused, was any plane safe to fly?

If that was commonplace, Kallstrom mused, was any plane safe to fly?

Every day, seven days a week, Kallstrom visited the hangar to see the center fuel tank emerging and to encourage the investigators and technicians who usually worked sixteen-hour days. Occasionally, Pickard would join him, and the two would scrutinize the shattered pieces of the big tank. The aviation investigators explained how they could see more clearly that the explosion had ripped through the front of the tank. Pickard listened as they spoke, but couldn't grasp what the aeronautical engineers were seeing. "Maybe it's because I'm an accountant," he told Kallstrom. "I just don't have the imagination." Kallstrom would clap his deputy on the back and say, "Damned if I can see it yet, either." Then he would look into the wreckage and ask one question after another, talking about baffles and wing roots or the coefficient of friction with the engineers.

"The only coefficient of friction I know," Pickard muttered to his boss, "is that I haven't shaved in three days."

Kallstrom had learned everything he could about missiles, bombs, and the workings of 747s. He also knew the names not just of his own agents but of the NTSB investigators and technicians as well. "How ya doin' today?" he'd ask. "Is that daughter of yours feeling better?" He had his problems with the NTSB brass in Washington, Loeb in particular—the cavalier reaction to the FBI's inquiry about the problems with refueling, for example, probably came straight from the top—but the experts in the hangar were working hard and not waving off anything. The respect Kallstrom communicated with his daily presence and questions was a powerful stimulus. He made it clear how much the FBI needed them. So one day in late August, when he walked in to find a number of the engineers saying their good-byes, he refrained from showing any irritation, merely mild surprise.

"Mr. Kallstrom, it's been great working with you," one of the engineers said, sticking out his hand. "I hope we'll meet again."

"Where are you going?"

The engineer belonged to a team Kallstrom had been counting on to start a full-scale reconstruction of the plane's interior. "Back to Washington," he told Kallstrom. "They don't see any need to do an interior mock-up."

By now, Loeb and Hall were convinced that the center fuel tank had exploded and destroyed the plane. Whether a refueling glitch had led to that explosion, or any of a dozen other possible mechanical or electrical failures the engineers had started to explore, struck Loeb and Hall as secondary issues. Their job now was to persuade the FAA to force airlines to eliminate the possibility of explosive vapors. One obvious measure would be to cool the fuel before it was put in the tank; another would be to fill all tanks before takeoff so that vapors would have less chance to build up; a third would be to inject inert gas into the tanks to displace volatile fumes, a system used on military planes. Loeb believed there was no way to "engineer out" all ignition sources, but this way, whatever the problem was, it simply could not recur. The vapors would be too cool to spark under any circumstances, electrical, bomb, missile, or even a meteor. Rebuilding the interior, Loeb and Hall felt, was a waste of time and money.

"Yeah, well, good luck, then," Kallstrom said, and wandered off. The engineers resumed packing their notebooks and tools. Each had his plane ticket already. By nightfall, they would be home in Washington.

Less than an hour later, one of the engineers heard his beeper sound. Washington was calling. An expression of stupefaction passed over the engineer's face as he checked in to hear that his plans, and those of his fellow NTSB investigators, had just changed. The engineers were to unpack their bags, cancel their plane reservations, and get ready to reconstruct the interior. They never did figure out who Kallstrom had called—he said nothing about it when he greeted them genially the next day, and they knew better than to ask—but clearly, he'd gone over Loeb's head.

To Kallstrom, reconstructing the interior would bring obvious, and essential, benefits. He wanted a clearer picture of what had happened inside the passenger cabin. He wanted to see the seats lined up in rows, the galleys and overhead bins put back in place. He felt it could only help in piecing together the puzzle. If a bomb went off inside the plane, or a missile passed through, surely the evidence of it would be visible. He wanted to see if there was any pattern to the interior destruction, and then wanted to compare the seat damage to passenger injuries to see if there were any other patterns.

By now, too, Kallstrom had spent enough time with the families of the victims to think that their grief would be eased if the interior of Flight 800 was reconstructed. He could imagine a day when they would come to the hangar, if they chose, and touch the seats where their loved ones had last sat. The families needed to know that everything possible was being done to explain the crash. If a cabin reconstruction helped prove that a bomb or missile hadn't destroyed the plane, that too would be reassuring to them.

Moreover, Kallstrom was convinced that if the FBI concluded that a mechanical malfunction was to blame, but failed to reconstruct the entire plane, conspiracy theories would flourish. The Warren Commission had let leads dangle in its investigation and prompted thirty years of fierce speculation about second shooters on the grassy knoll and Oswald as a pawn of the Cubans, the Mafia, or the Russians, all leading to a foolish movie by Oliver Stone. The mere thought of Stone made Kallstrom ill. *Platoon*, Stone's film about Vietnam, had enraged him with its focus on a few soldiers whose conduct was nothing like that of the Marines Kallstrom fought with, honorable men on an honorable mission. Like all conspiracy theorists, Stone looked for the worst and managed to find it, regardless of the facts. Kallstrom was determined to conduct this investigation so thoroughly, and so reputably, that no one would find a hook from which to hang a conspiracy theory. He owed that to the victims' families, to his agents in the field, and to the rest of the country whose best interests he had sworn to protect.

Still, with two months passed since the tragedy and no end of the investigation in sight, Kallstrom wondered privately if he had the stamina to see it through. At times, he felt as if he were back on the famous Hill Trail at the Marine officers' training camp in Quantico, his lungs and thighs burning, physically and emotionally spent with miles to go. But Hill Trail was one day of hell. This went on and on.

Most evenings now, Kallstrom managed to drive home. Along the winding Connecticut parkways, he cranked up tapes of his big-band favorites—Glenn Miller, Tommy Dorsey, and Louis Armstrong. To earn a few extra dollars and because he loved doing it, Kallstrom's father had played trumpet with local bands in Boston and on the Cape almost every weekend, and Jim had often gone to hear him.

From his father, Todd, the son of Swedish immigrants, he had acquired a strong work ethic, and the poise to hold forth onstage. His mother, Edna, a nurse, had named her middle child, born in 1943, after a knight: James Keith, an English ancestor. She had given each of her three children strong moral values and a nurse's compassion.

Home now was a gracious colonial in Connecticut where he and Susan were raising their two daughters, Erika and Krystel. When he'd met Susan he was a young agent in Baltimore, his first posting, and she was a secretary for the bank-robbery squad in the FBI's office in Baltimore where she had grown up. A year later, in 1971, Jim was transferred to New York, he and Susan were married, and they moved into their first home: a garden apartment in Connecticut, about an hour's drive from the FBI office.

And then—well, the years had passed more quickly than he could have imagined. Mostly he loved family life, enjoyed remodeling his house, and adored his two young daughters. He kept a Honda 750 motorcycle in his garage, and took it for a spin sometimes on a Sunday afternoon, dreaming of one day buying a Harley-Davidson.

Going home helped, but the pace of the investigation felt no less grueling for that, and Kallstrom felt tired in a bone-deep way he'd never felt before.

Tom Pickard was tired, too, and blamed himself for the investigation's lack of answers. Surely he could do better. Meanwhile, unknown to most of his fellow agents other than Kallstrom, he had been immersed in another major investigation that began before Flight 800 had fallen. Louis Freeh had come to him personally for help: For the first time in its history, the bureau appeared to have a mole. Aldrich Ames, the CIA agent who sold secrets to the Soviets that cost many of his fellow agents their lives, was under arrest. At first, the FBI felt Ames might have compromised certain of its own Cold War spy operations, but in analyzing computer files of those botched cases, an FBI espionage expert realized Ames could not possibly have known about these FBI cases in New York. Why had a promising lead dried up, or a would-be informant chosen not to cooperate after all? Those cases had been compromised, clearly by someone inside the bureau, who had apparently supplied information to the Soviets for a big payoff. Pickard had been working with two others, handpicked to investigate fellow agents, a task that depressed and appalled him. By the time TWA Flight 800 blew up, Pickard and his men had identified the agent they suspected was the mole. Now they had to build a case against him.

For Pickard's wife, a shy, West Virginian woman named Sharon to whom Pickard was famously—some might say uxoriously—devoted, the worst part of the investigations was that he could say nothing about them. A special STU-line phone had been installed in the master bedroom of the Pickards' New Jersey home, and Sharon had become ever more exasperated as it rang at all hours of the night, obliging Tom to conduct top-secret conversations he couldn't discuss with her. Once, Mary Jo White, the U.S. Attorney for Manhattan, had called at 2:00 A.M. to debate whether a suspect in another case should be arrested. For an hour, Pickard and White went back and forth: to arrest him or not to arrest him? Finally, Sharon, trying to sleep, could take no more. "Oh for God's sake," she shouted, "why don't you just shoot the guy?"

By now, Kallstrom's second deputy, Schiliro, had shifted his part of the TWA investigation back to Manhattan, while Cantamessa, Kallstrom's other senior person, remained at the Command Post in East Moriches supervising the divers and overseeing other tasks.

As if to torment the investigators, three hurricanes swept up from the south in quick succession that September: Edouard, Fran, and Hortense. None hit Long Island head on, but all brought fifteen-foot waves, shutting down the salvage operation for half of the month. Just before the first arrived, enough large wreckage had been removed that lighter, smaller pieces were exposed. The divers had intended to get to those pieces next, but currents from the hurricanes nudged them a yard or more from their resting places, then buried them in silt. Even when the skies had cleared and the waves subsided, divers found the silt dense enough to cut their visibility sharply, sometimes so much that they could not see their fingers unless they pressed them against their goggles. The light pieces became that much harder to retrieve, and the last of the bodies less likely to be found.

About half of TWA Flight 800 was in pieces in the Calverton hangar, but half remained below the waves. Along with that wreckage, or so it seemed, lay the answer to the mystery, perhaps buried in silt, perhaps dissipated already by the ceaseless corrosion of silt and salt water, or perhaps undiscoverable.

CHAPTER 13

PIECING THE PUZZLE

On early fall evenings at the Calverton hangar, the sky would darken and the stars appear by 7:30, when work subsided and the engineers began leaving for the day. Sometimes Hank Hughes, one of the NTSB investigators, would look up to find the place almost deserted, the big space silent, as the last cars trailed off along Calverton's country roads. Then he would walk over to the center fuel tank, his footsteps echoing faintly against the hangar's high-ribbed frame, and let his gaze pass slowly along its devastated shape, hoping to see an overlooked clue, a tiny telltale piece to make sense of the mystery. One night, he watched, astonished, as a black raven flew into the open hangar, circled above the tortured pieces of the fuel tank, then landed on them. Other workers noticed the raven too, and gathered silently to watch it watching them. It might not be a clue, the workers thought, but it certainly seemed an omen.

Hughes and the senior investigators to whom he reported—Jim Wildey, Deepak Joshi, and Bob Swaim—now felt sure the center fuel tank held the answer, but as its pieces came together, the hard evidence of a bomb or missile remained absent. Every day, one of the three would field a call from Dr. Bernard Loeb, the NTSB's brilliant but difficult director of aviation safety, second only to chairman James Hall in aviation issues. Loeb would be in his Washington office by 6:00 A.M., and soon want to know what the night's dives had yielded. He would still be in his office at 7:00 P.M., wanting to know what analysis on the latest pieces had shown. Every day, the trio had to report that nothing conclusive had materialized. Loeb was high-strung, not always considerate, and had a scientist's penchant for assuming he was right and everyone else was wrong. Yet in his own way, Loeb was as dedicated to seeking the key to the mystery as any of his colleagues, or his FBI counterparts. As the days wore on without an answer, he felt just as frustrated as they did.

At the beginning, Loeb had been almost sure that the crash was the result of a bomb or missile. But by the time most of the explosive chemical traces had proven to be Carlo the dog's training materials, he and his team at Calverton had changed their minds completely and now felt that the emerging center fuel tank indicated, without doubt, a mechanical or electrical malfunction was to blame. A center-fuel-tank explosion would have been catastrophic, they agreed, and very quick. Loeb knew the pilots had lost all power instantly. From at least one other aviation disaster, they knew that an exploding center fuel tank—a fuel-air explosion, as they called it—could do that. To Loeb, the central question was whether the fuel vapors could have been heated above 100 degrees, and thus be capable of exploding. Loeb and his investigators strongly suspected they could. The answer would not come until Boeing did simulation tests with real 747s in late August. Yes, the Boeing engineers would confirm to their own astonishment, the vapors could get that hot.

As he became convinced that a mechanical failure caused the tank to explode, Loeb became irritated, even angered, by the FBI's frequent statements about not ruling out a missile or bomb. The FBI, he felt, seemed to be perpetuating the notion that terrorism had taken out the plane because that, in a way, was what he felt the FBI wanted the answer to be. It would give them control of the investigation and offer the prospect of a handcuffed criminal led to justice. But this wasn't a disaster, Loeb felt, that was going to end that way.

For Loeb and the Calverton investigators—of the NTSB, but also Boeing, Pratt & Whitney, and, indeed, the FBI—the search for sense in a center-fuel-tank explosion began with a list of suspects: in this case, mechanical suspects. At the top of the list was a given: Volatile fuel vapors could be ignited either by a spark or an exceedingly hot surface. But what possible sources, inside the center fuel tank or just outside it, could have provided a spark or enough heat to ignite the volatile vapors? Unfortunately for the investigators, the answer was: almost none. The reason, intriguingly, had something to do with the May 9, 1976, midair explosion over Madrid of #N93118, the 747 that had come off the assembly line just ahead of the plane that would end as Flight 800.

As far as the investigators of that crash could determine, lightning had struck the left-wing fuel tank of #N93118, causing sparks to ignite fuel vapors. That was disturbing news. Thirteen years earlier, days after the assassination of President Kennedy, a Pan Am Boeing 707 had been hit by lightning that touched off an explosion of its left reserve fuel tank, breaking off its left wing. As a result, Boeing had taken what it felt were thoroughly protective measures against lightning and, in the process, against the possibility of fuel-tank explosions. One change called for more shielding of the volatile vapors inside fuel tanks from outside electrical connections that might be hit by lightning. Another required that the tanks be lined with materials that maintained lower temperatures than previous linings. Yet a third called for planes to be protected by "grounders" on their wings to help prevent lightning damage: The lightning would be drawn to the grounders, or static wicks, and then bounce off into the atmosphere, rather than into the plane. But then came the Madrid explosion. Standards, as a result, were tightened again.

Nothing, of course, could be done to keep lightning from striking in the first place or, when it did, from running along the wings that held the fuel tanks, or girdling the center tank located between the wings. But now every piece of wire outside the tanks was insulated or shielded, and surfaces were designed so that their temperatures remained at least 50 degrees below the minimum temperature capable—so many investigators thought—of igniting fuel vapors. The only electrical wires inside the center fuel tank were those connected to the fuel-quantity-indicating system, which included the fuel-measuring probes. They were not only shielded but designed so that their voltage remained ten times below that required to ignite fuel vapors. In the wake of Flight 800, NTSB investigators began wondering if high voltage from some external source might travel through these low-voltage wires nonetheless, at least for a split second before the low-voltage wires short-circuited, and act, in that split second, as an energy source capable of igniting hot fuel vapors. That was only one of many questions that began to be asked of the center fuel tank and its electrical conduits.

For nearly two decades after the 1976 Madrid midair explosion of #N93118, these tightened standards had appeared to help prevent fuel-tank explosions, whether from lightning or anything else—with one notable exception. On May 11, 1990, a Boeing 737 operated by Philippines Airlines at Manila's airport had exploded and burned on the tarmac as it was taxiing for takeoff, killing 8 and injuring 30 of the 119 people on board. The plane was destroyed by fire. The investigation found no evidence of sabotage. The cause, while not conclusively proved, was believed to be the ignition of combustible fuel vapors in the center fuel tank. Though investigators never found the exact ignition source, they speculated it was damaged wiring. Philippines Airlines had just installed lights to illuminate its logo on the wing, and the wiring connected to those lights ran past the center fuel tank. Perhaps that wiring had been damaged and caused a short circuit to spark the fuel tank.

The Philippines Airlines disaster, which had occurred not long after Loeb began his career at the NTSB, made clear just how catastrophic a center-tank explosion could be. Yet in that case, investigators studied seventy components in and around the fuel tank and found none defective. Since the standards were already as tight as the FAA felt it could make them, no new ones were imposed, or even suggested. The cause of the 737 explosion was ruled an inconclusive accident, and simply put to rest.

Amid all the variables, the investigators of Flight 800 knew one thing: The plane had not been struck by lightning, not on a perfectly clear evening with no rain clouds, much less thunder. Despite the clear weather, investigators did check with the weather bureau as well as comb radar tapes for signs of lightning—even heat lightning—in the area. They found none. But was Flight 800 a reprise of the 737 Philippines Airlines explosion? Did it suggest a pattern that would result in more jumbo jets blowing up in midair if the problem, elusive as it might be, was not discovered and solved? Or was Flight 800 the casualty of *another* fuel-tank glitch that bore no relation to the Philippines disaster and somehow had managed to occur despite all the protective measures taken by the FAA after the lightning strikes of 1963 and 1976?

To Bob Swaim, who headed the NTSB's wiring group, and his fellow NTSB engineers Wildey and Joshi, the fuel-measuring probes were the obvious first suspects to consider. The electricity that passed through them was only about five volts when the tank was full, nearly zero volts when the tank was close to empty, as it was on Flight 800. By comparison, a telephone beeper resting passively uses about five times that much current with one AA battery. Yet the probes were one of only two electrical conduits in the whole center fuel tank.

There were seven probes, or rods, that descended from various spots on the ceiling to the floor, a distance of about six feet. The small electrical wire within each probe led outside the tank to one of three fuel-quantity gauges in the cockpit that provided the measurement of the fuel in the center fuel tank. Also in the tank, electrically linked to the fuel-measuring probes, was a device called a compensator, which adjusted for different temperature conditions in the tank. It sat on the floor of the tank, submerged in fuel, linked by similar low-voltage wires to the fuel-quantity-indicating system. By mid-October, four of the seven probes, or probe pieces, had been retrieved. Some were darkened as if scorched by arcing. Was this the key? Had high voltage somehow entered the tank through low-voltage wiring that passed through the probes, arced, and sent a spark into the flammable fuel vapors? But the stains proved to be the polyurethane coating on the probes, which had been slightly burned in the fire that followed the explosion of the fuel tank, exactly what investigators would have expected to find from pieces of an exploded fuel tank. Once again a promising lead had fizzled, and the investigators, tensed for a breakthrough, sagged back in exhaustion. Deepak Joshi, head of the structures group, grew so tired and disoriented while giving a briefing to his workers one night at the hangar that he slipped into his native Hindi tongue for several minutes, his eyes all but closed. Finally he jolted himself awake and blinked to see a circle of utterly bewildered colleagues, themselves too tired to interrupt. "Oh, I am so sorry!" Joshi exclaimed, and started over in English.

As an experiment, Boeing's investigators decided to see if *any* amount of voltage could make the probes arc. They took some twenty-three-year-old probes from another jet and ran 3,300 volts through them, more than twice the 1,500 volts the equipment had been designed to withstand and absurdly higher than the five volts at which the probes normally operated. Even then, the probes maintained their integrity and failed to arc.

In the hangar at Calverton, investigators studied the fuel probes and compensators under high-powered optical microscopes that revealed the individual electrons of their surface materials. Everything appeared in order, given the heat they had sustained, except for an unusual black spot on one of the compensators that proved to be copper sulfite. At the Wright Patterson Air Force laboratory, investigators had found similar black spots on the fuel probes of military planes when maintenance crews reported fuel measurement problems on certain aircraft. Could the spot somehow conduct electricity from the compensator to the fuel vapor? Tests had shown the spots to be semiconductive, rather than highly conductive—as copper itself would be. Still, they could prevent probes from operating effectively. How had they come to be there and what could be done to prevent them? After much testing, the engineers at Wright Patterson argued that the buildup was caused by sulfur in the jet fuel that reacted with copper in the compensator and probes to form copper sulfite, just as sulfur in the air tarnishes household silver by reacting, forming silver sulfite. Over time, the process created a black or grayish mess that threw off the fuel probe measurements and might—conceivably—result in electrical arcing. The Air Force took the phenomenon seriously enough to continue studying it six years after discovering it, but it had found no evidence, in all that time, to suggest the possibility of arcing. The black spots were signs of aging and seemed unlikely to have any serious effect.

Investigators studying the center fuel tank at Calverton followed the electrical current from the probes through low-voltage wires that passed out of the tank, where they were stepped up to higher voltages, much as telephone signals are stepped up by transformers outside a home.

Many of the wire bundles near the center fuel tank had been destroyed in the fire that followed the explosion. Could a short circuit in one of those bundles have caused the explosion? It was a remote possibility, but one that three years later would emerge, partly from an inexorable process of elimination, as one of the likeliest causes. Of all the components on a 747, wiring was one of the few parts of the plane's operating system that was never replaced. Unlike a wheel or an engine, wiring was believed by some experts to last pretty much indefinitely. In fact, the conditions for an explosion-provoking short circuit made state lotteries look like safe bets. A high-voltage wire would probably have to cross a low-voltage wire at a point where the insulation of each was frayed. Only then could the higher voltage enter the tank along the low-voltage wire. Sparks or heat would then have to ignite the vapors inside the center fuel tank to cause an explosion—vapors that would have to be at least 100 degrees to become volatile. At Wright Patterson, investigators tried to ignite heated jet-fuel vapors by sending massive amounts of voltage through a low-voltage wire.

They couldn't do it.

And yet, in the months to come, NTSB investigators would wonder if both wires in a short-circuit scenario would really have to be frayed at the same point, or damaged at all. The voltage of a coated, undamaged wire could be made to induce a current into an adjacent wire, also coated and undamaged: transient voltage, the investigators called it. It was a process known as electromagnetic induction. It could occur, investigators speculated, by someone turning on a switch on the plane, beginning the flow of electrical current through a wire. Could transient voltage be sufficient enough in a wire near or leading to the center fuel tank to introduce a spark? This, to the NTSB investigators, would be new and mysterious terrain.

Along the floor of one hangar at Calverton, investigators untangled the masses of wiring brought daily, dripping wet, from the crash site. In all, a 747-100 contained 150 miles of wiring, most sections color-coded and branded every six inches with a hot stamp that showed where on a plane each wire ran. Bundles outside the center fuel tank that were recovered and that survived the fire were studied with special care. No fraying that would indicate a short circuit was found, though an engineer did notice that one of the hot-stamp marks had been imprinted so hard it penetrated the insulation of its wire and exposed a conductor. Had the hot stamp damaged other wires? Moreover, that conductor was near one of the three pumps that fed fuel from the center fuel tank to the plane's four engines, but there was no sign of electrical arcing in the pumps or wires in that area.

From the rear of the tank, a main wiring harness climbed up the left side of the plane into the area directly above the passenger cabin, then passed forward under the upper-deck windows on the left side of the plane before crossing over the plane's roof and into the cockpit. No sign of fraying was found in the seventy-five feet of wire that led from the tank to the cockpit dials. Inevitably, an airplane's wires did short out, an event as routine and usually as harmless as a lightbulb burning out in a home. Cockpit gauges were made to register these short circuits; automatic shutoffs and other checkpoints in the plane were designed to detour electricity around a short circuit and alert the pilots to report the blown wire or fuse upon landing. But on Flight 800, none of the cockpit gauges indicated even a routine blowout.

The plane's power cables were, of course, severed as a result of the center fuel tank's explosion. These were the plane's main arteries of electrical power, which ran from the cockpit directly toward the center fuel tank, branched in front of it, and continued down either side of the plane toward its tail. They powered the plane's controls and the lights in the passenger cabin and relayed the information to the black boxes at the rear of the plane. The explosion had severed the cables where they branched. At that instant, the cockpit went dark and the controls failed; the passenger cabin also went dark. But there was no evidence that a severed power cable had precipitated the fuel-tank explosion.

But the severed cables did provoke a new theory. Because the flight's cockpit voice recorder had stopped so abruptly, it had been seen initially as providing nothing more to the investigation than the near certainty that the cables had been severed when the plane exploded. In fact, some five minutes before the blast, a routine comment made on the tape about cross-feeding fuel between the engines to balance the plane now took on new meaning to some engineers. Perhaps a short had occurred in the electrical wiring in the number-four tank. The short might have generated a flame from the tank, which was on the wing; the flame might then have traveled back through the center-tank vent tube. There, it was believed, it could have touched off the fuel-air vapor in the nearly empty center tank. Investigators looked at the fuel tanks of other 747s and discovered that some of the wiring in the number-four fuel tanks of those aircraft showed signs of chafing, but with no such evidence on the wiring of Flight 800, this theory had to remain, for the moment at least, speculative.

In studying what else could have introduced a current into the center fuel tank, investigators looked at the fuel pumps just outside it—pumps that relayed its fuel through lines to the plane's four engines. There were two of these, plus a much smaller scavenge pump that kicked in when the fuel level in the center tank got too low for the big pumps to operate effectively. When divers retrieved both the larger pumps, safety board investigators took them apart and laid the pieces across a stretch of hangar floor, looking for any sign that one of the pumps' motors may have overheated. Perhaps a rotor had locked, or a bearing had worn down. They found nothing worse than the damage they would have expected after a bad crash. In neither pump was there even evidence of a tiny short circuit.

To the Boeing engineers, this was no surprise. The fuel pumps were designed to be explosion-proof. Neither flames or sparks were thought capable of passing through them. To be sure, Boeing put its pumps in a chamber filled with explosive vapors and forced some of those vapors into the pump's motor housing. Then the engineers deliberately introduced a spark, and exploded the vapors in the thick, metal housing. Even then, the explosion failed to spread to the vapors in the rest of the test chamber. The Flight 800 investigators checked the records of all planes that had experienced any kind of center-fuel-tank problems, including the 737 in Manila in 1990, and found that none had ever been caused by fuel pumps.

Nonetheless, FBI agents who had noticed the number of recent refueling problems in #N93119's service history were struck by the number of fuel-pump problems recorded in the plane's maintenance records. From July 1, 1994, to its final day of July 17, 1996, there had been twenty-six fuel-pump "write-ups," as the maintenance workers termed their reports. The NTSB investigators assigned no importance to the pattern—since the pumps showed no sign of damage. Moreover, the plane that had ended as Flight 800 had not yet complied with a Boeing service bulletin first issued on August 3, 1995, and revised on January 18, 1996, to make sure 747 fuel pumps did not cause a leak. The bulletin recommended that the airlines conduct careful inspections of the pumps as soon as possible, "since operators have sent reports of fuel leaks at the fuel boost and override jettison pumps." The advisory added that "reports tell that eight fuel pumps have been removed for that reason. The removed fuel pumps had been 34,000 and 67,000 hours. . . ." In one case, a leak in a plane undergoing routine maintenance had spilled onto an electrical short in a connector, causing a small fire outside the fuel tank.

In fairness, this was the only "Alert Service Bulletin" from Boeing that TWA had failed to follow through with #N93119, but perhaps it was the one that the airline shouldn't have ignored. After the crash, TWA declared that the plane had been scheduled to undergo the fuel-pump inspection and added that TWA's policy had always been that any Alert Service Bulletin from Boeing must be taken as seriously as a directive from the Federal Aviation Agency. The FAA saw nothing unusual in TWA's failure to inspect the plane's pumps nearly a year after receiving a bulletin: Other airlines, the FAA observed, had not yet completed the fuel-pump inspections of their fleets, either. But while the NTSB did not totally disagree with the FAA on this issue, some safety-board investigators found the FAA occasionally cavalier. To their minds, the FAA seemed at times like an advocate for the airlines, often reluctant to approve NTSB recommendations because of what it would cost the airlines and manufacturers to implement them. However, the NTSB investigators agreed that the unattended fuel pumps, though undamaged, could not be ruled out as a cause of the crash.

As for the small scavenge pump, it seemed to investigators a more feasible suspect early on for the simple reason that it couldn't be found, and never would be found. Did that mean it had exploded first, igniting the fuel tank? Perhaps, but powerful evidence argued against that possibility. In the cockpit, the switch for the scavenge pump indicated "off," when it was pulled up from the ocean. It was unlikely that the thrust from the crash pushed it into the "off" position. Furthermore, it should have been off during that part of the flight. None of the dial's components or electrical connections were faulty. At Wright Patterson, all the relay switches and circuit breakers that had provided power to the pump were thoroughly examined. Nothing amiss was found. Assuming the cockpit dial and switch were correct and the scavenge pump was off in the seconds before the explosion, no electricity would have been passing through it. If so, there was no chance it had caused the explosion.

From the beginning, many investigators had wondered if Flight 800's air-conditioning units might be implicated. The units had been secured from

Debris Field #3, closest to Kennedy Airport, indicating that they had been among the first pieces to fall as the plane exploded, but they showed no signs of having overheated or sparked. Could they have heated the fuel tank to such a degree that it had exploded on its own? This was hard to imagine, since the surfaces of both the tank and air-conditioning units were designed to be incapable of heating to more than the 400 degrees necessary for auto-ignition. Besides, 747s sat on hot tarmacs for an hour or more every day at airports around the equator, their air-conditioning units cranked up high. Those 747s never exploded. But when Boeing ran its Flight 800 simulation tests on 747s in the Arizona desert it learned, to its surprise, that the air-conditioning units could help heat center-fuel-tank vapors to above 100 degrees—hot enough to be ripe for a spark—although the tanks did not explode. Even so, the engineers no longer felt sure the tanks couldn't explode. The units would be put on to a list under the general heading of possible contributing factors.

Other even more remote suspects were also considered. Had a wheel brake caught fire as a result of a fuel-pump leak? The salvaged wheel brakes offered no evidence of such an event. Had tires routinely filled with nitrogen somehow exploded, detonating the fuel tank? There was no evidence of that scenario, either. Had a fire occurred in the hydraulic system, a portion of which ran behind the back wall of the center fuel tank? Again, salvaged pieces offered no evidence.

Certainly the fuel lines that ran from the center tank to the plane's four engines might have provided a path through which fire could travel from a spark or hot surface at a remote location. Eventually, many of the fuel lines would be recovered: not only from the center fuel tank to the engines, but from the tanks in the wings. None showed any evidence of a spark or flame. Of particular interest to investigators was the cross-feed valve that enabled the pilot to feed an engine from a different tank. Suspicions had arisen from the disconcerting comment on the cockpit voice recorder at 20:29:15: "Look at that crazy fuel-flow indicator there on Number Four." However, pilots who had flown TWA's #N93119 told investigators that that gauge frequently acted erratically. Some added that erratic behavior by the gauge was routine on other 747s, too. Nonetheless investigators examined the wiring that ran from the fuel-flow indicator into other systems, including a portion of wire that led, indirectly, to the center fuel tank, but found no indication of a problem. They found that a portion of the wire from the fuel-flow gauge ran in common with another wire that led to the tank. They wondered if a current from the high-voltage wire may have jumped into the low-voltage wire and created a spark inside the tank. No evidence of a problem was found, though they continued to study the possible scenario. No evidence of fire was found in or around the number-four engine either. As for the fuel-flow indicator itself, it took its reading not from the fuel tank—or its probes, or its lines—but from meters installed on the engines to show how much fuel the engines were using. Its role, in other words, was modest, and when it misbehaved, the reason was usually ice or some other incidental factor affecting its turbine performance for a short time. If the whole fuel system had faltered on Flight 800, several other indicators would have swung into action, too, but those indicators were fine.

By mid-October, with no tangible evidence of what may have created the spark that caused the explosion, investigators from the NTSB, and Loeb in particular, seized on a new theory. It was unlikely, but not inconceivable. Unlike other theories, it had the appeal of not requiring evidence. If static electricity had caused the explosion, there would be no frayed wires to indicate it, no short-circuited connectors, no charred fuel lines. Like the perfect crime, it would have left no clues.

Its effects were familiar to anyone who had ever walked across a carpeted room in stockinged feet and touched a doorknob to feel a light crackle and snap of electrical charge. Technically, static electricity occurs when a charged surface is brought close to another conductor. On a plane, fuel running through a metal fuel line might develop a static charge. Metal chips or fragments in the fuel would increase the likelihood. The investigators at Calverton began to wonder if static electricity might have occurred at junctures along the fuel lines that originated in the center fuel tank. A fuel line through the rear of the center tank was comprised of sections of tubing connected by metal fasteners called Wiggins couplers. What if one of these couplers had loosened or become damaged, so that the fuel flowing through it created static electricity, igniting the vapors in the tank?

In a world that produces an expert for every subject, there was, as it turned out, a leading authority on electrostatic charge in jet fuel. Dr. Joseph Leonard was based at the Naval Research Laboratory, where he had devoted thirty years to the matter. In 1970, two 727s had caught fire during refueling at an airport in Minneapolis, Minnesota. The incidents happened within weeks of each other, without an apparent explanation. In his investigation, Dr. Leonard found that the fuel trucks supplying the planes had developed an excessive amount of static charge before they rolled over to the planes, and then conducted enough of that charge during refueling to set the planes on fire. The problem eventually was traced to the airport's use of a new fuel-filter paper that had a significantly higher charging capability than its manufacturer had realized. When the fuel paper was changed, the problem was solved.

In an effort to create static charge from lengths of fuel line cinched by Wiggins couplers, Leonard sprayed Jet-A fuel through an ordinary syringe onto an isolated clamp. The highest voltage he could produce was 55 volts—not nearly enough to set off a spark.

At Wright Patterson, meanwhile, researchers tried to create enough static charge from Wiggins couplers and center-fuel-tank lines to produce enough voltage to spark. Eventually they boosted their charge to 650 volts, higher than anticipated, but well below the threshold of 3,200 volts needed to create a spark. By comparison, someone in stockinged feet walking across a carpeted room might create a static charge of 3,500 volts. Out of curiosity, the researchers introduced variables not present on Flight 800, including fuel that conducted static charge better than the Jet-A fuel used on Flight 800. By doing so, they achieved a voltage of 4,800. When they added water to the fuel, they reached 6,500 volts, but this was academic, since no such fuel had been used on Flight 800. Even that voltage failed to ignite the fuel in which it was produced.

Static electricity—the "invisible" theory—became a favorite of Dr. Bernard Loeb, who, much to the surprise of investigators in the hangar, declared one Sunday evening in early November on *60 Minutes* that static electricity was the likeliest cause of the center-fuel-tank explosion. "It's of significant interest to us right now," he told correspondent Ed Bradley. Loeb explained what a Wiggins coupler was, and offered the theory—suggesting that the NTSB as an agency had come to believe that a faulty Wiggins coupler could have caused a spark that exploded the tank. He neglected to mention that NTSB workers in the hanger had found no reason to believe that there *was* a broken Wiggins coupler on a fuel pipe running through the tank, or that static electricity had caused the blast. In fact, most of the pipe running through the center fuel tank had not yet been recovered.

Loeb then repeated the philosophy he'd voiced to his NTSB investigators. Whether or not static electricity had caused the center fuel tank's volatile vapors to explode, he said, the solution was simply to reduce the temperature of those vapors so that no mechanical malfunction—or, for that matter, no missile or bomb—could possibly ignite them.

"I don't really care what this guy's theory is," Kallstrom told Hall by phone the next day. "Just because he thinks X happened or Y happened or Z happened doesn't mean anything. We have to get to the truth. Let's stop talking about his opinion. We have a lot of experts in the world. We are not interested in their goddamned opinions. We are interested in facts."

"I know what you're saying, Jim," Hall replied diplomatically. "But it's also true that the NTSB had an obligation to the public to give its most educated theories a public airing as early as possible, and also to let the wider aviation community take a closer look at what might be a problem affecting other planes.

"We're no less interested in facts than you are," Hall added. "But we have more leeway to speculate because we're not bound by criminal legal standards."

"But these theories of his are myopic," Kallstrom shot back. "He hasn't got one scintilla of proof."

Tempers at the top would continue to flare, but at Calverton, the initial prickliness between NTSB engineers and FBI agents had by now all but van-ished. If Kallstrom's daily visits helped, so did the calm, evenhanded manage-ment of Kenny Maxwell who, like Kallstrom, worked even longer hours than his troops. So rarely did Maxwell get home to his FBI-agent wife in Newburgh, New York, that when he announced she was pregnant, there were widespread cackles of disbelief. Who was the father? they teased the good-natured Maxwell.

Working together helped—a lot—to ease ingrained suspicions. The NTSB engineers pictured FBI agents the way Hollywood did: as stern, macho types in black suits, wielding revolvers. They had to learn that agents rarely found themselves in shoot-outs. Indeed, far more often agents had to be as calculating and patient as scientists as they examined clues. The agents, for their part, had learned that NTSB investigators worked just as painstakingly—and, at times, even more unemotionally. Confronted by the horrible realities of TWA Flight 800, the FBI agents nursed strong feelings of frustration, sorrow, and anger at the thought that criminals might have downed the plane. The NTSB engineers, accustomed to plane crashes, talked clinically of factors like G-load, the gravi-tational force that would have pushed so harshly against falling passengers that no one could have survived.

As the two sides worked together, they learned to trust each other and became more willing to share information. As the weeks wore on with no relief in sight—and ever more wreckage to analyze and assemble—the investigators and agents grew weary together. One day, as a diversion, FBI agent Bill Barry took the whole NTSB group out to a firing range and fitted them with auto-matic weapons and shotguns. Most of the engineers had never held a gun before. The day at the range helped them blow off steam, and boosted morale. They needed that: Three months of intense analysis had not only failed to solve the mystery but augmented it. The center fuel tank occupied just one of the three hangars at Calverton. In another resided the far more ambitious recon-struction of TWA Flight 800's whole interior, from first class to rear galley, as the parts emerged from the sea.

The project needed more than the combined efforts of the FBI and NTSB. Cabin designers from Boeing and TWA had come to Calverton to refit every-thing from galley carts to overhead bins. Union machinists and aerospace workers matched seats and other furnishings to their blueprint positions. A Boeing engineer and an FAA specialist in "human factors" were there to point out all modifications of the cabin throughout its lifetime. Agents from FBI and from Alcohol, Tobacco, and Firearms studied the emerging tableau for any visual evidence of explosives.

The work began with blueprints and a roll of duct tape. A line of tape down the middle of the hangar defined the length, or spine, of the plane. Grids of tape on either side marked the cabin floor. Boeing's planes were measured in twenty-inch segments called stations; each square of tape became a station. Because every piece of the plane was numbered on Boeing's blueprints, the cabin reconstruction could begin to rise into three dimensions. About 40 percent of the seats still had their numbers affixed to them; positioning them was easy. The rest had lost their numbers, but in each case the damage could be analyzed and fit, like a puzzle piece, into the larger whole.

On his almost daily trips to the hangar, Tom Pickard would pause by the reconstruction to watch as more seats were added. The craftsman in charge, a New York State trooper, built a frame for each seat with two-by-fours and two-by-twos. If a seat was too damaged to stand, he used more lumber to set it upright. Here were the rows of three seats by the window, there the center rows of four across. There, too, was the carpeted aisle. Pickard would walk down the aisle as if moving among spirits, noticing the mangled galley and the lavatories. From his charts back at 26 Federal Plaza, he knew where each passenger sat. He would pause at these seats that children had occupied, touching the fabric of the cushions, trying to imagine the suddenness with which their young lives had ended. "You have a gap yet?" he would ask the worker, by which he meant some missing seats that might indicate the position of a bomb, or the entry of a missile. The investigators had noticed that seats toward the rear of the plane were highly fragmented, and that sixty-six seats had been damaged by fire, the results of the plane hitting the water in a fireball. "Nothing's jumping out at me yet," the worker would say. "But I keep looking . . ."

As the rows of seats rematerialized, at the rate of a dozen a day, another group of specialists matched the damage of each seat to the injuries sustained by the passenger who had occupied it, hoping that would offer clues to a bomb or missile. A Suffolk County police crime analyst integrated all the information on a burgeoning computer database that included digitized photographs of all the evidence. The team could actually watch a simulation of the plane explode on screen, then click to see how each passenger appeared to have been killed, based on the forensic evidence.

All this was reviewed by the team's senior medical consultant, Dr. Dennis Shanahan, and a team of pathologists from the Armed Forces Institute of Pathology. But Shanahan was puzzled. There was no clustering of injuries such as might occur in the proximity of a bomb. On none of the bodies were there any powder marks or discoloration to indicate a bomb at all. For what it was worth—and who knew; perhaps it would prove valuable—he had determined that on Flight 800, at least twelve people had moved out of their assigned seats into others before the plane took off: the usual scramble, on an overnight flight, for empty center rows where passengers could stretch out. Months would pass before investigators concluded, based on the wreckage, that the tank had exploded in a direction away from the cabin—toward the front and downward to the right. Eventually Shanahan would deduce why burns incurred by passengers inside the plane as it fell were surprisingly minor. That, he speculated, could be because most of the flaming fuel that enveloped the plane just before it hit the water was outside the plane. Shanahan had also determined that Captain Kevorkian had released the flight attendants from their stations just before the explosion occurred, so that they were presumably out of their seats and beginning beverage service. In fact, divers found the coffeemaker from the first-class galley in the "on" position; it was one of Janet Christopher's duties to put the coffee on. To many of the investigators, such details only underscored the horror of the human tragedy they were trying to dissect.

One of those was Hank Hughes, the NTSB investigator given to late-evening ruminations in the Calverton hangar. As reconstruction of the interior continued, he could almost feel the presence of the dead. Far from feeling frightened, he found the victims' spirits friendly and hoped to learn something that might prevent another such tragedy. Silently, he would convey some thought to one of the passengers—a simple greeting, perhaps, or a thought of condolence—and sometimes imagine a conversation ensuing, but he tried not to focus on any one passenger for long; that way lay depths of sorrow better left unfathomed. Instead, he pulled back to see the passengers as a group—a group he was struggling to help, wherever their spirits resided. Then he would wonder, as he drove home in the dark, whether work in the hangar was starting to unnerve him.

Hughes was a former Fairfax County, Virginia, police highway-accident investigator. He was familiar with death. For much of the last decade at NTSB, he had investigated aviation accidents and become an expert at restructuring them. Still, something was different about this one. The mystery was part of it, but so, too, was the time the investigators were spending on it, with no end in sight, while getting to know the victims better and better. Or maybe Hughes was burning out, which most air-crash investigators did sooner or later. So, thought Hughes grimly, did most highway-accident investigators. The work in the hangar had just had a tangible effect on Hughes' personal life. For several years, he had a girlfriend whom he loved, but was reluctant to marry: the usual commitment problem. Dealing every day with the wreckage of Flight 800, and with the waterlogged belongings of the victims, had told him how fragile life was, that it was not a dress rehearsal. Hughes stunned his girlfriend by announcing he was ready to get married—and early in the month, he went through with it.

Hughes was in the hangar on the day in late October when Charlie Christopher came to visit. Since Janet's funeral, the FBI agent had gone back to work in the New York office, and Charles, his son, had gone back to school and the Boys Scouts. But life was utterly different for them both. Along with his grief, Charlie was hugely frustrated by the enduring lack of clues to the case. He was determined to find and follow a criminal trail, no matter how faint. Kallstrom had to remind him, gently, that even if a trail appeared, Christopher would not be allowed to join in the pursuit. It was just too personal; some defense attorney may cry "conflict of interest." Instead, Kallstrom invited him up to the hangar, sensing that a visit to the cabin where Janet died would bring his old friend some peace.

As Hughes and the other investigators watched from a respectful distance, Christopher walked slowly toward the open cabin, with Kallstrom at his side. When he reached Janet's jump seat, he stood by it for some time, holding it with tears in his eyes. When he turned to leave in a kind of daze, Kallstrom held him in a powerful hug, and the two men wept together. Hughes, standing unseen nearby, felt suddenly guilty for witnessing such an intimate moment, but he couldn't tear himself away. Finally, Kallstrom and Christopher walked slowly in silence out of the hangar, their arms across each other's shoulders. As Hughes watched them go, what he thought was: It's not just me. Everyone touched by this tragedy is haunted by it, and the longer it goes on with no explanation, the harder it gets.

The enduring mystery disheartened the victims' families; it confounded Long Island residents to whom images of the crash night remained painfully vivid; inevitably, it dogged the politicians whose constituents these citizens were, or whose job it was, as members of one committee or another, to make sense of the unexplainable and decide whether or not to grant multimillion-dollar appropriations—for more reconstruction, more fully staffed time in the hangar, and for trawling. Curious as to what the hangar looked like, or simply wanting to do something, the politicians asked for on-site briefings. Respectfully, the FBI obliged.

Senators and congressmen, White House officials, foreign ambassadors, and diplomats would convene at an appointed time outside the hangar, like groups about to tour a museum. Their guide was usually Maxwell or, when very high officials arrived, Pickard or Kallstrom, who would tell them, before they entered, that investigators were working on three general theories at once—mechanical malfunction, a bomb, a missile. The dignitaries would shuffle about impatiently, having heard most of what the FBI had to say on the television news during the last three months. They wanted inside information; they wanted to know why it was taking investigators so long to explain what had happened to this airplane.

Once inside, the dignitaries would see the full-sized interior of a 747 stretching nearly a hangar's length. Its scale was daunting, and anyone who saw it felt small. They had come prepared to ask probing questions. Standing before the cabin reconstruction, the questions suddenly seemed pointless. They had heard talk of fuel tanks, and imagined tanks not much larger than the ones in their cars. The mock-up of the center fuel tank they saw in one of the hangars was large enough to hold all of them standing upright. They would be taken to see the plane's carpeting, its hundreds of segments arranged precisely in order on a hangar floor. They would stand next to the huge engines—at sixteen feet long, large enough to dwarf a man. They would see what was left of the cockpit, a tangle of torn and shredded wires. They would see a wing, charred and bent, and rows and rows of plane parts and pieces, as many as a thousand, most of which were mangled, twisted, and unrecognizable.

The tours usually ended back at the passenger cabin, where the politicians gazed silently at the reconstructed seats. Aware now of the magnitude of the investigation, seeing firsthand what it meant to retrieve the hundreds of thousands of pieces of a shattered 747 from the ocean floor and put them together here, they asked no questions at all.

Before they left, the visitors were taken to the second floor of the hangar, where the accumulating personal effects of Flight 800's passengers were stored. There they could see the clothing and suitcases, backpacks, cameras, teddy bears, and Saint Christopher medals that agents had cataloged and tried to match with the passengers who had owned them. On some of the effects, the visitors would note with a start, were traces of human blood, or the stench of seawater, jet fuel, and sea creatures. As they left, the visitors were stunned. "Good luck," they would say softly as the group broke apart. "Good luck."

But to some people who could not see the wreckage, and who could not see firsthand the dedication of the engineers and agents, and the vast effort to rebuild the center tank and reassemble the interior, the continuing absence of solid leads had begun to raise suspicions, and suspicions, in turn, provoked just what Kallstrom had most wanted to avoid: a rash of conspiracy theories.

CHAPTER 14

CRIES OF CONSPIRACY

At each of his news conferences, Kallstrom made a point of reciting a toll-free FBI phone number to solicit eyewitness accounts, leads, even wild hunches from the public. If anyone needed reminding of how useful a public appeal could be, the capture of the Unabomber on April 3, 1996, after years of false leads and frustration, would serve: only after *The New York Times* and *The Washington Post* published the Unabomber's lengthy screed against modern society at Louis Freeh's and Kallstrom's express request had David Kaczynski realized that the Unabomber was his own brother and, heartsick, turned him in.

Because Kallstrom was one of the few in the bureau with a thorough understanding of computer technology, and because he believed more than most agents in asking the public for help, he also advertised the FBI's online address, and set up a Flight 800 website. Some of the most intriguing leads came in that way, but in this first major FBI investigation of the online era, Kallstrom soon realized, the Internet could do as much harm as good, spreading conspiracy theories with digital speed through cyberspace.

Had the investigation issued tangible news, Flight 800 might not have provoked so many strange theories. But its lack of a breakthrough fed suspicions. In time, the conspiracy theories generated by the Internet would grow so various and bizarre that newspapers felt obligated to publish stories on them. As those stories, in turn, fanned more theories and created more theorists, the Internet would often seem to color the investigation more vividly, and more enduringly, than Kallstrom's dry acknowledgment that yet again "we have not moved the ball any farther down the field today."

Most of the theories began with a kernel of truth. The most alluring relied on pictures or audiotape, both of which could now be sent digitally. The murkier they looked or sounded on-screen, the more chillingly genuine they seemed. Some sites, for example, displayed grainy photographs of mail-pouch bags picked up from the ocean bottom. The implication, to an unsophisticated audience, was that Flight 800 had been carrying top-secret documents. In fact, international flights carry all sorts of mail, including diplomatic pouches; there was nothing unusual in Flight 800's mail load. Visitors to another site could download audio from a Coast Guard commander in the hours after the explosion saying, "One of our cutters heard Mayday, Mayday and that's all we heard." The suggestion was that Flight 800's pilots had radioed a distress signal in the seconds before the crash, and that investigators had covered that up. In fact, the Mayday call came from another pilot in the air at the time, calling out on behalf of the crippled plane. A third site found dark portents in the White House's carefully muted response to the crash. The website writer observed: "Even as White House spokesman Mike McCurry said 'no American official with half a brain' should be speculating about a missile attack, FBI agents were fanning out on Long Island's East End to chase down that very possibility," as if the agents were engaged in a clandestine effort that the White House was trying to conceal.

The theories soon spread across the country and beyond, finding a particularly receptive audience in France, partly because of the number of French passengers aboard Flight 800 and the tight control of the investigation by U.S. authorities. Frustrated and angry as the weeks went by with no break in the case, relatives and friends of the French passengers, along with other European families whose loved ones had died, took solace in Internet "evidence." Eventually, one of the documents made its way into the hands of an influential American in Paris who knew how to publicize it with maximum impact: the onetime press secretary to President Kennedy, Pierre Salinger.

In the thousand days of Kennedy's Camelot, Salinger had often been nearly as visible, in his role, as the president himself. Along with Ted Sorenson, McGeorge Bundy, and Arthur Schlesinger, Jr., he was a member of Kennedy's kitchen cabinet, counseling the president on the press during critical times such as the 1962 Cuban Missile Crisis. So widely respected was he that after Kennedy's assassination, Salinger ran for U.S. senator in California—and won. He served out a term, then joined ABC News as a correspondent based in Paris, where he occupied a cavernous, ornate apartment in which he entertained visiting journalists and held forth with a glass of wine in one hand and his omnipresent cigar in the other. The evenings were social, but also business: Salinger was now a consultant for the huge public relations firm Burson-Marsteller, which valued his wide network of contacts in the higher echelons of journalism and politics, both in Europe and the United States. That network, and his stature from the Kennedy days, attracted attention when he chose, in the fall of 1996, to say what *he* thought had caused the crash of TWA Flight 800.

Sometime in early October, Salinger was handed a copy of an unsigned document written, he was later told, by a former United Airlines pilot. The document was laced throughout with military argot. "TWA Flight 800 was shot down by a U.S. Navy guided missile ship which was in area W-105," the pilot's statement began. "W-105 is a Warning Area off the southeast coast of Long Island and is used by the military for missile firing and other military operations.

"Guided missile ships travel all over the world defending the U.S.," the statement continued. On July 17, 1996, "they were conducting practice firings up over the top of a Navy P-3 radar plane who [sic] was on a southwest heading about over the top of TWA 800. . . . The P-3 was a nonbeacon target (transponder OFF) flying southwest in the controlled airspace almost over TWA 800 and made NO calls to ATC. After the explosion, he [sic] continued his flight to the west and then called ATC and asked if they would like him to turn around and assist with the 'accident'!

"It has been a cover-up from the word go," the statement declared. "The NTSB is there in name ONLY. All announcements made by Mr. Bob Francis say absolutely nothing and notice that the FBI is always standing beside or behind Mr. Francis and it would appear that his job is to make sure that nothing is said that would give away THE BIG SECRET! It is time to end this farce and tell the public the real truth as to what happened to TWA 800."

To Salinger, these claims seemed too plausible to dismiss. Salinger was impressed, too, by the credentials of the source who gave him the document as if it were a top-secret missive. The source was an agent for the French intelligence service called the DGSE (Direction Generale de la Securité Exterieure), the French equivalent of the CIA, who said he had gotten the document from someone in the U.S. Secret Service.

When Salinger saw a story about TWA Flight 800 in *Paris Match* magazine that discussed the friendly-fire theory as a cause of the crash without mentioning information in his document, he considered going public with what he knew. The *Paris Match* story did include a reproduction of the Kabot picture— the snapshot of guests taken by Hampton Bays resident Linda Kabot showing guests on an oceanfront deck and a missilelike streak in the background. Salinger did not know this picture had been shown on the tabloid news show *Hard Copy*, which reportedly had paid the Kabot family $10,000 for its use. More to the point, he did not know that the FBI lab had examined the picture and concluded that the streak was from a plane picked up on radar and, as important, that the "missile" was in the wrong side of the sky to be near Flight 800. To Salinger, the photo and his new document appeared to add up to explosive news.

By the time Salinger decided to go public about Flight 800, he had woven a few more colorful strands into his story. On November 7, he announced his findings to an aviation conference in Cannes, saying he had obtained documents that convinced him that the U.S. government was responsible for the disaster. "The truth must come out," he told 150 executives of the Air Promotion Group, made up of 40 airlines, including American carriers.

This was a sympathetic group if ever there was one. If a missile could be shown to have downed Flight 800, the news would have two immensely cheering consequences for TWA in particular, and good news generally for the industry. The airline could not be held responsible for the explosion; and governments, rather than the airlines, would probably have to spend a lot of money to lessen the threat of another such incident. If, on the other hand, a mechanical malfunction was found to be the cause, TWA could be accused of at least poor maintenance. With a bomb, it could be accused of failing to ensure that the plane was adequately protected. Either way, it would face whopping civil suits from the victims' families and heavy costs to upgrade its entire fleet or its system of security at airports around the world. So, probably, would other airlines. With a missile, the carriers were off the hook.

Salinger told the excited crowd that the U.S. Navy had been testing missiles off Long Island the night the plane exploded. Generally, commercial flights remained above a 21,000-foot threshold except when approaching or leaving an airport, he said, so the Navy had seen no danger in conducting a missile test below that threshold. Unfortunately for Flight 800, a smaller commuter plane had appeared above it as it made its ascent, so air-traffic control had advised Flight 800 to remain at 13,000 feet momentarily to avert a collision. The controller's command had put Flight 800 in the path of a missile, possibly fired by a Navy cruiser conducting an exercise with a "P-3 radar plane." As for the P-3, Salinger suggested, its job in the exercise was to track the test missile. Clearly the plane's mission had been a classified one; just as clearly, the plane's crew had chosen to cover up the friendly fire after it occurred. Why else, he demanded, had the P-3 failed to communicate at all with air-traffic control? The plane's belated return to the crash site and offer to help in a rescue operation was doubtless a diversionary tactic, part of the unfolding cover-up. The documents on which he based these conclusions, Salinger averred, were "highly accurate."

Kallstrom learned of those statements from a reporter who called for his reaction to Salinger's claim that a Navy missile had brought down TWA Flight 800. Stunned, he managed only to say that he would have no comment until he learned more. His first call was to Louis Freeh, his second to Pickard, to have agents in Paris get right over to interview Salinger. That night, the FBI found Salinger at his son's apartment in Paris, and asked if he would meet with agents the next day at the U.S. embassy in Paris. Warily, Salinger agreed.

At the embassy, Salinger declined to show agents his documents, but reiterated his belief that a U.S. Navy ship had shot down the plane during a test firing. He couldn't provide the name of the ship, but said he was told the crew had been deployed out to sea immediately after the incident, as a way of keeping the matter quiet. Salinger added that he was on to other evidence. He had sources in high places, he said; there was a lot more that he would know soon. Both with the agents and with reporters who called him later that day, Salinger sounded sure of his information and adamant that he had done the right thing in publicizing it. When one reporter informed him that the document in question had been posted on the Internet for at least three months, Salinger brushed the comment aside. His own document, he declared, could not be the one to which the reporter was referring.

As Salinger was defending himself in Paris, Kallstrom was convening a news conference at FBI headquarters in Manhattan in the glare of international media coverage of Salinger's charges. NTSB chairman James Hall was en route to join Kallstrom, but his plane from Washington was delayed. Flanked by Navy admiral Kristensen and Brian Gimlett, head of the New York office of the U.S. Secret Service, Kallstrom stood before the microphones bristling with anger—as if he were about to announce a U.S. missile attack, not refute one. Salinger's report, he declared, was "just pure, utter nonsense." Kallstrom wanted to assure everyone, especially the families of the victims of TWA Flight 800, that no evidence of friendly fire had been found despite exhaustive investigation, and that no cover-up had occurred. As he began to explain how thoroughly the FBI, NTSB, Navy, as well as other agencies were sifting pieces of the wreckage for clues to a bomb, missile, or mechanical malfunction, Kallstrom was interrupted by an unkempt figure among the reporters. "The Navy is a suspect," the questioner called out. "Why should they be involved in the investigation? The Navy's a suspect."

"There will be time for questions. Not now. Do you understand?" Kallstrom shot back. The man continued to shout. "Remove him!" Kallstrom commanded, pointing to the man. Half a dozen police officers and agents hustled the ranting questioner out of the room.

In the initial stages of the investigation, Kallstrom continued, the FBI had determined that friendly fire was, as he put it, "highly, highly, highly, highly, highly unlikely." After a thorough examination of all military planes, vessels, and submarines in the area, the FBI had found nothing to change that judgment. "I'd add maybe five more highlys to that," Kallstrom said. "We have double-checked and triple-checked and looked from each angle, upside down, left, and right; we have left no stone unturned to assure ourselves beyond a reasonable doubt to a certainty that no military component or asset of this government was involved. Nor were they in a position to be involved."

Kallstrom assumed that Salinger had simply revived some tired allegations from the Internet, which the FBI had long since tracked to dead ends. But if the former press secretary had any further evidence to offer, the FBI would pursue it. "We're not going to sweep it under the rug," Kallstrom said. "We're going to look at everything. I want everyone in the world who has a viewpoint to tell us about it. We've received thousands and thousands of e-mails and telephone calls, and we've looked into every one of those." But Kallstrom rejected the most incendiary of Salinger's allegations. "The notion that someone in the government, the president of the United States or someone else, would have us hold off this type of information until after the Olympics—and then it was after the presidential debates, and then after the election—is just absolute, pure, utter nonsense," Kallstrom thundered. "It's outrageous. We would never do that. I would never do that. No one that works for me would ever do that."

Then, staring right into the television cameras, he said, "If this was an act of terrorism or a criminal act by some demented person, we want to find them, grab them by the neck, and bring them to the bar of justice. No one wants to do that more than us, no one. But the military of this country had nothing to do with this horrendous tragedy."

About an hour after the news conference, Kallstrom was back in his office, still steaming, when his secretary announced an urgent telephone call from Senator Patrick Leahy, a Vermont Democrat and the minority ranking member of the Senate Judiciary Committee, which oversees the FBI.

Kallstrom's heart sank. He knew how respected a figure Salinger still was in Washington. Was Leahy calling to say that Kallstrom had spoken too harshly or hastily? "Yes, Senator?" Kallstrom said. "Is something wrong?"

"Yes, as a matter of fact there is!" Leahy exclaimed. "I have Pierre Salinger sitting in front of me right now in my office with four little green Martians, about four foot tall each. And boy, do those Martians have a story to tell."

Kallstrom hesitated a second, then laughed so loud that Leahy had to hold the receiver away from his ear. The senator grinned. He had seen how angry Kallstrom was at the news conference, and decided that was a man who needed a laugh.

"God," said Kallstrom when he recovered, "did I ever need that."

———

The Salinger allegations had done real damage—damage that would not be undone by a single news conference. The public's faith in the investigators was now clouded, and many of the victims' families were deeply shaken. Over the next few days, family members deluged the FBI with angry calls, demanding the truth. "I let you into my home," said one father who had lost a daughter to the agent who had come to interview him. "We sat at my dining-room table. I discussed very personal things about my family with you. Now tell me, is what Salinger is saying true? Are you guys lying?" Trying not to betray how wounded he felt, the agent explained that Salinger had no new information, but the family member was unconvinced.

John Liguori, Corrigan's partner, got such a call himself from a woman he had met three weeks earlier. Atypically for an FBI investigation, the interviews of victims' families had been put off as long as possible, to give them time to heal and enable the agents to do background checks so as to save time at the actual interviews. Kallstrom also hoped that if they found out who was responsible for the disaster sooner or later, he could spare the families the invasion of privacy. But when the door had opened that day, Liguori saw the pain etched in that woman's face as plainly as if the crash had just occurred. It proved to be one of the most difficult interviews he had ever conducted as an agent, and now here she was on the phone, hurt and furious. "Please believe me," Liguori said softly. "I told you when we met I would not lie to you and I'm not lying to you now." But the woman was unpersuaded.

Though the prospect irked Kallstrom, the best way to disspell Salinger's allegations, he knew, was to deal with the man himself. From his Connecticut home the day after the news conference, Kallstrom called Salinger in Paris. Coolly cordial, he asked the former press secretary if he would share the additional evidence he said he had of a government cover-up of friendly fire. The FBI, said Kallstrom, stood ready to act on new evidence immediately, no matter whom it implicated. Salinger agreed to help, and volunteered that he was flying to New York on other business in a few days; perhaps he and Kallstrom could meet at that time. On the phone, the old press secretary sounded hesitant, almost meek—a far cry from his recent public statements. "I'm just trying to do the right thing for the United States," he said.

Not quite a week after his press conference, Salinger checked into a suite at the very comfortable Parker Meridien Hotel on Manhattan's West Fifty-seventh Street, where Pickard went to interview him on November 13, accompanied by Tom Corrigan, John Liguori, and Brian Gimlett of the Secret Service. Corrigan focused almost immediately on Salinger's PT-109 tie clip, evidently a gift from President Kennedy, who had given them to close friends as a remembrance of his near-death experience on a U.S. Navy boat in World War II. As the group settled into chairs in the suite's living room, Corrigan noticed the smell of a cigar in the ashtray, snubbed out, but still smoldering, with a thin trail still rising from it.

"Where's Kallstrom?" Salinger asked.

"He got tied up, and sent me in his place," Pickard said. That wasn't the whole story. By now, Kallstrom believed Salinger's charges were so preposterous that he didn't want to lend them the credibility that a one-to-one meeting with the head of the FBI's New York office would confer. Indeed, as an assistant director in charge of more than fourteen hundred agents, Kallstrom never conducted interviews; why break the protocol for Salinger? At the same time, he wanted to send a high-ranking agent so that Salinger couldn't claim the FBI was ignoring him. "I'm his chief deputy," Pickard added.

"Yeah, but Kallstrom is the one on television," said Salinger.

The agents found it odd that the furniture had been arranged in a semicircle, facing the door to the bedroom, which was opened just a crack. When a shuffling sound came from the other side, Pickard and Gimlett exchanged a wry glance. Someone, they suspected, was in the other room, probably taping the conversation. Pickard assumed that Salinger would try to bait them into making statements about the possibility of a missile attack on Flight 800—statements that could be snipped out of context and used to bolster a theory of government cover-up and conspiracy. "Whatever information you have to support your claims, any information you think we should pursue, we'd like to have it," Pickard said noncommittally.

Salinger showed the agents the two-page document he'd been given in Paris. He seemed genuinely surprised when the agents explained that the same document had been available to anyone who wanted to download it from the Internet since its posting on August 22 by a former United Airlines pilot named Richard Russell. "That can't be true," he said. "It went up after I publicized it." The agents shook their heads. Grimly, they told Salinger about the investigations they had conducted into all Navy vessels and crews in the crash-site area, and the research done to determine that no missiles could have been fired by a U.S. military asset from air, sea, or land. They told him about the radar maps from all commercial and military sources, and the transcripts of pilots, commercial and military, communicating with air-traffic controllers.

Salinger countered that he had talked to a passenger on an Air France jet that had taken off from Kennedy Airport just minutes after Flight 800 and followed the same flight path. The Air France jet had swerved wildly, the passenger recounted, in order to avoid a missile. The passenger, a female French dignitary, told Salinger she had gone to the cockpit to ask the pilot what was going on. The pilot had told her he had to take evasive action because a missile had been fired at them. Salinger said the pilot felt the whole area was under siege: a war zone. The pilot had told air-traffic control: "You know we can't go in there. It's too dangerous." In response, air-traffic control had told the pilot to take the evasive action he did, and that several passengers, besides the French woman, had been badly shaken up.

"Well, we'll check on it," Pickard said, jotting down the flight number—Air France 007—that Salinger mentioned. "What's the diplomat's name?"

"Oh, I can't give you that," Salinger said. "This person would be outraged if I gave her name to the FBI." He did, however, offer to help the FBI get the pilot's name.

In fact, the FBI and FAA had long since checked with the flight crews of every commercial plane flying in and out of Kennedy Airport on the night of the crash to learn of any unusual sightings made or precautions taken. There had been no such reports from Air France Flight 007 or any other flight.

The agents explained that the FBI had performed extensive interviews with many pilots in the air at the time Flight 800 had gone down. Surely, they said, these pilots would have told them about a missile attack, or the need to take evasive action to avoid being hit by a rocket. The air-traffic-control tapes, all of which had been reviewed, showed no conversations about evasive maneuvers, and the radar tapes from nine different sources showed no such maneuvers by any plane in the area.

"What about the P-3 plane?" Salinger demanded. "Why did they turn the transponder off so they'd be invisible to radar?"

Pickard explained that the FBI had looked fully into the Navy P-3 Orion, to give it its proper name, and come away satisfied that the plane was on an innocent mission that involved no use of armaments, either by itself or by the submarine—not the cruiser as Salinger believed—with which it had been conducting its exercise. The plane's transponder was off only because it had been broken for months, though in fact, it was working intermittently enough to show up as a beacon on secondary radar tapes. Naturally, primary radar also picked it up. Besides, Pickard added drily, the P-3's crew had been in direct radio contact with Boston air control since shortly after the plane left its base in Maine. Hardly a secret mission.

Pickard was curious to know the identity of the French intelligence officer who had provided Salinger his one actual document. Salinger refused to say. Pickard wondered which U.S. source could have procured this "top-secret document." Salinger said he didn't know.

In addition to the document, Salinger had a print of the Kabot picture. He produced it from a folder on his cocktail table. "What about that?" he exclaimed. The investigators told him they had received the picture long ago and determined that the angle of the object in the air was on the wrong side of the sky for it to have struck Flight 800. The "missile" in the picture, they added, was also traveling in the opposite direction. Salinger argued that perhaps this picture was different from the one the FBI had analyzed. His picture, Salinger felt, was evidence of a missile.

"What about the *Normandy*?" he added.

The agents told him the ship had been 181 miles south of the crash site when Flight 800 exploded, and not in a position to hit the plane with any of its armaments. Also, the agents had determined there was no test firing of missiles from the *Normandy* that night, as Salinger suggested.

By the end of the nearly two-hour meeting, Salinger's bluster had somewhat abated. He was obviously surprised that nothing he told the agents was new to them. "If I'm wrong, this stuff is going to break me," he said soberly.

Just as solemnly, the agents told Salinger how much pain his accusations of friendly fire had caused the families of the victims, how it had stirred doubts and confusion in their minds, and bred distrust between them and the agents conducting the investigation. Salinger acknowledged that, but said he felt obligated to come forward with information he'd been given, especially since it was, he was told, provided by a high-placed source in the Secret Service.

"Were you referring to the U.S. Secret Service when you spoke or the foreign service or possibly the French intelligence service?" asked Gimlett. "There is a difference, you know. The U.S. Secret Service guards the president."

"I know the difference," Salinger shot back. But on closer questioning, he admitted that he was not entirely sure that his French intelligence source had told him the document came from a U.S. Secret Service agent, rather than a French one.

The meeting ended with Salinger's promise to provide the agents with much more information. All he wanted, he said, was to help the FBI get to the bottom of this terrible mystery. But neither that week, nor in the weeks that followed, did he provide more information of any kind—nothing to supplement the one photocopy of the Russell document from the Internet. At the same time, he continued to make public appearances, flogging his "top-secret documents" and his talk of friendly fire to anyone willing to listen. For the agents, most of whom were old enough to remember Pierre Salinger with admiration as President Kennedy's press secretary, the rambling, red-thatched septuagenarian with his vague conspiracy theories appeared motivated not by the desire to do a "public service," as he put it, but to be in the public eye again—at whatever the cost to the investigation, the victims' families, and his own tattered credibility.

"I feel sorry for that guy," Corrigan said to Liguori as they left the Parker Meridien that day. "I don't think he gets it. He doesn't understand that what he's basing his reputation on is just a pile of crap."

"Yeah? Well, I don't," said Liguori. "Look what he's done to these families. He's ripped their guts out. And look what's he's done to all of us. He's made us out to be liars. Screw him."

When Pickard got in his car to drive home to New Jersey, he called Kallstrom to brief him on the meeting. "Salinger had nothing. Just Internet stuff. All he did was waste our time."

"What's this guy's problem?" Kallstrom asked. "Has he eaten too many rotten escargots, or is he just a moron?"

"Whatever it is, he's jerked our chains, Jimmy. That's all he's done."

As a result of the meeting, the FBI took another look at Air France Flight 007's flight from Kennedy Airport on the night of July 17. Agents reinterviewed the pilots, and this time they spoke to passengers, too. Pilots, flight attendants, and passengers agreed that nothing like what Salinger described had occurred. No pilot had observed any missiles in the area; no passenger had come to the door of the cockpit to make inquiries; the plane's course had not been changed to any degree, all of which was supported by the plane's radar and cockpit voice recorders.

However, within a week of Kallstrom's news conference on Salinger's accusations, a Pakistan Airlines pilot reported a streak of light across the sky off Long Island shortly after his takeoff in mid-November from Kennedy Airport. The pilot, Wajid Shah, said he saw it move three to four miles in front of and above his plane. A TWA plane behind Shah also reported seeing the light and was given permission to avoid the area.

Were these missiles, or had the pilots been spooked by Salinger's theories? A bit of both, it turned out. The FBI determined that the pilots had witnessed the Leonoid meteor showers: a volley of space dust and debris that creates bright streaks, like shooting stars, as it falls into the earth's atmosphere with pinpoint regularity every two years. Astrophysicists from around the country concurred that the Leonoid showers usually appear in New York skies in mid-November, lighting the sky with dashes of green, red, and orange that can look to civilians like missiles in the night sky. Experts at the New York planetarium confirmed that the showers had occurred in the sky exactly when the two pilots saw their streaks. Had such a streak somehow affected Flight 800? Anything was possible, but most scientists put the odds of a meteor shower as the cause of the crash in the same category as that of a New Mexico electrical engineer who propounded the "gas burp" theory, in which the plane might have been pulled down by a naturally vented methane cloud erupting from the earth; and the theory of a marine biologist that a herd of migrating whales might have generated an equally sizable, plane-devastating cloud of methane gas after a mass case of indigestion.

Nonetheless, the growing network of conspiracy theorists dismissed such explanations as glib cover-up stories, put out by a government desperate to hide the truth. From his Florida home, Captain Russell added Salinger to his list of e-mail correspondents, and the two struck up an alliance. Salinger was especially taken with Russell's latest evidence: a copy of a radar tape that had appeared, he said, mysteriously in his mailbox one day with no identification or postmark. Russell said that the tape showed an object moving toward Flight 800 at a rapid speed. Clearly, the theorists agreed, the object was a missile. And just as clearly, the American government was covering up the true story behind it.

By the time the media tired of airing Salinger's charges, the FBI and NTSB were more closely allied than at any other time in the four-month-old investigation. United in their indignation at Salinger's reckless charges, Hall and Loeb and other top NTSB officials spoke out forcefully against Salinger and in support of what Kallstrom had said in his news conference. Yet the new bond could not entirely assuage underlying tensions. Almost every day there were minor debates: how to proceed with a possibly key piece of wreckage, how to retrieve the wreckage now that the weather was becoming too cold for the divers, and what certain findings did or did not suggest. The weightier issues were money and time: how much more of each to devote to reconstructing the plane.

By now, the center fuel tank was far enough along for its shape to be clear. Yet enough pieces remained unsalvaged that aside from James Tobin, the hot-tempered FBI metallurgist now off the case, no one was able to say whether the tank had been struck by a missile or exploded by a bomb, or whether it had blown up for mechanical reasons. The reconstructed passenger cabin with its seats in neat rows on the floor of the hangar, its carpeted aisles carefully relaid, was an eerie reminder of the final split seconds of the passengers' lives. But it, too, raised as many doubts as it settled. While some seats were badly damaged, others appeared almost intact. At the same time, many seats had yet to be found. Even with the most sophisticated underwater sonar, there was only so much the Navy and law enforcement divers could do to retrieve the missing pieces any faster. Meanwhile, the investigators pondered what should be done with the wreckage that had been brought up. Was it enough to analyze the many pieces on their own, or should a full-scale reconstruction of the plane be undertaken instead? Or was that, as the NTSB's top brass had come to feel, a monumental waste of time and money?

At a meeting in early October at 26 Federal Plaza, Ken Maxwell, the FBI's supervisor of operations at the Calverton hangar, pulled a paper cocktail napkin out of his pocket and started poking holes in it with a pencil.

"Practicing to be a magician?" Kallstrom quipped.

Maxwell smiled briefly. "This is a frag pattern," he said, pointing at the napkin. A pattern like the one that would have been formed on a plane's fuselage if it had been hit by metal fragments in a high-velocity explosion. Maxwell ripped the napkin into pieces, then tossed them in the air. Kallstrom and the other investigators present watched the pieces come to rest on the wooden conference table.

"Can you tell me now where the holes are," Maxwell said, "or if they line up? And what their pattern is?"

Kallstrom laughed. The pattern, of course, would only be clear if the whole napkin was pieced back together.

For nearly three months, Maxwell had been surrounded by pieces of the plane, each day checking in more pieces retrieved by divers. In his gut he felt sure he was witnessing evidence of a horrific crime. He had heard the experts say the pieces showed no indication of a bomb or missile, but he knew they could find no evidence of a mechanical cause either.

With the napkin pieces still scattered on the conference table, Maxwell recommended that the entire center portion of the plane be reconstructed. It could be built out, he said, from the torn and twisted center fuel tank. The others agreed. They had urged such a project with Kallstrom for weeks. Several knew firsthand how helpful the reconstruction of Pan Am Flight 103 had proven to bomb investigators in Lockerbie. Kallstrom had resisted, hoping the fuel tank might contain the answer to the mystery, but now he nodded, too. "I think you're right, Max," he said. "If I asked myself, 'did a piece of shrapnel penetrate the fuselage, and did it then penetrate another layer before hitting the center fuel tank,' I couldn't answer that with these zillion pieces on the floor. And if I ask myself 'do these holes line up to show an entry and exit of a missile,' I'll never be able to answer that, either. We can't just look at this flat on the floor. We have to see it in three dimensions."

"No, just like the napkin, we will never be able to figure it out if we don't put this thing back together."

"Yeah, but I don't think the NTSB wants to do it," said Maxwell. "I think they're pretty convinced this is mechanical, and they don't want to spend the money."

"I'll work on them," Kallstrom said.

The concept was hardly a new one to Hall and his NTSB investigators, but reconstructions had been limited in the past to key sections of a plane that seemed likeliest to clarify the cause of a crash. This partial reconstruction seemed not only logical and efficient but saved money and time, which suited the NTSB, with its lean budget and small staff.

The NTSB had initiated the reconstruction of the center fuel tank when its singed and torn pieces revealed in August that the big tank had blown up. But the absence of any bomb or missile markings in the pieces assembled so far, coupled with the now-incontrovertible fact that the fuel tank had exploded, seemed to many to indicate mechanical malfunction—whatever that malfunction might be. As a result, the NTSB's top brass were dismayed to hear the FBI talk of reconstructing the entire center section of the plane, fanning out in all directions from the center fuel tank. To them, it defied logic; it made no scientific sense; and it would be very expensive. The day after his napkin meeting, when Kallstrom called Jim Hall in Washington to propose the project, the NTSB chief, not unexpectedly, balked. And in his own polite way sounded firmer than Kallstrom had ever heard him.

This was the same James Hall who, not long before, had come up to Calverton and talked about handing over the whole investigation to the FBI. But that was when the discovery of explosive chemical traces had made the crash appear almost certainly to have been a crime. With the news that those traces had apparently been no more than the remains of Carlo's bomb-sniffing test, Hall, like Loeb, saw the investigation in a fresh light. With no other evidence of a bomb or missile after nearly three months, the FBI was beginning to look less stalwart than stubborn. Why wasn't Kallstrom willing to concede the cause was mechanical? They felt the answer was that Kallstrom believed his FBI had to find the answer on its own, and that any answer the safety board came up with would lack the finality of an FBI conclusion.

As far as Hall was concerned, the balance of power had shifted, and rightly so. The NTSB knew how to conduct accident investigations. And it knew, from decades of experience with nearly 100,000 aviation crashes, that a full reconstruction was simply not required to do the job right. More than that, Hall, as well as Dr. Loeb and others in NTSB management, had come to feel that the FBI had stirred far too much public interest with its investigation of bombs and missiles. They felt that the FBI's public promises to pursue every criminal lead, leaving no stone unturned, was an overblown, unscientific response to the disaster. Without the FBI to gum things up, Hall and Loeb felt, the NTSB by now could have identified the center fuel tank as the culprit, listed four or five theories, made recommendations to the FAA on ways to prevent volatile vapors from overheating within all fuel tanks, and closed its books on another crash.

By mid-October, some NTSB officials in Washington were openly critical of the FBI's relentless pursuit of what they considered nonexistent criminal evidence. Kallstrom had told them, angrily, that whether the chances of terrorism were 90 percent or 10 percent, his investigation had to be no less thorough. He noted that law enforcement had a higher standard of proof than the NTSB. The FBI needed facts, not theories, to support its conclusions. He might have added, though he didn't, that nearly all the NTSB workers in the hangar wanted to go ahead with a full reconstruction, and viewed their superiors in Washington as distant bureaucrats who wanted to wrap up the investigation and cut their losses. But even Kallstrom's edited replies provoked more irritation. At a first formal meeting to debate the issue at NTSB headquarters in Washington, D.C., the tensions finally spilled over.

Kallstrom swept into the NTSB conference room eager to get started on reconstruction—perhaps even that day. Hall shook his hand warmly, trying not to show his apprehension. This was not a meeting to which he had looked forward. With his slight build and southern drawl, he resembled President Jimmy Carter: same sandy-colored hair, same mild manner and aversion to conflict, with a similar underlying streak of stubbornness that verged on anger. Hall was uneasy with the FBI chief who dominated a meeting by the sheer strength of his personality. "You don't talk with Kallstrom," he would complain to his staff. "You just sit and listen to him." But Hall was also determined to stand up to Kallstrom on reconstruction. Each chief had his seconds: Dr. Loeb and Vernon Ellingstad, director of the office of research and engineering, on Hall's side, and on Kallstrom's, Tom Pickard and Ken Maxwell. Kallstrom got to the point: Reconstruction was a must. "Not to do it would be crazy," he said. "It's a major investigative tool."

"I don't think it's necessary," Hall said evenly. "Frankly, my staff and I feel it would be a waste of taxpayer money, not to mention the safety board's time.

The sensible way to go is to reconstruct the one or two parts of the plane likeliest to tell the story."

"If you don't build the mock-up in a case like this," Kallstrom replied, "then the criticism will always be, and I think rightfully so, 'you didn't do everything possible to find the answers.' We'll be asked by reporters, 'Wouldn't the mock-up tell you things you did not know? How come you didn't build it?' To which I'd have to say, 'It beats the shit out of me.' "

One by one, the NTSB officials ticked off their other objections. The NTSB could not afford to pay even half of the $600,000 that reconstruction would cost; it would have to seek a congressional appropriation for it. In addition, the project would tie up dozens of NTSB engineers and other experts—for months. The cost in staff salaries, as well as the drain on expertise for other needs, would be considerable. Meanwhile, the NTSB and FBI would have to keep paying rent of $1 million a year on the hangar to the U.S. Navy, which had taken it over when Grumman downsized. And what would happen when the reconstruction was finished? Had Kallstrom thought of that? In all likelihood, the reassembled plane would have to remain in the hangar for years, under paid guard, to be pored over by lawyers and insurance claims adjusters, while the NTSB continued to pay rent on the space it occupied.

"We've never done this before, and yet we've managed to analyze thousands of plane crashes," Loeb said. "Why do it now?"

"We did it in Lockerbie," Kallstrom said, "and it proved immeasurably useful."

"Yeah, but that was because it was clearly your case," said Ellingstad. "Early on, you and Scotland Yard found out it was definitely criminal."

"It's just totally unnecessary," Loeb added. "I really don't see spending all that money for a publicity gimmick."

Kallstrom was stunned.

"Gimmick? How dare you say gimmick! This is not about goddamn publicity gimmicks. This is about 230 dead people! And don't you forget that."

Loeb nervously adjusted his wire-rimmed glasses a couple of times, but didn't retreat from his remark.

Kallstrom looked as if he wanted to leap across the conference table and strangle Loeb, but with considerable effort spoke calmly. "Well, for us this is a necessity, not an option. We feel that the FBI cannot get to the point of conclusively ruling out a bomb or missile unless we do this reconstruction." Then he looked directly at Hall. "We've been partners from the outset, but if you don't want to get involved in this project, the FBI will have to do it alone. This is not negotiable. I'm not asking you for authority. I am advising you on what we are going to do. We're going to build a mock-up, with or without you."

If the NTSB wanted to walk away, Kallstrom said, he would seek funding from Congressman Henry Hyde, chairman of the House Judiciary Committee, and Senator Orrin Hatch, chairman of the Senate Judiciary Committee, which oversaw FBI budgets in conjunction with Hyde's committee. Both had always been supportive of law enforcement needs.

Slowly, reluctantly, Hall nodded. Privately, he agreed with his senior staff that a full reconstruction was of no analytical use, and he was unhappy about begging Congress for money. At the same time, he was politically astute enough to realize how bad the NTSB would look if it refused to cooperate with the FBI on such a high-profile project.

"Well, gentlemen," he said with an enthusiasm he clearly did not feel, "if the FBI thinks this is important, then goddamnit, it's important. And we're going to do it." Ignoring their looks of disbelief, Hall told his two adjutants to get right on it.

Toward the end of October, at Kallstrom's urging, the same group met again at the NTSB's offices. Kallstrom wanted to know what they had done to move the process along. Were any companies contacted? When could the project get underway?

"Actually," Hall said in his gentle drawl, "we haven't really done much on it yet."

"Why's that?" Kallstrom asked.

"I've just been busy on other pressing matters."

Kallstrom was dumbfounded. "What the hell could you possibly be doing that's more important than the TWA crash? Please let me know so I can tell the American people."

"Well, as a matter of fact my people wanted to rethink this whole reconstruction issue," Hall said.

"What is there to rethink?" Kallstrom demanded.

Then Loeb spoke. "Frankly, I'm more convinced than ever that a reconstruction of Flight 800 is ridiculous," he said. "We know what happened to the plane right now."

"What's that, Bernie?" Kallstrom shot back.

"The center fuel tank blew up!"

"We all know that, Bernie. But why did the goddamn thing blow up? That's the question! We are not going to guess if this was a bomb or a missile. We're not in the guessing business. The FBI is not the Federal Bureau of Innuendo. We need to build a 3-D mock-up so we can be certain. How can you be sure a small piece of rocket warhead didn't penetrate that tank?"

Peter Goelz, Hall's closest advisor and a skilled diplomat, tried to soften Loeb's stance. "Bernie, maybe you should reconsider this. A mock-up can't hurt, right?"

"My people are the best experts in the world," Loeb insisted. "And if they say that it's not needed, then it's not needed."

"Let me remind you again," Kallstrom said acidly. "If you don't want to do a full reconstruction, we'll do it anyway." Then, turning to Hall, he softened his pitch. "Listen, Jim," he said, "we would much rather do this with you than without you. You guys are the experts. We need your help."

Hall was torn. He knew Kallstrom was right to want his help. Without the NTSB, the FBI would have an extremely hard time reconstructing the plane, but he was receiving tremendous resistance on the mock-up from his senior staff, especially from Loeb, an experienced aeronautical engineer to whom he almost always deferred on aviation matters. At the same time, it was known that Loeb had a huge ego and trouble taking in anyone else's opinion. Toward the FBI, and particularly Kallstrom, he had demonstrated a vehemence that even a few of his colleagues considered extreme.

"Look, we'll do it," Hall said reluctantly. Reconstruction, he felt, was not the proper course of action, but it could be viewed as politically correct. And political correctness, in whatever form it appeared, was a force best not confronted.

As the meeting broke up, Kallstrom was still stewing about Loeb's attitude. His gibes about reconstruction were just the half of it. For weeks now, Kallstrom had gotten second- and thirdhand accounts that Loeb was denigrating the FBI. The man was an aeronautics engineer, not a weapons expert, but that had not stopped him from making statements to the media that there was no evidence of a crime in TWA Flight 800, and that in his opinion neither a bomb nor missile could have downed the plane. His uninformed speculations were creating confusion in the minds of the families—and the public.

As Loeb waited for an elevator, Kallstrom told him he'd heard enough of his opinions on what might or might not have downed TWA Flight 800. "Let me remind you, Bernie, we do criminal, you don't," Kallstrom said. "You do accident. I don't comment on whether I think an electrical short caused this crash, and you are not to comment on whether you think it was a criminal act. Understand?"

"If a reporter asks my opinion, I see no reason why—"

"No," Kallstrom thundered. "I want you to cease and desist from giving any more opinions on bombs or missiles or explosive devices. Is that clear?"

Loeb nodded as if he understood, and as the elevator door opened, hurried aboard. For once, he had nothing to say in return.

———

To Kallstrom's amazement and fury, days passed without any action from the NTSB. Finally, the president's chief of staff, Leon Panetta, called a meeting in November of the FBI and NTSB for a formal update on the investigation, and to settle the issue of reconstruction.

Kitty Higgins, Leon Panetta's chief assistant and the White House liaison to both the FBI and NTSB for the crash investigation, was in daily contact with both agencies. She knew by now from both sides how hot an issue reconstruction had become. Feisty but empathetic, she had worked hard to help both agencies, and to help each partner appreciate the other's problems. In that time, she had come to feel there was something about TWA Flight 800 that distinguished it from other tragedies with which she'd been associated: the Oklahoma City bombing for one, the ValuJet crash for another. The investigators radiated a sense of mission the likes of which she'd never seen in Washington, and the victims' families, with whom she'd been in close touch, too, had been drawn to one another in a way that felt—Higgins could think of no other word to describe it—spiritual. But over time, Higgins had also heard far more complaints from the NTSB chairman than from the FBI or other involved agencies. And the truth was, she had begun to tire of them. She felt less like a coordinator, she confided to her boss, than a baby-sitter. It seemed to her that whatever the FBI wanted to do the NTSB would oppose, like a stubborn child, just to be contrary. About reconstruction, she knew money was not an issue: Congress had made that plain. Hall was using it as an excuse. On the other hand, she knew Kallstrom would sift through every grain of sand to find the answer if he could. Listening to Kallstrom about the importance of reconstruction, Higgins could not help but sympathize with his frustration. It was time, she agreed, to have the two sides argue their views before the chief of staff, and let him decide.

The meeting was held in the second week of November, in the Roosevelt Room of the White House. A long mahogany conference table with high-backed upholstered chairs was set off by a vibrant blue carpet and pale yellow walls. A fireplace dominated one side of the room, flanked by bookcases of leather-bound volumes chronicling military campaigns. On another wall, above a camelback couch, were life-size oil portraits of former presidents Franklin and Theodore Roosevelt, as well as one of Eleanor Roosevelt. The thick walnut double doors on one side opened directly into the Oval Office. For this meeting, they were closed. Instead, Hall, Loeb, and Kallstrom filed in from a door on the other side, followed, a few minutes later, by Panetta and Higgins.

Panetta, with his dark hair, spectacles, and soft-spokenness, exuded, somewhat incongruously, a gritty toughness. He was the one who had brought stern order to an energetic but wildly disorganized Oval Office: limiting access to a president whose door had been open to anyone who wandered by, curbing the marathon policy talks that Clinton loved but that devastated his schedule, paring the White House bureaucracy and making it work. He was not a man who liked to have his time wasted by intramural bickering. Having heard reports of the NTSB–FBI feud from Higgins, he started the meeting fairly sure of what he would conclude. But he began, after praising both agencies for the work already done, by asking for Hall's sense of how the investigation ought to proceed.

Hall ticked off the various theories of mechanical malfunction that the

NTSB had come to suspect as the likeliest causes of the crash. He explained why rebuilding the center fuel tank had been a good idea, and why going on to reconstruct the entire plane was a bad one. Essentially, he said, avoiding Kallstrom's gaze, it was scientifically unnecessary, and would be a waste of taxpayer's money.

"And, Jim? What do you think?" Panetta nodded to Kallstrom.

In a voice of studied calm, Kallstrom explained that the complete reconstruction of the center portion of the plane was crucial if the FBI was to reach a firm, incontrovertible conclusion on criminality. "I know that is what the families want," he said, "and I believe that is what the American people want."

"But do you think the cause is criminal at this point?"

"Honest to God, I don't know," Kallstrom said, "because we haven't completed the process yet. Just because no evidence of a crime has been found yet doesn't mean it wasn't a crime. The NTSB may very well be correct—that this tragedy was probably caused by a mechanical malfunction. I do not argue with that. It's just that we cannot rule out terrorism if we don't complete the criminal investigation. And we can't do that without building and studying a complete mock-up of the airplane."

Higgins, listening intently, glanced at Panetta as Kallstrom was speaking. She had worked with her boss for years; she could tell he liked Kallstrom's forthrightness. So could Hall and Loeb.

"We can no longer look just for big holes that big bombs make," Kallstrom went on. "There are all kinds of devious ways that terrorists can kill innocent people. Having a hunch that terrorism wasn't the cause, acting on a lack of evidence so far, doesn't give you a definitive answer. We don't operate that way. We have to be right." The alternative, Kallstrom added, was to invite decades of controversy and conspiracy theories, like those after the assassination of President Kennedy. Indeed, Pierre Salinger's antics were an indication of just the sort of reckless speculation Kallstrom feared.

Hall acknowledged that some absolute standard of proof might not be met without a whole reconstruction, but since they knew the center fuel tank had exploded, and they could find no sign of a missile or bomb in or around it or anywhere else yet, the cause almost certainly had to have been mechanical. Besides, there was a practical matter to be considered. The NTSB lacked the funds to do a massive, full-scale reconstruction of a 747. It would have to seek a special appropriation from Congress—a drawn-out, and not necessarily promising, prospect. The FBI, on the other hand, had a lot of discretionary funds it could spend on the project.

"Stop this nonsense that we've got all the money," Kallstrom said with exasperation. "That's simply not true. Every dime we spend on this we have to take from somewhere else, some other investigative fund. We are stealing from Peter to pay Paul. The notion that I have all this money to blow on the investigation is crazy. We just recognize that this is something we have to do and we'll find the money one way or another."

Hall then introduced Dr. Loeb as his top engineer, and solicited a second opinion.

"We just think it's a publicity gimmick," Loeb declared, visibly pleased at his pluck for daring to brave Kallstrom's wrath a second time and speak his mind to the president's chief of staff. Kallstrom said nothing, but the glare he gave Loeb was lethal.

"Let's stick to what good the reconstruction can either do or not do," Panetta said with a reproving edge in his voice. Privately, he had come to believe there was too much suspicion about TWA Flight 800 to leave any course of inquiry unexplored. Legally, he also knew how helpful a full reconstruction would be in ruling out (or in) a crime. Politically, it was a no-brainer. You didn't want the families accusing the White House of aborting the investigation into the deaths of their loved ones. You didn't want every other voter wondering if what happened to Flight 800 might happen to him the next time he boarded a plane because the White House had decided to save $600,000.

There was another reason. "This is something the president wants done," Panetta said. "I've talked to him at length about this. He believes the prudent thing to do is finish out the investigation. If the cause was terrorism, he wants it determined. If it wasn't, he wants to be absolutely sure what the cause really was. He wants it done—and he wants you to work together."

Hall stiffened, as if slapped. He had a close relationship with Vice President Gore; as an attorney, he had worked for Gore's father, a U.S. senator from Tennessee, as his chief of staff for a number of years, and he was a presidential appointee. "I work for the president," he said quickly. "I'll see to it that we do exactly what he wants."

When the meeting broke up, Higgins accompanied Kallstrom down the quiet, thick-carpeted hallway lit by polished brass sconces toward the West Wing exit. As he passed the Oval Office, he nodded to two Secret Service agents outside the door. After a few minutes, they reached the formal foyer of the West Wing, a surprisingly cozy room with upholstered sofas and chairs, elegant end tables topped by fine lamps, and several oil paintings of events in American history. "I really thought you were going to explode in there," Higgins said, as she shook Kallstrom's hand good-bye.

"I was all set to turn that conference table over," Kallstrom said with a laugh. "But out of respect for the White House, I decided not to."

And then, as Higgins watched through the panes of the West Wing's double French doors, Kallstrom cinched the belt of his Marine Corps green trench coat and strode off with the weight of a very, very tricky investigation balanced effortlessly, or so it seemed to Higgins, on his big broad shoulders.

CHAPTER 15

PROCESS OF ELIMINATION

Out at the crash site, the *Grasp* and *Grapple* rested at anchor, immense naval vessels that would have appeared to be guarding the coast if not for the cranes at either end, hauling up pieces of wreckage. Three months after the crash, helicopters still buzzed overhead in an almost constant aerial vigil, helping coordinate the salvage operation, while Coast Guard cutters and Suffolk County harbor-patrol boats ferried brightly clad divers from the salvage vessels to their latest coordinates.

When the salvage operation had begun—an eternity ago, it seemed—the Navy divers in their simple black wetsuits had scoffed at the fluorescent orange-and-pink suits worn by their FBI counterparts. "Gucci gear," the Navy divers called it: too stylish for them. On the buoys put out daily to show where wreckage lay below, the Navy divers scribbled good-natured insults with their waterproof markers about "Gucci men" and their designer clothes. As the air and water grew colder with fall, however, the joking stopped. Those fluorescent orange-and-pink suits were warmer—a lot warmer—than the standard Navy issue. Somehow, Kallstrom got the word. Overnight, the Navy divers received "Gucci suits" of their own, and were shiveringly grateful for them.

The FBI divers could remain at the local motels now that the summer season had ended. Bob Burkes, the nature lover among the FBI divers, had pitched his tent in the desolate Pine Barrens. But the Navy divers had lived the last three months on their ships, cut off from their families and friends, suiting up nearly every day for another surreal dive to the wreckage on the ocean floor. Only the powerful fringes of three hurricanes had kept them from diving. On those storm-tossed days, they either kept to their bunks, fighting seasickness, or passed time in rec rooms on the Navy support ship *Oak Hill*, watching sports on the big-screen television, calling home on cellular phones, getting haircuts, or even having a cavity filled at the onboard dentist. Fortunately, the storms did less to move seafloor wreckage than Admiral Kristensen had feared, and vital sites were all well marked before the hurricanes hit, but valuable days were lost. Now the waters were growing colder and choppier, the number of daylight hours diminishing. Clearly, the divers would have to stop soon.

The good news was that by now they had done almost all they could. The combined team of some 400 divers—225 from the Navy, the rest from the FBI, the Suffolk County, Nassau County, New York City, and state police, as well as the New York City fire department—had made more than 3,500 scuba dives, and roughly 650 dives by ship-spooled hose: more than 4,000 dives in all, not including more than 350 forays by remote-operated vehicles. By November 2 all but 16 of the 230 passengers and crew aboard Flight 800 had been found and brought up. Most of the plane's larger pieces had come up, too. In all, more than 85 percent of the plane had been recovered, a remarkable and unprecedented salvage operation. Now when the divers went down, they usually returned with fragments small enough to be carried by hand. Any of those might turn out to be the "eureka piece," as Kallstrom called it, but it was time for other means to be employed. The Navy had two suggestions: The seafloor could be vacuumed—literally—though the process would be cumbersome and, as with a household vacuum, suck up everything small enough to be absorbed, not just wreckage. The better bet, Kallstrom agreed, was trawling: dragging rakes and nets along the ocean floor to scoop up wreckage—and body parts—that remained. Scallop fishermen routinely trawled Long Island's coastal waters; the same commercial trawling operations could be employed for the investigation.

To Kallstrom, the worsening weather seemed to moot any debate about how to proceed. To James Hall and Bernie Loeb of the NTSB, the choice seemed rather less clear. Even as wrangling began on reconstruction, the NTSB heads challenged Kallstrom's view that trawling should be done at all. Surely the divers had brought up enough wreckage for the cause of the crash to be determined—or at least for criminality to be ruled out. And to Hall, Loeb's logic seemed more and more persuasive. Make fuel-tank vapors less volatile in all commercial planes and the tanks would not explode—period. Hall was also reluctant to again go to Congress with hat in hand to seek a special appropriation of $5 million—*five million dollars*—for trawling. But the standoff over trawling was settled much more quickly than reconstruction, despite its greater cost. The benefits of reconstruction were hard to prove in advance. With trawling, there was an easy case to be made: More wreckage would be found. Besides, members of the Senate and House Judiciary Committees had made it clear the funding would be made available to see the investigation to a successful conclusion and to try to recover all the remaining victims.

The divers' last day—November 2—began in the usual fashion. More than fifty divers checked sixty-one remaining targets and brought up what they found. Though many of the pieces seemed insignificant, one diver salvaged a two-foot-square piece of the center fuel tank, another a burned seat belt and an undeployed emergency passenger slide that had to be eased slowly up to the surface so that its pressurized canister would not explode.

The canister was a symbol of sorts. It reminded the divers of their extraordinary good fortune: Not one serious injury was sustained throughout this treacherous assignment. More than one diver had nearly drowned when a razor-sharp shard of metal sliced through his air hose, but in each case the diver had been able to advise the crewmen above to start oxygen flowing through an auxiliary hose. In other incidents, one sailor had broken a collarbone, another a cheekbone, and fourteen had decompression problems; for the largest Navy salvage operation since the aftermath of Pearl Harbor, that was a remarkable record. The lurking presence of hammerhead sharks also posed a threat. Though the sharks had been drawn by the scent of dead bodies, the absence of blood had kept them mostly at bay, but they were unpredictable. One day, several sharks confronted a pair of Navy divers and began butting them. It was a terrifying moment: If the sharks chose, they could end a man's life with one bite, and in the ensuing blood-frenzy, any number of divers might lose their lives. The threatened Navy men banged the hammerheads' snouts with heavy sticks brought for that purpose, and the predators swam off. Another day, a hammerhead butted one of the inflated dirigible boats, spinning it completely around. The helmsman raised a 12-gauge shotgun, ready to shoot if necessary, but the shark seemed to have vented his aggression, and slid away into the deep. These were the surprises, but every day, the divers had to combat some of the strongest currents in U.S. coastal waters and operate in the murk those currents stirred up.

In the early afternoon, the divers piled back into their inflatables for a last trip to the crash site. Instead of wet suits, they wore clothes. Instead of scuba tanks, they carried wreaths and carnations they had chipped in to buy at a local florist. Some had notes to the victims tucked in their jacket pockets. When they arrived at the site, the divers' boats made a wide circle like a floating wagon train around a campfire. The enormity of the tragedy of Flight 800 had remained vivid to them, day after day, though in order to work they had tried not to dwell on it. Now, as a Navy trumpeter played taps, they allowed themselves to think of the victims whose bodies they had brought up, whose backpacks or passports or sneakers they had salvaged, whose families, in many cases, they had consoled with their recoveries. The divers placed a white, red, or yellow carnation in the sea to mark each life lost and followed each flower with a prayer. As a final tribute, Commander Scholley, supervisor of the diving operation, read the Navy hymn over the marine radio, a traditional prayer for the death of a sailor. "Eternal father, strong to save . . . O hear us when we cry to thee for those in peril on the sea." Then there was a long moment of silence.

The divers felt mixed emotions as the ceremony unfolded. Robert Burkes, the FBI diver who preferred to sleep in a tent, was proud of having done a job that mattered. So many bodies had been brought up, helping so many families begin the healing process. So much wreckage had been brought to Calverton—literally hundreds of thousands of pieces. Even if none of it disclosed the cause of the crash, each piece narrowed the possibilities, and the trawling would complete the job. Surely, from some piece or pattern of pieces an answer to the mystery would emerge.

Lieutenant (j.g.) Stephane Blais, the Navy diver who had brought up one of the first bodies only to watch helplessly as it slipped back into the deep, had trouble mustering Burke's degree of optimism. All these dives, all that wreckage hauled up, and still not a single tangible clue to what had caused Flight 800 to go down. Almost every day, the divers had brought up some piece that looked promising to them, but by strict FBI protocol they handed the pieces over to FBI and NTSB representatives on each ship and neither saw nor heard any more about them—not even the FBI divers. Some pieces brought up had the FBI divers convinced at times that the pieces showed evidence of a bomb or missile. After each time they waited and waited for word of a crime. But none came. Perhaps they'd found the eureka piece after all, and the investigators at Calverton had overlooked its importance. There was value in the operation, Burke felt, but it was a more personal one, unintended by the FBI or U.S. Navy: Every diver on the assignment felt a keen new appreciation of the suddenness with which life could be taken away.

Back at the East Moriches Coast Guard station, Burke, his FBI dive partner, Mike Tyms, Blais, and the others stood on the wooden dock that had been the stage of such horrific drama the night of July 17. For a long time, they gazed out at an ocean that had refused to yield what they most sought. They spoke with the weariness and dull shock of men just back from war, unsure if they had won or lost. The memory of a child's library book, *What to See in Paris,* a man's wallet with family photos, a baseball cap entangled in seaweed—these vestiges of a firestorm in which not a shot had been fired were the images they talked about now.

With them was Joe Cantamessa, Kallstrom's "nothing is impossible" fellow agent in surveillance, who had spent these last four months in East Moriches as head of the FBI divers. About a month into the diving operation, Cantamessa had made a point of going down with the divers on a particularly murky day. He'd wanted to understand what they were going through, and he had earned their respect for that.

The trawling began two days later. Four fishing boats, supervised by the Navy, trawled just as they would for scallops and clams, dragging wide rakes along the seafloor that scraped everything in their paths into large nets. Initially, the plan was to trawl 25 square miles of ocean bottom, but soon the search was expanded to 40.5 square miles. Every area was trawled repeatedly, as many as 30 times, until the nets came up empty. As the solemn operation proceeded, the crewmen videotaped every inch of the seafloor they raked and reviewed the tapes again and again. Beside their monitors, they kept FBI-distributed pictures of missile launchers and components, as well as a picture of Flight 800's little scavenge fuel pump, one of the suspects in creating a spark to the center fuel tank, but neither missile parts nor the pump would ever be found.

By the end of April, when the effort ended, 13,000 trawl lines would have raked 19,000 square miles of ocean bottom. That, according to Captain Chip McCord, the Navy's supervisor of salvage, was the equivalent of dragging up the interstate highway from New York to Los Angeles six times. In all, the effort would recover more than two tons of wreckage: 2 percent of the plane. The hauls would contain parts, at least, of each of the sixteen missing bodies, including, eventually, a human foot, still in its Timberland boot—all that was ever found of twenty-nine-year-old James Hurd III. From DNA analysis, Charles Wetli's staff at the Suffolk County morgue would be able to make the last of their positive identifications shortly after the one-year anniversary. At Calverton, investigators would surmise that despite the trawling, perhaps 2 percent of the plane's pieces would remain scattered on the seafloor. To recover 2 percent of a jumbo jet was still a considerable amount, but recovering 98 percent was a remarkable and heroic achievement.

On shore, the investigation felt becalmed. Hundreds of FBI agents remained deployed on it in Manhattan; scores more worked at Calverton testing debris, and the NTSB had eighteen working groups, still trying to identify a mechanical cause, more than the agency had ever assigned to an aviation disaster before. When trawling began, the odds against finding a clue in forty square miles of ocean were, as Kallstrom knew, depressingly high. Unless the eureka piece turned up unexpectedly, the FBI now faced the most difficult and frustrating kind of investigation: to prove a negative. In proving that something did not occur, nothing could be overlooked. Every single avenue of inquiry would have to be pursued to its bitter end, if only to show no evidence of a bomb or missile. It was an enormous undertaking and one in which none of the investigators knew where it would take them or if their attempt to prove the negative would turn up a positive in the end.

In this dreary interregnum, with Pierre Salinger's reckless charges still reverberating in the media, Kallstrom lost his right-hand man to a promotion no one could have refused. Just before Thanksgiving, Tom Pickard moved down to become head of the Washington field office. At the same time, he was promoted to be an assistant director of the FBI. Though the call was an honor,

Pickard said good-bye with a sense of guilt and regret. He felt he was leaving his job undone. "I hate to leave you now," he told Kallstrom glumly. "We're at a critical period here."

Kallstrom shrugged. "You need to move on, Tommy. I hate to lose you, but you can't turn this one down." Besides, Pickard's replacement in the New York office was a man in whom Kallstrom had confidence: John O'Neill of the Washington terrorism unit, who had already played a significant role and was thoroughly familiar with the case.

The farewell party for Pickard at Harry's Bar in the lower level of the Woolworth Building in downtown Manhattan was, in fact, two farewells in one: George Andrew, the very well-liked agent who never hesitated to say just what was on his mind, had been assigned to head the Omaha, Nebraska, office. At the party, Kallstrom gave Pickard a Steuben glass apple on behalf of the New York office, and told the mostly law enforcement crowd how much he'd miss his number-two man. "I could always depend on Tommy to clean up the carnage I started," Kallstrom said, to laughter. "I always knew Tom would say 'But, boss, we really can't do that.' And I would always say 'Tom, you'll find a way.' " Brian Gimlett, head of the Secret Service in New York, gave Pickard a more useful present: a bulletproof tuxedo vest. "You'll need this to protect yourself from Washington politics," he joked. And to Andrew, Gimlet gave a warm hat with ear flaps like the one cartoon character Elmer Fudd always wore. "It's cold out there," Gimlett warned. "You'll need it."

Within a week of starting his new job, however, Pickard managed to close out another investigation that had haunted him far longer than Flight 800. With his team of two fellow agents, he had been able to confirm the identity of the mole who in selling out the FBI had done damage to a few big espionage cases in New York. He was Earl Edwin Pitts, an FBI career agent who in 1990 had been transferred from New York to FBI headquarters in Washington to work in national security. Dealing with Soviets was his specialty; as it turned out, spying for them was his other great skill. He had been doing it, the agents determined, since July 1987. Pickard was so sickened by the discovery that he refused to be one of the arresting agents and let agents from his office arrest Pitts at Quantico, where at his request he had been assigned as an instructor at the FBI academy. Confronted, Pitts showed no emotion. "I want a lawyer," was all he said. A year later, he pleaded guilty, claiming that in the 1980s his salary of $45,000 had left him in such financial straits that he had to supplement it by trading information to the Soviets for cash. Just forty-three years old, he was sentenced to twenty-eight years in a federal penitentiary.

With the Pitts arrest on the front pages and no eureka pieces emerging at Calverton, the NTSB in December—five months after the crash—made a number of formal recommendations to the FAA, which increased already-existing tensions between the two agencies. To avoid a repeat of Flight 800, the NTSB advised that temperatures in all center fuel tanks should be kept lower; tanks should be kept full to prevent vapor buildup; and nitrogen should be pumped into the tanks to keep the fuel-air mixture less volatile, a very expensive series of solutions. The FAA had an opposite view: Better to "design out" all possible ignition sources from the center fuel tank, the agency suggested, and reduce the possibility of a spark that could set off the volatile vapors. The FAA's solution would be much less expensive for the airline industry to implement.

FAA experts found some of the NTSB recommendations to be costly, impractical, and potentially hazardous. Pumping nitrogen, an inert gas, into fuel tanks would reduce the volatility of vapors. This was done in military planes to safeguard them, particularly during an attack. But the practice would be expensive on commercial fleets as well as impractical, since nitrogen is not readily available in airports throughout the world. Addressing the NTSB recommendation that tanks be filled at the outset on planes traveling from west to east, the FAA suggested that doing so could lead to a potentially dangerous situation when the aircrafts landed. Since most of the fuel would not be burned due to wind currents, the aircraft would be landing with a heavy load and a full tank, creating a dangerous condition.

Therefore, the FAA recommended, eliminating all possible ignition sources was the best way to protect center fuel tanks from explosion. The NTSB countered that "designing out" ignition sources was a stopgap measure; a spark could come from numerous sources, making it impossible to eliminate every one. Make the tank safe no matter what happens, Loeb argued, and then the problem would be solved forever. The underlying tension was all too clear. Some at the NTSB continued to feel that the FAA was too sympathetic to the airlines and the airline manufacturers. They felt that the issue was mainly the FAA's unwillingness to take on the airline industry; in particular, the NTSB had been critical of the FAA for being too slow to force the airlines and manufacturers to move on what the safety board viewed as important safety measures.

The NTSB has no power to force the airlines to implement changes, nor does it want that kind of regulatory authority. It is content with its mission of investigating accidents, and making recommendations for improvements that might prevent future ones.

On the other hand, some officials at the FAA consider the NTSB a small, independent irritant with no power, an ombudsman that the FAA can heed or ignore at its own discretion. Some at the FAA feel that at times the NTSB does not have the full picture, does not grasp how long it takes to implement change, the numbers of people who have to be convinced, and the cost involved.

The FAA has mandated changes proposed by the NTSB in the past; others they found unnecessary or likely to create further problems.

———

On December 4, 1996, TWA held a memorial service meant to show that its own bureaucracy, slow as it might have been to react in the days after the crash, was now fully sensitized to the families' losses, and in particular wanted to honor the victims whose bodies had not yet been found. The gesture, as with so much of what TWA tried to orchestrate, missed the mark.

Fourteen of the fifteen families in question gathered in a tent at Pinelawn Memorial Park in Farmingdale, Long Island, about an hour's drive west of the crash site. Fifteen empty coffins were lined up to represent the missing bodies. The family members gave mementoes, notes, and photographs to funeral directors, who placed them in the coffins. Among those gathered were TWA executives, Kallstrom, Bob Francis, Admirals Kristensen and Linnon, and Suffolk County's police chief, Joe Monteith. But to the families, the service seemed manipulative. "This is closure for TWA, not for us," said Cyndi Hurd to a reporter after the service. (All that had been found so far of Hurd's twenty-nine-year-old brother James Hurd III was a suitcase, a pair of sandals, and one of his ties.) "They want all of us to go away. They want to bury this whole thing." TWA spokesman John McDonald thought this criticism, shared by most of the other families, was unfair. "It seems we are criticized no matter what we try to do," he said with a sigh. If and when the last fifteen bodies were found, he added, the cost of burying them would be borne by TWA, as had been the funeral cost of all the other passengers and crew to date. But if the airline had hoped to console the families with its gesture, it clearly failed, and the fact that it had been staged so close to the holiday season only added to their sorrow.

For Kallstrom, the holiday season offered the chance to make a more tangible gift of remembrance to one of Flight 800's grieving family members, one that had the aura of a Christmas miracle.

It was the day after the crash that a sharp-eyed Coast Guardsman had spotted a small burgundy box bobbing in the water and plucked it out to discover it held an engagement ring. Photographs of it, held by the stunned guardsman, had been published in a story about the crash in France's *Paris Match* magazine. There, a friend of the fiancé who had been carrying the ring made the connection, and called the woman for whom it had been intended.

Julie Stuart was still at home in Connecticut—and in shock—when she got the call. On July 17, she had put her fiancé, Andy Krukar, aboard Flight 800, intending to join him the next day in Paris for a meticulously planned romantic weekend, the culmination of which would be the moment that Krukar placed the $15,000, 1.6-carat diamond ring on Julie's finger. In the days after the crash, she had been too grief-stricken to notice the picture of the ring in several Associated Press news stories, but when her friend in Paris alerted her to it and sent a copy by overnight express, she cried out in amazement on seeing it. She and Andy had picked out the ring together. There it was, still in its burgundy box. She felt sure that Andy's spirit had helped recover it, and wanted her to have it as the symbol of their love cut short.

Getting the ring back had proved harder, however, than finding it on the open seas. Because she was not yet Andy's next of kin, Julie had to offer conclusive evidence that the ring—recovered item number 26—belonged to him, then prove she was legally entitled to it. She presented the jeweler's bill, the canceled checks, and the jeweler's elaborate description of the ring to TWA officials. When they balked, Julie wrote letters to the FBI, NTSB, even to President Clinton. Finally, she went with Andy's sister, Marge Gross, a former TWA flight attendant, to the Smithtown Sheraton for one of Kallstrom's daily press conferences and cornered him when it was over. Kallstrom promised he would look into the matter. When her story checked out, he called her and promised she would have the ring by Christmas. On December 23, in a ceremony in his office at 26 Federal Plaza, he made good on that pledge.

Accompanied by members of Andy's family as well as her own, Julie nervously slipped the ring on her finger and dissolved into tears. "I wish it was the way it was supposed to be, with Andy putting it on," she managed at last. "But still, I'll treasure it for the rest of my life." She looked up at Kallstrom through her tears, and then turned back to the family members behind her. "He's the only one who would listen to me," she said. "He's the one who got it back."

Christmas in the hangar was difficult, but investigators tried to make the best of it. They cut down a huge evergreen, put it in a corner, and decorated the branches by attaching green, red, and yellow tags used to mark the debris fields where the wreckage was found. By December 20 they had stopped sending home personal belongings that were recovered, indentified, and released. One of the last to go was the big stuffed Tweety Bird that Coast Guardsmen had spotted bobbing in the water the day after the crash. Agents had wrapped white tape around his torn leg and propped him up on a front table in the hangar, buoying the spirits of everyone who saw him. Shortly before Christmas, investigators had received a letter from a French family explaining that a daughter killed in the crash had purchased a Tweety Bird in America on vacation and asking if it had been found. Some items were still being held as potential evidence, but Kallstrom agreed the Tweety Bird hardly needed to be kept on that account. Off it went.

The investigators did have plenty of real wildlife to keep them company during their long days of work. The Canada geese had decided to stay for the season. A few of them paraded around inside the hangar as if they owned the place. They named one Andy, and he would waddle around nipping at the shoelaces of the investigators as they worked.

Soon after meeting with Julie Stuart and her family, Kallstrom flew out to Calverton to wish everyone in the hangar a Merry Christmas—and send them home to have one. Giving Julie Stuart her ring had pleased him enormously, but it was one of the few upbeat moments he'd had of late. Ever since 1967, the holiday season stirred mixed feelings in him.

About forty-five of those days came together, one after another, in the awful Christmas bombardment of Alfa 3 in December 1967.

At the start of that month, Kallstrom's platoon was dug into bunkers with other contingents of the First Battalion, Third Marines, in the middle of the demilitarized zone, where they were forbidden by Washington politicians from advancing toward a large phalanx of North Vietnamese gunners who were dug in just across the Benhi River. Daily, a squadron of B-52 bombers pummeled the North Vietnamese artillery positions with air attacks that were virtually ineffective against the enemy guns burrowed out of reach of the American bombs. The North Vietnamese army could not see the Marines, but knew they were daring them to make the fatal mistake of crossing over the river into the south. On Christmas Day, the enemy delivered a present to the American troops—1,000 rounds of artillery and rockets. The B-52s reciprocated with a relentless counterattack, dropping 1,000 bombs, which briefly lifted the Marines' spirits. But the North Vietnamese had dug a network of tunnels some 50 feet deep. When the bombers came overhead, the North Vietnamese scampered underground and survived.

The Marines' foxholes were four feet deep and seven feet wide, like mass graves, Kallstrom thought. By Christmas Day, they were wet, infested with mosquitoes, and visited occasionally by snakes. Set up like sitting ducks in a seeming stalemate, the Marines nursed bitter visions of Washington bureaucrats—starting with Secretary of Defense Robert McNamara—sipping Jack Daniel's in their Georgetown town houses while issuing orders that jeopardized the lives of young troops barely old enough to order a beer. Thereafter Kallstrom would harbor a sharp disdain for Washington bureaucrats—armchair leaders, as he called them—and "in the rear with the gear" politicians. He would identify fiercely with frontline troops, whether they were Marines in wartime or FBI agents and NTSB investigators in an air crash investigation.

One day not long after that brutal Christmas of 1967, enemy artillery trapped three of Kallstrom's Marines in a foxhole, literally burying them. Kallstrom and his Navy medical corpsman ran over to the foxhole across an open field, dodging incoming artillery; dug out the buried men with their bare hands and dragged them to safety. For that, Kallstrom was awarded the Navy commendation with Combat V medal. The Navy corpsman got a Bronze Star, a higher medal for the same incident, for a reason that both men understood: As the Marine officer in charge, Kallstrom's heroism was more *expected*. Kallstrom understood that perfectly. It was part of the Marines' esprit de corps, a spirit that only those who had served could feel. The esprit de corps, he would repeat softly. The sacrifices men made for one another on the field of battle, the love they felt for one another under the most adverse of circumstances—these would remain the high points of Kallstrom's life, long after the triumphs of his FBI career had appeared to eclipse them.

On this Christmas nearly three decades later, Kallstrom was haunted by images so incongruous with the lights and caroling of Christmas that it was hard for him to pretend he felt any Christmas spirit. Still, he stood by the big Christmas tree in a corner of the hangar and looked out with a smile at the hundreds of agents and other workers assembled to hear him speak. He thanked them all for the work they had done, for fighting an honorable war with the unknown to find the truth. He was proud of them, he said, his voice cracking. They should know their country was proud of them too.

For all gathered, the moment was an emotional one. But in the high-vaulted hangar, amid the thousands of pieces of twisted wreckage, and the ghostly aisles of reconstructed plane seats, even a voice as strong as Kallstrom's seemed to dissipate in the vastness of the space around it.

With the new year, trawling and reconstruction became the FBI investigation's twin prongs. By now, NTSB investigators believed the center fuel tank had been the primary explosion that caused Flight 800 to crash, and would have preferred just to address that problem and close the investigation. Kallstrom and his investigators wanted to make sure that an initial explosion had not occurred elsewhere—perhaps caused by a missile or bomb—and then sparked the center fuel tank.

As the FBI saw it, both trawling and reconstruction were vital to advancing its criminal investigation. Not until all, or almost all, of the plane was salvaged and reassembled would any certain judgment about criminal cause be possible to make. Among the missing pieces that might be especially helpful was the whole left side of the center fuel tank, half of its right side, a big chunk of fuselage in front of the tank, large pieces of the plane's underbelly, and the lower portion of a front cargo area. Pieces they did have revealed that Flight 800's front cargo hold, like the center fuel tank, had ripped apart. No evidence of a bomb or missile had been found, and in all likelihood the hold located in front of the center fuel tank had been damaged by the tank's forward wall exploding into it. But until the rest of the cargo hold was found, its destruction by a bomb or missile could not be ruled out. There were so many other sections of the plane with question marks on them that needed to be examined in three dimensions before they could be discounted with any certainty. The investigators also wanted to know why part of the plane where the fuselage and right wing connected had landed in Debris Field #3—the one closest to Kennedy Airport—indicating it was among the first pieces to fall off, and thus near the ignition source. Had an explosion occurred outside the center fuel tank after all?

Kallstrom's Calverton manager Kenny Maxwell, his integrated team of analysts, and NTSB and Boeing engineers got to work in earnest on reconstruction. Extrapolating from blueprints, they laid out a full-size grid of the plane in one dimension, then put salvaged pieces in their appropriate places on the floor. Fortunately, Boeing had numbered nearly every part of its 747s—all except certain generic rivets and screws. Even the wiring was marked every few inches. The marking had helped the manufacturer assemble the plane properly in the first place and allowed for easy replacement of parts. In the event of an accident, of course, the pieces could be that much more easily identified. For this reconstruction, Boeing also brought in experts to help put broken pieces together, and closely consulted with the 747's original designer, who also visited the hangar.

The next step was to construct a metal scaffolding and stretch a skin of wire netting from post to post so that actual plane pieces could be put in their three-dimensional place. As the plane's life-sized skeleton took shape, the workers below took to calling it "Jetasaurus Rex." The smaller pieces could be brought up ladders and put in place by hand. The larger ones were hoisted by a crane once used by Grumman to build F-14 fighter planes. The more pieces the experts succeeded in placing, the more quickly the remaining pieces fitted into the gaps, but the process was a daunting one. More than 95 percent of the plane had been recovered.

Meanwhile, Kallstrom sent agents to France and other European countries to conduct family interviews that had been delayed, in deference to their grief, as long as possible. Corrigan and agent Pam Culos flew to Paris on January 17, exactly six months after the disaster, on a 747 that would have been TWA Flight 800 except that the number had been changed to Flight 824. Through a schedule of nearly forty interviews, all emotionally draining, the agents would try to keep in mind Kallstrom's instructions: Be sensitive and, aside from classified information, don't hold anything back. As with the other agents in France, Corrigan and Culos each had an agent-translator assigned to them.

Corrigan's last interview, in Chalet, France, was the most painful of his career. While Culos met with other family members in the area, Corrigan went to talk to parents who had lost their forty-year-old daughter in the crash. The parents had received letters from the medical examiner's office in Suffolk County but, because the letters had been in English, they had gone unread. That troubled Corrigan, who knew that the letters the FBI had sent to the European families advising them that agents would be contacting them had been translated. But Chalet was a village, and the only person the family knew who might translate the letters was a schoolteacher away on leave.

Slowly and carefully, Corrigan's FBI agent–interpreter read the letters aloud in French. The parents remained calm until they heard the words "We have not identified any body parts of your daughter." At that, the father slumped in his chair. He had had no idea that his daughter's body was not whole when he buried her.

Corrigan did his best to boost the parents' spirits. He stayed with them for five hours, telling them about his own three boys, all under the age of five. By the time he was ready to leave, Corrigan had made some headway, or at least he hoped so. As he stood at the front door, the father said, "I didn't trust the Americans. In fact I never really liked Americans. But now you and your agent have made such a difference."

"*Merci beaucoup,*" a grinning Corrigan said in his finest New York accent. The father smiled back warmly. And then he held Corrigan for a long moment.

On February 17, the families of the victims—mostly American but many Europeans as well—were to come for a tour of the hangar on the seven-month anniversary of the crash.

Kallstrom knew it was going to be a tough weekend. For many of his agents at the hangar, the visit would be their first personal contact with the families. At a meeting at FBI headquarters in New York, he told some forty agents in attendance, "We need to be there for them. I am not telling you to act in a certain way, as if to cry on cue. I am telling you to be professional, but if someone is having a hard time, go up and put your arm around them, absolutely."

"But Jim," one agent said, more bewildered than anything else, "that is just not what we do. That's not what we're about."

Kallstrom was impatient. He knew agents were trained to be detached, but in the FBI, as in the Marine Corps, they had to learn to be flexible. "Listen to me," he said. "If all we do in our minds is the myopic job of investigating and fail to realize that our mission involves more than that, in this case with the world as well as the families, then you, sir, do not have a very clear vision of what the FBI is all about. And if that is what we did in the past we were dead-ass wrong, understand?"

Snow was falling out at the hangar as the families arrived for their tour. More than a few nursed a new cause for anger at TWA: The airline had not granted them reduced bereavement fares to fly to New York for the tour. For dozens of families, the full airfare was more than they could afford. Many had lost their principal wage-earners, and were experiencing new and frightening financial straits. TWA's decision looked even more niggardly when other airlines offered the reduced fares the families had sought. TWA's representatives argued that the airline had already spent millions of dollars on hotel bills for the families at the Ramada Inn in the weeks following the crash, and for each of the victim's burials. But the families were still furious—as were FBI agents and NTSB investigators, who passed a hat in the hangar that weekend, taking up a collection of $3,000 to buy the families lunch and dinner Saturday at the Smithtown Sheraton Hotel, where they were staying.

Family members were asked to sign a release that they would not sue for mental distress from what they saw. It was a lawyer's prerequisite, but hardly necessary in practical terms. The families simply yearned to see the shattered vessel where their loved ones had last been alive.

As they walked in, the family members passed a large sign mounted on an easel. Along with statistics detailing how many pieces of the wreckage had been salvaged and put together, the sign noted in large print on the bottom that the construction was being funded by the NTSB; a line of much smaller type beneath mentioned that the FBI had also contributed to the project. The family members were immediately struck by the enormity of the reconstruction; the images of devastation were everywhere. A mountain of wiring and crumpled debris several stories high occupied one area; this, the families were told, was the plane's former cockpit. The massive wings, charred and bent, angled away from the chewed-up fuselage. Twisted cargo containers, monstrous tires, scores of scorched and contorted pieces lined up waiting to be identified and joined to the reconstruction—all underscored the violence of what had occurred seven months ago to the day. The strong stench of jet fuel, dead fish, and seawater thickened the air.

By contrast, the nearly completed reconstruction of the interior cabin was strangely, surreally neat. All 21 of the crew seats and nearly 400 of the 433 passenger seats were in place, though parts of many were missing. Some were represented only by their steel frames. Others lacked headrests, or legs, or seat cushions. Some were hardly damaged, still intact with the small buttons in the armrests that turn on the overhead lights, operate stereo headsets, or call a flight attendant. At either end and in the middle stood the rebuilt galleys and lavatories. Hank Hughes, the ruminative NTSB worker who had sensed the victims' spirits in the hangar, was the manager of the team just finishing the cabin reconstruction. It pleased him to know the interior was helping the FBI search for damage patterns an explosive might make, but for Hughes, as for the families gathered around it, the interior was a sacred shrine to the victims.

Joe Lychner was there, a tall figure familiar to many of the others for the public advocacy he had begun to perform on their behalf and for aviation safety in general. His handsome features looked drawn now, and haunted. The Breistroffs—Michel, his wife, and daughter—clung together, shrouded by the same palpable melancholy. Heidi Snow stood alone, her relationship with the Breistroffs strained. Julie Stuart was there wearing Andy Krukar's ring. But others had stayed away, unable to face the devastation and the surreal sight of the plane under reconstruction. Jackie Hettler and Pam Karschner stayed home, but their husbands went. Ann Dwyer had considered coming, but Ron felt she was yet too fragile to view the shattered plane. Charlie Christopher, who had already seen the hangar, stayed home with Charles.

The family members who had come gathered silently around the reconstructed interior, stunned by the physical reality of the crash. No one needed to tell this audience which seats their loved ones had occupied on TWA Flight 800. Everyone knew. In twos and threes, the family members gathered by whatever number was emblazoned on their minds and offered silent prayers. There were so many tears and so many tormenting questions, not so much about the way it happened or even why, but about how fast. For some victims, mostly those whose seats were damaged to a degree as to be unrecognizable as such, there could be little doubt that death had come in an instant. But for others one could not be sure whether death had come in seconds or in minutes. Because the seats were potential evidence in the ongoing criminal investigation, the visitors were asked not to touch or sit on them, but they were invited to hand over pictures and flowers to FBI agents, who placed the mementos on the seats for them.

Judy Sorenson knelt in the spot where her husband, Rod Foster, had been last seated on the plane. He'd been a corporate pilot going to France to fly back a new airplane for his company. Foster was her second husband to be killed in a plane crash. Both husbands had been pilots.

As she knelt there with her grown daughter alongside her she thought about her last good-bye to her husband. They had stood together in the driveway of their Sharon, Connecticut, home. He had just taken the top off her convertible. He told her his trip would be a quick twenty-four-hour turnaround, and he would see her the following night. "Remember, you're mine," she teased him. "I know," he said. "And you remember you can look but don't touch." They both laughed and then kissed good-bye. She drove away and went to work. It was the last time she saw him. Judy was lost in her thoughts when suddenly a voice from behind her said, "We'll find an answer, Judy. We'll find an answer. I promise you." She turned and saw Kallstrom, tears in his eyes, kneeling behind her and her daughter.

At the end of the following day, Hughes picked up all the flowers and took them to East Moriches. There, the Coast Guard took them to sea and scattered them over the crash site. The photographs were put on a board and displayed in the hangar. Soon after, letters from the families, addressed to the investigators, began to arrive at the hangar. Many were written in French, Italian, even Arabic, thanking the investigators for trying to make sense of the crash.

For all the comfort the visit to the hangar provided, the families were reeling from the version of events submitted by TWA and Boeing lawyers in response to the many civil suits some of the families had brought against them. TWA lawyers had cited a 1920 law called the Death on the High Seas Act, a law enacted to compensate widows and orphans of seamen lost in international waters. Previously, shipowners had not been liable for lives lost at distances greater than one league (three miles) from shore. As a result of the 1920 law, shipowners were obligated to pay full wages to the widows of seamen lost beyond the three-mile limit. The Act was a show of mercy enacted by a compassionate government before the days of workmen's compensation. Seventy-five years later, the lawyers for TWA and Boeing were claiming that the act limited their liability to the families to lost wages *and nothing more*. Therefore, the lawyers claimed, the Death on the High Seas Act covered only able-bodied, wage-earning workers and provided nothing for the death of a child, for example, or an unemployed spouse, or a grandmother or grandfather, none of whom would have been found aboard a commercial ship in international waters. Thus, the lawyers claimed that no compensation was due to the families of children and retirees lost on TWA Flight 800. The crowning insult of this defense was that Flight 800 had gone down some nine miles from shore—just beyond the 1920 line of demarcation, whose validity under the Act had recently been upheld by the U.S. Supreme Court in a similar case: On January 16, 1996, the Court had ruled that under the Act, the 747 Korean Airlines Flight 007 could limit its liability in the case of its plane that had been destroyed by Soviet fighters over U.S.S.R. airspace in 1983, killing 268, including some Americans.

Kallstrom and Bob Francis held a press update at the Sheraton Hotel to mark the seven-month anniversary of the Flight 800 crash. Kallstrom said the FBI was continuing "to run down every lead, conduct every interview, and do every experiment necessary" to find out whether this disaster was the result of a criminal act.

One reporter shot out that maybe the FBI should pull out of the probe. There doesn't seem to be any sign of a bomb or missile, the reporter said.

"We're not a bunch of quitters. We don't walk away," Kallstrom said. "I can understand people's frustration that we can go to the moon and Mars, and yet these guys can't figure this one out. It is not from lack of trying, or lack of expertise, or of professionalism." He said that the reconstruction of the airplane was just in the infant stages, trawling was continuing, and there was a lot of testing being done by experts throughout the country.

Before the press conference, Kallstrom had briefed family members on the FBI's investigation, as did NTSB officials. He reassured them that he intended to keep his promise to them to stick with the investigation until he was convinced that he had done everything conceivable to determine whether the disaster was caused by a terrorist or saboteur.

As the larger reconstruction took shape, a new sense of excitement rever-berated in the hangar. As each section of the plane was put in place, experts could judge the pattern as part of the whole. A jagged hole in the fuselage might correspond to one on the other side, indicating that a missile had passed through, or a tear may indicate a bomb. A reconstructed wing might show the passage of a spark-lit fire after all. That none of the pieces told such a story scarcely dampened the investigators' enthusiasm. Perhaps the next ones would.

As the plane was filling out, the FBI's chief chemist, Steve Burmeister, flew up from Washington to do some on-site analysis of his own. From below the skeleton frame, he could actually see how the explosion had blown out the for-ward wall of the center fuel tank—and see, too, how the force pushed down-ward, splitting the plane's spine, and how the skin of the fuselage had peeled back. The pieces he analyzed in the vicinity of the fuel tank looked like bits of a smashed potato chip that had been put together again. As one after another failed to reveal any explosive residue, however, Burmeister became more con-vinced that a bomb or missile had not downed the plane. This was clearly, as he put it, the source point of the explosion. If it contained no residue, or signa-tures in the metal, how could the cause be criminal?

As Burmeister looked for chemical traces, Kallstrom's independent metal-lurgist, the recent Alcoa retiree, studied the patterns of matched-up fuselage fragments. Dr. Barry Shabel was a distinguished metallurgist. For months, he scrutinized every metallic inch of the reconstruction, looking especially for toothlike tears that might be evidence of a high explosive. In all, investigators found 117 such fractures, but they were spread around the plane, many in areas nowhere near the center fuel tank or the forward section of the plane. To Shabel, that suggested the patterns had been caused as the plane broke apart rapidly, tearing the metal. Nonetheless, more than two thousand other pieces of metal were being studied for damage by high explosives. Investigators laid all these possible suspects on the hangar floor and cataloged them, then poured the findings on all of them into a huge computer database, so that markings could be compared and cross-referenced. Occasionally, the eureka piece would seem to emerge for a moment, but then it would join the lengthening list of dis-counted others.

Along with metal markings, investigators studied some fourteen hundred holes of one size or another, some about an inch in diameter, most likely caused by rivets flying through the cabin and fuselage as the plane came apart in the air. None of the holes studied so far suggested the kind of high-velocity pene-tration that a bomb or missile would have made. Some were large enough to indicate the kind of hole a missile would have made in passing through. But none of the holes appeared to line up to show entry and exit of a missile. There *were* areas of the plane with wide gaps where more than a foot of fuselage skin was missing. For instance, a piece of skin about five feet by two feet was missing from an area on the left side of the plane below the windows. But none of the pieces around the gap showed damage that would indicate a bomb or missile.

Every morning as he arrived at the hangar to supervise the reconstruction, Kenny Maxwell would call out, "Today's the day! Today's the day we find out what happened!" But as Jetasaurus Rex grew without yielding an answer, his rallying cry began to seem hollow to other agents. Was it buried somewhere deep in the wreckage, he would wonder? Was it sitting right over his head? But he felt sure they would find the answer. As one of the agents investigating the World Trade Center bombing, Maxwell had stood beside the crater caused by the explosion and seen how clearly it denoted a bomb. Now he stood in the Calverton hangar every day for eight months and knew nothing. He had seen many things, as an investigator, that aroused his suspicions: twisted chunks of metal, some with spiked tooth damage; burn marks in seats; mysterious holes in the fuselage. The explosives experts had explained every case away.

Many of those experts, even some in the FBI, now felt as Burmeister did: that the lack of evidence seemed to rule out a bomb or missile. But Maxwell just trusted his gut, and his gut said terrorism.

Meanwhile, investigators in the hangar kept refining the center-fuel-tank reconstruction as pieces came in. The front and aft cargo sections were also being reconstructed. No evidence of an explosion in either had surfaced in all these months, but they remained one of the likeliest venues for a bomb and so had to be studied until all doubt was disspelled. The large air-conditioning units that might have overheated the center fuel tank as the plane idled on the tarmac occupied a place of their own, too, and were subject to much the same scrutiny. Meanwhile, amid all these projects, miles of wiring stretched in various directions, to be disentangled and analyzed, inch by inch, for signs of damage.

One especially dramatic phase of the investigation occurred one late night in February when the lights in the hangar were shut off as some twenty investigators gazed up at the dark, hulking fuselage and FBI agent Sue Hillard Capozzi hung above it in a small steel seat, dangling from a crane. She was wearing jeans, a T-shirt, and running shoes, and she held a wand that focused a beam of ultraviolet light on the razor-sharp metal of the jumbo jet. As she beamed the wand at the plane, she tried not to think about dropping the $20,000 instrument.

Capozzi was searching for chemical residues that might indicate a missile or bomb—traces that only ultraviolet light would reveal. "I've got something over here," she shouted, moving the ray of light back and forth. "Over there beneath the cockpit." She directed two investigators to the exact spot where the light glowed. The FBI scientists, including Burmeister, clambered up tall ladders to take a swab. Carefully, they placed the sample in a plastic evidence bag that would be shipped to the FBI lab in Washington for analysis.

Before the night was out, Capozzi found more traces, enough to fill several evidence bags. The samples were sent to the FBI laboratory. To the agents' chagrin, nearly all proved to consist of body fluids that had dried on the surface of the wreckage. None of them indicated chemical explosives.

Far from the hangar, other tests were ongoing. At the naval research lab in Arlington, Virginia, Dr. Joseph Leonard, the world expert in electrostatic charging of fuels, conducted test after test to try to produce static electricity in hulking center fuel tanks sent over by Boeing. So far, he had not managed to exceed his modest mark of 55 volts—not nearly enough to set off volatile vapors. In a stretch of desert outside Tucson, Arizona, missile experts from China Lake fired missiles and other armaments into a junked 747. As FBI agents including Kenny Maxwell stood by, warheads were also detonated next to the fuselage and in various places aboard the plane, all so that the specialists could confirm the marks, or "signature," that a high explosive would leave on the civilian aircraft. That wreckage was then compared to the pieces of Flight 800 to see if there was a match or even similarities. None of it was consistent with wreckage accumulating in the Calverton hangar.

The growing number of indications that Flight 800 had *not* been downed by a missile or bomb hardly constituted news. But in the resulting vacuum, conspiracy theories multiplied much more freely, and to the astonishment of Kallstrom and his agents, the most effective purveyor of them—the one they thought they had shamed into silence—was back in the limelight again.

On March 6, 1997, Pierre Salinger along with Ian Goddard, a private investigator, and Mike Sommer, a former investigative reporter, released a report claiming the government had gone to great lengths to cover up the truth that a U.S. missile had accidentally downed the airliner. It alleged the missile was either of a kinetic-energy or continuous-rod design, capable of eluding radar. Fired during a secret U.S. Navy exercise off Long Island, the missile had been intended to strike a Tomahawk missile but hit the plane instead. In his report, which he said a team of ten experts had helped him compile, Salinger alleged that witnesses monitoring the Navy exercise heard a male voice say, "Oh my God, I just hit that plane," along with the voice of a sailor confessing to his father, "Dad, we shot it down."

As further evidence, Salinger cited Captain Russell's radar tape—the tape that Russell claimed had appeared one day in his mailbox that showed a missile streaking toward Flight 800. As further proof, he revealed a shocking memo sent by a high-ranking member of the NTSB to the FAA on November 15,

1996, complaining that on the night of the crash, a radar tape with a mysterious blip had been sent to the White House before the NTSB could examine it. The memo was about the Kennedy Airport tape that had contained an anomaly that turned out to be a computer glitch—the anomaly that no other radar tapes had disclosed. It was true that the NTSB had been irked by the FAA's decision, in the tense aftermath of the crash, to rush the tape to the White House before showing it to the NTSB first. And Kallstrom agreed with the NTSB, but that was old news now. If Salinger had another tape in his possession, one that showed some different "ghost blip," then that blip was probably the P-3 Orion going through the area with its broken transponder.

Salinger's other new claims were simply off the wall. He declared that an F-14 fighter plane had been in the area; there was none. He said the USS *Kearsage* was carrying live missiles and conducting an exercise in the area. But the *Kearsage* lay off the coast of Virginia on July 17, more than 200 miles away. Salinger also suggested that a U.S. Navy missile might have detonated outside Flight 800's fuselage, causing the crash—this, presumably, if his first theory proved unsound. But investigators found no evidence of missile damage on Flight 800's fuselage to support such a claim. And Kallstrom and his investigation had discounted friendly fire.

One of Salinger's newer claims was that an eyewitness had been found—a man named Thomas Dougherty—who actually saw a missile strike the plane. But that was not how Dougherty described his impressions to Suffolk County police three days after the explosion. Dougherty told officers he was leaving a restaurant on Dune Road in Quogue when he heard what he thought were two claps of thunder. He said he looked toward the ocean and saw an orange-white glow shrinking as it moved away from him. The glow, he said, was rising skyward from southwest of his position. He thought it was a flare or fireworks. Then, when it reached its peak, it became a "whitish glow." He said he saw an object drop into the ocean. Then he heard more thunder and saw an orange ball of flame dropping toward the ocean. He did not see it hit the water because his view was obstructed by houses along Dune Road. But Dougherty had said nothing about a missile to his questioners.

A few days later, Salinger convened a news conference in Paris to call for a congressional investigation into the missile conspiracy theory, based on the conclusions he had reached with Goddard and Sommer. But the real object of the conference appeared to be the promotion of a newly published paperback book by James Sanders, a retired California policeman and automobile-accident investigator. At the news conference, Salinger and his colleagues changed certain details of their story again by suggesting that Flight 800 had been shot down in error by a U.S. Navy missile which had "lost its lock-on and was probably chasing a drone missile or the Navy P-3 Orion." Again, they invoked the radar tape that Captain Russell claimed to have found in his mailbox and other such "evidence." They now felt they could prove a government conspiracy.

Kallstrom called the claims "ridiculous" and "based on erroneous chatter on the Internet, so-called witnesses—most of whom deny what he claims they said to him—and just plain false information." When Salinger had first surfaced with his claims, Kallstrom believed the old political insider had made a foolish but honest error in going public with his Internet claims. Now he felt that Salinger was spouting stories he knew to be false just for publicity. Kallstrom was furious. He asked the U.S. Attorney handling the Flight 800 case, Valerie Caproni, to consider whether Salinger and other such theorists might have violated the law by fabricating information and obstructing justice. Meanwhile, he sent Florida agents to visit Captain Russell as well as James Sanders, who was now living in Virginia.

The agents, armed with a court order, confiscated Russell's radar tape and asked how he procured it. The tape proved to be a copy of one from Long Island's MacArthur Airport, which did not show a missile, as Russell had claimed, but the projection of a distant commercial plane that appeared to be in the vicinity of Flight 800. According to radar experts, the "ghosting" had probably occurred when the reflection of a commuter plane bounced off the aluminum siding of a warehouse near the airport and showed up on radar as a "ghost blip." This was another "ghost blip" like the one on the Kennedy screen. It failed to show up on any other of the nine radar tapes of Flight 800. The MacArthur "ghost blip" showed up on only one or two radar sweeps. On subsequent sweeps—a matter of seconds—it was gone. Even a speeding missile would have left more of a radar target than that.

Sanders, for his part, was questioned closely about a piece of seat fabric from Flight 800 that somehow had come into his possession. He had had the fabric tested by an independent California laboratory and concluded, based on the lab's findings, that it contained chemicals consistent with fuel residue from a missile that he claimed had struck Flight 800. This new "evidence" was the underpinning of his book, *The Downing of TWA Flight 800*, which also rehashed the theories propounded by Salinger, Russell, and various websites devoted to the crash. Sanders had no experience studying plane crashes or debris from missile attacks. He did, however, have a wife who was a TWA employee, and who appeared to have heard much intriguing speculation from "insiders" at the airline. Later, when Sanders and his wife were indicted for possession of evidence stolen from the Calverton hangar, a TWA pilot assigned to the hangar admitted that he had stolen the fabric and given it to Sanders. The FBI confiscated the fabric from the California lab where it had been tested for Sanders.

For Kallstrom, the most maddening claim by Sanders was that the reddish-orange stains found on some of the seats were consistent with missile fuel and thus provided clear evidence that a missile had shot down Flight 800.

In August, Maxwell had noticed the foreign substance on some of the seats, and had FBI chemist Steve Burmeister on the next flight to New York to examine it. Burmeister took large swatches of the stained fabric back to the FBI lab in Washington, where he worked all night testing it. His conclusion was that the reddish-orange chemical was upholstery glue. Burmeister double-checked his findings with the seat manufacturer, who confirmed that the substance was glue. Kallstrom did not stop there. He had agents obtain the patent and formula for the glue and compare its elements to the chemicals found on the seats. They matched. The residue was glue.

Investigators concluded that as a result of the crash, many of the tray tables on the seatbacks were ripped off, exposing this substance. To make yet another check, Kallstrom had investigators tear off the tray tables still attached to some of the seats. More of the reddish-orange substance was seen. Samples were sent to the FBI lab and to the manufacturer again, and it was reconfirmed that the substance was upholstery glue.

———

By late April, the trawling nets were coming up empty at last. Trawling was abandoned. The reconstruction team had done nearly all it could, too. In just three months, the semblance of an entire 747 had been constructed on the hangar floor from more than 876 pieces of wreckage. It weighed more than 60,000 pounds, and was 94 feet long. In another hangar resided the passenger cabin, with its seats, lavatories, and galleys. One NTSB metallurgist, James Wildey, spoke for both agencies when he declared, "I can safely say that this is some of the most examined metal there is anywhere in the world, especially between the nose section and the aft section. Literally every inch, every quarter inch of the fracture in the fuselage skin, and the frames and the stringers and the center fuel tank in the wing center section, every inch of that structure has been examined in great detail. We have looked at the surfaces for evidence of hot gas erosion, of pitting, and of other features that might be associated with bombs or missiles."

Wildey concluded they had found no such evidence.

The FBI's experts who had measured holes in various pieces of wreckage now climbed up to measure the relation of holes to each *other*, using string to see if exit and entry holes lined up as if a missile had passed through them. They looked for correspondence between smaller holes, too, that might have been left by a Stinger missile, or made by a missile exploding just outside the plane. They knew that a 747 jumbo jetliner is not flimsy, and that a small hole in its skin would hardly bring it down unless it could be related to some structural damage elsewhere. Even so, they kept looking, and figuring, and thinking. For those in the investigation as well as the families of the victims, the maddening absence of tangible clues was offset somewhat by the visit to the hangar in February. No less important was the opportunity they had, on April 2, to honor the divers who had worked so hard to recover their loved ones' bodies, in an FBI tribute at the naval base in Norfolk, Virginia. From Montoursville, a caravan of families drove through the night to attend it. The families were moved as much by gratitude as grief. The remains of all sixteen of the Montoursville children and all five of their adult chaperones had been found by the divers. At the naval base, the parents hugged the sailors. Gary Hettler reflected the feelings of the group when he said he would have driven to California to offer his thanks. At the ceremony, the sailors were dressed in impeccable Navy whites as each set of parents sought out the diver who had brought up their son or daughter and asked question after question. The simplest detail of a child's body as it was found was, in its way, a solace.

Rear Admiral Edward Kristensen, who had headed the Navy operation at the crash site, talked with the families. "Usually if a sailor is not complaining, he's not happy," Kristensen said. "But I never heard one complaint, one grumble, up there."

Kallstrom was there too, along with several agents. During the formal ceremony, he compared the divers to World War II heroes. "If you read about the great battles in our military history, many of the same elements are present here in the diving expedition. American forces put their lives on the line," he said. "All the pep rallies in the world, all the patriotic speeches in Congress, all the motivational talks by law enforcement leaders, never, ever carry the day. It's the troops and the people on the battlefield that carry the day."

Afterward, Kallstrom spent more than two hours speaking with small groups of family members. The Hettlers were among them. Would Kallstrom come visit them, they asked? "Absolutely," he said. Ten days later, he did.

In the months since the crash, Kallstrom had spoken often to the Hettlers, passing along updates as soon as he heard it so that they, in turn, could disseminate it to the other Montoursville parents. He had taken special care to keep them posted during Salinger's disconcerting appearances, assuring the parents that his charges and those of Sanders and others were groundless. As the Hettlers knew, the small picture of their son was still taped to Kallstrom's computer, a special incentive to solve the mystery at last. A scholarship had been set up at the Criminal Justice School at Northeastern University, which Rance had been scheduled to attend.

On a gray, chilly day, Kallstrom flew down in a small FBI plane to the Lycoming-Williamsport Airport, just outside Montoursville, where Gary Hettler picked him up in the family van for the short drive to his sprawling, ranch-style home. Rance's black Blazer S-10, the one he was supposed to take to college two months after his trip to Paris, was parked in the garage, a CD of Garth Brooks still in its stereo.

The Hettlers, like so many other families of Flight 800 victims, had left much of their loved ones' belongings untouched, as if they were still living at home. Clothing remained on hangers in closets, stuffed animals remained propped up on the beds, and books were unmoved, sometimes open to the last page read by the victim. In Joe Lychner's home, the bedrooms of his two little girls remained as if they had closed the door and gone off to school for the day. At the Christophers', Janet's white running shoes sat atop her dresser. When Charlie retrieved her little red Toyota from the employees' lot at Kennedy Airport, he found them on the floor under the steering wheel. After a flight, she would take off her high heels and slip on her comfortable shoes for the drive home to Pennsylvania. For months after the crash, the sneakers sat on the front seat. Finally, Christopher put them on her dresser. That was as far as he felt he could move them.

When Kallstrom stepped into the Hettler home, he saw just how large a presence Rance remained. Over the fireplace was a photograph so large that his face seemed life-size. Other pictures around the room showed him playing football and basketball, and running track.

The Hettlers took Kallstrom to a restaurant where they were joined by Pam Karschner and her husband, Dale. As Kallstrom talked about the investigation the parents listened intently, but he could tell some of the details were passing over them. None of the details would bring their children back. Heartbroken, they could only try to hold themselves together for the sake of their other children.

After lunch, the Karschners headed home, and Kallstrom returned to the Hettler home for some homemade angel food cake and coffee while Jackie offered to show Kallstrom more family photos in a den down the hall. They filed past the closed door to Rance's room. No one outside the family had been allowed inside it. Jackie paused at the door and, glancing toward her husband, put her hand on the knob. "You can go in," she said softly.

Kallstrom beheld the room of a serious athlete with track-and-field ribbons displayed alongside Little League baseball trophies. A picture of the Montoursville Warriors football team featured a smiling Rance in the middle of the front row. On one of the mint green walls hung a framed collage of twenty baseball cards. On a nightstand rested a Bible with a pale burgundy cover.

"I played high school football too," Kallstrom said softly. "I feel like I know him."

Jackie indicated the clothes still on his bed, the clothes he had decided at the last minute not to take as he filled his backpack—navy blue shorts and a white

T-shirt flecked with gray paint were hanging on the inside doorknob. Rance had been painting the family's house all summer and planned to finish the job when he returned from Paris. Nine months later, one side of the house was still unpainted.

"Would it be all right with you," Kallstrom asked, "if I spent a few moments alone in Rance's room?"

The Hettlers exchanged another look, then nodded. Slowly, Kallstrom closed the door, so quietly that the Hettlers, heading down the hall, didn't hear it click shut. Standing on the light blue carpet, Kallstrom felt he was in the room of a younger version of himself—almost, in a way, in his own past. He stood in the center of the small room for several minutes and looked around. Finally, he settled on a picture of Darryl Strawberry. Rance, his mother explained, had rooted for Darryl through the athlete's struggles with drugs and a difficult marriage. Strawberry was the fallen hero who might rise again, if only he tried hard enough and if enough young fans kept their faith in him.

The future Rance had planned was evident from the Northeastern Criminal Justice cap on the dresser, a big step toward becoming an FBI agent. Kallstrom remembered Jackie saying how Rance had told her, "Someday I'm going to come home wearing an FBI cap, and you're going to be so proud." Kallstrom sat for a moment on the edge of Rance's bed, looked down at his loafers, and saw a beat-up pair of Nike sneakers, their long laces dirty and drooping on the rug. If fate had taken another turn, Kallstrom thought, he too might have died in a plane crash at Rance's age, his dreams unfulfilled, his life cut short. Instead, he was fifty-four years old and had seen so much. The Marines, Vietnam, twenty-five years in the FBI, marriage and two wonderful daughters. He looked around Rance's room and recalled exactly how he had felt at that age, just out of high school when nothing could stop him. He took a deep breath and said a little prayer to himself. "Okay, Rance, now's your big chance. If you can help us out, do it. Okay, bud?"

A few minutes later, Kallstrom regained his composure and opened the door. He found Jackie and Gary Hettler in the kitchen. It was time for a trip to the cemetery.

The grave site was at a high point on the cemetery grounds. Kallstrom followed the Hettlers up to a gray stone with lettering below Rance's name that read WE LOVE YOU, BEAR. Beside it lay the grave of Amanda Karschner. Her headstone contained one of her favorite phrases: THE BEAUTY OF THE ROSE IS NOT MEASURED BY THE LENGTH OF ITS STEM. Then Kallstrom walked through the cemetery visiting the graves of each of the other children from Flight 800 who were buried there. All the stones bore the same date of death.

CHAPTER 16

POINT, COUNTERPOINT

The clap of a wooden gavel brought the congressional subcommittee on aviation to order shortly after 9:30 A.M. on July 10, 1997. In a long, stately room lit by two brass colonial-era chandeliers, members of the subcommittee settled into seats around a high, horseshoe-shaped dais with gavel-wielding chairman Republican John Duncan of Tennessee at their center. The audience filled the room, their briefcases and handbags spilling into the aisles. In the front rows sat officials of the NTSB and FAA in their conservative suits. Families and friends of the victims of TWA Flight 800 comprised a more varied group behind them. Mothers and fathers of the children of Flight 800 as well as other family members and the public had waited more than an hour in the hallway outside to be admitted to this proceeding. Ranged along a wall stood journalists and cameramen, their bright lights making it all too clear that these hearings had aroused intense interest around the world. For the first time since Flight 800's fiery end nearly a year before, the NTSB and the FBI would be opening themselves to cross-examination about the investigation—explaining why, despite the tens of millions of dollars at their disposal, they had failed to determine exactly how the plane had gone down.

The subcommittee members were as eager to hear answers as anyone in the audience. Month after month, their mail had brought passionate letters from voters questioning why the crash remained a mystery and worrying that other such crashes might occur. Along with the FBI, members of Congress had also fielded theories and rumors from pilots, mechanics, scientists, professors, and more, many of them laced with impressive technical jargon. The suspicion was that some branch of government—the FBI, the military, the White House— had engaged in a massive cover-up of a state-sponsored terrorist or friendly-fire attack. Even TWA officials had told congressional aides they suspected wreckage was being spirited away by the FBI from Calverton to a secret hangar in the dark of night. At least one member of the committee, Republican James Traficant of Ohio, was sure a cover-up *had* occurred and that the FBI had participated in it. Having consulted for hours with one of the most vocal of the conspiracy theorists, Traficant was just itching to get Kallstrom in his crosshairs. He knew his specifics; he had his questions lined up; he was *ready*.

Kallstrom flew unaccompanied on the 6:30 A.M. shuttle from New York to Washington and jotted notes on the short trip for his opening remarks. He had no need of a proper speech: For almost a year of press conferences, addresses to grieving families, and White House briefings, he had managed without one. But he did have a message. Almost wistfully, he gazed out the window and wondered how to convey the dedication that hundreds—thousands—of agents, investigators, scientists, engineers, divers, and police had brought to this investigation. He wanted Congress to appreciate the humanity and love of country that had driven investigators to work so hard that they jeopardized their personal lives for a greater good. Anyone on the subcommittee who appreciated that would know how absurd the notion of a cover-up was. Anyone who understood the analysis conducted on the smallest piece of wreckage would realize how much progress the investigation had made, even if the cause remained a mystery. So many plausible theories had been ruled out, so much rank speculation dispelled. But in the glare of television cameras, as Kallstrom well knew, members of Congress could grandstand and pontificate, preferring sound bites to common sense. He would need all his powers of communication to keep the deliberations from descending into a cross fire of accusations and conspiracy theories.

Two senior agents, John Collingwood, head of the FBI's Public and Congressional Affairs Department, and his assistant, Barry Smith, were waiting for Kallstrom at National Airport and drove with him to the Rayburn House Office Building, across the street from the Capitol. Yet when he pushed open the tall, heavy, wooden doors of the second-floor hearing room, Kallstrom entered alone. That in itself was enough to surprise the audience and committee members who were just then taking their seats: Other high officials were arriving with their entourages. Kallstrom's breezy confidence set him apart, too. Other officials looked solemn or tense as they mulled over statements and points they wanted to make. As Kallstrom saw faces he recognized, he waved and smiled warmly. When he realized where the families of the victims were sitting, he made straight for them. Many he hugged. Each he asked about, his eyes fixed on whoever was responding. The family members thanked him for pressing on with the investigation and felt buoyed, as always, by Kallstrom's bristling energy. Just as palpably, their presence energized him. He told them he was still optimistic; a cause would be found. Meanwhile, he would see them again in a few days, he confirmed, at the memorial service on Long Island to mark the one-year anniversary.

Finally, Kallstrom took his place at one of the two witness tables that faced the panel. At the other table sat Dr. Bernard Loeb, Kallstrom's NTSB nemesis, and James Hall, the NTSB's chairman, along with Peter Goelz, the NTSB liaison to the grieving families, whose heartfelt empathy had earned him considerable gratitude. Before he took his own seat, Kallstrom greeted the NTSB men, as well as FAA officials to their right, firmly shaking their hands. He knew that the subcommittee members had heard talk of a rift between the FBI and NTSB, and that they would likely ask about it. Kallstrom believed that the agents and NTSB investigators had done a tremendous job together, considering the obstacles. Fundamentally, the agencies were still a united front. Or so he hoped.

Kallstrom had testified before Congress several times previously, and had enjoyed his appearances. He liked getting his message out, and he knew he communicated well. He had an unguarded manner and spoke effortlessly, whether to a television camera, a large group, or a congressional subcommittee. The tough questions he'd sometimes fielded, even hostile challenges on occasion, did not upset him. He loved the duel. The harder the question, the more opportunity he had to defend the record. In February, Kallstrom had been testifying before a congressional subcommittee on wiretapping and digital telephony when California congresswoman Anna Eshoo turned for a moment to the matter of TWA Flight 800. "I, along with millions of Americans, was riveted to my TV screen with the tragedy," the congresswoman said, "and I have to tell you that you gave me a lot of confidence. You gave people the truth, you're solid and. . . ."

"I appreciate that," Kallstrom said. "Telling the truth is one of my great faults," he added with a laugh, a little embarrassed by the comment.

"I couldn't mean it more," Eshoo insisted. "I may not agree with everything that is going on with the agency in some of these other areas, but I want to express that to you. And it is a lot of gratitude. You're to be . . ."

"Thank you, ma'am. We had a great team."

". . . the way you conducted yourself."

"Clearly, it wasn't me."

"Well," said Eshoo, "it's no wonder you have a great team. They have confidence in you. They have a great leader."

As he looked at the panel before him today, Kallstrom wondered if this would be the last time he testified before Congress as a leader of the FBI. He was fifty-four years old, three years from the bureau's mandatory retirement age of fifty-seven. He dreaded the thought of leaving public service and someday working for a private corporation where budgets and bottom lines determined the important decisions of the day. Compared to nabbing Mafia bosses and terrorists and grappling with mysterious air disasters, the private sector was not an enticing prospect. Let the subcommittee members do their worst, he mused. The truth was he would savor every minute of it.

The hearing's ostensible purpose was to review the work the FBI and NTSB had done on the investigation to date and to inform legislators and the public alike as to where the investigation was headed. The underlying agenda was to examine the friction that had arisen between the two agencies as well as the growing strain between the NTSB and the FAA, which so far had declined to adopt the safety board's recommendations of the previous December for greater fuel-tank safety. Perhaps, as the various agencies aired their grievances about one another, mistakes or even a cover-up might come to light.

Hall spoke first, and began by introducing twenty-three NTSB investigators who had worked on the investigation. "I wanted them to have the opportunity to meet y'all," he observed, "because y'all represent the people we're doing the work for." Then he moved to defuse the issue of conflict among the agencies. "Let me say, I know there has been comment in the press about the disagreement. I'm sure that's going to be discussed more. But let me say that for a year, the FBI, the FAA, the U.S. Navy, the Coast Guard, and local and state officials in the state of New York have all worked side by side, shoulder to shoulder, on this investigation. I'm proud of each and every employee."

The legislators listened to this hokum with unconcealed impatience, and then began their questioning. Their greatest irritation, clearly, was with Dr. Loeb for what many viewed as his overreaching, even irresponsible public comments about possible causes of the crash. Congressman Roy Blunt of Missouri said he had heard Loeb tell the media that the recommendations made to the FAA about center fuel tanks could have prevented the Flight 800 disaster. "Was that a misquote, or do you really believe that?"

"That is not a misquote," Loeb answered, leaning over to speak into the lone microphone on the NTSB's table. "That is an accurate statement. I believe that. The team that is behind me believes that. I don't do these things off the top of my head. I base them on what our investigators state. And our investigators are backed up by the leading fuel expert, the leading static experts in the country."

James L. Oberstar of Minnesota, the ranking Democrat on the committee, took Loeb to task for his interview a month earlier with ABC's Sam Donaldson in which Loeb told Donaldson that Flight 800 might never have exploded if the commercial airline industry had followed the lead of the military and made sure that the fuel-air mixture in the center fuel tank was not flammable. "This explosion could have been prevented?" Donaldson had asked during the televised interview. "Yes, it could have been," Loeb had answered. Later in the interview, Donaldson asked Loeb if the airline industry had corrected itself since Flight 800 or if "that could happen again this summer?"

"It absolutely could, Sam," Loeb answered.

"Do you think the public is going to stand for that?" Donaldson asked.

Replied Loeb: "I personally hope—I know our board feels the same way—that the public doesn't stand for that, that the public lets the FAA know that this is unacceptable."

In fact, the subcommittee members now knew that the FAA had grounds to disagree with the NTSB's position. The FAA experts counseled that the wiser course was to eliminate any ignition sources that could cause a spark, rather than make the fuel-air mixtures in the fuel tanks less volatile. Oberstar was irked that Loeb, as the representative of a nonpartisan government agency, would lobby brazenly against another agency on television, and he was furious at Loeb's casual prediction that another plane might go down at any moment in the same way as Flight 800 had. Unless Loeb had hard facts to support his claim, he was guilty of trying to panic the public about air travel. For years, when the Democrats had ruled Congress, Oberstar had chaired this subcommittee. Loeb's behavior, he thundered, did not at all reflect the NTSB that he had once known.

Congress and the American people, Oberstar went on, relied on the NTSB for its "dispassionate, objective, reasoned, scientifically sound, and meticulous analysis of accident data at the accident site and in the laboratories, not in the TV studios. Not with the somewhat alarmist rhetoric with which Mr. Loeb discussed this subject recently in a television interview. In an era and an arena of finites, it is inappropriate to talk of absolutes. And it is uncharacteristic of the NTSB. Be the prod and the goad that you are supposed to be. . . . Don't engage in this kind of activity. It's a disservice to the NTSB."

"Thank you, Congressman," Hall said politely. But before he could say more, Congresswoman Patricia Danner added that she fully endorsed Oberstar's observations and added one of her own. "I would suggest to you, Mr. Hall, that you determine who is going to be the spokesman for your department, and see that they speak for the department and not for their own personal self-aggrandizement."

Hall nodded meekly, and added that the NTSB had only 360 in staff and little money for public relations. In 1996, he noted, Flight 800 and the ValuJet crash in the Everglades had ranked as the number-one and number-five biggest news stories of the year—in an election year, at that—necessitating countless press conferences and interviews. Inevitably, a few misstatements would be made. With Flight 800, the media's demands and the dangers of misstatement had been heightened by conspiracy theories. "You've heard a lot of talk about cover-up. Mr. Kallstrom and I constantly have to deal with, you know, what are you hiding and what are you doing. I made the decision to put Dr. Loeb on television because he has a very able technical background. I am sure Dr. Loeb and I both wish maybe we'd been in the cutting room with Sam Donaldson when he decided what he'd put on the air," he said. "But those mistakes are made. We apologize for them. We're doing the best we can. We'll try to keep that to a very minimum in the future."

Loeb was furious and pushed a scribbled note under Hall's nose. It said: "Are you going to let her *fry me* like that? *Say something!*"

After several moments, when he got the opportunity, Hall smoothly added that he had not realized Danner's remark on self-aggrandizement was directed at Loeb. "Dr. Loeb has spent twenty-five years in public service," Hall said. "He is a civil servant, not a political appointee. . . . I hope you would not share the opinion that anything that he did was self-aggrandizement. He did what I asked him to do as a public servant to keep the American people informed."

"Well, you know, in Washington," Danner said acidly, "each person has their own opinion. I just heard a colleague say that he virtually is assured in his mind that it's a mechanical failure. And I certainly don't agree with that, either."

"No, ma'am, but the nice thing about America is that everybody gets their opinion . . ." Hall said.

If Hall's remarks disappointed the subcommittee members, he managed at least not to exacerbate matters by losing his cool. Kallstrom, for all his experience with congressional committees, was taken aback by his own first interlocutor, Congressman Ray LaHood of Illinois. "If you set aside all of the technology and technical information and vapors and all of this stuff, Mr. Kallstrom, do you think there will ever be a day when you wake up and tell the American people what exactly happened to this flight?"

Kallstrom was infuriated. *Wake up? Where the hell did this big mouth come off? While he'd been pondering in his ivy tower on Capitol Hill, hundreds of FBI agents and others had worked their asses off for a year to solve this mystery. And as for the notion of tossing aside science in the investigation of a plane crash—that was rich, really rich.*

"Mr. Congressman, let me give you a nontechnical answer—an emotional answer," Kallstrom said, keeping his temper in check.

The investigators, the FBI agents, the police officers, the Coast Guard people, the people that brought the bodies ashore, the people that were there, the people that have the tragedy in their face, the people that related to this professionally and emotionally, everybody wants the answer. We don't quite know the answer yet because we're not done with the process.

Now my agency and all the law enforcement agencies that support us are charged with answering the question—was this criminal or wasn't it criminal? And we don't want to rush to judgment on that. It's not like we are standing around waiting to have a good time to say it.

So the answer is, we couldn't agree with you more. We couldn't agree with the families more. We want that answer ourselves. If this was a criminal act, we don't want the cowards that did it to have one more hour, one more day, one more week, or one more month, obviously. It may very well be that some sophisticated different type of dastardly technology that we have not seen before was used here. We don't know. But the significance of standing up and making an opinion on whether this was or wasn't so, in our view, is important, that we have to be right. We have to measure ten times and cut once.

The room fell silent as Kallstrom spoke. But LaHood appeared unmoved. "So the answer to the question, Mr. Kallstrom, is that you believe some day you are going to wake up and tell the American people exactly what happened?"

"I don't know what you mean by 'wake up,' " Kallstrom said tensely. "But some day I think, the FBI . . ." He paused, weighing whether to take on LaHood directly. "If by 'wake up' you mean we're asleep and are going to wake up, I don't agree with that," he said in his low, gravelly voice, trying to disarm the congressman by maintaining an agreeable tone. "But if some day we're going to know whether it was criminal or it wasn't, I believe we will. And the next point is, I believe some day we'll know exactly what happened. Because I think NTSB has the best science in the world on this. They have a bunch of experiments and tests that are on the flight path. I think we'll know. I think the probability is we will know."

LaHood posed the same question to Hall. When would the cause be determined? "Is it going to be a year from now? Two years from now? Five years from now? A month from now? When is it going to be?" Hall said he would hope everything could be completed by the second anniversary, but noted that the NTSB was approaching the third anniversary of the USAir crash in Pittsburgh without an answer.

As LaHood listened to Hall's reply, he noticed that Kallstrom had been staring at him angrily. Kallstrom, in fact, was ready to choke him for what he took to be an unwarranted criticism of his investigators and the entire law enforcement team.

LaHood turned back to Kallstrom. "I don't want you to believe that the term that I used, 'wake up,' meant that you'd been sleeping at the switch," he acknowledged gruffly. "Contrarily, I don't at all. I respect very much the work you have done and all that the agents have done. The fact that you have so many experienced people working on this I think gives us assurances that you will give us the answer."

"Sir, let me just say, I know you didn't mean that," Kallstrom said, visibly mollified. "I just wanted, for the record, to make a point, for all the thousands of people that have worked around the clock on this thing."

Satisfied, LaHood surrendered the floor to Ohio congressman James Traficant, a former sheriff with long black sideburns, wispy, flyaway hair, and a sixties-style, light-colored suit. "I would just like the panelists to answer my questions yes or no," he began. "If you can't, just say you can't answer it. First question for Mr. Hall. Hypothesis and theories and opinion are not facts, is that correct? Hypothesis is theory, correct?"

"Yes," Hall answered slowly.

"To this point, has any physical evidence, conclusive forensic physical evidence, appeared to prove that a mechanical failure caused the explosion of the center fuel tank? Yes or no?"

"We're looking at that," Hall answered.

"I want a one-word answer," Traficant snapped.

Traficant was grandstanding, but he also believed that this yes-or-no style of interrogation was the best way to flush out truth from obfuscation. He had used it to good effect during his ten years as head of his home county's drug program. He believed he knew a liar when he saw one. He felt he could direct a witness toward the truth by precluding equivocation. So far in this hearing, he felt he had not heard the truth—not when Loeb was speculating about electrical malfunctions that may have caused the tank to blow up, and not when Hall was saying the NTSB did not yet know what had happened to the aircraft.

For months, Traficant had chewed over his suspicions with William Donaldson, a retired U.S. Navy commander who traded conspiracy theories with Russell, Sanders, Salinger, and others. That a cover-up had occurred was, to them, a given. But why? If a state-sponsored terrorist attack had occurred, why would the FBI, the NTSB, and the White House want to cover it up? Could the missile have been fired by a friendly state in error? Or was it a case of American friendly fire that the government was concealing? Traficant's suspicions were focused on the explosive chemical traces found on board the plane. He wasn't buying the FBI's discovery that a dog-training exercise had produced the traces.

"Mr. Kallstrom, were there in fact traces of PETN and RDX found in that plane wreckage?" Traficant asked aggressively.

"There were explosive chemicals found," Kallstrom replied, obviously amused by the congressman's blunt style.

"Isn't it a fact that PETN and RDX are widely known as components of SEMTEX?"

"Yes," Kallstrom answered.

"A terrorist substance?" the congressman pressed on, going in for the kill.

"Yes."

"Isn't it a fact that the plane was underwater for several weeks, at least?"

"Yes."

"Other than the theory of the dog having placed these residues of such chemicals on the plane, is there any other evidence of any kind that would support in any way the chemicals getting on that plane?"

"There are other remote possibilities, yes," Kallstrom said.

"Basically, very remote, would you say?"

"Yes," Kallstrom said.

"Let me ask you this," Traficant continued in his blustery manner. "Is there any evidence that documents that this wide-body 747 was in fact visited by a dog at St. Louis?"

"Yes," said Kallstrom.

"You have a general gate number, or do you know for sure that the dog was on that plane?"

"We know for sure," said Kallstrom not quite sure himself what Traficant was trying to get at. "We have the report of the St. Louis Airport police department that documents the training, very specifically documents the training, documents the packages that were put on, documents the—"

"My question, not to interrupt you: was it conclusive that a dog was on this plane that blew up?"

"Yes."

"Okay fine. Now, Mr. Kallstrom, we have the presence of PETN, RDX. We now know the manner in which the plane broke apart. The flight data recorder contained no hint of a mechanical malfunction. With that background, isn't it a fact that the potential of a terrorist act is very prominent here?"

"Absolutely, and that is why we have done what we have done. And why we are continuing to do what we are doing."

"Now for the FAA," Traficant said, turning to the FAA's Guy Gardner, who sat at a table with Hall and Loeb. "Isn't it a fact that you have issued your own analysis of this crash? Yes or no?"

Gardner was surprised that his agency was being brought in so abruptly. "We issued an analysis," he agreed.

"An analysis. Isn't it a fact that your findings differ from the NTSB report?"

"No, sir."

"It is not?"

"No, sir."

"Is it a fact that you are resisting the recommendations of the NTSB?"

"No, sir," Gardner replied again. The FAA's official position was that it was studying the NTSB recommendations.

"Relative to aircraft design and operational changes?"

"No, sir," Gardner insisted.

"I have one last question for Mr. Kallstrom," Traficant said, unimpressed. "Isn't it a fact that where the dog was to have visited, that is not the part of this plane where the precursors of SEMTEX were found?"

"That's not true," Kallstrom said. "And if I could just add for your information, it is very important where the packages were put, Congressman. And the test packages that we looked at, that were in very bad condition, that were unfortunately dripping those chemicals, were placed exactly above the location of the airplane where we found the chemicals on the floor."

"Mr. Kallstrom, let me just say one last thing. There is nobody that has better science and forensic evidence in dealing with criminal activity than the FBI. And the point that I would like to make is, and one last question, yes or no, have you determined with absolute forensic proof whether a mechanical failure or a mechanical condition produced this explosion?"

"Absolutely not."

This was not, as it happened, the first time Traficant felt his own government had duped its people. He believed the investigation of Pan Am Flight 103 was also a cover-up. Sources had assured him that the bomb had been placed not by Libyans but by a faction of the PLO in an operation bankrolled by the Syrians. He felt that the Bush administration, in an effort to recruit the Syrians for the coalition against Saddam Hussein during the Persian Gulf War, had ignored Syria's role in the bombing, and instead blamed Libya, which supported Iraq.

In the case of Flight 800, Traficant was unpersuaded that Kallstrom and Hall had given him honest answers. Surely, he thought, they were hiding *something*. With the blessing of subcommittee chairman John Duncan, Traficant would continue to investigate suspicions surrounding the crash with the assistance of his chief of staff, Paul Marcone, for nearly a year. He felt certain that some low-level agent or military person would come forward to tell what had really happened to Flight 800, if only he kept on the case. It had happened with investigations he had conducted previously into covert operations and he hoped this time would be no different.

Congresswoman Patricia Danner's district encompassed St. Louis, including the world headquarters and the main hub of TWA. If the government was indeed covering up a criminal cause, especially friendly fire, the airline could avoid civil suits brought by the victims' families and might not have to pay even the pittances stipulated by the Death on the High Seas Act. Instead, TWA could sue the government itself and probably win. Taking Traficant's lead, Danner bore in on the drug-sniffing exercise on board a TWA plane parked at a gate in St. Louis. How could the FBI be sure that Flight 800 had been that plane? "Both Congressman Traficant and I," declared Danner, "would like sent to our offices immediately the plane number, not just the gate, but the plane number."

Danner then turned to eyewitness accounts which Salinger and others claimed the FBI had ignored. Was it true, she asked, that the FBI had failed to interview certain eyewitnesses who called in to report their observations?

"Ma'am, just to give you some idea, forty-eight hours after this tremendous tragedy we had close to seven hundred of our agents doing interviews," Kallstrom said.

But how much emphasis had the FBI placed on them, Danner wanted to know.

"Well, I made reference to the fact that we talked about the missile from almost the beginning of this tragedy. I wasn't even back to my office yet when we had information through the FAA of air crews that were reporting things in the sky. Not one witness ever said 'missile.' But by that morning after the tragedy, we had upwards of one hundred people on their decks, golf courses, driving, whatever they were doing out there, in different places in boats, standing on bridges, who described to us events in the sky which we took very, very seriously.

"And we had a missile theory," Kallstrom added. "We talked about it at the first or second news conference. The missile theory had two legs, terrorist or friendly fire. We said there is a possibility a missile shot down this plane. I think that is the first time anyone has ever said that in the United States."

"Have you interviewed all of them?" Danner asked about the eyewitnesses.

"We've interviewed all of them, most of them more than once and some as many as three or four times, yes."

Danner appeared skeptical. Like Traficant, she had heard myriad rumors and theories propounded by conspiracy buffs, all of which recycled the charge that key eyewitnesses had seen or heard things the FBI had ignored. This made for compelling speculation, but set against the thorough interviews of eyewitnesses in the 302 reports and the hundreds of FBI agents on the case, the speculation simply fell apart. Every person who contacted the FBI in the days after the crash had been interviewed. Not one of those accounts, as Kallstrom observed, described an actual missile. Over time, some eyewitnesses' memories had been embellished by speculation in the press about a missile as the possible cause, and Pierre Salinger and other conspiracy theorists had even found at least one eyewitness willing to swear he had seen a missile after all. But investigators had the interview reports to show that no such account had emerged in the weeks after the crash—soon enough, in other words, to be credible.

If Traficant and Danner had come to the hearing with private agendas, so, in a sense, had Kallstrom. He wanted to squash these rumors. He got another chance to do that when Congressman Oberstar asked him if the FBI was standing in the way of the FAA's and the NTSB's work on the crash by failing to complete its investigation.

"I can't think of anything we do that would in any way slow down anybody," Kallstrom declared. "We're providing tremendous support for this investigation, the security of all of the materials, the Calverton hangar, communications, all kinds of things. I mean, if your recommendation is for the FBI to leave before we've done our investigation . . ."

"I didn't say that, and you know that," Oberstar interrupted.

"Maybe Mr. Hall would comment on this," Kallstrom said, turning to look the NTSB chairman squarely in the eye.

Hall looked befuddled. If he had insinuated to others over the past year that the FBI had impeded his agency—and there were many, beginning with White House liaison Kitty Higgins, who said he had—he had done so in private, away from Kallstrom's challenging presence, and certainly far from the glare of public scrutiny.

"Congressman," Hall said, "I think, as I've indicated throughout the testimony, we've worked together side by side in a very cooperative fashion. Obviously, with a criminal investigation, there are certain, what's the word on evidence, trial rules of evidence, rules of evidence, and handling of evidence that have been followed. The only thing that we would not be in a position to do until the FBI does complete its investigation is have a public hearing, and open our public record. But I don't think in any other way joint participation would have an impact on our investigation."

Kallstrom beamed. Now the truth was on the record. Kallstrom was weary of suggestions from the NTSB that the FBI should quit the investigation because there was no evidence of a crime, and hoped that Hall's admission would end such talk.

Kallstrom told the committee that over the next ninety days, the FBI would continue a wide range of tests. In particular, it would detonate junked aircraft with directional shape charges and high-speed particle-missile warheads to determine if either kind of explosive could have ignited the center fuel tank. Investigators would also keep studying the hundreds of holes, slits, punctures, and penetrations in the reconstructed wreckage, and new specialists were being brought in to review everything yet again. In addition, the FBI would revisit many of its 270 eyewitness accounts in an attempt to correlate what they had seen and heard, from their various locations, of Flight 800's explosion and descent as they were now understood in painstaking detail from the nine radar accounts of the crash. If any of those accounts failed to square with the facts, the FBI would investigate them further, but if the accounts all correlated with what had occurred after the plane exploded—if the various streaks were *results* of the explosion, not missiles precipitating it—that would be just as important to know.

"From the beginning," Kallstrom said, "the FBI's investigative purpose has been to reach what I have called critical mass, to gather sufficient evidence to allow us to state, with a high degree of certainty, whether this tragedy was the result of a criminal act, and if so to determine who was responsible and bring them to justice. . . . All our efforts to date have failed to uncover any credible evidence that the loss of Flight 800 was the result of a criminal act."

For its part, Hall said, the NTSB was working with the FBI on this latest notion of high-speed particle penetration—not from certain kinds of missiles, because that fell under the aegis of possible criminal causes, but as a consequence of what Hall called "space junk," or even a meteorite. Meanwhile, the NTSB was refining its four likeliest scenarios for what had caused the center fuel tank to explode: the scavenge pump; static electricity; the fuel-quantity indicating system, including the fuel probes; and the tank's electrical conduits, or both frayed and undamaged wiring. As a safety measure, the agency was also conducting tests on Jet-A fuel—the kind used in all commercial aircraft—to better understand its volatility, and planning to explode full-scale models of 747 center fuel tanks. If Flight 800 remained a mystery, there was still much that the agency could learn from it to prevent such an air disaster from occurring again.

Most panel members praised the FBI, the NTSB, and the FAA for their work as the committee and its witnesses broke for lunch. When the hearing resumed that afternoon, the families would be heard.

The families had no angry questions to direct at the FBI or NTSB. A few still suspected that *some* sort of cover-up had occurred, though if it had, they felt, the military was probably to blame, and had misled the FBI and NTSB along with everyone else. The families knew how much both agencies had done to try solve the mystery. They considered Peter Goelz of the NTSB a supportive friend, and saw Kallstrom as their hero.

They did want Congress to appreciate the full horror of how their loved ones had died, and their own anguish, hoping that Congress might tighten air-safety and airport-security standards further. But their priority was to persuade Congress to amend the Death on the High Seas Act to exclude aviation disasters. The families were furious that TWA and Boeing had seized on this legal relic, and they were asking Congress to amend the act retroactively. At the very least, they wanted Congress to bar the airlines from using the act in future crashes.

One of the first to speak was Frank Carven, brother of Paula and nine-year-old Jay's uncle. "Last July, TWA told the families of those who were passengers on Flight 800 that their loved ones had died," Carven said. "This July, TWA is telling those same family members not only that their loved ones are gone but that they have no value in the eyes of the law. The airlines and other defendants are for all intents and purposes shielded from any liability. No one is liable, no one is accountable. This situation is unacceptable.

"To this date," Carven added, "no one can really explain to me in any rational terms why an individual who perishes in an aviation disaster less than three miles from our shore has value, while an individual who perishes 3.1 miles from our shore has no value. . . . Individuals recover for loss of a loved one in a car accident, people recover for spilling hot coffee on their laps, families recover for the loss of a loved one in any aviation disaster which occurs less than three miles from our shores. The victims of TWA Flight 800 seem to have been lost twice, once at sea last July and again in the courts of justice of this great country. Please do not abandon the families in their time of greatest need."

As Joe Lychner leaned toward the microphone, the crowded room fell silent. "One year ago today, on July 10, I was the luckiest man in the world," Lychner began softly. "I had a great home and a loving family, including my beautiful wife, Pam, who was thirty-seven, my daughter Shannon, who was ten, and my daughter Katie, who was eight. We had it all. I had recently started a new position with my company, and that's why I was not with my family when they boarded TWA Flight 800 for a short stay in Paris.

"One year ago, on July 17, one week from today, a combination of an original design deficiency in the Boeing 747 center fuel tank and the age of the twenty-five-year-old TWA aircraft killed my entire family. I must apologize in advance to the other family members who are here today, but I feel that I must describe to you my nightmare so that you can walk in my shoes for just five minutes. My life was cast into a living hell that will last until the day I die."

And then Lychner told the packed room how he imagined his family had died. "Imagine your family sitting in row 43 in the right rear section of the 747. Your eight-year-old daughter sitting by the window, right next to your wife. Your older daughter, who is ten, is sitting across the row in the middle section by herself. As they take off your daughter is so excited to be going on her first international flight. As they take off there is a sense of relief because the air-conditioning units are finally starting to cool the cabin. Then it happens— the loud bang that first seems so unreal and out of place. But in an instant your wife knows that something is very wrong. She reaches for your eight-year-old daughter and holds her tight. She turns to reach for the ten-year-old but she is too far away. She sees fear in her daughter's eyes but there is nothing she can do. The initial explosion was big, but not big enough to kill your family instantly. They are sitting too far in the back of the plane. Now everyone is screaming.

"For thirty seconds the plane holds together; there is hope in their minds that they may be able to make it back to Kennedy Airport or at least make a water landing. Then the plane that is going four hundred miles per hour starts to fall apart. The front part of the plane falls off and the cold night air rushes down the interior. Everything in the plane become airborne. Your family is terrified beyond words.

"Your ten-year-old is trying to get low in her seat to protect herself. Your wife is clutching your eight-year-old, as she turns to see your ten-year-old daughter hit by a piece of airborne luggage traveling at four hundred miles an hour. Mercifully, your ten-year-old is now dead. Then the plane starts to rapidly fall apart. The sides of the plane disappear and your wife and eight-year-old, still alive and strapped to their seats, are thrown from the plane. . . . When they hit the water their ordeal is finally over, but my hell has just begun."

Experts had assured Lychner and other family members that their loved ones had died almost instantly, without pain—but this failed to mitigate the horrifying images that haunted Joe Lychner, especially since he found the passenger seats relatively undamaged. Who could say with certainty that the passengers had not suffered horribly, for thirty seconds, or a minute, or two?

"After their bodies are recovered," Lychner continued in the hushed room, "you swear that you will find the people who did this to your family and bring them to justice.

"Now imagine this. A room full of corporate lawyers employed by Boeing, TWA, and their insurance carriers, strategizing on how to limit their companies' liability for killing 230 people. They happen upon an antiquated law that was written in 1920, known as the Death on the High Seas Act. They believe that they have found a legal loophole which will allow them to make a claim that over half of those 230 people on the plane are worthless.

"They are responsible for the deaths of 230 people. The distinction between the plane going down nine miles offshore rather than three miles has no bearing on the value of our family's lives. Please do not let Boeing and TWA elude justice."

William Rogers, Jr., from Montoursville, wiped tears from his eyes as he recounted what his seventeen-year-old daughter Kimberly, an honors student with enough credits to graduate from high school a year early, meant to him. "Kim always gave, she never took," he said. "I'm a brittle diabetic, which means I can't control my sugar levels very well, and I have several associative diseases as a result of diabetes. Twice she saved me from what would most certainly have been a diabetic coma.

"How much was she worth to me? Twice my life. What has the loss of her companionship meant to me? Everything. She was my nurse and cared for me with all that she had. She cannot be replaced, and I have no one else left to take care of me. I lost my best friend and the person who loved me unconditionally, as I loved her in return."

As for the airline industry, Rogers declared, "It cannot be allowed to continue to hide behind this law. . . . They cannot hide or excuse themselves, for we see them for what they are: number crunchers caring only for profit. . . . Our daughter Kim was a human being, not a ticket stub. I ask you to honor her accomplishments as a human being and to treat her with the respect she deserves."

The testimony from the tearful families brought an emotional end to the hearings and, for the committee members, searing images not easy to forget. Too often, such hearings produced little more than transcripts and resolutions, but the impact of the families would have a tangible effect: Within days, the aviation subcommitee would vote to support the amendment the families sought to the Death on the High Seas Act.

The mystery continued, but at least the families' seeming victory at the subcommittee hearing was heartening, as the first anniversary of the crash approached.

CHAPTER 17

THE LONG GOOD-BYE

During the spring and summer of 1997, a number of chillingly realistic tests were run in the United States and England. At a remote site 110 miles north of London, a retired Air France Boeing 747-100, the same model as Flight 800, was pressurized to simulate flight conditions at about thirty thousand feet. The FBI attached to the center fuel tank directional bombs—shape charges. The charges were set off; the tank blew up. The center-fuel-tank pieces were retrieved and studied. They bore no resemblance to those of Flight 800. In an Arizona desert, the FBI also set off missile warheads next to scrapped 747s to compare the resulting damage to TWA Flight 800 wreckage and to form a database that the bureau could use for any future cases of possible bomb or missile destruction of a commercial jet. The signature of the Arizona damage bore no relationship to the wreckage of Flight 800.

Once again, the FBI was "proving negatives." But on the afternoon of July 14, 1997, just before the first anniversary of the crash, another test, conducted by the NTSB, proved a "positive" at last.

A Boeing 747-100, an exact duplicate of TWA Flight 800, rolled down runway 22-R at New York's Kennedy International Airport. The ensuing flight incorporated every characteristic of the doomed plane, from its weight equivalent of 230 passengers and crew—and their luggage—to the settings of every gauge on its instrument panel.

The plane was outfitted like a heart patient undergoing a stress test. More than two hundred sensors were attached to the center fuel tank, each leading to a machine at the rear of the aircraft that recorded levels of temperature, pressure, and vibration inside and outside the tank. These data were collected by an onboard team of experts from NTSB, FAA, Boeing, and TWA. Dr. Bernard Loeb declared before the test that he wanted to learn everything that went on inside the center fuel tank: its exact temperature, how much it vibrated in flight, and whether the vibrations affected the temperature or volatility of the vapors inside. Loeb's latest suspicion was that the vibrations might form a mist that in turn might provoke a greater mix of air and fuel, so that the vapor became volatile enough to explode under certain circumstances. For the FBI, the NTSB also monitored the plane's exterior for any unanticipated hot spots. The idea was to identify locations on a commercial aircraft, other than the engines, where temperatures might be high enough to attract a heat-seeking missile.

As the plane lifted off from the same runway Flight 800 had used nearly a year before, its gross weight matched that of the doomed plane precisely. Its center fuel tank held fifty gallons—the same quantity Flight 800's had contained. Moreover, the fuel was taken from a 747-100 that had just arrived from Athens, as Flight 800 had on July 17, 1996. This was to be the first of nine such tests conducted that week.

For the pilots and investigators onboard, the first test flight was eerie enough. On one of the subsequent ones, a crew of Boeing test pilots actually mimicked every move of Flight 800's crew. First they took the plane up to 35,000 feet and brought it into Kennedy Airport at the same time that Flight 800 had arrived from Greece. As soon as the test flight landed at Kennedy, the plane's number-one and number-three air-conditioning units were turned on—and remained on for three and a half hours. All preflight operations, such as fueling and loading baggage and food, were done at the same time they had been for Flight 800. The plane was pushed back from the gate and began to taxi at the same time as the original flight, and it took off within one minute of Flight 800's departure time. At 87 degrees, the outside temperature was 16 degrees warmer than it had been on the night Flight 800 took off. Other than that, everything was identical.

Following the flight path of TWA Flight 800, the crew leveled off slightly at 6,000 feet, then brought the plane up to 13,000 feet, leveled off again, and dropped slightly to 12,800 feet before rising to the exact spot in the sky where Flight 800 had exploded. The test crew reached the location within ten seconds of the moment when Flight 800 had blown up.

To the crew's surprise, as the plane rose to 14,000 feet, the temperature of the center fuel tank reached 120 degrees at the rear and 127 degrees in the middle, the highest temperature reached during the flight; as the plane continued to rise into cooler air, the temperature fell.

These temperatures showed that the fuel-air mixture in Flight 800's center fuel tank could certainly have risen above 100 degrees, the temperature at which an ignition source could cause vapors to explode. This was not the answer to how Flight 800 had crashed, since the source of the spark that might have ignited the vapors was still a mystery. But after a year of leads, rumors, speculation, and countless scientific scenarios based on remote possibilities, it was a verified, incontrovertible fact that went straight to the likeliest cause. At the least, it suggested changes were in order for the fuel-air mixture in all 747 center fuel tanks—changes that would inevitably be mired in politics, legal maneuvering, and financial concerns.

———

For the families, this new information would come as welcome news. On the anniversary of the crash, hundreds of family members participated in four days of ceremonies in Manhattan and on Long Island, trading technical details with the grim expertise the year had taught them.

The Hettlers and the Karschners arrived together. On their first night in New York, the two couples forced themselves to see the Broadway show *Beauty and the Beast* with their daughters, in an attempt to lead normal lives for the sake of their surviving children. Afterward, they strolled down Broadway together. Suddenly, Jackie Hettler froze and dropped to the sidewalk in tears. "What's wrong?" Pam Karschner cried. Jackie pointed to Times Square's large electronic newsboard. On the building's giant screen was Rance Hettler's face; on the occasion of the anniversary, a news show was flashing photos of the Flight 800 victims.

During the weekend, a memorial was unveiled at St. John the Divine Cathedral: a bronze panel inscribed with the names of the 230 victims on a wall beneath a stained-glass window depicting the *Titanic*.

One event among those held on Long Island was conducted at the cemetery at East Moriches. After a simple service, 230 doves were released into the sky. The families then filed over to a nearby memorial garden that had been paid for with $60,000 raised by the residents of East Moriches. At the entrance was a sign: FLIGHT 800, FOREVER IN OUR HEARTS. A granite arch was inscribed with the names of all 230 victims. Leading up to it was a pathway that contained 1,200 bricks, each engraved with remembrances from families, friends, and strangers. One brick seemed to capture the scope of the tragedy with a single phrase: IN THE BLINK OF AN EYE.

Finally, in the late afternoon of July 17, the families attended a memorial service on an ocean bluff near Smith Point State Park to mark the moment the plane had gone down a year before. The gathering included hundreds of relatives and nearly as many investigators—FBI, NTSB, Boeing, and TWA employees, Suffolk and Nassau County police, and New York City and state police.

After the ceremony, Kallstrom approached one family member on the boardwalk who he knew was keeping his distance. Michel Breistroff, whose son Michel, the hockey player, had died in the crash, had been talking with other French family members. Generally, the French were convinced that a missile had brought down the plane and that the U.S. government was covering up the truth; Breistroff, Kallstrom knew, was a particularly adamant advocate of this view.

"Hello, Michel," Kallstrom greeted the tall, distinguished-looking man shaking his hand firmly. "I want you to know how much it means to me and everybody else who worked on this that you and your family made the trip."

Breistroff squinted at him skeptically. "I'm glad I came," he said in somewhat halting English, "but I'm not sure of the purpose. I think I just had nowhere else I could think of being this weekend."

Breistroff's highly successful business career had lost all meaning for him in the last year. His son's death had left him almost paralyzed with grief and deeply embittered toward the U.S. government, which he was convinced was covering up a hideous missile disaster. "I want more than anything else to learn what caused this tragedy," Breistroff said stiffly, "to understand what my son died for."

"Then let me tell you," Kallstrom said. He put a big hand on Breistroff's back and guided him gently to a wooden picnic bench off the boardwalk, where the two could talk in private. Rather than sit side by side, the two men straddled the bare bench, facing each other in a direct, even confrontational manner, like diplomats negotiating a treaty.

"Michel, it looks like an accident, a tragic explosion that ruined a lot of lives. And I'm just about the last person in this country to concede that," Kallstrom said. "From the start, I could not accept that this was an accident if there was a chance in hell that it was not. I would quit my job tomorrow if someone forced that on me.

"At the same time, we have not finished our investigation. I intend to do every last thing to make sure that an explosive device or a missile did not take down this airplane before I go out and declare publicly this was not a crime. But we see absolutely no evidence of a bomb or missile." He added, "We're still looking. You can count on that."

"I want to believe you, but I can't," Michel said. "It's a missile. That's what I believe. If you say it is mechanical, show me the proof, then I will believe it."

Breistroff was repeating what he had heard in France from Pierre Salinger and his group, and from others, about friendly fire and a cover-up by the American government.

"Michel, listen to me," Kallstrom pleaded. "We wouldn't do something like that. We just wouldn't do it. And we didn't just take the word of the military. We did our own investigation."

Kallstrom could see that Breistroff was devastated by a hurt that Kallstrom could only imagine. Looking at him, Kallstrom could appreciate why the public had seized on the missile theory. It made sense of the unknown. But the theory did not square with the facts.

"We investigated the hell out of a missile," Kallstrom said. "We didn't find a missile in the water. We didn't find a missile when the eyewitnesses said they saw something in the sky. We didn't find forensic evidence of a missile. We didn't find anything in the metallurgy to indicate a missile. We haven't found anything that points toward a missile."

"What about the books?" Breistroff asked. Like *The Downing of TWA Flight 800*. "What about Salinger's claims? What about the eyewitnesses?"

"Some people are hyping the books," Kallstrom replied, "promoting conspiracies to make a quick buck off this tragedy, doing their demented PR stunts. As for Salinger's eyewitnesses, we talked to all those people in the days after the crash. None of them mentioned missiles at that point. If they now say they saw missiles, their memories have probably been colored by all the articles they've read about missiles and conspiracies.

"The truth is that I can't tell you what happened," Kallstrom continued. "We don't know what happened to this airplane. But we do know one thing, this plane was not brought down by friendly fire."

Breistroff looked at him, wanting so much to believe.

"Michel, all I have is my words, my voice, and my eyes to tell you the truth," Kallstrom said. "You have to judge whether you think I am being honest with you or not."

"All that matters to me is knowing the truth," Michel said. "My life is over now. I sit in a chair at night and go to bed at two A.M. When I get up in the morning, it is not daylight for me, but only darkness again. I want to trust you, but there are people higher than you that may be pulling strings."

"Michel," Kallstrom insisted, "there is no way in hell that if a Navy missile or any other missile shot this plane down it could ever be hidden from me. I promise you that. And believe me, if anyone ordered me to be part of a cover-up, I would like nothing better than to expose them. No matter who the cowards were. I would stand up and tell the whole world about it."

There was a long silence. Breistroff held Kallstrom's gaze awhile, then hung his head. Kallstrom put his hands on the other man's shoulders. Then, spontaneously, the two men embraced. Breistroff buried his face in Kallstrom's shoulder and sobbed.

When they parted, Kallstrom could see family members along the shore tossing flowers into the water, etching names in the sand, making their peace with the sea. He squinted a little and saw Charlie Christopher and his son walking toward the ocean.

For Kallstrom, the anniversary brought back memories, good and bad, but mostly bad. He glanced at his watch: 8:30. A year nearly to the minute since Flight 800 had exploded off these shores.

8:31.

He was sweaty, and tired. He turned slightly and saw a few family members a distance down the beach and thought of the loss that had brought them there.

He recalled the shock and sadness of those first twenty-four hours, bringing the bodies off the ocean. The memories of going to Kennedy Airport and talking to the families. Memories of the morgue and the tour that Dr. Wetli had led him on, past body after body after body.

As Kallstrom stood at the ocean's edge, watching the waves roll up the beach, he thought, We have all learned a long hard lesson in life and about our existence and frailty on this planet.

8:32.

And yet there were good memories as well, Kallstrom knew, from the very first minutes. People who pitched in without looking for credit or merit badges or promotions. The divers who had risked their lives day after day, and the investigators, hundreds of them working so much harder and longer than they ever had before.

8:33.

Kallstrom turned back to see some of his agents who had sojourned through this strange year with him. They were leaning on the warped-wood railing of the boardwalk in the distance: Schiliro, O'Neill, Cantamessa, Maxwell, Herman, Valiquette. To have worked so hard and come up with no cause, no culprits, was a great frustration. But there was something more, something the agents could not fully express but that Kallstrom understood: In pursuit of the truth, man's love for his fellow human beings was perhaps the only sure truth that had been found in this disaster. In a way that none of the agents on the boardwalk could even articulate, it was an ennobling truth, a truth that embraced them all.

Kallstrom's beeper sounded. He looked down for the number read-out. *Pickard.* In Washington.

Kallstrom took his cell phone from his pocket and punched in Pickard's number.

"Just wanted to see how you're doing there," Pickard said. "How's it going for you?"

"Tom, just how, when we've done everything humanly possible, can we not have the answer?"

"You just never know, Jimmy," Pickard said. "Maybe someday someone will walk into an American embassy and announce they know the secret of Flight 800."

"But maybe, Tom, just maybe we'll never know."

They talked for a few more minutes before saying good-bye. Kallstrom looked out at the ocean again. In the distance, he noticed a plane heading out over the calm water. On its wing he saw what he thought was a flash of light. *What the hell?* But no, it was just the last rays of sunset reflecting off metal, glistening in the deepening sky. "They're going to make it," Kallstrom whispered aloud. "They're going to be fine."

EPILOGUE

One evening in October 1997, Jim Kallstrom was driving home from 26 Federal Plaza when he realized, halfway up FDR Drive, that it was time to end the investigation of TWA Flight 800. The thought hit him as he looked over at the Empire State Building, its tower bathed in orange light for Halloween. Another holiday, another season, another change of temperature and landscape with no breakthrough in the investigation. And yet, Kallstrom thought, a threshold had been reached. One study after another had piled up, from a great variety of experts, none of which provided evidence of a bomb or missile.

The latest study had provided him the answer to the most perplexing question of the entire investigation. It was the CIA's report, six months in the making, on the most haunting aspect of the investigation: the 270 eyewitness accounts of a missilelike streak in the sky at the time of the crash of TWA Flight 800. If these eyewitnesses had not seen a missile in the sky that night, what *had* they seen?

At Kallstrom's request, the CIA examined all the eyewitness interviews conducted by the FBI since the explosion; many eyewitnesses had been interviewed more than once. In conducting its analysis, the CIA used global positioning satellite data collected by the FBI to determine exactly where each of 240 eyewitnesses had been standing, and correlated his or her line of sight and observations with data from Flight 800's cockpit recorder clock as well as sensors from U.S. spy satellites that had recorded the final explosion of the plane. The remaining thirty eyewitnesses told investigators that they were unsure of what they had seen or were too far away to have provided useful observations. The CIA concluded that the eyewitnesses had not seen a missile but had witnessed the crippled plane itself in various stages of breakup after the center fuel tank had exploded.

The CIA experts started with an obvious premise: *Sound travels more slowly than light,* which is why you see the lightning of an electrical storm before you hear the thunder. At a distance of about ten miles from shore and an altitude of three miles, the sound of a center-fuel-tank explosion took, the CIA deduced, at least forty seconds to reach the shore. Of the 240 eyewitnesses, 58 reported hearing a loud explosion first and then looking out toward the horizon. Each of those witnesses had observed a streak descending. What they saw, the study showed clearly, was the plane in the last nine seconds of its forty-nine-second final ascent and fall, after the sound of its initial explosion had reached them. Though the other eyewitnesses failed to report hearing an explosion, most of them also saw a streak descending. Either the sound was blocked by objects in front of them, the CIA concluded, or they simply failed to hear a sound that did, in fact, reach them. Either way, they, too, were seeing the last seconds of Flight 800's fall.

As for the twenty-one eyewitnesses who claimed to have seen a streak rising, the CIA determined that they had happened to look out over the water after the explosion but before the sound of the explosion reached shore. What they saw was the plane climbing after its nose had fallen away—a bright, rising streak of fire like the fireworks display to which many eyewitnesses compared it—as the plane's engines consumed the last of the fuel already relayed to them. That final ascent, the CIA calculated, lasted for about twenty of the plane's final forty-nine seconds. Then, with all electrical power cut off by the explosion and no additional fuel flowing from the dead lines, the engines sputtered and stalled.

From radar as well as the satellite sensors, the CIA determined that after the explosion the plane climbed from 13,800 feet to about 17,000 feet, where it peaked, then went into a very steep and rapid descent. While the jet was still a mile up in the sky, its left wing broke off, spilling a cascade of fuel that burst into a massive fireball seen by eyewitnesses as far as forty miles away and detected by infrared sensors aboard U.S. satellites. The timing of the fireball as recorded by those sensors perfectly matched the observations of the many eyewitnesses who saw it: about forty-two seconds after the initial explosion. The initial explosion was determined to have occurred within a fraction of a second before the black boxes stopped recording. Approximately seven seconds after the fireball, the plane hit the water.

The observations of airborne eyewitnesses did nothing to alter this picture. Dwight Brumley, the Navy electronics-warfare officer aboard USAir Flight 217 at the time of the explosion, had reported seeing a small aircraft pass under his plane, followed about ten seconds later by a small, flarelike projectile traveling in an east-northeasterly direction. Radar pinpointed the coordinates of both USAir 217 and the small commuter plane passing near it just before Flight 800 exploded. The CIA determined that Brumley and a fellow passenger saw the flarelike projectile just as Flight 800's voice recorder cut off with its awful click. They didn't hear the explosion because they were sitting in a pressurized cabin, but they did see fire spreading from the plane, which was in fact the "projectile." Captain David McClain, piloting an East Winds commuter plane at 16,000 feet at a distance of twenty-five miles from Flight 800, had reported a white light on the 747 that might be, he thought, a landing light left on. McClain, the CIA concluded from its time chart, had seen the initial stages of the breakup of the plane after it had exploded and was afire. So had the Air National Guardsmen, Major Fritz Meyer and Captain Chris Baur. As for Thomas Dougherty, the eyewitness whom Salinger had promoted as having seen a missile, he had almost certainly been one of the few eyewitnesses to see the first explosion. As investigators knew, the plane's engines had carried it several thousand feet higher before it fell out of the sky and incurred its second explosion. The two explosions were the two claps of thunder Dougherty told FBI agents he had heard.

"From a distance of nine miles or more, this may have looked like a missile attacking an aircraft," the CIA concluded, "but nothing in their statements leads CIA analysts to conclude that these eyewitnesses in fact saw a missile. Indeed, several eyewitnesses who suspected that they had watched a missile destroy the aircraft were puzzled that they hadn't actually seen the aircraft before the missile hit it. The airliner should have been visible to any observer witnessing a missile approach it. So the eyewitnesses almost certainly saw only the burning aircraft without realizing it. To date, there is no evidence that anyone saw a missile shoot down TWA Flight 800."

Kallstrom reported in his final news conference on November 18, 1997, that the FBI had spent roughly $20 million on its sixteen-month investigation of TWA Flight 800. Its agents had conducted 7,000 interviews and pursued 3,000 leads. Its scientific investigators—along with explosives and missile specialists, independent metallurgists, and aeronautical experts from the NTSB—had inspected one million pieces of wreckage; studied more than 1,400 penetrations, slits, or holes in the reconstructed plane; measured and analyzed 259 gaps in the fuselage; and taken more than 2,000 swabbings of potential chemical traces. They had found no evidence of high-explosive damage, either from a missile or a bomb. They had found only damage that was, as Kallstrom put it, "consistent with the overpressurization of the center fuel tank, the breakup of the aircraft, the fire, and the impact of the aircraft into the ocean."

Kallstrom described how the FBI had investigated, and finally dismissed, the possibility of friendly fire. "In all cases, no weapons were fired. In all cases, no ordnances were capable. In all cases, no weapons were expended." He tried, in the strongest language, to discount suspicions about missiles and rejected arguments that unexplained radar pointed to the likelihood of a missile. "Never was, never will be," he said.

As for the red residue from the seat cushion that was claimed by missile theorists to be rocket fuel, Kallstrom reconfirmed it was contact adhesive glue.

"We know that for a fact. We know the manufacturer's formula, which is patented. And we know without a doubt that it's adhesive that holds the back of the seats together, not rocket fuel, not residue of a rocket. Never was, never will be."

Kallstrom refuted Salinger's allegations point by point. The "missile" cited by Salinger on radar returns from the Islip airport, the USS *Normandy*, the Linda Kabot picture, the Heidi Krieger picture—all were invoked one last time and put to rest. With some grim satisfaction, Kallstrom added that Salinger and Ian Goddard, a fellow conspiracy theorist who pushed his theories on the Internet, had backed off from their claims. Salinger had called Kallstrom just two weeks before to say that he "was giving up the conspiracy theory." While not admitting specifically that he was wrong, he said he would no longer speak out publicly about it. Goddard had apologized to the Navy and the victims' families, declaring in an Internet posting that he had made "a big mistake" in promoting the Navy-missile theory.

Kallstrom left open the possibility that the FBI would return to the probe. "If something comes up, we are going to jump into it with both feet as quickly as possible," he said. "We are not writing a big 'closed' on it and putting it in some dusty safe somewhere." But for now, he concluded, the FBI investigation of TWA Flight 800 was over without having determined why the plane had exploded, but having painstakingly proven a negative: that the cause of the crash was not criminal.

———

Kenny Maxwell, head of the FBI's operations at the Calverton hangar, knew there was no proof of a crime but felt there were several unanswered questions, and hoped that the NTSB would continue to pursue them. Maxwell, a dogged investigator, continued to wonder why pieces of one of Flight 800's wings had been among the first parts of the plane to fall, and he wondered if a bomb or missile and not the force from the center fuel tank could have blown the wing off. He wondered, too, why so few of the bodies had significant burns. Dr. Shanahan, the forensic pathologist from the Armed Services Institute of Pathology, had spent months correlating injuries to each passenger's position in the plane; one of his preliminary theories was that the explosion had moved in a direction away from the cabin, which would seem to discount the possibility of a shape-charge bomb. However, he also speculated that the breakup of the plane might have begun before the tank blew up, spilling bodies out before they could burn. Shanahan's initial theory suggested that there was an explosion somewhere else in the plane, possibly a bomb or a missile, that then set off the fuel tank. Kallstrom and his team had taken Shanahan's report seriously, but it was outweighed by almost every other analysis and study and unsupported by any physical evidence on the plane of a bomb or missile.

Maxwell also felt he and the investigators failed to reach an adequate explanation for the traces of explosive residue found on the heavy canvas curtain in the rear cargo bay of the plane. That was one place where the police officer conducting Carlo's bomb-sniffing test had not put explosive chemicals. To Maxwell, the traces lent added significance to the fact that the door to the rear cargo bay had never been found, and that there were spiked-tooth tears in the thin aluminum skin adjacent to it. In high-grade steel, such tears would seem to indicate high-explosive damage greater than could be explained by the explosion of the center fuel tank. But the rear cargo bay doorway was made of thinner metal, so that tears alone could not be construed as physical evidence of a missile or bomb. FBI scientists suggested that the explosive traces could have been carried to the rear cargo hold through the plane's air-conditioning venting system, or that there may have been other dog testing conducted, either in the United States or overseas by foreign law enforcement, and no record was found.

Maxwell did not believe the crash was necessarily criminal, but these questions continued to haunt him—indeed bother him to this day.

Kallstrom heard the theories and reviewed the studies, but he felt that on balance they failed to measure up. "There is no perfect investigation," he told Schiliro and others. "That's why you never know the answer until you do all the work and then review all that you have and make a decision. There will always be things that do not go along with the bulk of evidence."

In the case of Flight 800, those inconsistencies are small in comparison to the questions that were answered, the possibilities that were discounted.

———

The FBI investigation into TWA Flight 800 ended a week after Ramzi Yousef's conviction in a federal court for masterminding the plot to bomb the World Trade Center. It was his second conviction for terrorism: In an earlier trial, he had been found guilty of placing the bomb on a Philippines Airlines plane that killed a Japanese businessman in December 1994, and plotting to blow up a dozen other U.S. jetliners. On January 8, 1998, he was sentenced for both cases. He received 240 years for the World Trade Center bombing and a life sentence for the Philippines Airlines bombing. "Yes, I am a terrorist and am proud of it," Yousef proclaimed at his sentencing. Terrorism, he said to the judge in the trial, is "the only language you understand."

On April 3, 1998, Eyad Ismoil, the World Trade Center accomplice whom Tom Pickard had brought back from Jordan after tense negotiations, was sentenced to 240 years in prison for his role in driving the bomb-laden van. Abdul Hakim Murad, Yousef's accomplice in the Philippines Airlines bombing, was sentenced on May 15, 1998, to life in prison without parole.

One theory put forth by a terrorist expert is that the crash of Flight 800 may have dissuaded one group of terrorists from carrying out its threatened acts of violence against the United States. This was the so-called Movement for Islamic Change, which faxed an alarming ultimatum from "The Jihad Wing of the Arabian Peninsula" to the London offices of *Al Hayat* newspaper the morning before the crash. The theory was that the crash might have upstaged the radicals' plan—or served their purpose by appearing to be the terrorist act they had intended to carry out. Subsequently, the FBI would link this group to Osama bin-Laden. On August 7, 1998, bin-Laden's confederates would orchestrate the bombings of United States embassies in Kenya and Tanzania, all but destroying both buildings and killing 224 people and injuring more than 5,000. Quick work by the FBI and CIA teams dedicated to tracking bin-Laden and his network would link the bombing suspects to bin-Laden himself. As a result, President Clinton would approve a retaliatory attack of cruise missiles on a Sudanese factory alleged to be used by bin-Laden for building biological chemical weapons, as well as an attack on an Afghan terrorist camp. The Sudanese attack was one element of the "contingency plan" President Clinton had "dusted off" in the tense hours after Flight 800 went down—but only, as one senior White House advisor put it, a "peanut" compared to what the United States would have unleashed if it had proven conclusively that the destruction of TWA Flight 800 had been a state-sponsored criminal act against Americans.

A month after the FBI ended its investigation of Flight 800, the NTSB staged a week of public hearings to issue its own findings to date. In theory, the NTSB's investigation would remain open until a probable cause was identified or new evidence appeared to suggest the cause was criminal after all. In truth, safety board investigators privately held out little hope of ever knowing exactly why TWA Flight 800 had exploded.

The NTSB now accepted as a given that Flight 800's center fuel tank exploded after a spark was introduced to ignite its volatile vapors. But where *had* the spark come from? Static electricity, Dr. Bernard Loeb's pet theory of the previous year, seemed unlikely after scientists at Wright Patterson laboratories had proved unable to produce a single scenario under which static electricity could have caused a significant spark. The more likely suspect was some portion, as yet undiscovered, of the plane's 150 miles of wiring.

At first, the investigators had assumed that two wires would have to be frayed and crossed for a short-circuit to occur. But they also talked of the phenomenon called transient electrical fields. Between two wires that ran parallel—wires that were not touching at all nor damaged—electricity might still manage to arc, or migrate. As of spring 1999, the safety board is still studying

Flight 800's wires, trying to determine if and how a spark or surge of high-voltage energy from a high-voltage wire could have entered the tank through low-voltage wiring in the fuel-quantity indicating system that leads into the tank. The NTSB has learned that wires do corrode or chafe as planes get older—enough to raise speculation that a combination of factors involving wiring in the fuel-quantity indicating system possibly created a one-in-a-million catastrophe.

Still, chairman James Hall stressed in the hearings the measures that the safety board had recommended to the FAA that might prevent such an explosion from occurring ever again. Keeping the center fuel tanks filled on eastbound transatlantic flights, keeping air-conditioning units off during much of the time a plane was on the tarmac waiting to depart, and using inert nitrogen gas as an additive in the tanks—all would lower temperatures in the center fuel tank.

The FAA was still examining those recommendations, but many of its experts believed that some of the NTSB's suggested measures were impractical, expensive, and might lead to other safety problems. For example, filling the center fuel tank of a 747 full on an eastbound transatlantic flight would add weight to the aircraft and, because of the push from the eastbound tailwind, the aircraft would land with a full tank, a potential safety hazard. As for air-conditioning units, the FAA *had* suggested—but not ordered—that airlines install, on applicable 747 models, insulation between the air-conditioning units and the center fuel tank. But there was still no evidence, the FAA observed, that the heat from air-conditioning units had contributed to the crash of TWA Flight 800. The FAA also suggested that pumping nitrogen into the fuel tank might prove to be costly and impractical. Nitrogen and the equipment to pump it into the tanks are not available in most airports around the world. The FAA was studying the use of a less volatile fuel than Jet-A, and has directed airlines to inspect wiring, especially wiring in and around the center fuel tanks, more carefully.

Since then, the FAA has taken other tangible steps. In July 1998, two years after the crash of Flight 800, the FAA ordered that center fuel tanks of older Boeing 747s be inspected. Reports of worn fuel line parts on newer 747s prompted the FAA to broaden its mandate a month later to include all 747s. The FAA also ordered airlines to keep more fuel in the center fuel tanks of 747s on eastbound flights because a prematurely aging part in some fuel pumps might cause sparks and ignite vapors, though this particular part, the agency added, could not have provoked the center fuel tank explosion of Flight 800 because the larger fuel pump in question had been recovered undamaged.

Separately, on October 1, 1998, the FAA announced a program to learn whether it should limit the service life of wiring in commercial planes. By then, another terrible crash had highlighted the potential risk of faulty wiring in older planes. On September 2, 1998, Swissair Flight 111 fell into the ocean off Nova Scotia, Canada, killing all 229 people aboard. The cause, investigators suspect, was heat damage and electrical arcing in an overhead cockpit panel as well as in the plane's avionics circuit bay—problems, in both cases, of faulty wiring. On January 28, 1999, the FAA issued a directive requiring airlines to inspect all MD-11 planes, of which Flight 111 had been one, for wiring and insulation problems.

The FAA has reasoned arguments for each of its policy stances, but the heads of the NTSB are not persuaded. The investigation of Flight 800 has left the two agencies deeply skeptical of each other, with some at the NTSB convinced more than ever that the FAA's decisions are weighted by its reluctance to take on the airline manufacturers and concern over how much each new safety measure will cost the airlines. The FAA's cost-benefit analysis puts a value of $2.7 million on each passenger, suggesting that any measure costing more than $621 million—230 lives lost times $2.7 million—should not be adopted unless a clear cause and effect can be established.

In the case of Flight 800, no such cause and effect have been discerned.

Both at the NTSB hearings and in the months since, Boeing has acknowledged that it may have to make changes in the fuel systems of its 747 planes and other models to ensure better protection of the tanks. In fact, Boeing has already made several changes, including the installation of a flame arrester on the scavenger pump as a precaution against spark or fire. The company has also agreed to study ways to reduce the flammability of fuel. But it has learned that it would cost the airline industry an estimated $60 billion to switch to a fuel with a flashpoint of 140 degrees, 40 degrees higher than the flashpoint of Jet-A fuel. The company has issued several 747 service bulletins because of the Flight 800 disaster, advising airlines to inspect fuel tanks and their complementary parts during each plane's next major maintenance. Service bulletins between 1997 and 1999 largely centered on the fuel-quantity indicating system. The company recommended inspecting the fuel probes in the center fuel tanks and replacement of any probes that held wiring against them with a metal clamp. Flight vibration, it found, can cause damage to the insulation in the wire bundles. Boeing is working on a service bulletin and wire kit for separating fuel quantity systems for those operators who choose to install wire separation. Boeing is also considering new ways to insulate the air-conditioning units beneath its center fuel tanks, exploring ways to flush hot vapors from tanks that are less than full, and weighing whether to relocate fuel probes outside the center tank.

These measures are still being studied.

In December 1997, as the NTSB hearings were winding up, James Kallstrom announced his retirement from the FBI. To fellow agents, he had said more than once that he planned to buy "one of those stainless-steel hot dog wagons—no stress, no deadlines, no reporters. Get a television set and watch the Red Sox games and sell hot dogs on a sidewalk. Yeah, that is what I am going to do." But at fifty-four, three years shy of the FBI's mandatory retirement age, he accepted a top executive position at MBNA America Bank, an international bank and one of the world's largest credit card issuers, based in Wilmington, Delaware. "I don't leave because I want to leave," Kallstrom declared, "but it is time for me to think about other responsibilities." Foremost among those was putting his two daughters through college.

To the conspiracy theorists set on believing that dark forces were at work behind the investigation of TWA Flight 800, Kallstrom's decision to leave the FBI appeared weighted with significance. Perhaps he had left in the middle of the NTSB hearings because he was embittered by the cover-up in which he'd had to participate. Such theorizing struck Kallstrom as absurd. He had been offered the MBNA job and many others before the crash of TWA Flight 800 but had declined then to accept any of them, first because he had just been appointed head of the New York office—the best job in the FBI, he thought—then, after the crash, because he wanted to see the investigation to its conclusion.

Kallstrom's retirement dinner in January 1998 was a huge hotel-ballroom affair with fifteen hundred paying guests, but in two ways it resembled the intimate Friars Club dinner held to honor Ray Kelly on July 17, 1996, the night that Flight 800 had crashed. Nearly everyone from that earlier dinner was at this large, warm, festive farewell. And among them was Ray Kelly. At the Friars Club, Kallstrom had toasted Kelly. Now it was Kelly's turn to toast Kallstrom.

"There are few episodes, thank God, in the history of America where a single catastrophic event captures the imagination of the nation and the world and fills it with trepidation, fear—with the feeling of uncertainty," Kelly told the crowd of mostly law enforcement and corporate leaders. "One of these events was the bombing of the World Trade Center. Another was the Oklahoma City tragedy. And the third was the crash of TWA 800. In these pivotal moments, the country yearns for something or somebody to reassure it, to come to the fore. In the case of Oklahoma City, I think it was the image of the firefighter carrying that infant victim, symbolizing the massive emergency response. It showed a caring community. In the case of TWA Flight 800, Jim Kallstrom emerged as the symbol of that strength and that caring. When you saw that face on the TV screen you knew that no stone was going to be unturned to find out what happened to that airplane because Jim Kallstrom was on the job.

"There was significant pressure to just get it over with, but not for Jim Kallstrom," Kelly added. "Jim was there for America and the world when it needed a reassuring presence. He delivered. He brought dignified closure to a terrible American tragedy."

Another tribute to Kallstrom, significant in its own way, came from Dr. Bernard Loeb of the NTSB. After all the wrangling between Kallstrom and the heads of the NTSB over the issue of reconstruction, Loeb acknowledged, a bit grudgingly, that Kallstrom had been right to push for reconstructing the whole plane. Loeb hadn't expected it to solve the mystery, and it hadn't, but it had helped investigators see that it was not a crime, and helped minimize the spread of baseless conspiracy theories. The heads of the NTSB had never been involved in a case that stirred dark currents of paranoia on two continents; at the FBI, Kallstrom had come to appreciate how destructive those currents could be. He was right, Loeb conceded, to try to contain them.

Yet despite all the FBI has done to show that no bomb or missile took down Flight 800, conspiracy theories continue to proliferate. Some theory-spinners read dark meaning into a memo sent by Kallstrom to NTSB chairman James Hall, asking the NTSB not to explore criminal aspects of the investigation at the hearings. Conceivably, Kallstrom wrote, new evidence might emerge suggesting that the crash was a criminal act after all. He said he was concerned about protecting the integrity of the piles of evidence the FBI had accumulated and did not want to create a new body of evidence for any potential trial, which testimony at the hearing could surely do. Conspiracy buffs cite Kallstrom's letter as evidence that the government was trying to suppress information about the criminal investigation.

At the time of the NTSB hearings, three conspiracy buffs were charged with crimes related to the theft of a swatch of seat-cushion fabric from TWA Flight 800 that they claimed had contained residue from missile fuel. Terrell Stacey, a TWA pilot who had worked at the Calverton hangar, pleaded guilty in U.S. District Court in Uniondale, Long Island, to theft of government property for giving the fabric to James Sanders, the former California police officer who later claimed that an independent laboratory had tested the fabric for him and found it to contain chemical residue found in missiles. By then, the FBI had shown conclusively that the residue was glue. Sanders and his wife, Elizabeth, were convicted by a federal jury of aiding and abetting and conspiracy in connection with the theft of fabric, potential evidence in a crime, stolen from the hangar.

On the second anniversary of the crash, conspiracy buffs found a new face in William Donaldson, a retired Navy pilot who held a news conference sponsored by a conservative political group called Accuracy in Media to claim that Flight 800 had been downed by two missiles. One, he said, was launched from a boat just off Long Island, the other from a second vessel farther south. The missiles, he said, had exploded just off the plane's left wing. They were airbursting antiaircraft missiles, Donaldson suggested, probably fired by terrorists against the United States.

Donaldson is a member of the Associated Retired Aviation Professionals, founded in 1998 by a group that believes TWA Flight 800 was brought down by a missile and not by a mechanical malfunction. In a one-hundred-page report, Donaldson claims that some eyewitnesses reported seeing a missile in the sky and that the FBI is suppressing those observations.

In the report, the NTSB and FBI come in for equal portions of blame. Donaldson notes that there were no mechanical problems with the plane prior to the crash, that Captain Terrell Stacey had flown the aircraft the day before it exploded and it had performed normally. Furthermore, Donaldson believes that senior FBI agents witnessed the jet's explosion and chose not to make their observations public. A special FBI forensic dive team, he said, was used to prescreen pieces of wreckage on the seafloor before Navy divers were allowed to salvage them, presumably to put aside pieces that showed missile damage. Later, he said, agents dismissed the residue of high-chemical explosives found in various places in the cabin of Flight 800 by concocting the story about Carlo the police dog and his bomb-sniffing test.

Most of this was a rehash that fell apart on scrutiny. The lack of serious mechanical problems on the plane before its last departure hardly ruled out a mechanical problem on Flight 800. Other than Ann DeCaro, who used the word "missile" in the context of fireworks she thought she'd seen, no eyewitnesses had used the "m" word in their initial interviews. One FBI agent—George Gabriel—was in a boat, fishing off Long Island, at the time of the crash but was miles away and saw only what he thought may have been an oil tanker on fire. There was no special screening for FBI divers; FBI agents had simply logged in wreckage brought up by divers as a standard chain-of-custody procedure on a criminal investigation. No FBI divers were in the water before the Navy arrived. The story about Carlo the dog was, sadly, all too true. Many agents would have liked nothing more than to learn that chemical traces proved that high explosives had hit the plane; that was the whole thrust of the FBI's criminal investigation.

Donaldson made other charges. He declared that the tail of Flight 800 had failed shortly after the nose came off, proving, he said, that a massive outside force had brought down the plane. He also claimed that shortly after the explosion an unidentified surface radar target had fled the scene of the shoot-down at thirty knots. Both charges, however, were baseless. A failing tail was beside the point: The exploding center fuel tank had severed the plane's power lines.

After that, none of the plane's parts had functioned. Radar tapes had picked up a boat about twenty-five feet long that was approximately 2.9 miles south of the crash site when the plane exploded in midair. The FBI has not continued to seek this vessel because there is no evidence to indicate the plane was brought down by a missile.

Of Donaldson's main theory, that two antiaircraft missiles had hit Flight 800, there was simply no physical evidence, despite the recovery of 98 percent of the plane.

Donaldson's theory or any other conspiracy theory, no matter how compelling or convincing, that a missile shot down Flight 800 ignores the fact that absolutely no physical evidence of a missile or a bomb was ever found. The reconstructed fuselage showed no telltale exit or entry holes that lined up, no markings or signatures consistent with a missile or missile warhead. And despite the months of diving operations and further months of trawling, no missile or missile components was found amid the wreckage on the ocean bottom. At the Calverton hangar, scores of experts from around the world inspected the plane. These included missile experts who design and develop missile systems, others who manage the missile programs for the U.S. government, military experts from China Lake and Red Stone Arsenal, as well as independent FBI-hired metallurgists and explosives specialists who spent months examining the reconstructed fuselage. Not one saw any evidence of missile damage to the plane.

Donaldson concluded his report by calling for congressional hearings. He was joined in his call by retired admiral Thomas Moorer, chairman of the Joint Chiefs of Staff during the Vietnam War. This call, however, was sorely undercut by the long-awaited report on TWA Flight 800 by Congressman James Traficant of Ohio. As his grilling of FBI and NTSB officials at the aviation committee hearings had shown, Traficant strongly suspected a government cover-up, either of friendly fire or a terrorist attack. Over the months following those hearings, he had consulted often with Donaldson, who helped his staff work up questions for Kallstrom, Hall, Loeb, and other witnesses and theories as to what sort of missile might have hit the plane. As Donaldson kept coming up with new, and seemingly more bizarre theories, however, Traficant and his staff had cooled on him. When the retired commander had declared, after nine months, that a Canadian frigate had shot the plane down, they stopped returning his calls. The experts at China Lake and Wright Patterson, on the other hand, had impressed Traficant's investigators with their knowledge of missiles. Richard Bott of China Lake told them he was impressed with the thoroughness of FBI efforts to pursue the missile theory. "No one has uncovered a single piece of solid evidence or testimony from a participant in the [NTSB and FBI] investigation that points to a cover-up or any nefarious activity on the part of our government," Traficant concluded. Nor was there any evidence that a missile or bomb had destroyed the plane.

Donaldson, at least, believed an enemy power or terrorist had attacked TWA Flight 800. Other conspiracy buffs, against the overwhelming weight of evidence compiled by the FBI in its investigation, continued to believe that a friendly-fire cover-up had occurred, one perpetrated to hide the government's complicity in the deaths of 230 innocent people and—so went some versions—to keep secret some advanced missile system that the U.S. government did not wish to disclose to foreign powers.

Kallstrom was no longer surprised by such theories. Generally he was not offended by them either; he understood that the enduring mystery of TWA Flight 800 would lead to all kinds of speculation and rumor, most of it well meant. That, he often said, was part of what he prized about America, the right of its citizens to voice opinions and challenge their government. He disdained only those theorists who appeared to be acting cynically, using the tragedy to promote themselves and make a quick profit. Well-intentioned or not, though, the conspiracy theorists seemed to defy common sense.

"Logically," Kallstrom would shake his head and say, "it is inconceivable that there could be a cover-up, given the thousands of people who had access to the airplane pieces brought to the hangar. Somebody would slip up or leak information to the media—motivated by money, principle, or a guilty conscience."

Kallstrom knew that the teams of people that included TWA employees that worked on the crash investigation might want to show that the plane had been brought down by a missile to escape liability. The people with access to the airplane also included Navy divers, law enforcement divers, Navy crews, the U.S. Coast Guard, the FAA, the NTSB, the ATF, the TWA pilots association, the Airline Pilots Association, the Airlines Stewardess Association, the Mechanics Union, Pratt & Whitney, Boeing workers, trawler workers, private contractors, down to the cleaners who swept the floor of the hangar. There were NTSB-type accident investigators from Russia, France, England, Canada, Australia, Singapore, and outside contractors. And those people all had wives and husbands, relatives, friends and coworkers—multiplying the numbers who would have had to keep a secret.

"And why," Kallstrom added, "would the FBI have pushed so hard to reconstruct the plane over the objections of the NTSB if it was colluding in some friendly-fire cover-up? If it was a cover-up, you'd say, 'hey, not such a good idea.' Why would the FBI have insisted on the extensive trawling operation that brought up two million pounds of debris over a four-month period? There weren't any divers on the bottom deciding what went into the fishing nets that were brought to the surface. Wouldn't you want to keep as many pieces buried on the ocean bottom?"

Why, for that matter, continue the investigation for sixteen months? A smart person conducting a conspiracy would certainly have sealed the Calverton hangar and allowed only a small number of FBI or government workers in there. So why give so many people access to the Calverton hangar—such easy access that even a TWA pilot was able to steal evidence from the aircraft for a friend to use to promote yet another missile conspiracy theory? And, he adds, not one of the conspiracy theorists has even seen the wreckage, yet they say they know this plane was brought down by a missile.

"You can say this plane was brought down by the man in the moon taking a leak," Kallstrom declared, "but the bottom line is there is no evidence of a missile."

———

Undeterred by such logic, filmmaker Oliver Stone is preparing a television movie on TWA Flight 800. The director, whose depiction of the Vietnam War in *Platoon* infuriated Kallstrom, and whose refashioning of history in *JFK* and other movies was so abhorrent to the FBI chief, announced his intention in the fall of 1998 to explore unanswered questions about the crash.

"The FBI came up with a conclusion, and it is not one I agree with," Stone declared. "You have to pay attention to what eyewitnesses saw—the streaks of light. There were a lot of witnesses, just like the Kennedy assassination. A lot of people said bullets were fired from the grassy knoll. How could we ignore that? But we did."

"The real facts," retorted Kallstrom in a public reply, "are glossed over by the likes of Mr. Stone and others, who spend their lives bottom-feeding in those small dark crevices of doubt and hypocrisy."

At the time, Stone had not begun filming his movie, but ABC Television was planning to air it. The ensuing outcry appeared to startle both the director and ABC's executives. Strong objections were lodged with ABC by the victims' families and by the NTSB. Journalists in ABC's news division were also upset, since Stone's movie was to be sponsored by the network's entertainment division. Given Stone's penchant for presenting conjecture as fact, the journalists feared that the film would further erode the line between entertainment and news already blurred by various newsmagazine programs. Chastened, ABC announced it would not air Stone's film after all; in the spring of 1999, the director was reported to have interested at least one cable network in airing the film.

———

Amid the charges of conspiracy buffs, a persuasive voice raised the possibility that electromagnetic interference, or EMI, might have downed Flight 800 after all. Writing in the April 9, 1998, issue of *The New York Review of Books*,

Harvard philosophy professor Elaine Scarry observed that U.S. military planes at various times appear to have transmitted enough EMI to damage other military planes or helicopters. An Air Force study conducted in 1988 by Colonel Charles Quisenberry concluded that EMI might be capable of shutting off a plane's fuel system or causing a plane's computer controls to issue a "false" instruction, such as to raise the wing flaps. Was it unreasonable, Scarry asked, to imagine that EMI from a military plane or helicopter might affect a commercial jet?

The FBI had looked at EMI and concluded that neither on the night of July 17, 1996, nor at any other time had a commercial plane anywhere in the United States appeared to be affected by military EMI. The FBI found no vessels or aircraft in the area with the equipment on board to produce strong EMI. It concluded that the strongest electromagnetic field in the area at the time of the crash would have come from the radar tower at Kennedy Airport, a distance away. But Scarry observed that the author of a NASA study on the subject had speculated that EMI could occur very infrequently, targeting one plane rather than others in a particular area because of a confluence of factors including the kind of electronic systems a plane was operating by and the kind of composite materials used in certain airplane bodies.

The NTSB had also looked at EMI as a possibility, but on the theory that Flight 800 itself might have produced its own electromagnetic field, causing a short circuit that sparked the center fuel tank. But the safety board found no indication that EMI had played a role. Investigators believe that if an external source had been present the crew would have experienced a loss of control and would have communicated that condition. The flight data recorder and cockpit voice recorder revealed nothing. Scarry cited the crew member who minutes before the explosion had said, "Look at that crazy fuel-flow indicator." That, she theorized, may have been an indication of massive EMI. But while NTSB investigators continue to examine that condition, they feel sure that other irregularities would have appeared in the instrument panel, eliciting reactions from the pilots, for EMI to be a factor.

At a hearing of the Senate Judiciary subcommittee on administrative oversight on May 10, 1999, Senator Charles Grassley, an Iowa Republican and one of the FBI's most vociferous critics (he had exposed problems at the FBI's Washington laboratory some years ago), accused the bureau of having a blind fixation on finding evidence of a bomb or a missile, a fixation that may have unnecessarily prolonged the investigation. He also charged that the bureau lacked the skills necessary to investigate a plane crash and cooperate with other agencies. Notably, no other senator on the subcommittee actively participated in the hearing, which consisted largely of complaints by three NTSB workers, an ATF agent, and the outspoken metallourgist William Tobin, now retired from the FBI laboratory. They all criticized the FBI for refusing to stop the investigation into the bomb and missile theories when hard evidence failed to turn up in the weeks and months after the disaster. One NTSB metallurgist said that the views of those investigating a mechanical cause were largely ignored, and all three said that they were overwhelmed by the FBI's presence. Tobin testified that he was convinced early on, even after explosive traces were found, that a bomb or missile did not take down the plane. In fact, soon after these traces were found, he told Senator Grassley, he felt he had to "fall on the grenade" for the American people in order to stop the FBI from declaring the crash a crime. Despite Tobin's fears, James Kallstrom says that "at no time did I ever contemplate going out and declaring this a crime with the scant information we had."

Also at issue was whether an ATF report, issued months after the crash and concluding that the cause was mechanical, was possibly withheld from the NTSB by the FBI. In response, the FBI produced a letter from Kallstrom indicating that the report had been sent to NTSB chairman James Hall days after Kallstrom received it. Just prior to the hearing, a senior NTSB official said that the board had been privy to the contents of the ATF report for months before it formally received it from the FBI, and while it agreed with the report's conclusion, it did not agree with the ATF's scientific findings on which the agency had based that conclusion.

Kallstrom, who was not at the hearing, called it "a kangaroo court of malcontents. . . . If they want to criticize me and the law enforcement team [for] working too hard, too long, and doing too much, that we stayed the course and did a thorough investigation, I will wear that as a badge of courage." He added that for the ATF to conclude that the cause was mechanical months after the crash, while tons of the airplane remained on the ocean bottom and before the plane's reconstruction was complete, was preposterous. "They chose not to follow the investigative process. The fact that they may have turned out to be right in the end is irrelevant. Even a stopped clock is right twice a day.

"The NTSB showed up at this massive investigation with only six people. If it wasn't for the hundreds of law enforcement investigators who worked so hard, nothing would have been investigated. Can you imagine if we hadn't pushed to look at every possibility, no matter how remote, and had relied only on a magnifying glass to do our search, and this turned out to be a crime, but because of a slipshod investigation we overlooked it? It's easy now to look back and criticize us for being too thorough since it turned out not to be a crime."

Kallstrom added that the ATF report, written before the investigation was complete, broke the basic rules of criminal inquiry. Had the explosion turned out be a criminal act, he said, the report could have been used by a defense attorney and jeopardized a prosecution.

Also in May 1999, James Hall asked the House Aviation Subcommittee to grant the NTSB statutory control over any future aviation investigations in which a crime was suspected.

For the families of Flight 800, the approaching third-year anniversary of the crash has meant more time to heal, in some cases to start new lives. Charlie Christopher recently retired from the FBI. His son, Charles, is a cadet at Valley Forge Military Academy who aspires to be a Marine fighter pilot; like his mother, he loves to fly. The Hettlers and the Karschners go to a lot of state basketball games together; each family has a daughter who plays for the championship Montoursville high school team. Both families continue to struggle with their losses; at the Hettlers' house, Rance's room is still untouched, its door kept closed. Heidi Snow has started a twenty-four-hour Internet and phone support group for grieving families of plane crashes, called the Air Crash Support Network. Michel Breistroff has established an athletic scholarship at Harvard in memory of his son. Ron and Ann Dwyer run a horse arena named after their daughter; the arena includes programs and facilities for handicapped children. On Valentine's Day 1999, Joe Lychner proposed to a Houston native, Brenda Bragg; he feels after much soul-searching that his first family would want him to build a new life. "Not to do so," he said, "would make me a victim of the crash." He and his new wife will probably move to a new house. Since then, he has received yet another call from the Suffolk County morgue, informing him that yet another body part of one of his daughters has been identified, and asking him what he would like to have done with it. He is opening the grave a third time.

Several of the crash victims' family members, among them Frank Carven, brother of flight attendant Paula Carven and uncle of Jay, have lobbied actively to bring about changes in the Death on the High Seas Act. Though the amendment they successfully promoted was before the House Aviation Subcommittee in the summer of 1997, it has not been voted on in the subsequent three sessions of Congress and still awaits action. In Manhattan U.S. District Court in June 1998, the attorneys for the families argued that the plane went down in U.S. territorial waters, not in international waters. They noted that in 1983, by executive order, President Reagan had extended the territorial waters of the United States from three miles to twelve miles, and that the Death on the High Seas Act did not therefore apply to the victims of TWA Flight 800, which went into the water nine miles off Long Island. Judge Robert Sweet later ruled that the Flight 800 accident did not in fact occur on the high seas, thus making the families eligible for greater damages should they pursue and win their civil lawsuits against TWA and Boeing. Sweet also declared that the families could pursue damages for emotional stress and suffering on behalf of their nonworking family members, including the children.

The ruling is being appealed.

———

Even in his new job, Kallstrom is never more than a phone call away from his old one. For him, as with so many of the investigators, life will never be the same after Flight 800.

"It was a very traumatic time, a very sobering time," Kallstrom says. "I can talk about it now. I couldn't, then, when we were expecting a terrorist act. It was not obvious to a nation or the world that we were at such a high state of alert in the United States.

"I think the FBI accomplished its mission," he says now. "We successfully answered the question: Was this caused by a crime or wasn't it? We withstood the forces pulling on us from both sides, those that wanted us out because they thought the answer was simplistic and those who wanted us in. I think we took the right course in making very certain of our conclusions. And I am very proud of that and of all the investigators I worked with."

Kallstrom's former FBI boss, Louis Freeh, says that Kallstrom brought a great asset to the investigation that the FBI and the country needed: leadership.

"Jimmy's got courage and credibility with the agents and the respect of other law enforcement departments. The important thing is that he is not afraid to make a decision. And in my opinion he made all the right ones in this case."

Kallstrom knows the work was unique for the FBI. "A lot of what we do is the darker side of life, yet the size and scope of this grief surpassed anything I have ever been involved in," he says. "I've never seen so much tragedy, seeing one thousand–plus people in one place who just lost a mother, or father, or son, or daughter, and in some cases whole families. We couldn't bring any of their lives back, but we could try to find out what happened to this airplane."

Kallstrom says he has no lingering suspicions that the crash of Flight 800 might have been a crime. He is 99.9 percent certain, he says, that the crash was *not* a crime. "The toughest judge of that question was us, the entire law enforcement team," Kallstrom says. "With all our heart and soul, professionalism and experience, we had to find the truth. We did it for ourselves first. We had to live with the results of our effort." He is eager for the NTSB to identify a probable mechanical cause. After all, he observes, nearly three years have passed since the crash.

Can it happen again? This is a question that occurs to Kallstrom every time he boards a plane himself. "I always have thoughts when I get on a plane," he says. "A tiny voice in my mind says I hope this plane doesn't crash. Anytime you get up to thirty to forty thousand feet, I think most human beings have that voice in their heads asking the same question. Having been this close to the aviation industry, however," he says, "I think air travel in this country is the safest form of transportation. It is statistically the safest."

The images Kallstrom still sees in his mind are not so much the victims' bodies being brought in by boats or the sad faces of the rescuers who found nobody to rescue. Instead, Kallstrom sees, as he is prone to do, heroes responding with courage and compassion. He has learned that a disaster of life-and-death dimensions tends to transform its observers, so that the trappings of a material world matter less to them than helping humanity.

Out at Calverton, the devastated body of TWA Flight 800 still occupies a hangar. In the months since the reconstruction was finished, many families of the victims have urged the NTSB not to consider destroying the plane when its investigation is done. In its own brutal way, the plane stands as a tomb—the sacred burial place for their loved ones. Others have asked that it be preserved as a national relic. For now the plane remains in the hangar, where its maintenance costs the NTSB $4.5 million a year.

Curiously enough, however, a number of parties are now vying for the wreckage, to use it as an extraordinary full-scale teaching tool for aeronautic students and aviation experts worldwide. In fact, the reconstruction was designed to separate in three large pieces and thus can be transported easily.

Wherever it ends up, it will stand as an eerie testament to the most mysterious aviation disaster in U.S. history.

ACKNOWLEDGMENTS

In the end, *In the Blink of an Eye* resulted from the willingness of the FBI to open itself up to a journalist. Clearly, the book would not have been as revealing without the bureau's full cooperation and trust that this would be an honest portrayal of the investigation and their work. I am enormously grateful to FBI director Louis Freeh, assistant director James Kallstrom, and all the FBI agents and members of the FBI–NYPD Joint Terrorism Task Force who assisted me. These investigators spent time patiently (although their patience wore thin at times) answering my questions and explaining their roles in the Flight 800 investigation, as well as sharing their thoughts, frustrations, and observations. Most of the investigators prefer not to be acknowledged publicly, but I do hope they will accept this general recognition with my heartfelt thanks. No thank-you, however, to these men and women would ever do them justice.

This book would not exist without the faith and commitment of Jason Epstein, whose wisdom and brilliant editing made all the difference. Jason understood the importance of the Flight 800 story long before it became obscured by lurid conspiracy theories; that sort of speculation only strengthened his resolve that the investigation merited a full airing in a sober setting.

I am tremendously grateful to Larry Neumeister, my collaborator and colleague, who has been with me on this journey every step of the way from the first days of the crash. He helped clarify the vision, and provided strength and inspiration throughout this great challenge. Working with him has been one of the most unpredictable, fulfilling, and fun experiences in the world. He is a journalist committed to the truth, and a true friend.

Michael Shnayerson came into the project at a moment when it needed a sure hand, someone studied in the art of story and structure. Working long days over several months, he provided direction, organization, and advice that demonstrated his talent, experience, and determination to shape the manuscript into a stronger narrative. He was always there for me, and I appreciate everything he brought to the project.

This journey would never have started without the decision of Sam Boyle, New York bureau chief at the Associated Press, to commit a reporter full-time to the story until it was clear that nothing more could be done to learn the truth. He never tried to steer the facts to a favored direction, preferring to let the story tell itself and trusting the reporter to find the truth, even if the truth was not as tantalizing as it first appeared. He personifies the highest ideals of journalism. Thanks for all support from the New York bureau, the finest reporters in the country. Two members of the New York bureau should be singled out: Tom Hays for his help and insightful suggestions, and Larry McShane for being there whenever he was needed. And a word of gratitude to the Associated Press, whose commitment to fairness, honesty, and objectivity continues to hold it up as the world's greatest news organization.

My thanks as well:

To attorney Jay Acton, who provided sound guidance in navigating through the complicated world of publishing; on stormy waters he was a lighthouse beacon that kept me focused.

To my agent, Kathy Robbins, one of my earliest supporters, who saw that the story had great value when it was in its infancy. She offered sage advice during crucial periods. And to her assistant David Halpern, who gave constant encouragement and was always eager to help.

To the Random House family, particularly Ulf Buchholz, Jason Epstein's assistant, who offered patience at the most stressful moments, keeping the project rolling steadily toward completion; Kapo Ng, the jacket designer, whose artistic hand wrapped the book in dignity; and Tom Perry and Liz Fogarty, for bringing the book to the attention of the public with style.

To Edward Burke, who helped launch the project and stayed by my side throughout.

I would also like to thank the many law enforcement investigators from the FBI and from the Suffolk Country, Nassau County, New York State, and New York City police departments who were interviewed either for my AP reporting on the investigation or specifically for this book but whose names do not appear in the final version. Their contributions to the book and to the overall Flight 800 investigation were no less helpful or significant.

Many others also gave generously of their time, counsel, and information to help this story be as accurate and complete as possible. I would like to thank them for their full cooperation. Among them are investigators and officials of the National Transportation Safety Board, the U.S. Navy, the U.S. Coast Guard, the Bureau of Alcohol, Tobacco, and Firearms, the FAA, Boeing, TWA, Suffolk County, the U.S. Attorney's Office, the Joint Chiefs of Staff, and the White House.

It would take twenty pages to name all those who helped complete this journey. They know who they are and what their contribution has been, but because of space or by their request they are not listed here. I send my special thanks to those people as well as to the following individuals for their assistance and support: Joe Monteith, Ben Mevorach, Darrell Mills, Don Phillips, Joe Valiquette, John Collingwood, Ed Allen, Jack Ballas, Barry Smith, Dick Torykian, veteran 747 pilot Chuck Beam, James Catterson, Drew Biondo, Steve Horvani, Priti Chohan, Jeff Drach, Ann King, Rick Lazio, Peter King, Carolyn McCarthy, and Russ Young.

A special thank-you to the families who lost loved ones, for sharing painful emotions at moments when it had to be uncomfortable, and for seeing that there was value in not hiding their grief from the rest of the world. The family members have shown courage, heart, and beauty, and demonstrated how life doesn't end even when the worst cards are dealt. There but for the grace of God go any of us.

I cannot find the words to adequately describe my profound gratitude to my family, who are truly the wind beneath my wings. I am humbled by their understanding and boundless love.

The members of the FBI–NYPD Joint Terrorism Task Force assigned to the TWA Flight 800 investigation

Tom Pickard FBI
John O'Neill FBI
George Andrew FBI
Pasqual D'Amuro FBI
Neil Herman FBI
Tom Lang FBI
John Haughic NYPD
Bob Pritchard NYPD

Steven Bongard FBI
Joe Cordaro NYPD
Tom Corrigan NYPD
Pam Culos FBI
John Dew FBI
Sal Emilio ATF
Ken Engelhardt NYPD
Tracy Fortin FBI
Christina Gust FBI
Rich Karniewicz FBI

Tony Lamantia   FBI
Lu Lieber   FBI
Dom Magro   N.Y. State Police
Scott Metcalf   FBI
Jennifer Leonard   FBI
Steve Hughes   U.S. Secret Service
Christopher Munger   FBI
Jim Minor   U.S. State Department
Ted Otto   FBI
Pete Robustelli   INS
Frank Shulte   FBI
Reuben Scott   FBI
Kim Thompson   FBI
Christopher Voss   FBI
Gary Wheeler   FBI

FBI AGENTS ON THE "HANGAR CREW"

TEMPORARILY ASSIGNED TO THE

TWA INVESTIGATION TASK FORCE

Ken Maxwell
Brad Morrison
Terry Sweeney
Bob DeSantis
Dan Boyer
Bill Barry
Mike Driscoll
Sue Hilliard
Marty Finn
Bill Didie
Rondie Peiscop-Grau
Jim Lomanto
Paul Ramondi
Reid Roe
John Swanson
Dennis Smith
Gary Luker
Johan Ianuzzi
Olaf Raumberger
Gerry Fornino
Steve Wager

INDEX

ABOUT THE AUTHOR

PAT MILTON is a correspondent with the Associated Press in New York.

ABOUT THE TYPE

This book was set in Photina, a typeface
designed by José Mendoza in 1971. It is a
very elegant design with high legibility,
and its close character fit has made it a
popular choice for use in quality
magazines and art gallery publications.